Jam
Factory

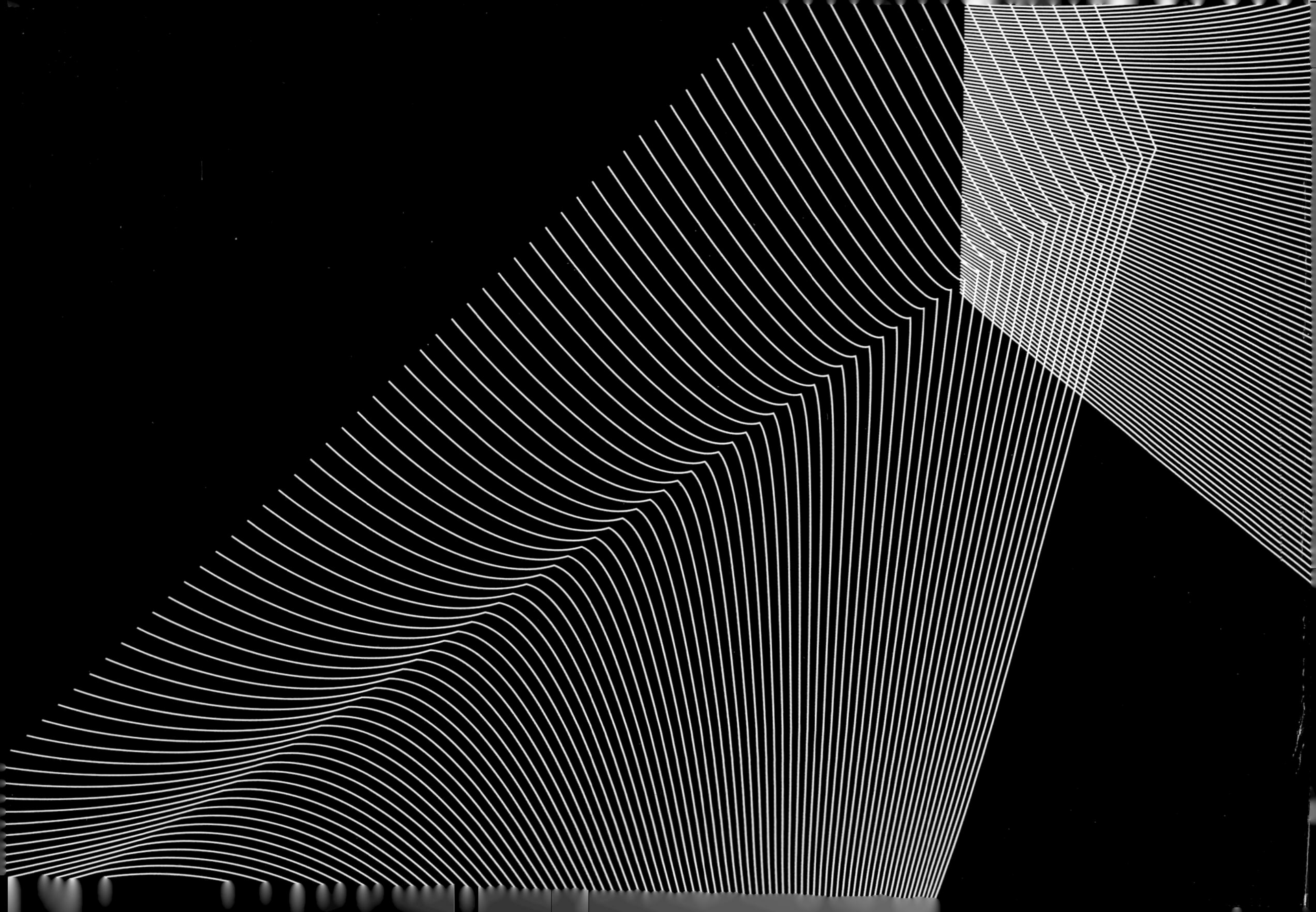

STEEL

STEEL: ART DESIGN ARCHITECTURE
Edited by Margaret Hancock Davis
Published by JamFactory, Adelaide

First Published in Adelaide,
Australia in 2017

Published to coincide with the exhibition *STEEL: art design architecture*, shown at JamFactory, Adelaide from 17 February to 23 April before touring nationally.

Jam
Factory

Published by JamFactory
19 Morphett Street, Adelaide SA 5000

www.jamfactory.com.au

ISBN 978-0-9807910-9-9

Curator:
Margaret Hancock Davis

Catalogue Editor:
Margaret Hancock Davis

Copy Editor:
Joan-Maree Hargreaves

Art Direction and Design:
Stephen Goddard, Project Two

Printed in China for Imago

All measurements have been given height before width before depth, or height before diametre, and are in millimetres.

Government Support
This exhibition is supported by the Visions regional touring program, an Australian Government program aiming to improve access to cultural material for all Australians.

JamFactory acknowledges the support of the South Australian Government through Art South Australia and the assistance of the Visual Arts and Crafts Strategy, an initiative of the Australian, State and Territory Governments. JamFactory's Exhibitions Program is also assisted by the Australian Government through the Australia Council.

Australian Government
Visions of Australia

ADELAIDE SOUTH AUSTRALIA
Government of South Australia
ARTS SOUTH AUSTRALIA

Australian Government | Government of South Australia
THE VISUAL ARTS AND CRAFT STRATEGY

Australian Government | Australia Council for the Arts

Design Sponsor
TWO
PROJECT TWO

CONTENTS

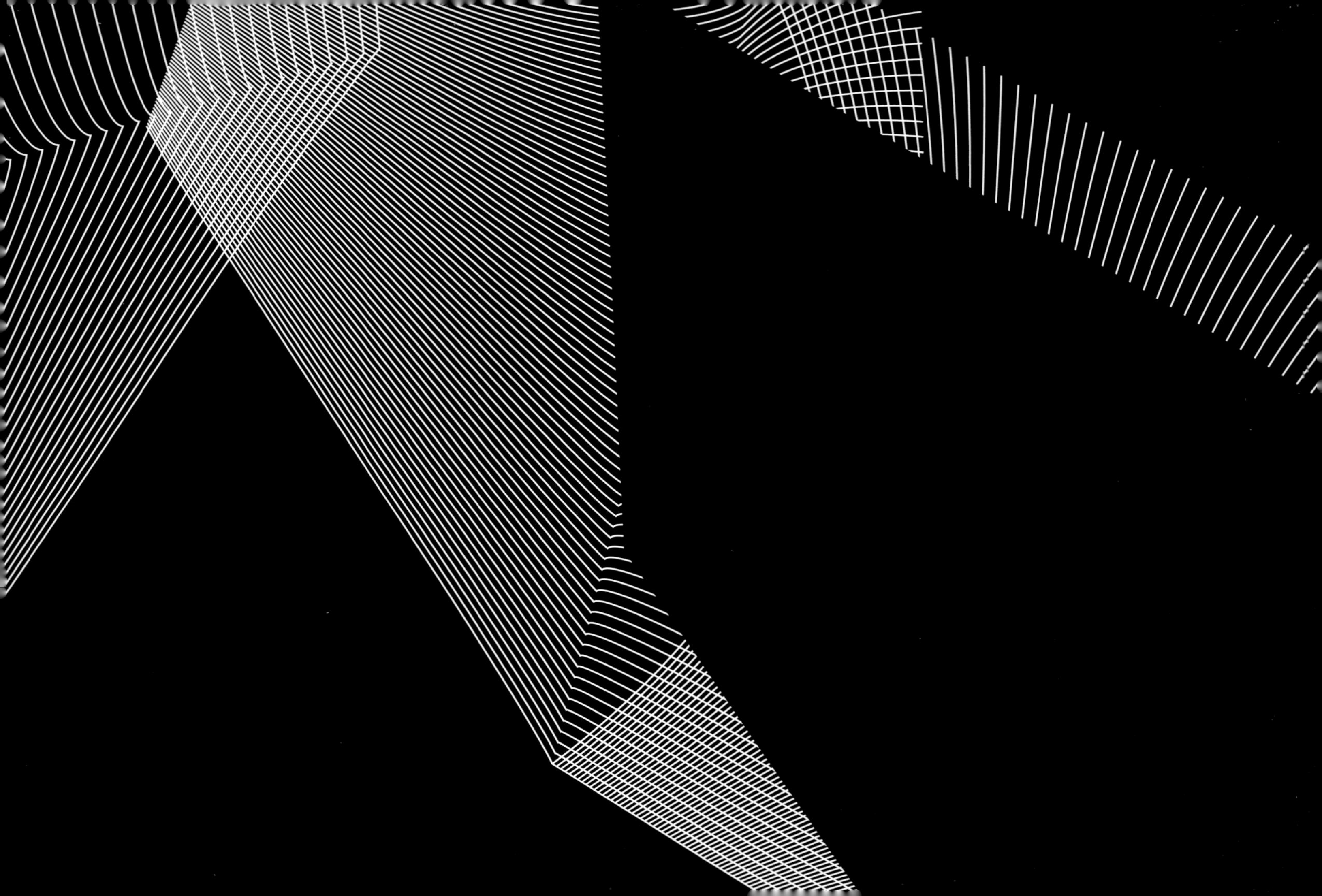

FOREWORD

BRIAN PARKES

CHIEF EXECUTIVE OFFICER
JAMFACTORY

STEEL: ART DESIGN ARCHITECTURE explores innovative and outstanding ways that steel is being used by artists, designers and architects in Australia in the 21st century. The exhibition is the third in a series of innovative material-based exhibitions, which began with *WOOD: art design architecture* in 2013 and continued with *GLASS: art design architecture* in 2015. Both exhibitions toured extensively across Australia and we are delighted that the *STEEL* exhibition will be shown in 14 venues nationally over almost three years.

JamFactory is a unique not-for-profit organisation located in the Adelaide city centre. It supports and promotes outstanding design and craftsmanship through its studios, galleries and shops, and is recognised nationally and internationally as a centre for excellence.

Jewellers and metalworkers have been working with steel in JamFactory's workshops since the mid 1970s and since the establishment of our current Jewellery and Metal Design Studio (within our purpose-built building in 1992), steel has become one of JamFactory's primary production materials. The studio's workshop facilities include a lathe, a milling machine, hydraulic presses, rollers, linishers, a guillotine, forging and welding facilities, drill presses and other equipment to enable a wide range of methods of working with steel and other metals.

This exhibition marks the 25th anniversary of the Jewellery and Metal Design Studio – one of the four studios in which JamFactory offers its intensive two-year, post-tertiary Associate training program. Over 25 years the studio has produced some outstanding alumni and has been led by influential practitioners: Greg Healy, Rik Barnsley, Sue Lorraine and current Creative Director Christian Hall.

The studio is also a busy production facility that designs and produces successful products – including several made from stainless steel – for retail and wholesale markets,

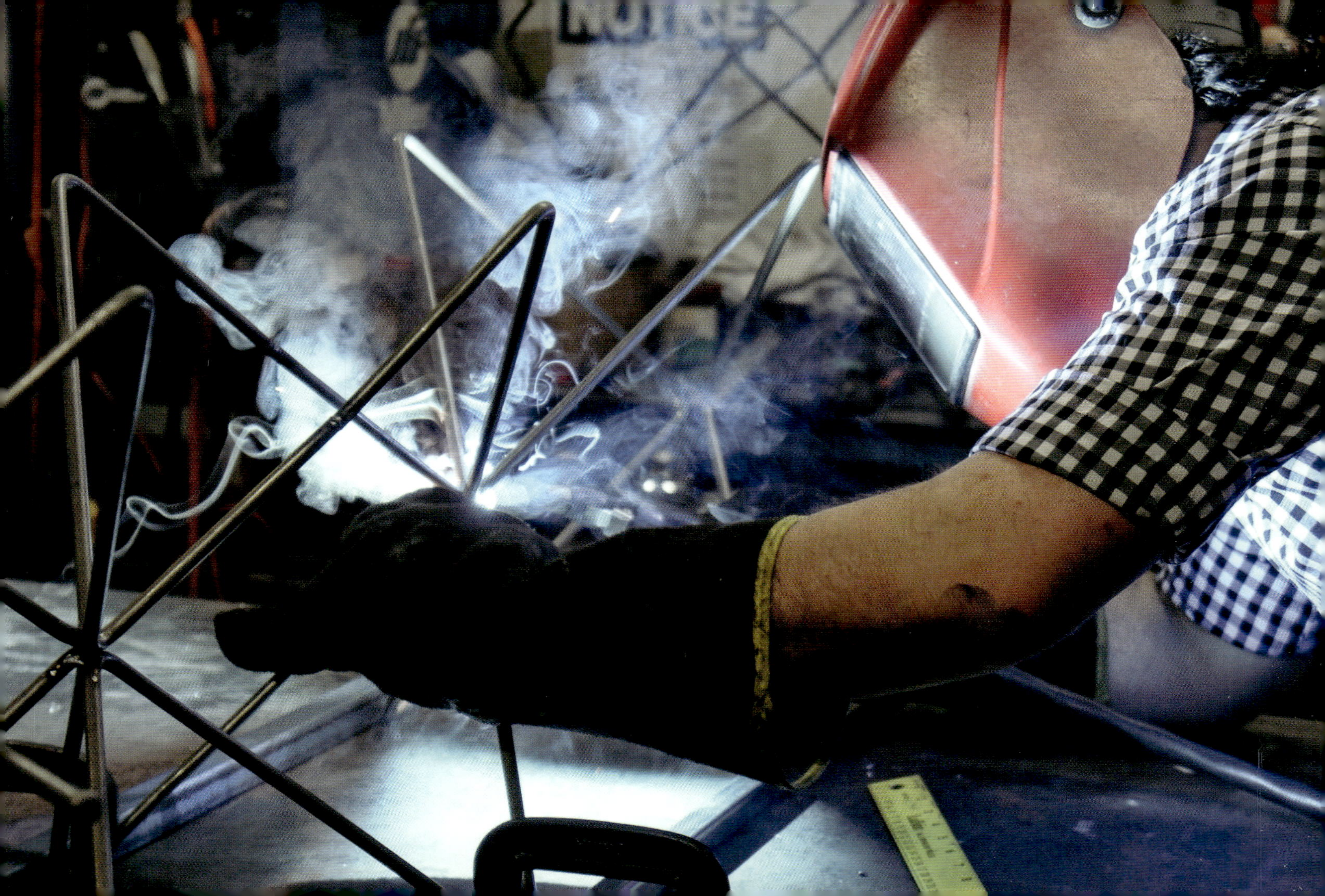

along with a broad range of bespoke commissioned work including awards, corporate gifts, jewellery, lighting installations and public art projects. The studio is regularly engaged by artists, designers and architects to prototype and produce products or components for new projects. Each new job that comes into the studio provides fascinating training opportunities and experiences for the training Associates.

I would like to take this opportunity to thank the 29 exhibitors in *STEEL: art design architecture* for their willingness to participate and for allowing us to present their works. These influential artists, designers and architects, drawn from across Australia, were selected over a 12-month research period and it is the diversity of work and stories represented that makes this project so rich.

I would like to particularly acknowledge the exhibition's curator Margaret Hancock Davis for her tireless work in realising the ambition of this significant project – including securing substantial funding, selecting and liaising with the exhibitors, writers as well as stakeholders, developing and editing this exciting publication and managing the complex logistics for such a major tour.

A key feature of this exhibition has been the design and fabrication of the display furniture and related elements. The exhibition design has been led by independent Sydney-based designer Stephen Goddard, with additional input from Christian Hall and a group of Associates from the Metal and Furniture Studios.

Stephen Goddard has also designed this wonderful catalogue and we thank him for his significant personal contribution to this and the previous two exhibitions in this series, which as a collection stand as evidence of an outstanding collaborative relationship that we plan to continue to build on into the future. I must also thank copy editor Joan-Maree Hargreaves, as well as all of the contributing writers and the many photographers whose work has helped to create such a beautiful publication.

An exhibition of this scale requires much support, and I would like to acknowledge the principle funding that JamFactory receives from the South Australian Government through Arts South Australia, and from the Commonwealth Government through the Australia Council for the Arts. The development of the exhibition and its extensive national tour has been greatly assisted by additional Commonwealth funding through Visions of Australia, and I thank the Minister for the Arts, Senator the Hon Mitch Fifield, for this crucial support.

We hope that this exhibition will inspire audiences around Australia to consider the social, cultural, economic and creative possibilities of steel, to think about our historical relationship to it, and to consider its evolving role in the 21st century. ■

◂
Christian Hall welding
Mesh Shelving, 2015.
Photo: courtesy the artist

OVERLEAF
The Australian Plantbank,
Australian Botanic Gardens,
Mount Annan,
New South Wales, 2014
Photo: John Gollings

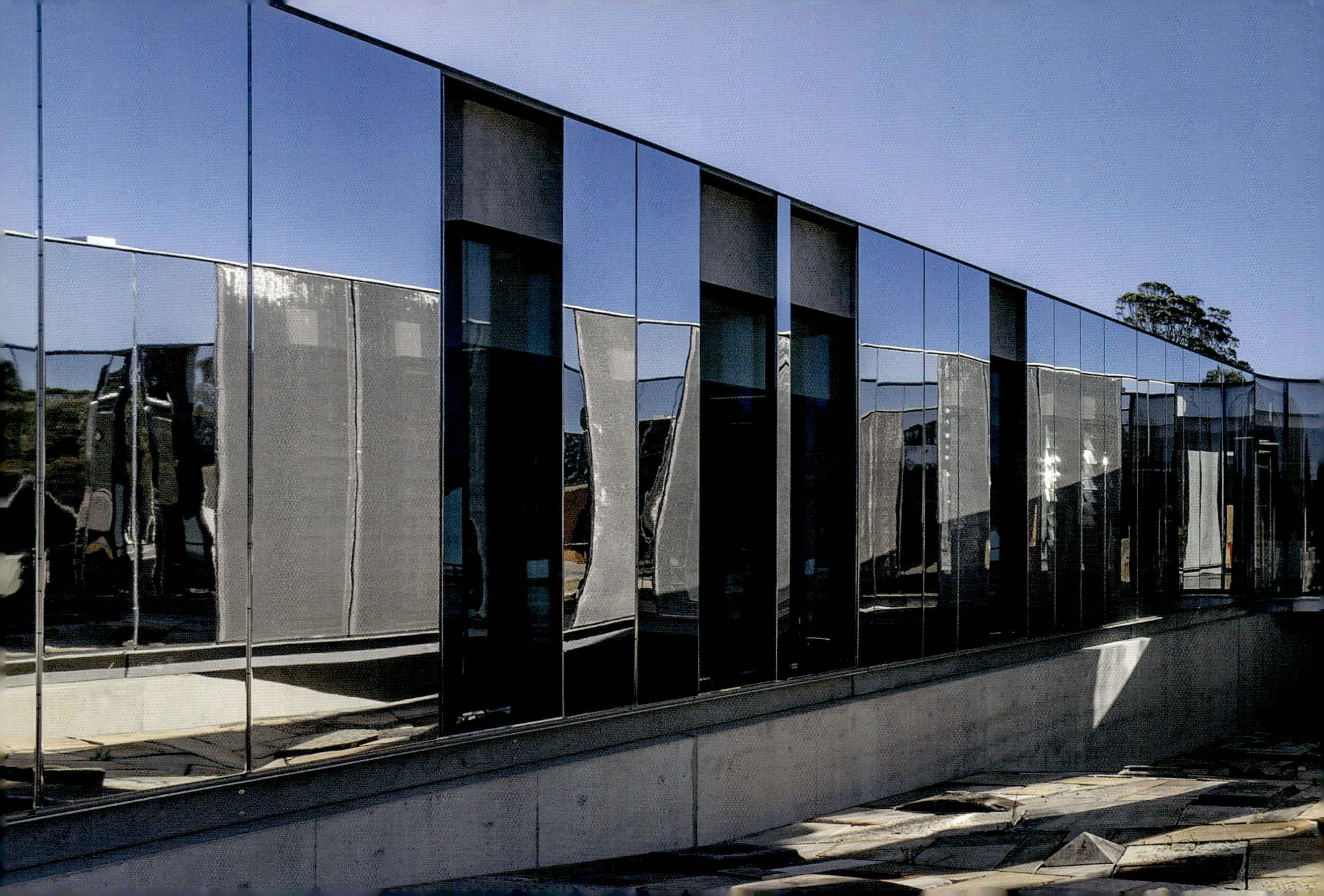

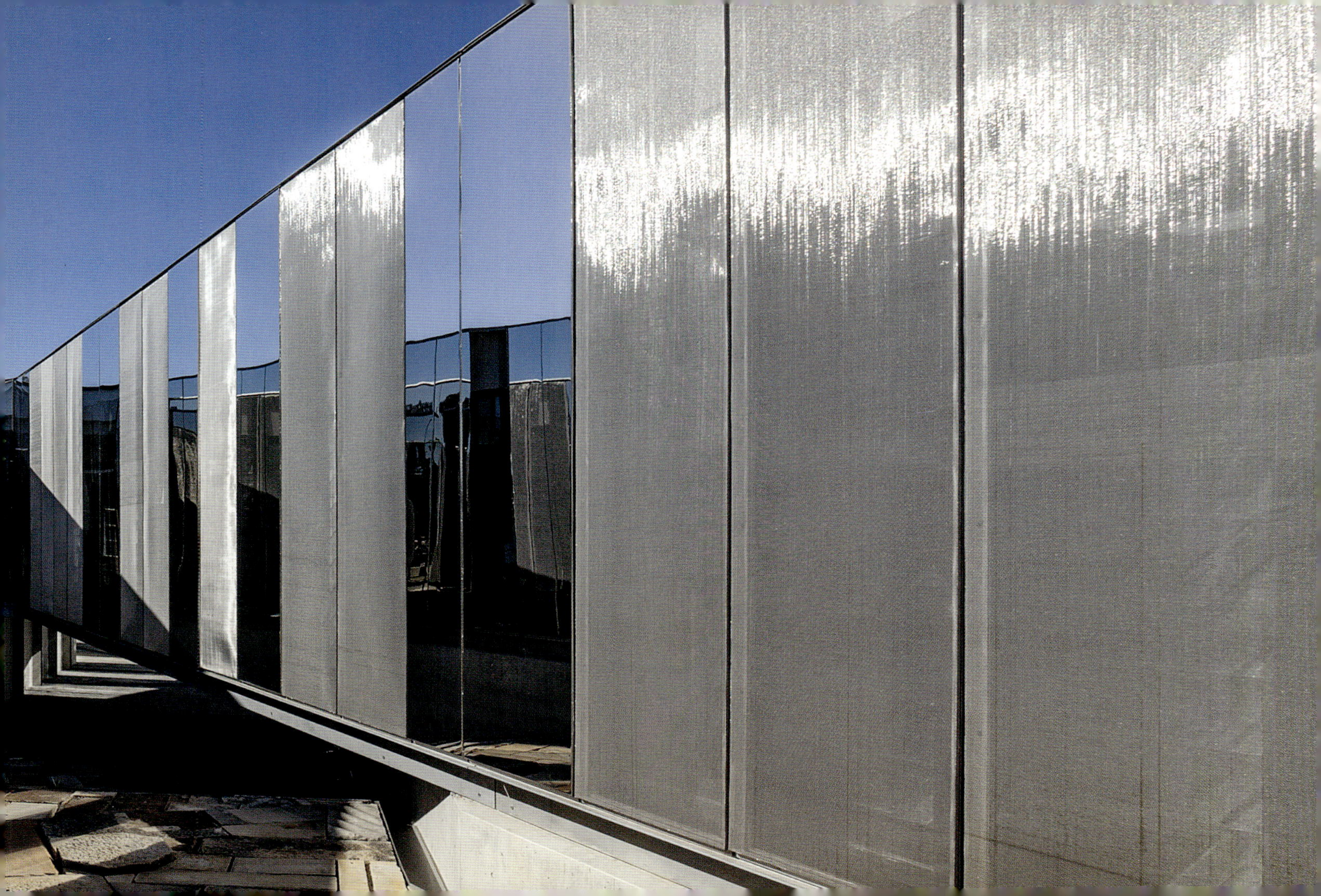

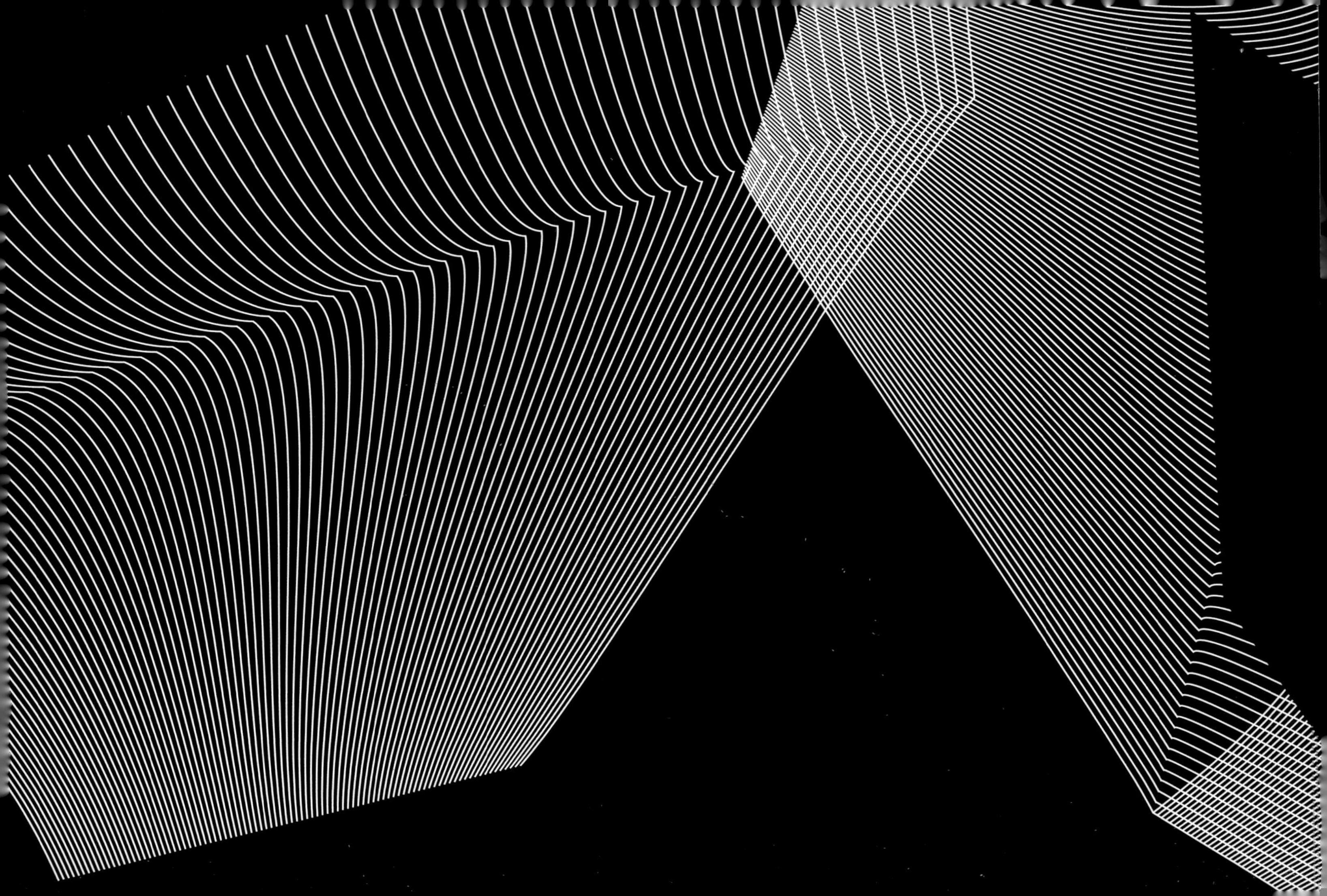

STEEL: ART DESIGN ARCHITECTURE

MARGARET HANCOCK DAVIS

'THAT'S ALL the motorcycle is, a system of concepts worked out in steel. There's no part in it, no shape in it, that is not out of someone's mind... I've noticed that people who have never worked with steel have trouble seeing this—that the motorcycle is primarily a mental phenomenon. They associate metal with given shapes—pipes, rods, girders, tools, parts—all of them fixed and inviolable, and think of it as primarily physical. But a person who does machining or foundry work or forge work or welding sees "steel" as having no shape at all. Steel can be any shape you want if you are skilled enough, and any shape but the one you want if you are not.'[1]

Steel is a medium rich in human history. An alloy of iron and carbon, steel dates back to 4,000 years ago and traces the technical and cultural development of multiple civilisations. First forged in hand-made furnaces, steel production and its subsequent use, expanded in the 17th century with the technical innovations of blister and crucible steel. By the 19th century the Bessemer[2] and Siemens-Martin processes heralded in the era of mass steel production.

Today steel is one of the most ubiquitous materials in the world. It inhabits the landscape of our bodies, our domestic spaces and our built environments. A material that ranges from raw and functional to lustrous and decorative – steel blurs the boundary between utilitarian and precious. Its affordability and durability has made it so pervasive that it is often overlooked. Just think of an average day: you may awaken in a house or apartment block whose structural form is made of steel; head to the bathroom where you turn steel taps for a shower under a steel shower rose; next to the kitchen to open your stainless-steel-covered fridge, turn on your steel kettle, and eat breakfast with utensils made from steel; before leaving in cars, motorbikes, trains, trams or buses, over bridges and on tracks, all of which contain some steel.

Throughout Australia, major towns are fundamentally linked to the history of production of steel. For 84 years the BHP steel works in Newcastle, New South Wales, created a city within a city, employing up to 12,000 workers at its peak. Bluescope's Port Kembla steel works located south of Sydney continues to operate today be it only with one blast furnace currently in operation, a far cry from the 1980s when its workforce reached 22,000 workers across a huge site serviced by four train platforms. Meanwhile the uncertainty of Arrium's steel works in Whyalla, South Australia continues to be in the news since being placed under administration in April, 2016. However it is not only the production of steel that has seen towns develop throughout the nation, the prospecting for iron ore[3] spurred mining settlements throughout remote areas of the country including Iron Knob in South Australia through to the remote Pilbara region of Western Australia.[4]

Steel has also played an essential role in the development of Australia's design vernacular. In the hands of skilled Australian designers and makers, steel has become an essential material that helps articulate a national character and contributes to our distinctive material culture.

For the many thousands of varieties of steel, one seems intrinsically connected with the Australian identity, that being corrugated steel sheets known as corrugated iron. Synonymous with Australia's rural and mining landscapes, whilst also forming an essential part of the classic "Aussie" backyard, as sheds, chicken coups, out houses, and water tanks, corrugated iron is durable, strong, adaptable and light. It is for these reasons that it is used or interpreted by contemporary architects, designers and artists including exhibitors featured in *STEEL: art design architecture*.

Simon Laws's *The Drew House*, 2010 (pg 67) takes its cue from the architecture of Queensland's cane growing region around Bundaberg. The dramatic visual language of the sugar cane mill, its large-scale boilers and turbines juxtaposed with the beautiful silhouettes of the corrugated iron water tanks and stands, finds form in this holiday home. Built to be a luxury type of camping for the Drew siblings, the house operates as sculpture on a bushland site camped at by the family for many years. Located near the beach, the building aims to celebrate its environment allowing its occupants to be in touch with their surroundings. The building is designed as a series of interconnected pavillions and walk ways. Assembled in Brisbane the pavillions were scaled to fit a semi-trailer and transported to the site. With the house positioned to capture natural airflows, the south easterly breeze creates a passive cooling system without the need for air-conditioning.

DesignByThem is a Sydney based design-company established in 2007 representing and producing the work of Australian designers. Founded by industrial designers Sarah Gibson and Nick Karlovasitis, it has a design first approach that is reflected in its culture and products.

Every design is carefully considered, developed and curated to ensure it meets the requirements and standards of good design. DesignByThem creates a playful collection of fun and functional furniture and lighting. Made of mirror polished stainless steel, *The Corro Bowl*, 2011 (pg 138) is a beautifully refined corrugated form accentuating steel's inherent strength and fluidity.

Lorraine Connelly-Northey (pg 169) is a Waradgerie woman from Swan Hill in north-west Victoria who finds inspiration in the land of her childhood and her mother's tribal boundary, where the Mallee meets the Murray River. The strong cultural practice of weaving is translated in Connelly-Northey's work which transforms found materials such as rusted sheets of corrugated iron, steel barbed wire, fencing mesh and other agricultural detritus into traditional forms including koolimans (coolamons), narrbongs (dilly bags) and interpretations of possum skin cloaks. Her choice of materials from our frontier and colonial past reminds us of Australia's fraught history with our First Nation's peoples – the fence being both a physical barrier used to contain and control Aboriginal people living on Missions and as metaphoric symbol of Aboriginal people being trapped within a white society, unable to express their culture and traditional way of life.

Australia like most countries has many cultural tropes and myths surrounding its identity. In addition to the traditions of our First Nation's people, Australian identities have been forged through many lenses: from our aforementioned colonial frontiers and our convict past with its bushranger legends, to our Anzac traditions of courage and sacrifice, to our counter-culture surfer icons of the 1960s and 70s, one of the most mythologised "Aussie" representations. Trent Jansen looks to these myths to create designs through a process he describes as design anthropology. Researching human behaviour to layer concepts into his forms, Jansen's *Tidal collection*, 2015 (pg 253) for Tait conjures long laid-backed summers spent relaxing at the beach or by the pool. The steel-wire forms of the lounger, sun lounge and chair references the shape waves take as they make their way to shore, knowledge surfers capitalise on to catch the perfect wave.

Part of the Australian story is our history of migration, where people from around the world have moved to make a new life in this country, adding to our diversity and multiculturalism. Mari Funaki (pg 175) and Kensuke Todo (pg 153) both made this journey from Japan. Funaki is remembered and revered as one of Australia's leading contemporary jewellers and advocates. Working almost exclusively with mild steel or gold, Funaki heat treated her steel objects and jewellery to form a rich blackened surfaced that was then oiled and sealed with wax. This deep black references the industrial world whilst giving the work a strong graphic quality. Like 3D drawings in space, her works contain intimate interior spaces that

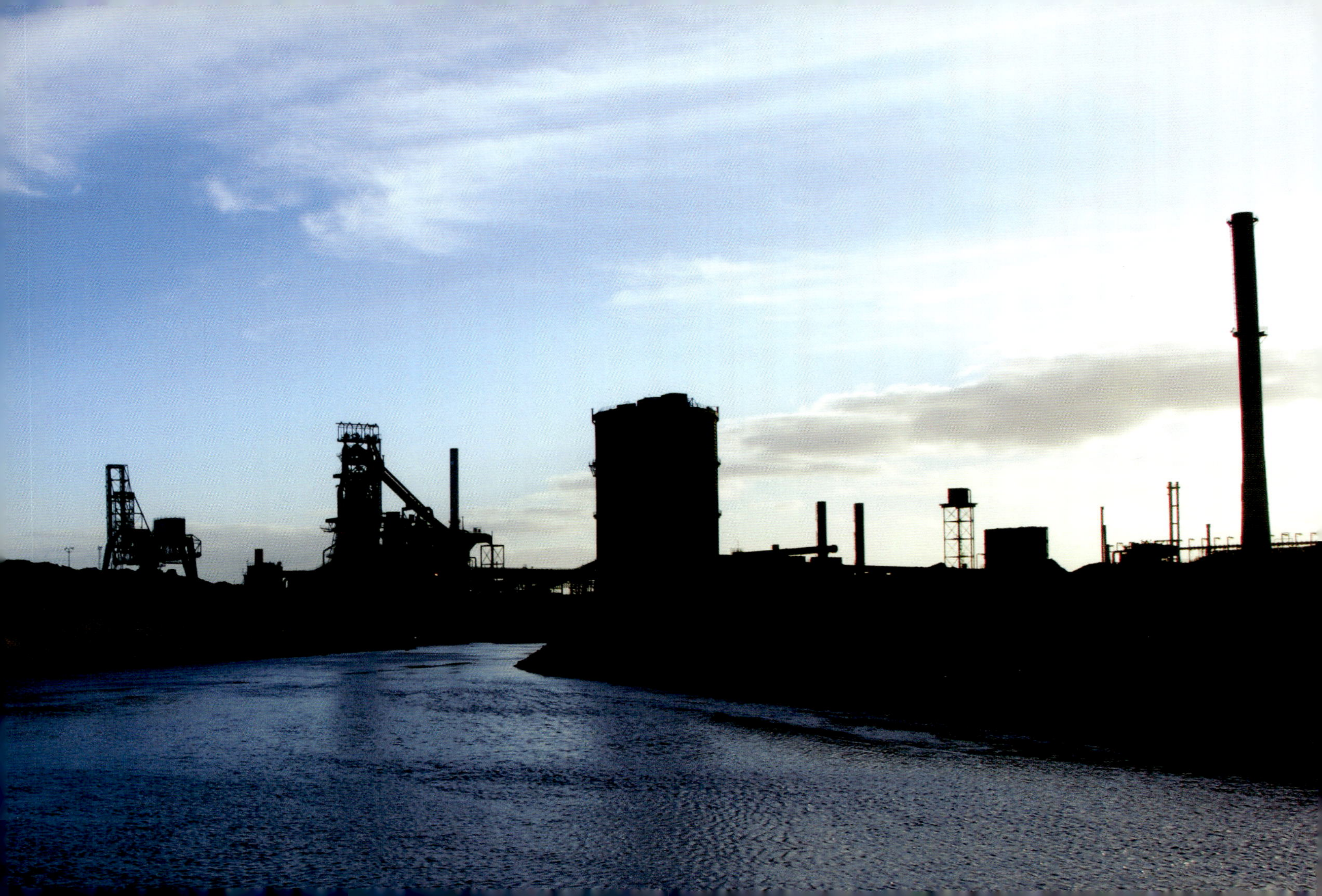

have the capacity to 'stir our imaginations or trigger something from our memories.'[5]

Memories play an important role in the work of Todo. Todo is a gifted drawer and sculptor whose works express a sense of longing for his place of birth. He notes that the work he makes in Australia would not be possible in Japan. In Japan he would be surrounded by the cultural motifs he uses. It is only with distance that these items are rendered metaphorically to reflect and preserve the comforts of home. Interestingly both Todo and Funaki use a pared-back palette of materials and colours that admirer's of their work may infer as a nod to a Japanese aesthetic.

[redacted]

◀ Arrium Steel works in Whyalla, South Australia.
Photo: Sean A. Kelley

Preservation can take many forms. The Australian PlantBank, 2014 (pg 85) designed by BVN is situated in the Australian Botanic Gardens, Mount Annan, on the outskirts of greater Sydney, New South Wales. Part of a global network coordinated by the Royal Botanic Gardens, Kew, England, known as the Millennium Seed Bank Partnership, The Australian PlantBank houses both the Domain Trust seed bank and research laboratories, which specialise in horticultural research and conservation of Australian native plant species, particularly those from New South Wales. Located in a part of the garden between a threatened and rare remnant section of Cumberland Plain native woodland and the garden's nursery that propagates species (including the famous Wollemi Pine), the building is designed to embrace the woodland, acting as a mediator between the natural and the man-made. Steel is used throughout the building with polished steel panels reflecting the building's surroundings, and the bushfire-resistant-mesh covered louvered windows enabling the building to open up to natural airflows.

Ecological practices often lead to discussions of sustainability and recyclability. Steel is the most recycled material on the planet, recycled more than all other materials combined. Its overall recycling rate stood at 88 percent in 2012.[6] The amazing metallurgical properties of steel allow it to be recycled continually with no degradation in performance from one product to another. The recycling of steel can be seen in the beautifully crafted knives of master knife-maker Barry Gardner (pg 73). Gardner is one of those makers that knows their "ah ha" moment – for him it came 24 years ago whilst visiting a gun trade show in Adelaide. Trawling through the many stalls he came across one showing a group of knives made by the stall-holder. From that day he knew that this was what he wanted to do. Slowly developing his skills through trial and error and through research into Japanese knife-making practices, Gardner creates hand-forged knives desired both nationally and internationally. Working mainly with Damascus steel, he tiers up multiple layers of molten steel sourced from old files and band saw blades that he then reworks, twisting and folding the steel to create the distinctive patterns revealed once the knife is submerged in an acid bath.

From an ancient craft, to one that works with modern technology to realise its final result, Maureen Faye-Chauhan's (pg 191) intricate mild steel brooches are produced through the manipulation of 3D images in advanced computer-aided design programs and laser printing. Describing her practice as artistic, she notes that 'part of the creative process is bringing forth something from nothing: ideas develop, a drawn line closes to become a shape, and through the manipulation of space, that shape becomes a form.'[7] Working with fundamental geometric patterns found in nature's building blocks, Chauhan relies on repeated elements and the strength of steel to create her light and complex forms.

Architects, designers and engineers work with steel because it offers high performance at a reasonable price and depending on the processing, steel can have an extremely long life. Steel's ability to maintain its integrity whilst spanning large distances sees it used in the construction of bridges throughout the world. The oldest steel bridge, for example, has spanned the River Severn in Great Britain for over 230 years. Like bridges, the roof-spans of a modern stadia use steel. The sophisticated and award-winning Adelaide Oval Redevelopment, 2013 (pg 113) by COX Architecture in association with Walter Brooke and Hames Sharley, creates three pavilions within the treasured Adelaide parklands. Its striking diagrid pavilion roofs are made possible through the use of steel, as Patrick Nees, Director at COX Architecture notes: 'Steel as a material has allowed us to design structures that achieve a lightness and elegance that are defining characteristics of Adelaide Oval. Spanning further and doing so with strength and the least amount of material could only be achieved with steel. The use of steel allowed the design team creative freedom to achieve the dynamic forms that are now synonymous with Adelaide Oval.'[8]

The diagrid structure finds new form in the work of Australian-born, London-based designer Brodie Neill (pg 79) and the work of Adelaide-based designer-maker Christian Hall (pg 91). Produced by Italian manufacturer Marzorati Ronchetti the limited edition *Reverb wire chair*, 2012, in mirror-polished stainless steel is a reinterpretation of Neill's earlier design *Reverb chair*, 2009. Inspired by the reverberation of sound, the conical vortex of the original nickel-plated hand-formed aluminium chair is made lighter and more complex in this steel mesh iteration. For Neill, 'The mesh amplifies the vortex and the flowing contour lines and maps out the conical shape of the chair's expanding geometry.'[9] Christian Hall also plays with the diagrid translating the form across scales from the intimate sculpture of jewellery through to furniture solutions including shelving units and room dividers.

Steel mesh is used for both practical and aesthetic reasons in the award-winning Waterloo Youth Centre, 2013 (pg 105)

[redacted]

▸ Worker tending to the molten iron as it flows through the trough, Blue Scope Port Kembla Steelworks, New South Australia.
Photo: Sylvia Liber, Fairfax Media

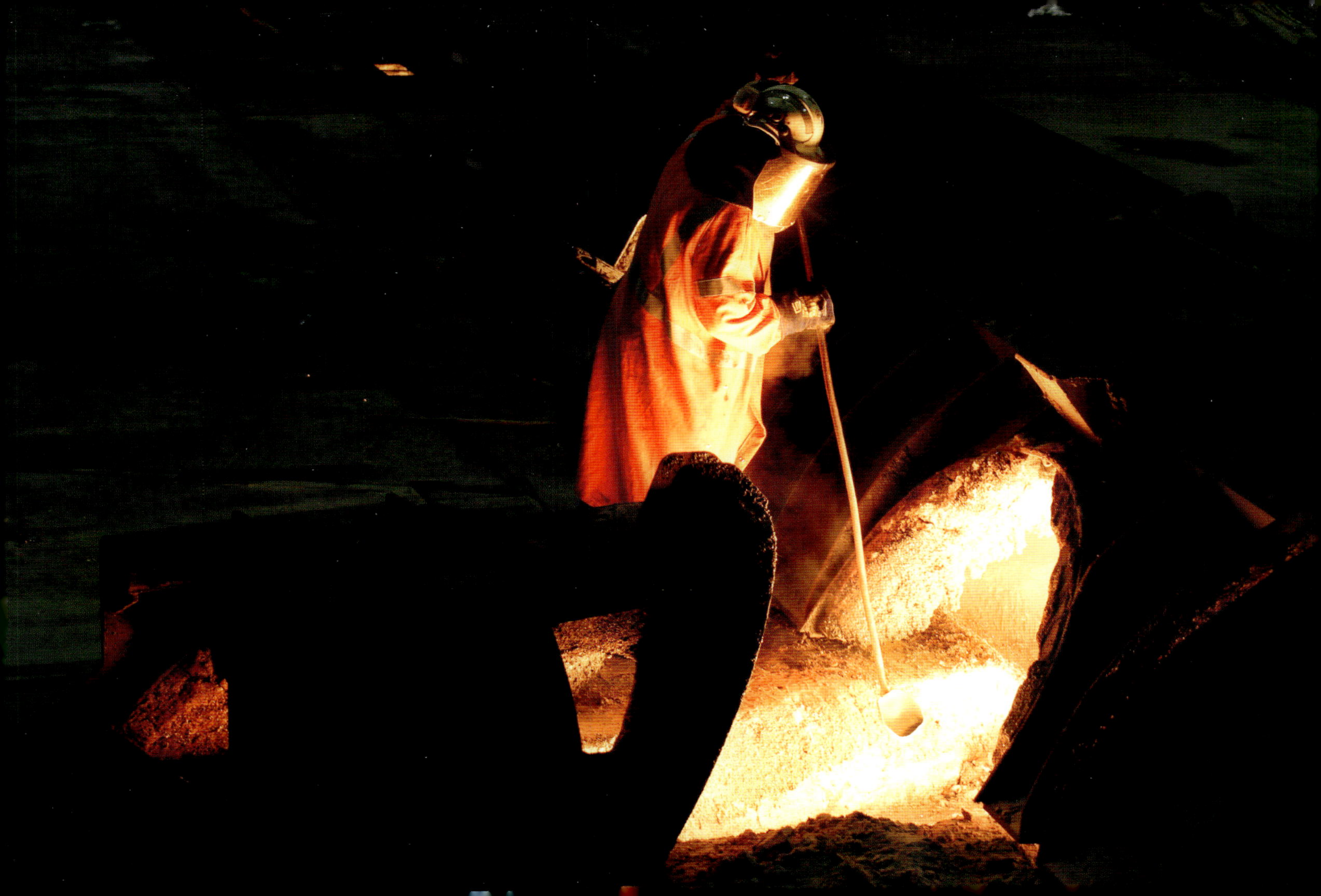

designed by Sydney-based architect firm Collins and Turner.Dramatically crowned with a cantilevered mesh, the building takes cues from the Snowdon Aviary in London Zoo. Revitalising a converted amenities block that houses WEAVE (formerly South Sydney Youth Services), the durable freestanding mesh structure acts like a beetle's hard carapace protecting the building from vandalism whilst creating an expanded floor plan that includes a private rooftop garden and light filled central void.

The facades of buildings have the potential to take many forms – architecture firms often choose to collaborate with artists to create beautiful solutions to design problems. Looking for a unique solution to shroud a five-storey car park, part of the Royal Domain Tower on St Kilda Road, Melbourne, studio505 approached Melbourne-based paper artist Geoffrey Nees (pg 141) to create an artwork that could be translated at this large scale. Working with paper for more than 20 years it was of interest to Nees to instil part of the non-uniformed nature of the hand-made into the facade. Steel's light, durable and malleable qualities allowed the resultant design of spiralling mandalas or starbursts, made up of 25,000 perforated petals, to be laser-cut then hand-folded over a three week period.

Making one material act like another is core to Dan Lorrimer's practice (pg 127). Like Nees he works sheets of steel as is it were paper, folding and manipulating it with hydraulic presses. He is an artist that uses processes that reflect his concepts – the collided and crumpled sculptures speak of geological tectonic forces that form our mountain ranges and deep ocean trenches. The folded form finds a bold translation in the *Armour Screen*, 2012 (pg 164) by korban/flaubert. Partners in life and design, architect Stefanie Flaubert and metal specialist Janos Korban established korban/flaubert in 1993. Their practice is all about metal, in particular, steel. They readily speak of the alchemic magic of transmuting soil into a precious but finite material, describing their works as artefacts that came from the Earth and that one day may return to it.

The idea of returning to the Earth, dust to dust, speaks of decay. Rust or the oxidisation of iron is synonymous with the red soils of Central and Western Australia, as well as the dust storms that roll eastward to the coast. Importantly it is the colour of blood, formed by the oxidisation of iron in the hemes of our haemoglobin. Weathering steel, best known by the trademark CORTEN, capitalises on this rich copper red colour. The distinctive 'patina' of weathering steel is the result of copper chromium alloy steel developing a protective surface layer of oxidisation when exposed to the atmosphere. Utilising corten, leading Australian sculpture and public art specialist Matt Harding's *Seeds of Thought*, 2015 (pg 188) speaks of binaries – regenerations and decomposition, strength and fragility, interiors and exterior – all are explored in this series of works.

The studio of Tony Hobba Architects (pg 247) is located on the Surf Coast of Victoria. Living and working in the unique landscape of the Great Otway National Park and the famous surf beaches including Bells Beach informs the work of the practice. Hobba notes that through their work they wish to act 'sensitively to the natural environment, its power and its vulnerability'[10] and this ethos is perfectly expressed in the Third Wave Kiosk, 2012, in Torquay. The Kiosk's predominant exoskeleton is constructed from recycled sheet piles typically used for seawall, bridge and pier construction. Left in their original state, the reddish brown and yellow oxides of the folded steel structure harmonises with the natural contours and colours of the coastline.

Bringing together art, design and architecture in this publication and the exhibition it accompanies allows us to think upon the links and similarities between the creative processes, problem solving and design thinking undertaken in these various disciplines. It reveals that many of the concerns that drive these innovative uses of steel engage the themes of identity, locality, materiality and sustainability. A material of such great potential, steel influences nearly all aspects of our lives, rendering the ingenuity, craftsmanship and skill of those working with it practically invisible. Through the selected 29 examples, *STEEL: art design architecture* unearths just some of these possibilities. ■

1 Pirsig, R. M., *Zen and the Art of Motorcycle Maintenance An inquiry into Values*, 1974, Chapter 8, pp. 104-05.

2 Invented by English inventor Henry Bessemer, in 1856, the Bessemer process removes impurities from the pig iron by oxidation with air being blown through the molten iron. The oxidation raises the temperature of the iron mass and keeps it molten. The Bessemer process was superseded by the Siemens-Martin method. Open hearth or the Siemens-Martin process decreases the molten materials exposure to nitrogen which makes steel brittle. Open hearth has subsequently been replaced with the oxygen converter method of steel production. The last open hearth steel works closed in China in 2001.

3 98% of the world's mined iron ore is used to make steel.

4 Western Australia is rich in iron ore with 89% of all of Australian deposits found there.

5 http://www.ngv.vic.gov.au/wp-content/uploads/2013/02/Mari-Funaki-media-release.pdf, accessed July 2016.

6 http://www.steel.org/sustainability/steel-recycling.aspx, accessed July 2016.

7 www.mfayechauhan.com/, accessed July 2016.

8 https://www.bluescope.com/about-us/bluescope-news/2015/11/recognising-the-versatility-of-steel, accessed July 2016.

9 http://www.designartmagazinecom/2013/02/designer-brodie-neills-limited-editions.html, accessed July 2016.

10 Statement provided by Tony Hobba to writer.

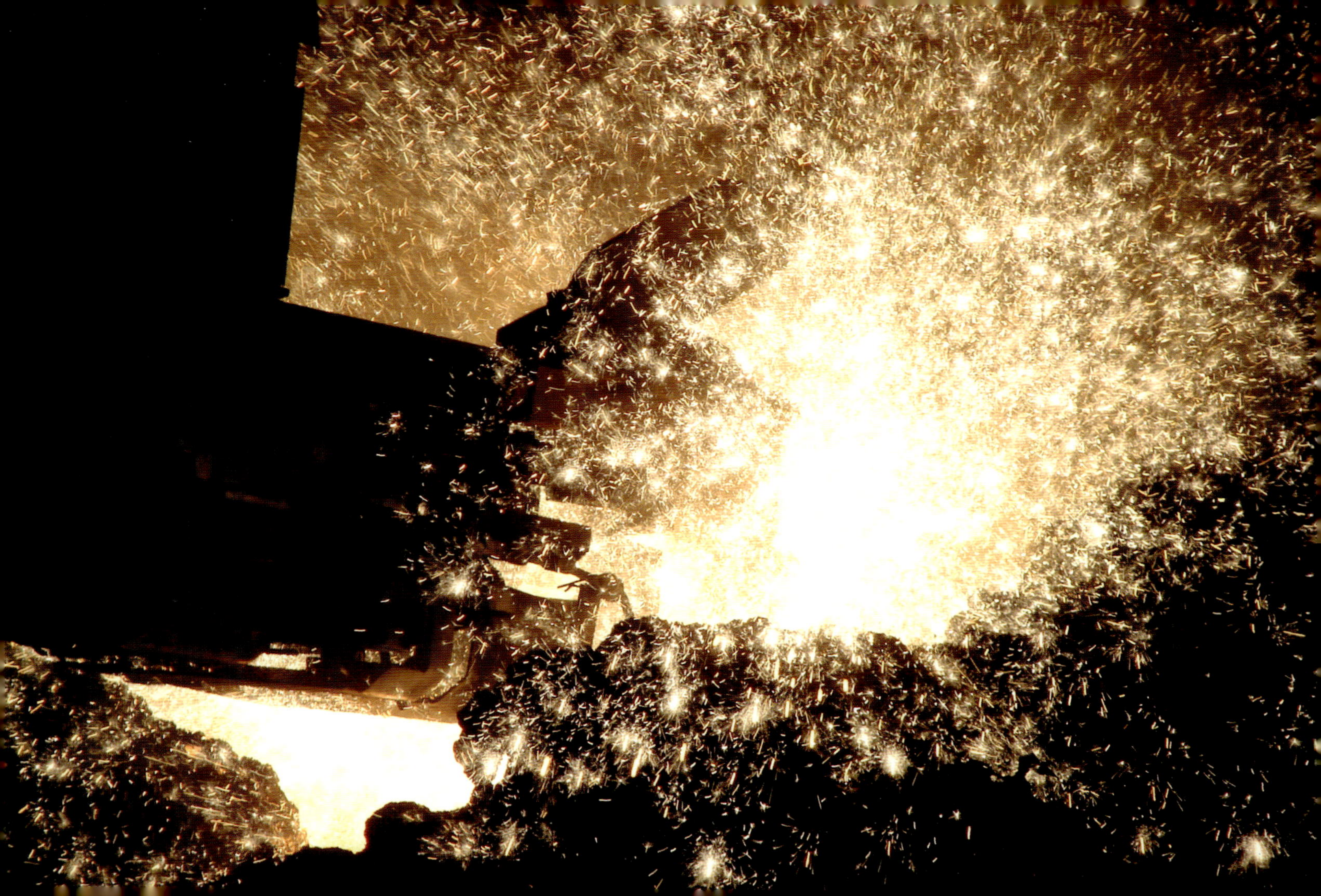

STRANGE IRONY

MARK THOMPSON

WHEN WE TALK about steel, we first need to come to terms with a sense of time that is immense and sprawling, almost inconceivably so. The Earth's past is to be found in layers of geological strata, the Cenozoic, Mesozoic, Paleozoic, Proterozoic and more. Digging deeper reveals that our world is unthinkably ancient, its early formation stretching back some four-and-a-half billion years to the Hadean Eon, soon after the Earth had begun existence as a disk of intensely hot dust and gas.

Roll forward another two billion years to the end of the Archean Eon when much of the Earth's iron ore, and hence our steel, was laid down in banded iron formations. Every piece of steel in this exhibition and in our daily lives has, at some stage been a part of this ancient prehistory. With our puny lifespans of threescore and ten years or so, we struggle to grasp the immensity of geological time. And here's the real kicker: this timespan is generally only talked about in the retrospective sense. It's even more challenging to conceive of geological time as *prospective* – geological time that stretches off into the future. Consider the fact that our Solar System (and the Universe for that matter) is not due to cease existence for quite some time yet. The Sun, for instance, won't run out of hydrogen for another five billion years.

So regardless of however we may dream that the human race will evolve, with the steady remorseless ticking of the geological time-clock, one day all we humans have ever made and known will be compressed into a few millimetres of rock strata. That's what inevitably happens here on our constantly changing Earth: over the millennia whole continents roam around its surface, grinding and crushing into each other. Volcanoes and earthquakes violently destroy landscapes. Countless eons of rain steadily wear whole mountain ranges down to mud. So one future day, some visitors may arrive here and detect a curious, wafer-thin strata in the planet's geology, the remnants of our Anthropocene era.

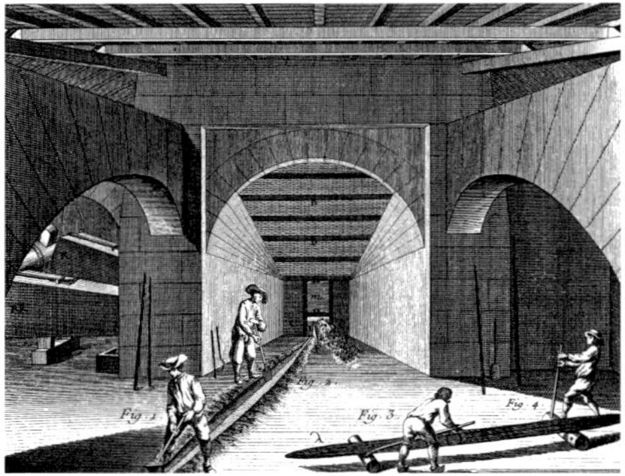

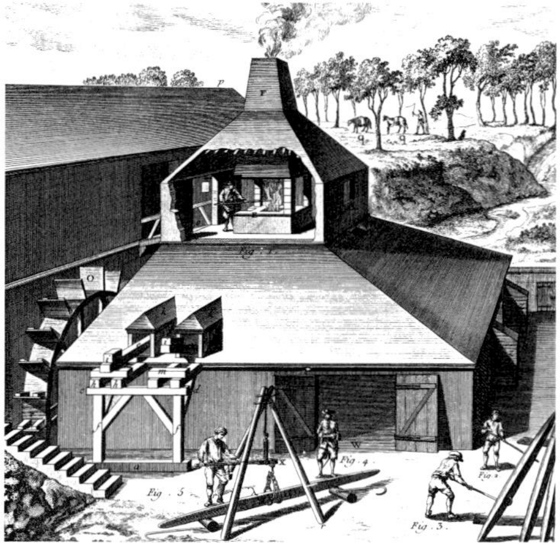

It will be made up of the detritus of human existence, every building we ever made, every car, every knick-knack, every work of art, every consumer 'durable'... all crushed and squashed flatter than a pancake. These visitors will likely conjecture: 'Who were these creatures?' And, 'Why is there so much iron in that thin strata?'.

When the European invaders came to Australia in the late 18th century, they did so at a pivotal time: the Industrial Revolution's first tentative steps were just bursting into an explosion of social and economic change. Iron and steel-making were already 4,000-year-old processes, which had sprung up, quite separately, all over the world. Steel weapons in particular had driven this progress, and the making of steel from iron was an arcane and even secretive process.

In many cultures around the globe, the worker of iron and steel has been a figure set slightly apart from the community in which they live. Often the smith is a feared and remote character, not just for his obvious strength but also for his esoteric powers to transmute hard metal into useful tools and weapons.

For much of the last 4,000 years, the making of iron and steel was a fairly small-scale operation. That was all to change in the 18th and 19th centuries, when inventions such as the Bessemer process and other subsequent developments blew oxygen through carbon-rich molten pig iron to remove excess carbon and other impurities to produce steel. Suddenly, the making of steel was possible on a very large scale.

The resulting product was far more malleable and versatile than brittle cast iron: the properties of steel enabled it to be drawn, forged, milled, rolled, tempered, annealed and hardened. It was now possible to create tools that made more tools, ever sharper, ever more accurate, ever cheaper. These new steel-making methods were rapidly scaled-up to make steel far cheaper and in effect, threw the switch on the Industrial Revolution.

Steel-making towns such as Sheffield and Birmingham in Britain, where steel-making had been almost an artisanal craft, soon became huge and productive cities. These new cities,

PREVIOUS PAGE
Blast furnace in action Arrium Steelworks Whyalla, South Australia. Photo: Sean A. Kelley

the 'dark satanic mills' of William Blake's famous poetic reference, churned out everything from cutlery and tools, to gravity-defying bridges.

Small artisanal steel-making enterprises – the kind we might call 'craft' now – were soon bludgeoned out of existence by big steel, driven out by a new class of commercial entrepreneur and innovator. The ingenious worker tinkering with all these exciting new ways of working metal eventually became a new occupation with almost shamanic powers: the engineer. Engineers seized on the increasing capacity to create tools and technology – drills, lathes and mills, with ever-finer tolerances, common standards and measurements. Tools could be used to make even better tools and implicit in this technology was a belief in constant improvement and the virtue of reason. Steel was both literally and metaphorically the mainspring of the Industrial Revolution: once wound up it has kept going, still unwinding centuries later to a yet unknown end.

In Australia, half a world away from the dramas of the Industrial Revolution, those first European invaders eventually managed to wander inland. They found that the interior of the country was harsh, dry, dusty and red...

◀

Engravings shown the process of iron-making in France in the 1850s sourced from Denis Diderot's *Pictorial Encyclopaedia of Trades and Industry*. These images predate the modern manufacture of steel by almost half a century.

▶

Camel train in the Far North of South Australia. The camels are loaded on both sides of their saddles with semi-circular sheets of iron, c.1911. Photo: courtesy State Library of South Australia

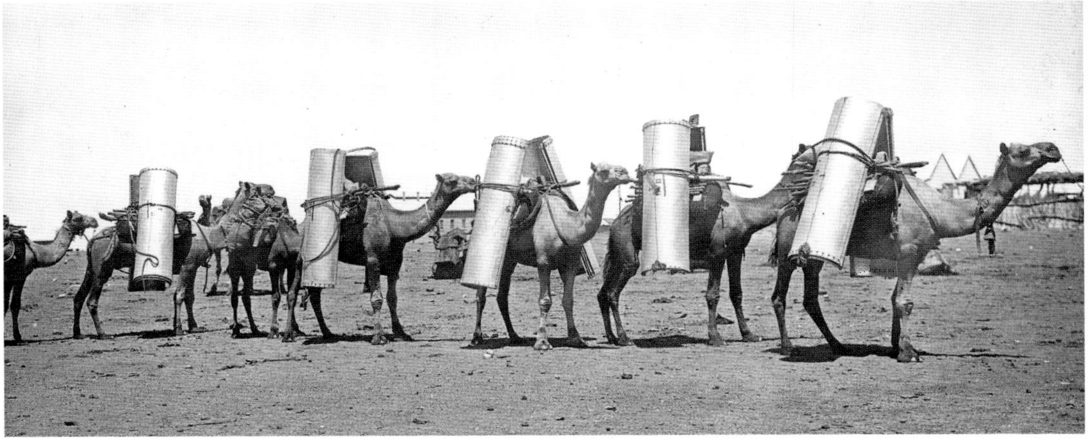

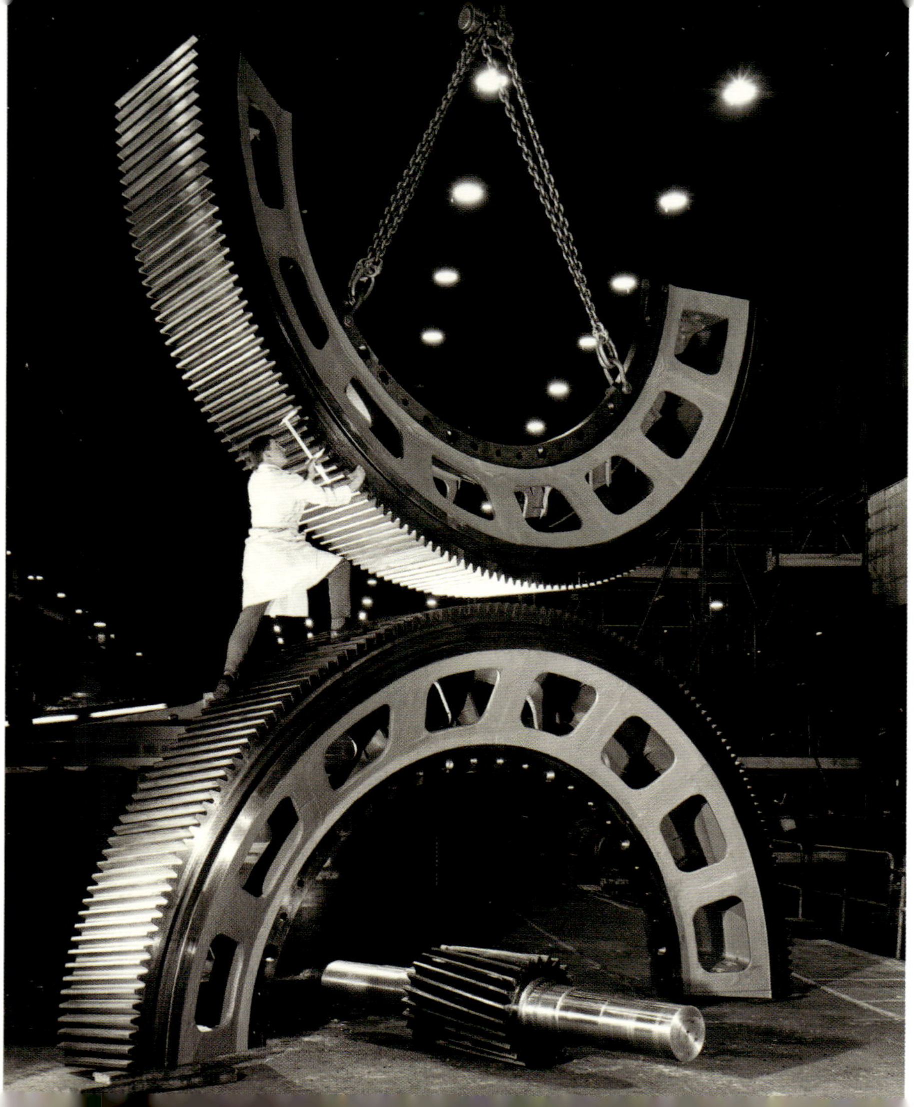

the apocryphal 'Red Centre'. It's not a huge exaggeration to say that Australia is, in part, literally made of iron: much of the colour of the red dust that typifies central and northern Australia is due to the presence of iron oxide.

In more recent times, we have become the world's biggest iron ore exporter – we do have nearly a third of the world's economically extractable iron ore. And despite the recent downturn in world steel production, our annual exports are still worth many billions of dollars. Digging up whole mountain ranges of iron ore, principally in Western Australia, and packing it off in ships to make steel in Asian blast furnaces has kept us in rather nice comfort for the last half-century. Our own steelmaking industry has never reached the potential offered by this immense resource. It is now in a steady rate of decline, the source of considerable national anxiety for many people worried about our ability to be masters of our national destiny.

Steel is loaded with meaning: it is about certainty, permanence, and durability, and lends itself to a strange appeal to patriotism and masculine virility. Yet, oddly, it also comes with a certain sentimentality. In Australia, rusting steel is now a symbolic motif laden with meaning: it tells of the stoic endurance required to survive a harsh landscape, even as it is slowly rusting away, reverting to the red dust from which it came.

Perhaps the ultimate alchemy in our red landscape is to cook that dust at high temperatures so that it may return, rolled and fluted, as sheets of corrugated iron, or perhaps drawn into great lengths as fencing wire. It's a curious property of both of these steel bush essentials, fencing wire and corrugated iron, that they contain an inherent musicality. The sound of stretching fencing wire in the wind can be eerily beautiful, like an immense Aeolian harp lost in a lonely paddock. Or to twang taut fencing wire when it is recently strung is to hear waves of sound travel up and down the fence line, bouncing back from a distant strainer post. And to listen to the first rain drops pinging on a corrugated iron roof is a delight. Then the steady transition to a gentle patter then a low drumming, rolling, continuous singing as the rain gathers in strength – and you are safe and sound under that one-millimeter-thickness of rippled steel. For this sound, for the elegance of corrugated iron as a design solution, it is impossible to deny the essential almost Zen-like beauty of this most prosaic of building materials.

Despite the hubbub around digitally-based technologies such as 3D printing, steel, in large quantities, is still at the core of our human-made world and will be for many years to come. As a world-transforming enterprise, nothing comes close to the impact of iron and steel over the last couple of centuries. That transformation is not universally good: the heating of our atmosphere and oceans from burning the immense quantities of coal required by our grand dreams of industrial production is now challenging our certainties. There is now a price to pay, first for the Industrial Revolution and then the subsequent deluge of low-cost consumer goods that it triggered.

Our ability to fashion some rusty red rock into steel gave us great capacity and convenience, but in getting there we may have sown the seeds of our destruction. In our pursuit of the wondrous possibilities steel offers us, we may have inadvertently cooked the planet.

Thus paradoxes abound with steel. Its lustre and polish are undeniably beautiful yet carry a sinister freight: historically its production methods were honed in the making of swords, gun barrels and weapons. It seems both ancient and permanent, yet it emerges from the dust and eventually reverts to its rusty origins. The making of steel objects is a human craft that outgrew itself and became the universal industrial and technological material: the ultimate symbol of the Anthropocene era. ■

[redacted]

◂
Wolfgang Sievers, *Gears for Mining Industry, Vickers-Ruwolt, Melbourne*, 1967
gelatin silver photograph,
599 x 474, National Gallery of Victoria, Melbourne, purchased through the Victorian Arts Board, 1972
(PH129-1972)

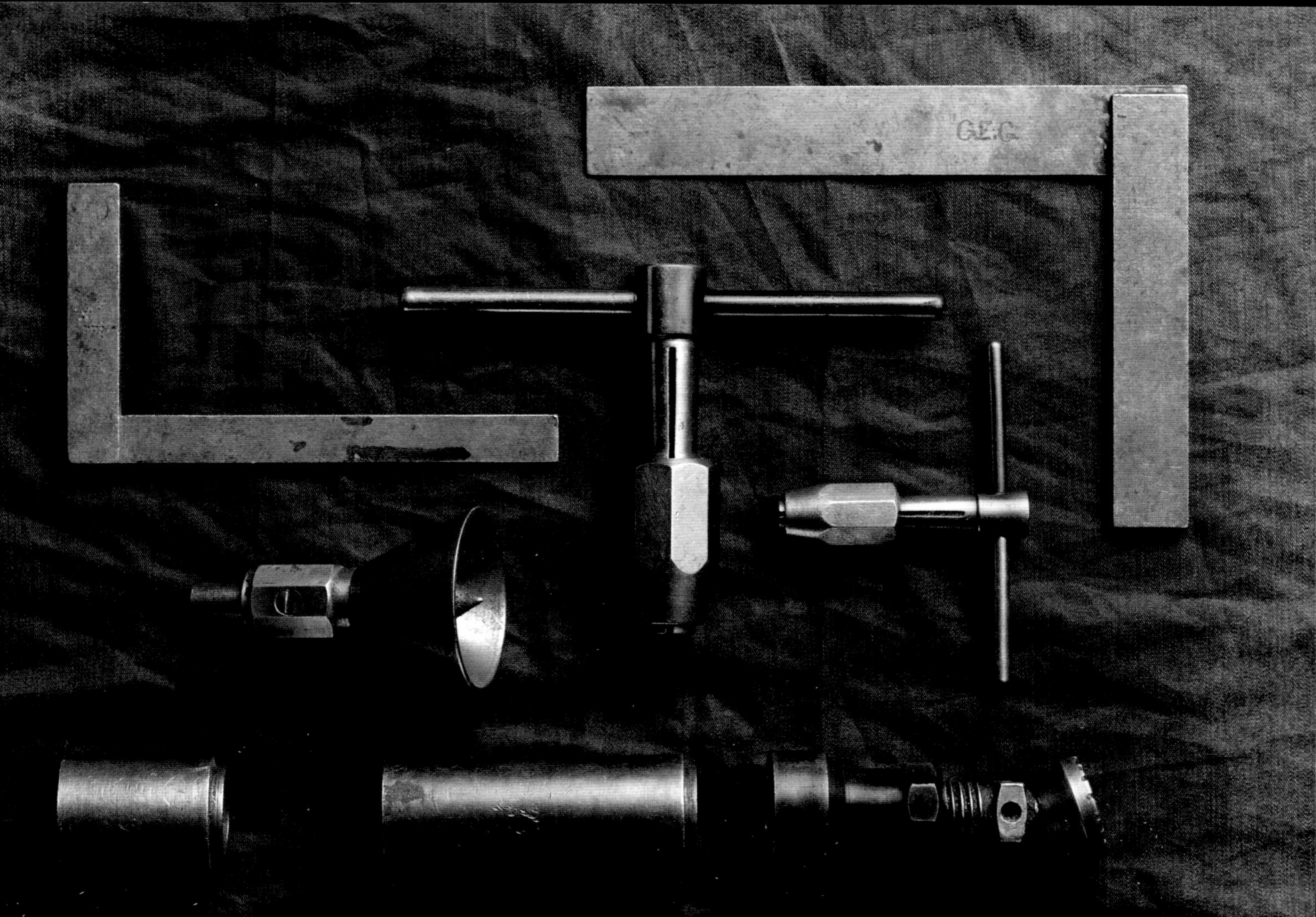
G.E.C

A BALLET OF GIANTS

STEPHEN GODDARD

'TURN YOUR RADIO UP and if you can still hear the noise, come back and I'll see what I can do.'[1]

My grandfather, George, was a mechanic and a very funny man. Trained as a fitter and turner, he eventually ran a local garage in Ross, a classic main-street-with-a-church-on-the-hill town in the midlands of Tasmania. More distinctly I remember him as highly skilled in the art of manipulating metal. He paired this with the inventiveness you needed to solve problems – pragmatic issues, often of repair. A mechanic. An inventor. Possibly a designer-maker, if he were alive today.

As children we spent a lot of time at Ross. George's garage had (still has, albeit in need of repair of its own) a clattering system of belts run from a central lineshaft. This network of drill presses, a metal lathe, grinder and air-compressor was run from a single electric motor, with tools engaged as needed by the pull of a lever or two.

Like my great-grandfather Ted, I've always understood timber. I know how you can shape it and finish it. I have a sense of the tolerance and of the possibility. For George, metal was as malleable as soft King Billy Pine, the material of much of my own childhood craft. Small handles for thread taps; devices for jacking small jobs; set squares manufactured and stamped with his initials; or the product of his ground-up craft – a petrol cap or replacement lever for his pre-war BSA motorcycle.

My father Graeme is equally inventive and also a craftsman. He followed somewhat in George's footsteps, training five-nights-a-week at the Hobart Technical College and supported by his daytime work as a cadet engineer in the drawing office at Humes Steel Division. What followed was a 50-year career as a mechanical engineer and works manager for Humes Steel Division, later known as Steel Mains, and in the company's final years as his own business partnership, Tristeel Engineering.

The centrifugal concrete pipe making that Walter Hume made famous was originally a patented system for finishing ornamental steel fence panels (dip them in paint and then spin them around – fast – to rid them of the excess and achieve a perfect finish). In a moment of inventive thought, Hume saw that this might apply to the manufacture of concrete pipes. Following his 1923 patent of a method to roll steel sheet, and by a logical and iterative process, the steel pipe, often concrete-lined, emerged.[2] Equally inventive were the significant advances that Hume made in automatic arc welding, research that continued through the life of Humes Steel Division and Steel Mains.

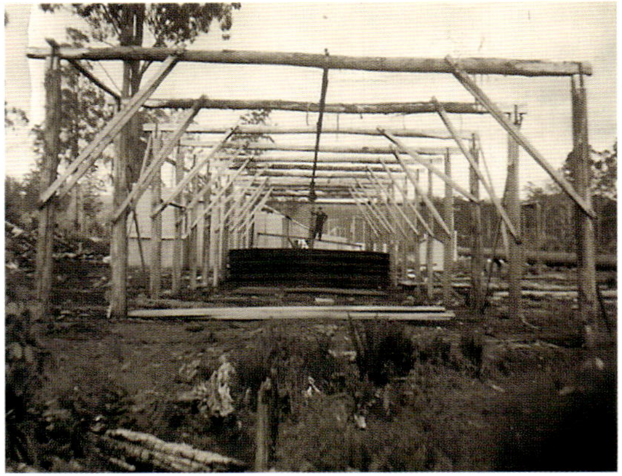

Humes moved into Tasmania and established a purpose-built timber-framed steel factory on site in the bush in 1936 to build and lay Tarraleah Line 1.[3] These are the penstocks (pipes for conveying water to power stations) that still feed one of the network of hydro-powered electricity generation stations for which Tasmania is famous. The pace of work was voracious. In the space of 15 months, a canal, civil works, power station and the first pipeline (with surge tower) was completed by 1,000 workers living in tents and camps on site. In 1946, the rapid growth of the business saw the building of the Derwent Park factories that I remember from my childhood and teenage years. These were the home to Humes and Steel Mains, and where the bulk of Tasmania's penstocks were built over the next half-century or so.

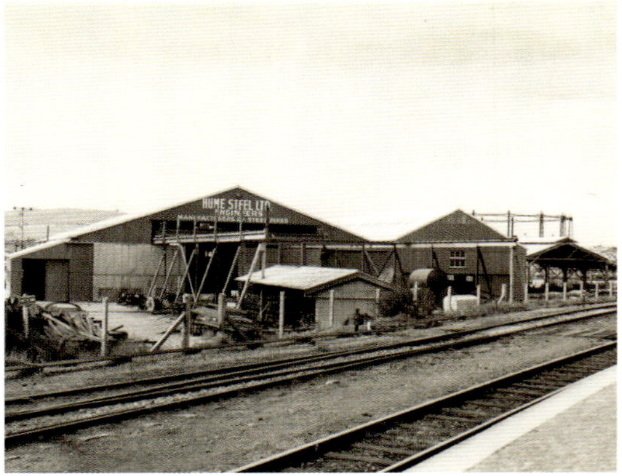

The Derwent Park factories were a playground for the many weekends of our childhoods, and have remained a strong memory. Unlike my younger brother, I didn't become an engineer, but I've never been able to separate my own design work from a love of making. Over time I've embraced the balance of the evolving nature of design practice with the endurance of craftsmanship – whether that be in the creation of sets for theatre and television as it was in my early days, or the bulk of my work as a communications and exhibition designer as it is now. The marriage is sometimes odd – a need for design innovation balanced against the idea of the heirloom.

[redacted]

◀

Outdoor steel storage and timber- framed gantry at the original Hume Steel Ltd. factory in Tarraleah, Tasmania, c.1935.
Photo: Ron Vagg

◣

Hume Steel Ltd. factory in Derwent Park, Tasmania, c.1950.
Photo: unknown

[redacted]

◥

Factories at Humes Steel Division in Derwent Park looking toward Humes Concrete Division, 1968.
Photo: Graeme Goddard

▶

Hot gas ducting loaded on rail cars to be taken to Goliath Cement plant in Railton, Tasmania, 1968.
Photo: Graeme Goddard

PREVIOUS PAGE
Small tools handmade by George Goddard in the 1930s.
Photo: Keith Saunders

The Derwent Park factories were formed around a pipe-manufacturing production line. The lower shop was where steel sheet was cut, prepared, edged, and in some cases descaled in cold acid. The giant steel plates would make the short trip by semi-trailer to the largest shop – the one I remember most distinctly. It was here that it was rolled and welded to make penstocks that averaged a 12' diameter and 30' length. Smaller pipes, concrete-lined using Hume's ingenious method, formed the backbone of production all year around. It is only with time that I've come to understand the masterplan of how the nine acres of factories worked in complete harmony.

Sparks, the electrician, had his workshop in the corner of that largest shop floor and I always saw him as a quiet ally. Dad would save scrap cable from the copper recycling bins to fuel my homemade projects. I loved lights, motors and inventions, all of which I ran from a 12-volt car battery. Every new box of scrap represented fresh possibilities – another part of the backyard to be potentially 'wired up'. The measure of my productivity was the length of time I was able to work before I flattened the battery and it needed to be recharged.

Whilst pipes were the mainstay, Steel Mains manufactured an endless array of large, custom-designed objects. At the time I saw them as sculptural, divorced as they were from their final installation and with any actual use a complete mystery to my creative arts and dramatic mind.

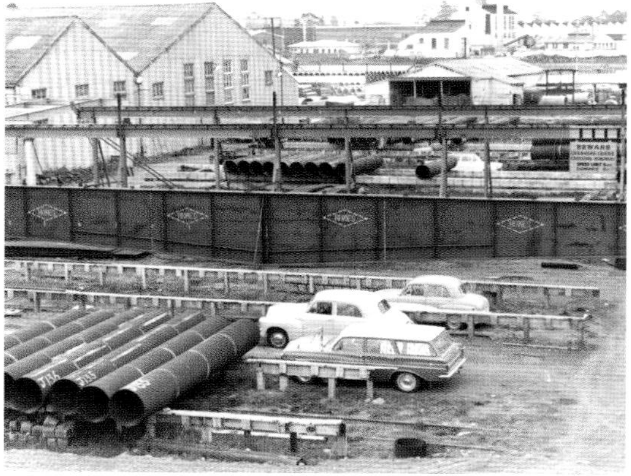

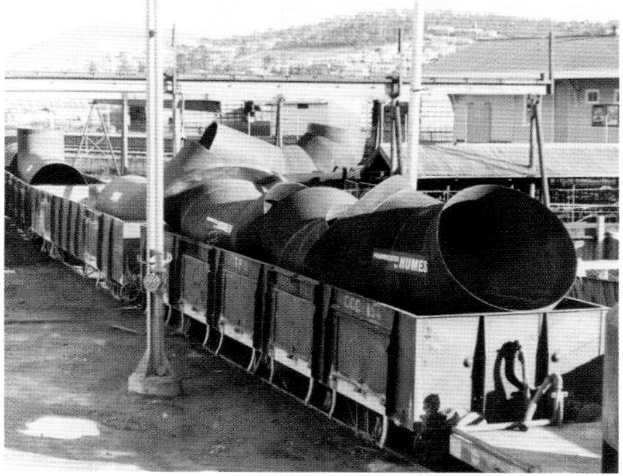

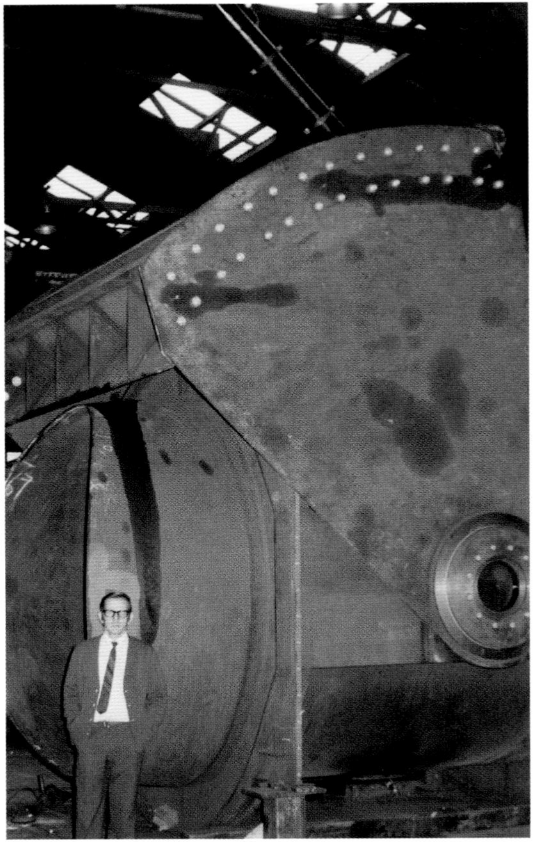

They were simply large steel forms that would float and turn on the factory floor as they were crafted, assembled and disassembled in the likeness of warehouse theatre sets. Gantry cranes would load and move them for fabrication, painting and delivery, playing the role of the stagehand.

As sculptural items, there was an aesthetic that I came to understand and enjoy. It was one of angular asymmetry, divorced from what we might consider classical beauty. These were the disjointed shapes of heavy industrial engineering, which left a cacophony of scrap metal remnants throughout the factory site. With care and instruction we were allowed to roam and play, which has given me a great tolerance and joy for places of manufacture. I still believe I grew up with an odd perception of what might constitute beauty, or indeed, the seams in which we might find it.

The factory floor was a ballet of giants. What belied these huge constructions was an extraordinary accuracy, which was lost on me at the time. The scale of manufacture was opposite to the delicate tools in George's garage, but the attention to detail was still microscopic – 20/1000 of an inch, maybe a bit less, or maybe a bit more. But not a lot, any way you looked at it.

Reflecting on these times with my father recently, we talked about inventiveness – that same problem-solving necessity that defined my grandfather's thinking. As we looked through images, the immediate appeal to me was often

◂

Graeme Goddard standing in front of a large radial gate manufactured for the Gordon Dam in Tasmania, 1976.
Photo: unknown

▸

Inside the main shop at Hume Steel Ltd in Derwent Park with large pressure vessels under construction, mid-1950s.
Photo: unknown

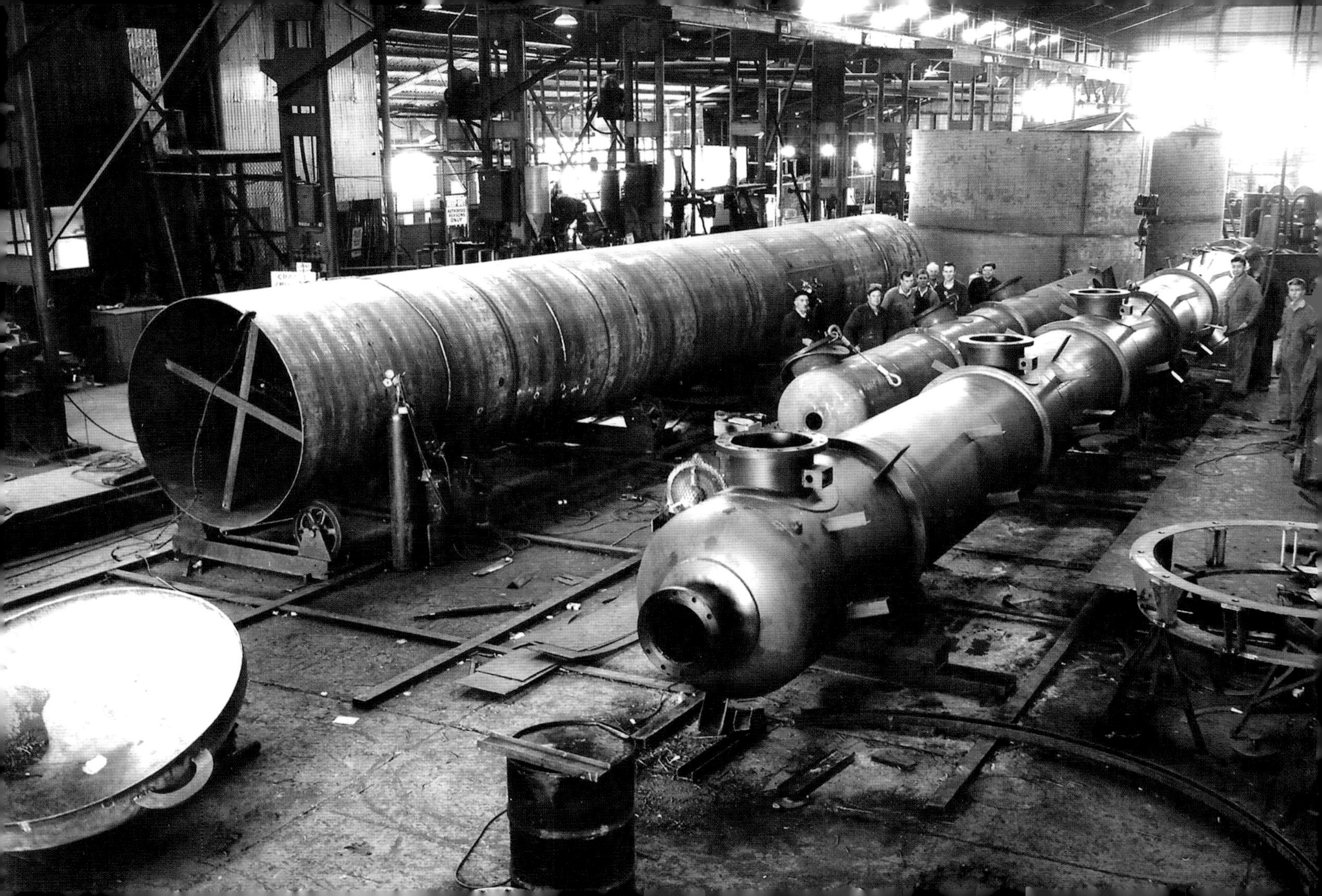
AUTHORISED PERSONS ONLY

[redacted]

The final steel girder being lifted into place during the repair of the Tasman Bridge, Tasmania, 1976. Photo: courtesy David Young, John Holland Construction

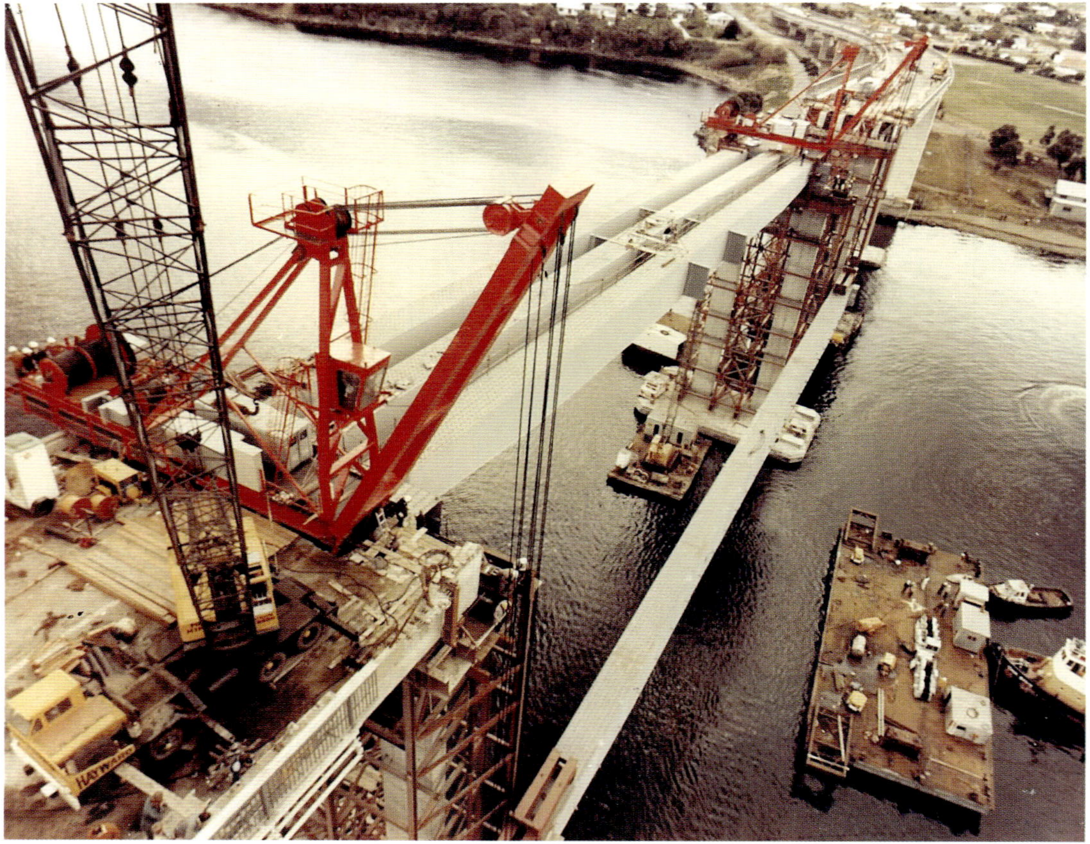

aesthetic or in awe of scale. Dad would explain the invention that the pictures contained. One showed a part of a substantial radial gate, used to drain water from the Gordon Dam during its construction in the 1970s. A belt grinder, pulled back and forth on a pendulum by a wire machined the arc surface of the gate, accurate to within just a few thousandths of an inch. It now seems makeshift, but in fact comes from the perfect logic of knowing intimately how a material works.

In my memory of the small city of Hobart, Steel Mains seemed important. Perhaps it was that the company would sometimes make the evening news, as roads were closed for the biggest objects to be hauled. Or perhaps that the factory was integral to the rebuilding of the Tasman Bridge. The bridge partly collapsed in 1975 after being struck by the bulk-ore carrier, Lake Illawarra, killing 12 people and leaving the city largely bisected for a number of years.[4] Memories of this period are vivid. At Wilkinson's Point I climbed inside the giant steel girders that were being assembled there, to be barged down the river into place.

Tasmania struggled for many years to move beyond the large-scale industry that sustained it, into the micro and cultural industries for which it is becoming increasingly and internationally known. In poetic and circular history, Wilkinson's Point is now home to the spectacular pavilion designed by architectural firm Room 11 that cantilevers over the Derwent River as part of GASP!.[5] In my eyes, the pavilion has a shape reminiscent of the bridge girders launched onto the water in that very place. A coincidence I'm sure – but memory, interpretation and contemporary culture in joyful collision nonetheless. Through its rose-coloured glass wall the view is to the rusted corten walls of MONA[6], which sits just a few minutes walk from the house I grew up in (and where I had a workshop of my own).

The ferry trip to MONA passes under the Tasman Bridge and past the Electrolytic Zinc Works (built from much of the odd shaped plant that Steel Mains created). Meandering past GASP!, my childhood house and finally to the museum, somewhere out to the left is INCAT.[7] This is high tech industry, situated on the foreshore not far from where Steel Mains once hummed. The plant still manufactures giant wave-piercing catamarans in aluminium for clients the world over. With that our conversation turns to innovation – the opportunity for Tasmania, with its rugged west coast, to lead the way with wind power – the fresher, younger child to those penstocks and wood-stave pipes.[8] There's hope yet, should a government take leadership and embrace the significant potential.

Dad's factory and George's tools are at opposite ends of the spectrum of manufacture in steel. They both remain a defining influence – the powerful patina of place, fine art of craftsmanship and connection to material. Above all, it's the sense of inventiveness and ingenuity that propels my thoughts beyond the dangers of nostalgia, into a celebration of thinking and making. ■

1 In August 2016, I visited my father Graeme at home in Tasmania. This and other anecdotes in this piece form part of the recollections we discussed in an oral history conversation, and that have been added to an ongoing personal memoir he is keeping.

2 Port, L. with Murray, B., *Australian Inventors*, Cassell Australia Limited, NSW, 1978, pp 87-93.

3 Tarraleah is a small town in the Central Highlands of Tasmania, and home to one of Australia's first hydro-electric power schemes.

4 http://www.ccc.tas.gov.au/page.aspx?u=1086, accessed August 2016.

4 Glenorchy Art and Sculpture Park, http://gasp.org.au/, accessed August 2016.

6 Museum of Old and New Art, http://www.mona.net.au/, accessed August 2016.

7 INCAT is a private company, still with a portion of shares owned by founder Bob Clifford, amongst others. http://www.incat.com.au/, accessed August 2016.

8 Wood stave pipes were formed from straight lengths of timber tapered on their sides and held together with steel bands to form a circular pipe. The principle is somewhat like the manufacture of a barrel.

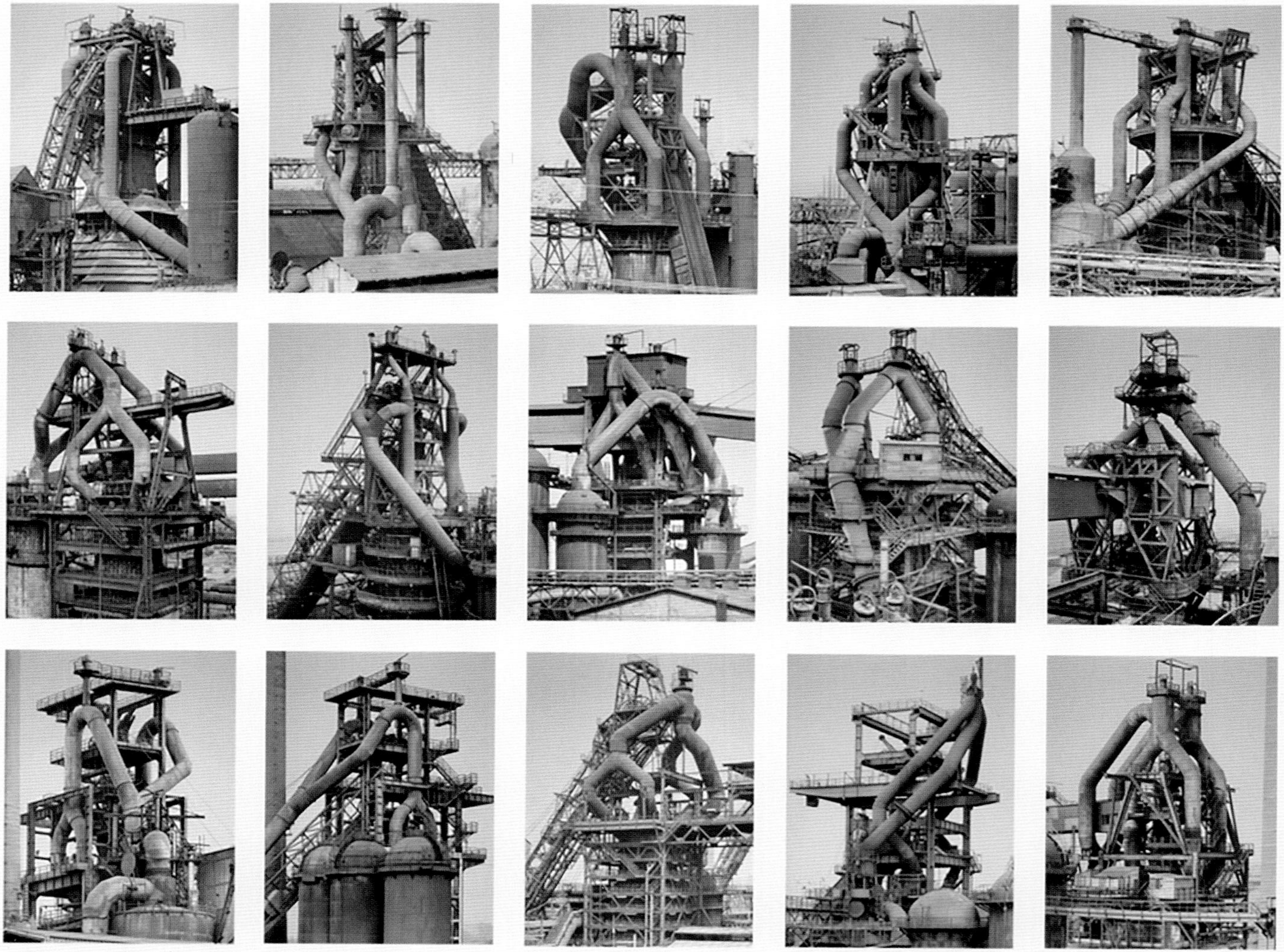

WORN STEEL

KATE RHODES

GERMAN ARTISTS Bernd and Hilla Becher[1] became famous for their photographs of the machines of industry: coal bunkers, blast furnaces, mine tipples, water towers, lime works, steel mills. They worked from the 1960s until the turn of the century, across Europe and the United States, making black and white photographs that straddle the worlds of archival documentation and conceptual art. The resulting photographs are systematically formal, making portraits out of non-human subjects. They are also dense in detail and presented both in their books and exhibitions in a grid format to encourage comparison between the typologies – turning viewers into lay industrial anthropologists.

At each site the Bechers also created overall landscape views of an entire plant, which show how the individual structures connect. The landscape images of steel mills, for example, show the storage tanks, the cooling towers, the winding towers that haul the iron ore, and the blast furnaces that convert the ore into metal. But these better-known typology images give little sense of the smog and toxicity we associate with steel mills and coal mines and in this way they reproduce our limited relationship, and equally limited knowledge for anyone living away from industrial centres, of how our cities are powered and how industrial products are made. However, the Bechers' landscapes expose billowing clouds of white from monolithic cooling towers and blast furnaces. They give us a sense of the visual and sensual impact that a sprawling steel mill has on its environment and what a world unto itself steel production creates within a community.

In Australia, steel is constantly making headlines. Currently, an over-production of the metal in China is seeing prices and demand for local raw materials and finished steel products plummet. Australian steel plants are continuing to close furnaces, making the labour of thousands of people redundant. The Bechers' images, made over the course

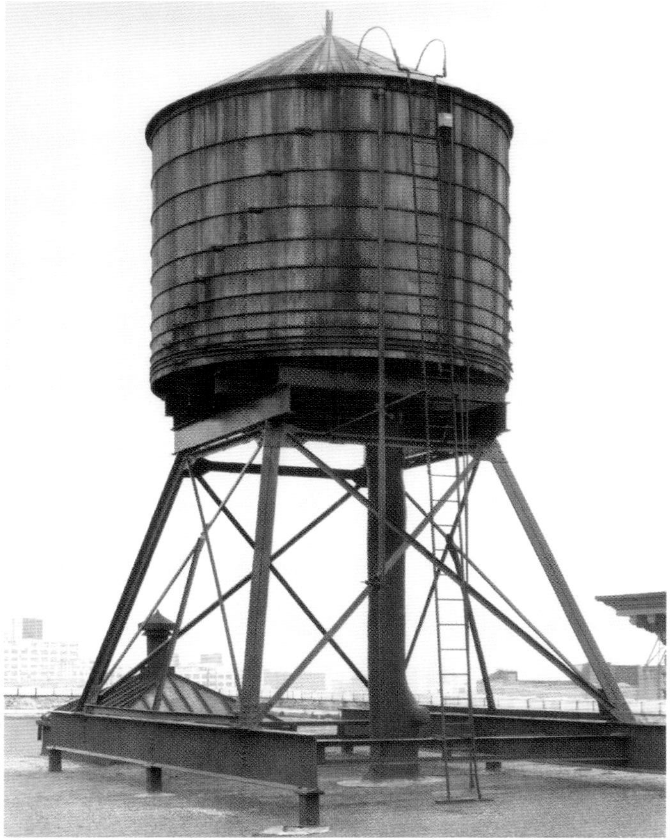

of 40 years, long pre-empted this moment and even from the time they began photographing in the 1960s, the project has existed as a kind of an archaeology of the decline of industry in the West. The demise of these typologies – shuttered as the industrialised economy continues to evolve – was precisely what instigated the Bechers' picture-making in the beginning.

STEEL AND JEWELLERY

Steel's industrialised production drives its fascination, selection and interpretation for many jewellers. For makers, steel is inexpensive, malleable and easily built into forms. It is strong but also light, meaning that very fine sheets of mild steel can be tamed to perform complex moves that other materials with less tensile strength would fail to hold.

At the time the Bechers began photographing industrial plants in decline, contemporary jewellers began to respond to Modernism's design aesthetic – described by the jeweller Susan Cohn as 'the use of industrial materials, clean simple lines, [and] an absence of decorative detailing apart from elements like rivets or screws'.[2] It was a period of emotionally detached jewellery objects[3] and a swathe of makers keen to bring ideas to the fore and who eschewed the seductiveness of gold, silver and costly gemstones or pearls associated with jewellery as a luxury item.

It was the second turn against the use of jewellery's traditional family of materials since the revolutionary avant-gardists of the Art Deco, Bauhaus and Constructivist period experimented with stainless steel, glass, eggshells, ivory and other unusual materials in the 1920s.[4] These makers were fascinated with the achievements of technology and championed jewellery reflecting their Futurist-inspired view that 'the salient characteristic of modern life is speed'.[5]

PREVIOUS PAGE
Bernd and Hilla Becher,
Blast Furnace, 2003
15 black and white photographs,
1734 x 2394, BHB-795 (15),
courtesy of Sonnabend Gallery,
New York
© Estate Bernd and Hilla Becher

◂

Bernd and Hilla Becher,
Water Towers: New York City: Broadway / Spring St., 1979
black and white photograph,
915 x 737 cm, BHB-20026 (1),
courtesy of Sonnabend Gallery,
New York
© Estate Bernd and Hilla Becher

Steel finds it hard to shake its architectural, urban, cold, industrial pedigree and jewellers often tap these qualities of the metal to make work that is minimal and structural looking and which comments on the human-made world. But these industrial qualities also make steel a challenging material for the jeweller to handle: steel can be difficult to solder as it oxidises and can require specialised, industrial equipment to manipulate it. Steel can also be hard on the wearer: sharp edges can damage clothes and skin, it requires more maintenance than gold and silver and doesn't like to get wet.

But it is here the alchemy of the jeweller's craft comes to the fore – to take this industrial material and change its appearance, feel and meaning while retaining something of its core characteristics. Japanese-born, Melbourne-based Mari Funaki's (1950-2010) work in blackened mild steel is one of the best examples world-wide of the rewards of successfully manipulating the challenging and shape-shifting complexity of steel. Funaki's work is at once of nature and of the factory – bending and stretching containers suggest insect-like forms with their long gangly legs but they are finished in deep, non-reflective, unerring industrial black. Some works, as curator Robert Cook notes, are half insect and half building structure, objects that keep evolving so that 'the relation of the built to the organic is not one thing or another: it is part of a shifting continuum'.[6] Indeed it was an encounter with a beetle while out walking with her young nephew that would become a potent reference point for some of Funaki's most important works, coincidentally just after she had discovered steel's multiple possibilities.[7] Such delicate play and such long, reaching and articulated 'arms' and 'legs' in Funaki's thin steel containers and objects would not have been as possible in another material.

For jeweller Otto Kunzli, Funaki's works are also reflective of the built world and seem to create interior spaces for imaginary inhabitation. As he suggests, they could be models for architecture.[8] He proposes that her works require their simple titling – *Bracelet*, *Ring*, *Brooch*, *Container*, *Object* – as if they were so constructed, so sculptural, so removed from jewellery and the body that we need direction as to their placement and purpose.

The unyielding blackness of steel was attractive to Funaki for its precise distinction.[9] Funaki's preferred steel was sourced from Tokyo then cut to size, the initial shape assembled, folded and soldered in place, sandblasted clean and then blackened, over many attempts, with a torch – transmuting from blue, purple, brown to black – before a final oiling (using machine oil) and waxing (with floor wax).[10] Funaki's containers, bracelets and brooches are constructions – and a description of their making process would seem just as apt at a worksite. As Cook writes: 'ostensibly crisp and rather formal in feel, there is also a profound darkness in her work as it appears both animal- and architectural-like in its continual organic/inorganic formation and re-formation'.[11]

AN AWKWARD BEAUTY

This shape-shifting quality is also highlighted by curator Jane Devery, who describes Funaki's 'ambiguous and undecipherable' work in terms of an 'awkward beauty'.[12] This description is a useful lens for thinking about what steel's character lends to some other examples of contemporary jewellery that also seem to grapple with the push-pull effect of imperfection peculiar to the use of steel. Very often this imperfection is explored not in opposition to beauty, but as its other face.

Inari Kiuru is a Finnish-born artist and designer who lives in Melbourne. Her work includes objects, images and mixed-media installation drawn from her research into post-industrial landscapes. Using steel, enamel, paint and gold, Kiuru decodes the gritty surfaces of Melbourne's suburbs. In her earrings, made of galvanized steel, the 'imperfect' figures not as the absence of form or the representation of asymmetry, disharmony, disfigurement or deformation (qualities opposed to conventional associations beauty has with balance and integrity), rather, it is present in order for us to recognise and highlight beauty's special qualities. Kiuru matches her use of galvanized steel and its mottled and patchy exterior with gold, enamel and paint and uses steel to reflect on the aesthetic contradictions of the urban world around her.

Likewise, Kate Wischusen, also based in Melbourne, chooses mild steel and enamel for their ability to echo found locations in the urban landscape – creating jewellery as a kind of metropolitan memorial. Her brooches become worn souvenirs that archive the eroded, misplaced or disrupted state of urban markings.[13] Material and surface experiments allow for the creation of memories and marks from traffic on the steel frame, which are then worn away.[14] In a not dissimilar way during the 19th century, clothes-makers and repairers referred to the wrinkles in the elbow of a sleeve as 'memories', too many of which reduced the value of the garment.[15] Like those 19th century garments, Wischusen's objects are replete with the signs of wear and tear and as a result also reflect signs of a haunting loss. Their simultaneous rough-smooth surface reveals layers of material character and surface effects – a cutaway cross-section of the city capturing both creation and deterioration in the striking 'flaws' – the scratches and scrapes that remain after erasure. Wishchusen's works thus openly ask how imperfection might feed our understanding of jewellery and its real and symbolic value.

These bodies of work reconfigure traditional ideas around beauty within a new system and hierarchy of aesthetics. At a time when the gloss of beauty has largely faded into distrustful notions of ostentation, relentless novelty and the ersatz, imperfection – the worn, the uneven, the disfigured – might be understood as signs of humbleness

▸
Mari Funaki, *Bracelet*, 2006
mild steel, heat coloured,
110 x 110 x 55, private collection
Photo: Jeremy Dillon, courtesy of
the Estate of Mari Funaki

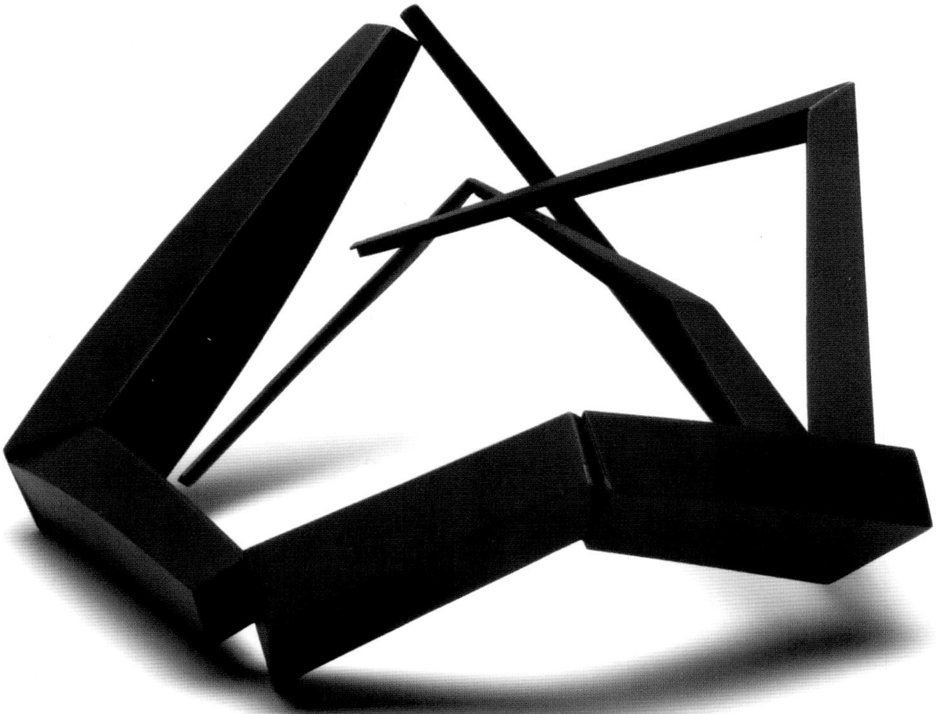

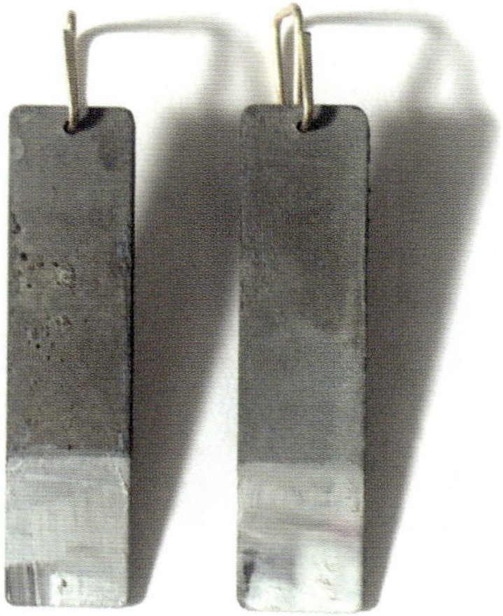

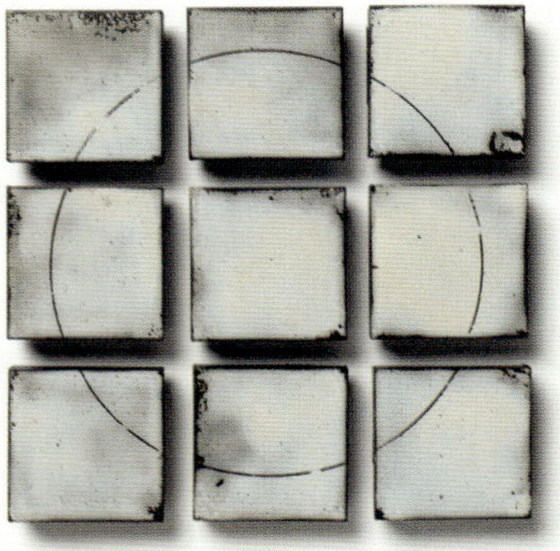

▸

Inari Kiuru, *Earrings* from the *Industrial lightscapes* series, 2016
heat oxidised galvanised steel, paint, 9k gold hooks, 10 x 50 x 0.5
Photo: courtesy the artist

▸▸

Kate Wischusen, *Disconnect*, 2014
mild steel, stainless steel, vitreous enamel, 160 x 160
Photo: Jeremy Dillon

and authenticity. These makers seem to seek a more demanding view of beauty and use jewellery's special character – its intimacy with the body – to maintain an uncertainty around such core traditional drivers of how we decipher jewellery's worth.

But perhaps surprisingly, in spite of these examples, steel – as a stand-alone material – rarely features in the work of emerging jewellers today. Is it because steel is the material that their teachers and established jewellery luminaries use? Instead, many emerging Australian designers are choosing plastic, resin, rubber, wood, fibre and found materials in the company of traditional gold, silver and gemstones. It may be argued that the material in which jewellery is made, be it cheap or very expensive, should feed into its meaning. Indeed while Funaki is one Australia's best-known jewellers, and someone who skilfully used steel, she also regularly used gold for all of its inherent physical characteristics and conceptual associations – its ability to reflect and offer openness and outward expression.

Ideas-driven, materially inventive jewellery remains the most exciting work in the field today. Makers who experiment and participate in debates and who test the edges of jewellery practice through the work that they create, in turn feed the conversation about jewellery paradigms. Both the values of jewellery and jewellery's value is informed through makers' choices of materials, and they are necessarily interdependent. As even this brief look at steel shows, a maker's material choices can have a profound impact not just on the performance of a work but on what messages that work sends to and from its wearers. ■

Thank you to Melanie Katsalidis (Pieces of Eight), Katie Scott (Gallery Funaki) and Meredith Turnbull for their conversations in research for this essay. Thanks also to Max Becher for his generous and helpful comments regarding his parents' work.

1 Bernd Becher: August 20, 1931 – June 22, 2007. Hilla Becher: September 2, 1934 – October 10, 2015.

2 Cohn, S., 'A Brief Contemporary Jewellery History', in Susan Cohn (ed.) *Unexpected Pleasures: The Art and Design of Contemporary Jewellery*, Rizzoli, New York, 2012, p. 226.

3 den Besten, L., 'The Trouble with Beauty' in Susan Cohn (ed.) *Unexpected Pleasures: The Art and Design of Contemporary Jewellery*, Rizzoli, New York, 2012, p. 102.

4 Ludwig, R., *Schmuck-Design der Moderne / Modern Jewellery Design*, Arnoldsche, Germany, 2008, p. 18.

5 Ludwig, R., *Schmuck-Design der Moderne / Modern Jewellery Design*, 2008, p. 18.

6 Cook, R., 'Keeping the secret's secret' in *Mari Funaki Works 1992-2009*, Art Gallery of Western Australia, Perth, 2009, p. 9.

7 Frontispiece, Mari Funaki, Gallery Funaki, Melbourne, 2007.

8 Otto Kunzli, Mari Funaki, Gallery Funaki, Melbourne, 2007.

9 Cook, R.,'Keeping the secret's secret', 2009, p. 6.

10 Cook, R., 'Keeping the secret's secret', 2009, p. 8.

11 Cook, R., 'Keeping the secret's secret', 2009, p. 5.

12 Devery, J., *Mari Funaki: Objects*, National Gallery of Victoria, Melbourne, 2010, p. 6.

13 http://victoriancraftaward.org.au/kate-wischusen/, accessed August 2016.

14 http://victoriancraftaward.org.au/kate-wischusen/, accessed August 2016.

15 Evans, C., *Fashion at the Edge: Spectacle, Modernity and Deathliness*, New Haven and London: Yale University Press, 2003, p. 257

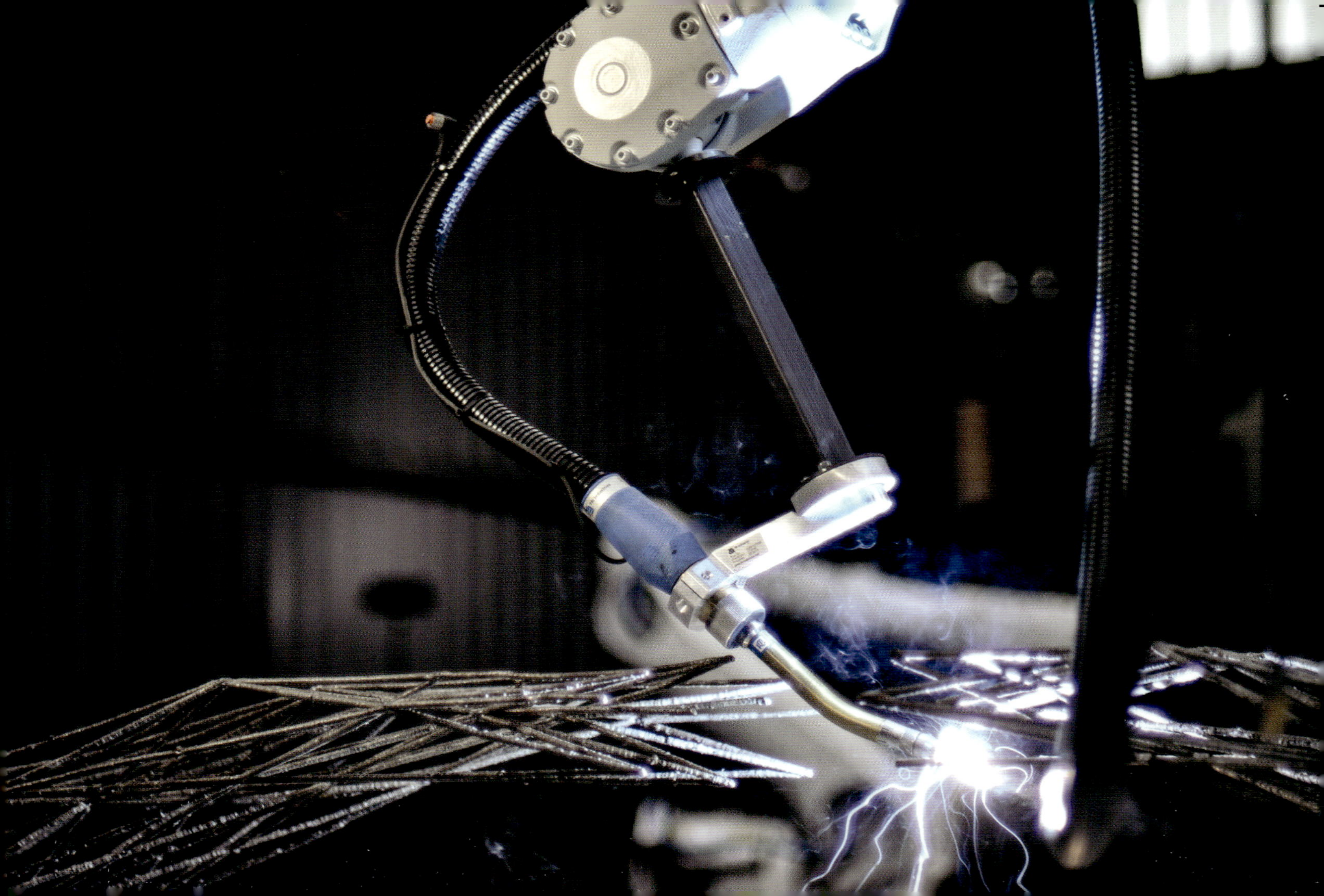

FROM STRENGTH TO STRENGTH

PENNY CRASWELL

STEEL IS SYNONYMOUS with strength. The largest mega-structures in the world – from the tallest building, the Burj Khalifa in Dubai, 2009, to the longest bridge, the Danyang-Kunshan Grand Bridge in Beijing, 2011 – are made of steel. Even more importantly still, these architectural feats are all made possible because of steel. In buildings, steel is most often used as a structural support – in load-bearing frames, columns, beams, bracings, skeletons and supports. Even those that present facades of glass, timber, brick or concrete are often built on a foundation of steel, invisible beneath the surface. This most extroverted of materials, strong and bulky, becomes the silent partner to other materials – a steadfast support to often-enormous loads.

Considering its reputation as a strong material, it is surprising to realise that when steel was first introduced, it was viewed with suspicion. Prior to English engineer Henry Bessemer's invention in 1856, which allowed steel to be made reliably, quickly and inexpensively, steel production had been imperfect, with structures built with iron being highly susceptible to rust and corrosion. The Bessemer Process, in combination with the invention of industrial galvanisation (which protects steel with a thin layer of rust) allowed for structures never seen before. One of the first large structures to test the strength of this new steel was the Brooklyn Bridge, which in 1883 was the first suspension bridge supported by steel cables – a design that had its detractors back then, but has since proved the test of time, and inspired countless examples like it all over the world.

MODERNISM AND STEEL

Since industrial production made steel a 'super-material', it has become ubiquitous. As well as being used in buildings large and small, bridges, dams and other infrastructure, steel can be found in railways, planes, ships and cars. It is also in our homes, from appliances

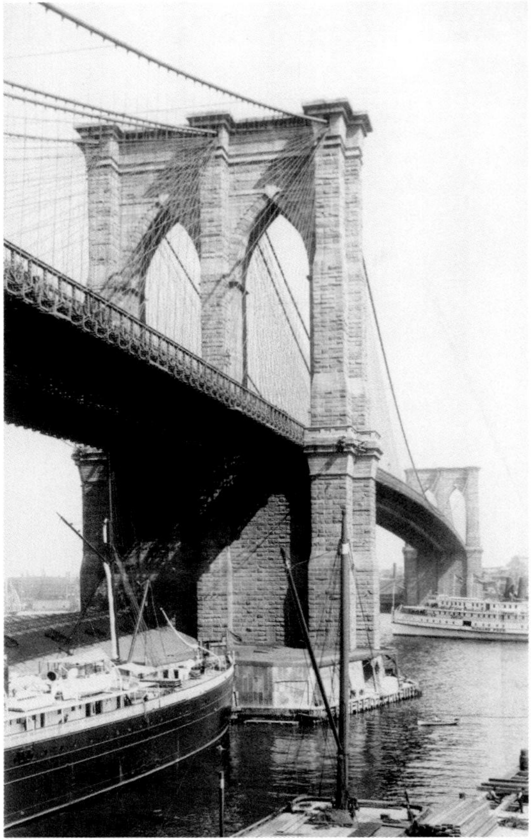

to furniture, lighting to cutlery. Starting with the industrial revolution and gaining momentum throughout the 20th century, steel continues to be symbolic of progress and the future. It stands for something powerful, modern, functional, utilitarian. Aesthetically, it can be gleaming and shiny, or it can be ugly, dirty, brutal and even cruel. The building boom of skyscrapers that began in Chicago at the end of the 19th century before moving to New York and around the world, was reliant on the material, creating an entirely new architectural aesthetic of steel, glass and concrete. This aesthetic spoke of Modernism – steel itself was seen as inherently new. Polish-born, US architect Daniel Libeskind describes his first impression of America as being tied up with this aesthetic: 'I came to America as an immigrant. You know, on a ship, through the Statue of Liberty. And I saw that skyline, not just as a representation of steel and concrete and glass, but as really the substance of the American Dream.'[1]

The use of steel in furniture is also inexorably linked with Modernism – Marcel Breuer displayed his now famous tubular steel chair, *Wassily*, at the opening of the Bauhaus in 1926, inspired by Mart Stam who was the first to experiment with the material in furniture design. In the same year, Eileen Gray designed the E-1027 circular table using tubular steel in combination with glass. These bold new designs marked a milestone in furniture design – shifting from bespoke crafted pieces made by hand to industrially-manufactured, mass-produced products. They represent a paradigm shift in furniture design – not only in materials, but in aesthetics and in meaning, following the modernist mantra that form follows function. Walter Gropius, the founder of the Bauhaus, wrote in 1923 that industrial production was 'the most modern means of design,'[2] while Breuer noted 'this metal furniture is to be nothing more than a necessary device for modern-day living.'[3]

The *Tolix* chair soon followed – first created in a metal workshop by French designer Xavier Pauchard and registered in 1932, the chair was also symbolic of a new approach to furniture. Like the Bauhaus, the intention was to make mass-produced furniture that was therefore affordable to all. Here, steel was a utilitarian material, selected for its price point.

PREVIOUS PAGE
Mx3d Bridge, Joris Laarman Lab, 2016
The first bridge spanned the Oudezijds Achterburgwal canal in Amsterdam.
Photo: Adriaan de Groot

It was also symbolic of the Modernist break from tradition, utilising industrial processes and engineering to create new aesthetic forms. Since the *Wassily* and *Tolix* chairs, tubular, stainless and sheet steel have become common materials for product designers making furniture, in what has been described by Museum of Modern Art Curator Paula Antonelli as 'perhaps the single most important innovation in furniture design in the 20th century.'[4]

FUNCTIONALISM AND AUSTRALIAN IDENTITY

Modernism in architecture in Australia was closely tied to functionalism – an approach that used rational planning to design buildings that were specific to Australia's climate. Here, steel was seen as an efficient material – Architect and Interior Designer Raymond McGrath claimed in a 1936 issue of *Australian Home Beautiful* magazine that: 'Efficiency is the keynote. The day of concrete, stainless steel and glass is at hand, together with planning based on scientific, as apart from social, considerations.'[5]

Even before Modernism, steel had an essential role in traditional Australian architecture in the form of corrugated iron, which was used heavily in rural buildings from sheds to housing. In contemporary practice, this Australian vernacular architecture, has been reinterpreted and is now most often built with steel – although it is still most often referred to as corrugated iron. Architecture critic Philip Drew describes the re-emergence of corrugated

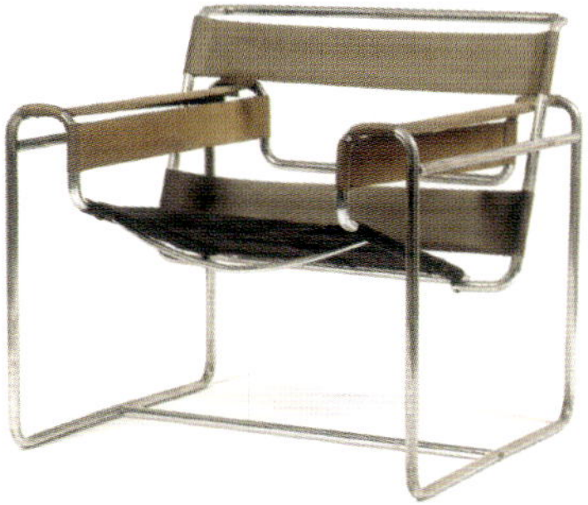

▶

Marcel Breuer, *B 3/Wassily*, 1925
cold bent, nickel-plated tubular steel, polished-yarn fabric, 725 x 765 x 695
© Vitra Design Museum
Photo: Jürgen Hans

◀

Brooklyn Bridge, c1896
photographic print, albumen, 737 x 305,
Copyright 1896 by Geo. P. Hall & Son, general photographers, No. 157 Fulton St., New York Geo. P. Hall & Son

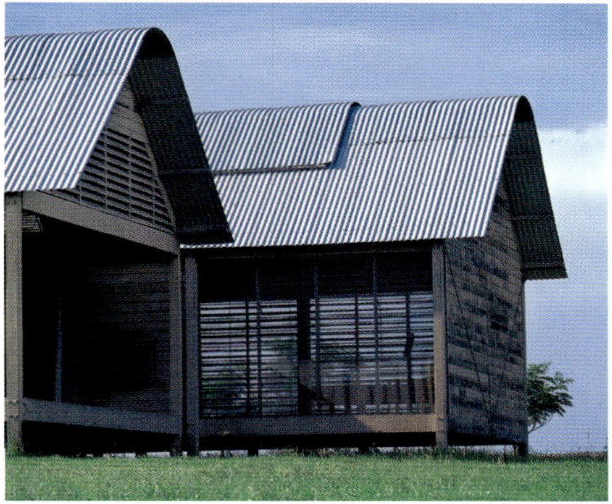

▶

Marie Short / Glenn Murcutt House, Kempsey, New South Wales 1974-75 and extended 1980
Architect: Glenn Murcutt
Photo: Anthony Browell courtesy Architecture Foundation Australia

iron in contemporary Australian architecture as tied to Modern functionalism, a movement that prioritises the utilitarian over the aesthetic. He writes: 'In using identifiably Australian methods and materials, the corrugated iron house was the logical result of Modern Functionalism, which has a further virtue that it can also be seen as indelibly Australian.'[6] Drew in particular notes the use of corrugated iron by Australian Pritzker Prize-winning architect Glenn Murcutt in his buildings, largely residential. Murcutt, interested in using the least amount of steel possible for the frame of his houses according to the principles of Mies van der Rohe, made his architecture uniquely Australian by using corrugated iron and other Australian materials. 'What Murcutt has remarkably achieved is to elevate corrugated iron and make it look elegant and noble in a way that was inconceivable before then.'[7]

Interestingly, despite being known for his corrugated iron forms which the Pritzker jury noted was inspired by 'the native Australian wool shed,'[8] Murcutt himself claims that the reference to traditional farm sheds is not his main inspiration. Instead he suggests he is more interested in referencing Aboriginal shelters: 'The iconography of Aboriginality is of far greater interest to Murcutt, when he discovers later that his roof profiles bears resemblance to that of bark-covered structures.'[9]

Regardless, Murcutt's work has inspired a range of buildings that use corrugated iron within the Australian landscape. Designed by Casey Brown Architecture, Crackenback Stables, 2016, in New South Wales's Snowy Mountains provides a contemporary reinterpretation of the Australian farm shed, with two architectural forms clad in corrugated zinc and aluminium alloy-coated steel. This surface wraps the walls and the roof of the building, with the alignment of the corrugations parallel to the roof pitch, emphasising the structure's trapezoidal form.

Functionalism and the use of steel aren't limited to architecture in Australia. Designers, craftspeople and artists around the country spend their days in the workshop forging and welding steel. In Tasmania, John Hounslow-Robinson has become world renowned for creating some of the best knives in the world, with famous chefs as customers. Forged by hand, these knives are intricate and beautiful, with most taking an average of two days to make, while some take longer and are made of up to 1,000 layers of steel. Although the end result of the process is an object of beauty, Hounslow-Robinson's work is also a perfect example of functionalism – focused on creating a blade that is strong, sharp and has exceptional longevity. In creating these knives, Hounslow-Robinson lives simply, immersed in his craft like the blacksmiths of times past. Far from the mass-production of modernism and the Bauhaus, his craft is personal and beautiful, despite the cold, hard, rational, and even brutal nature of the finished blade.

[redacted]

▸
Casey Brown Architecture,
Crackenback Stables, 2015
Crackenback, New South Wales
Photo: Rob Brown

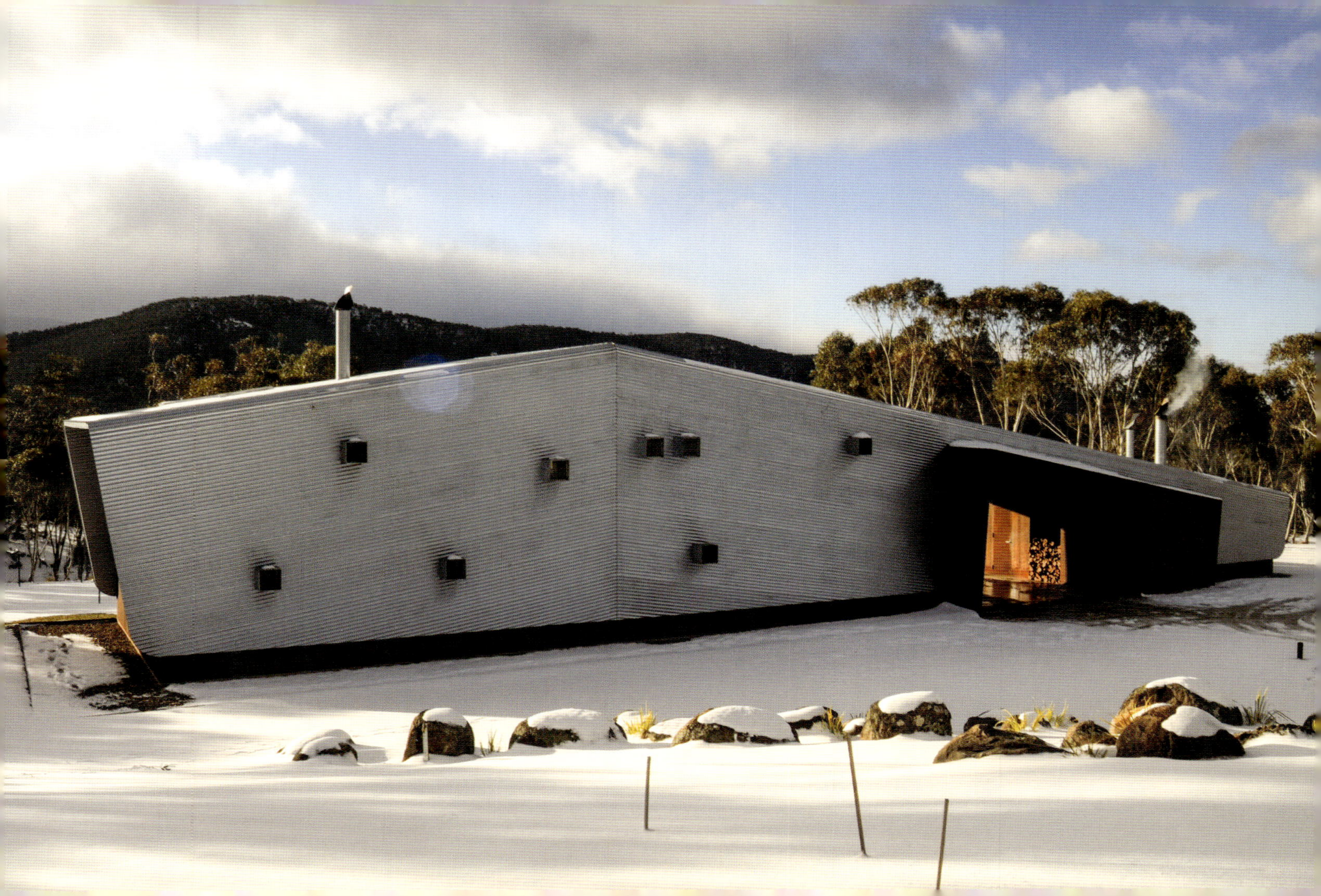

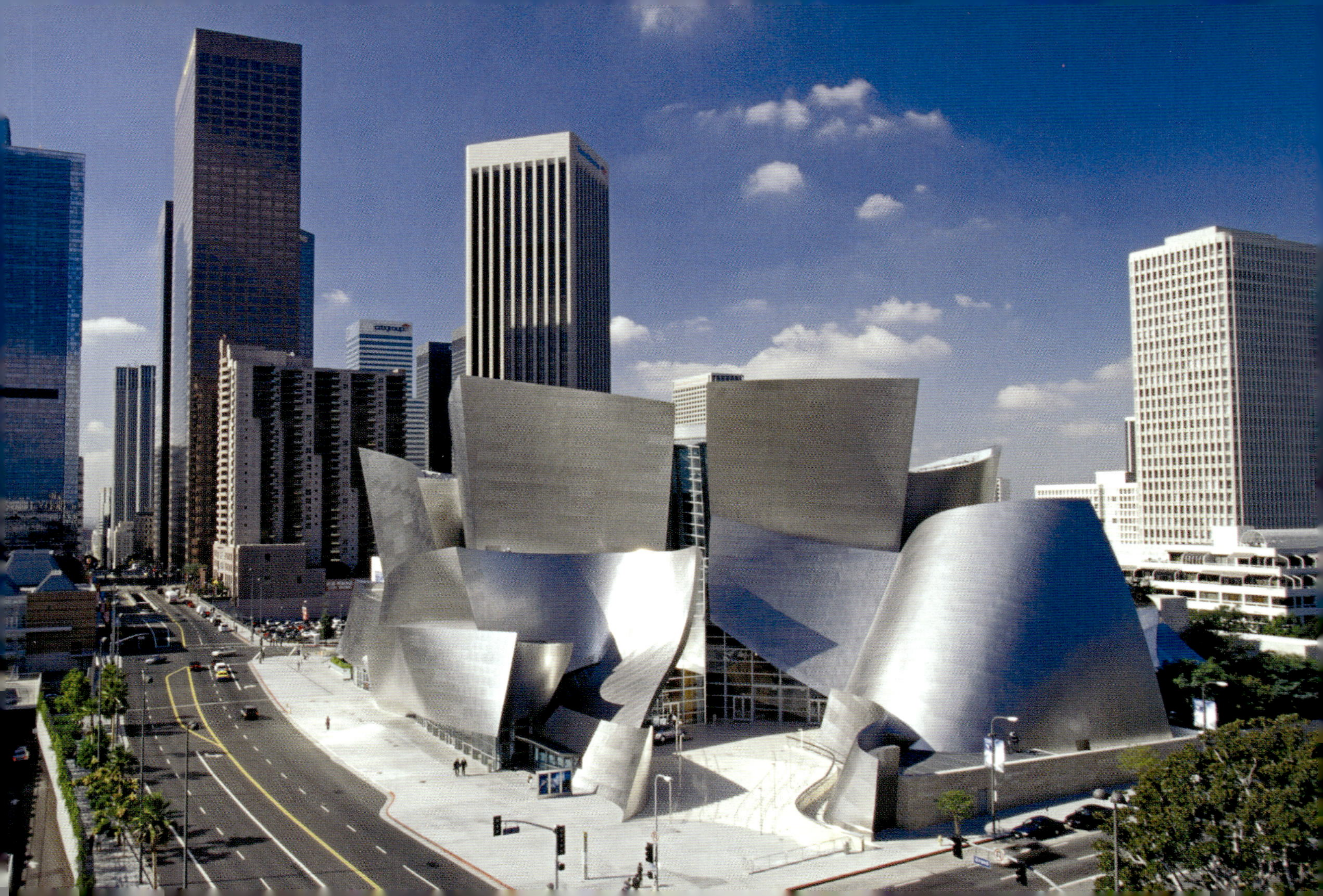

[redacted]

◄

Frank Gehry,
Walt Disney Concert Hall, 2003
Grand Ave, Los Angeles, CA.
Photo: courtesy of Gehry Partners, LLP

ARCHITECTURAL STEEL

Steel's strength and flexibility, along with other acoustic, thermal and earthquake-resistant features, has enabled incredible feats of engineering, including long spans in architecture that allow huge expanses as well as unusual shapes, sizes and forms. The diagrid is an example of innovative steel structure – a framework of diagonally intersecting beams, most often constructed in steel, that require less structural steel than a conventional steel frame. Norman Foster's Hearst Tower in New York, 2006, and 30 St Mary Axe (the Gerkin), 2003, in London are the most well-known diagrid buildings, while in Australia, One Shelley Street in Sydney by Fitzpatrick and Partners also features a diagrid, eliminating the need for internal columns and internal structural cores. In the case of One Shelley Street, the internal structure of the building, with meeting pods jutting out into the void, would not have been possible without the diagrid exterior, an architectural and engineering solution that offered new possibilities for design and form both externally and internally.

One of the most ground-breaking architectural monuments in terms of form and structure is the Guggenheim Bilbao, 1997, designed by US architect Frank Gehry – a building which relies heavily on steel. The curving shapes, formed by a steel skeleton, were completely revolutionary at the time. The curves themselves added to the strength of the construction, with the engineers asking Gehry to exaggerate these curves, if anything, to increase the building's strength. For the facade, Gehry originally chose steel because Bilbao was a steel town – but the effect was not what he had envisaged: '...we built twenty-five mockups of a stainless steel exterior with different variations of the theme,' explains Gehry. 'But in Bilbao, which has a lot of rain and a lot of grey sky, the stainless steel went dead. It only came to life on sunny days.'[10] Instead, Gehry used titanium on the Bilbao building for aesthetic reasons, and stainless steel on the facade of the Walt Disney Concert Hall in Los Angeles 'where there is so much sun and it doesn't die.'[11]

Stainless steel had been used on building facades before, including the famous Chrysler building, 1930 that features gargoyles in the shape of American eagles, stepping spires with a stylized sunburst pattern and other motifs inspired by Chrysler cars, such as radiator caps and ornaments of car wheels. More recently, in New Zealand, the Len Lye Centre building, designed by Patterson Associates, presents a series of repeating, undulating steel forms that curve in horizontal folds like a large curtain that reflects and distorts everything in its vicinity. Here, the reference is to the artist himself, Len Lye, a sculptor whose steel-motion compositions are kinetic works that feature pulsating ellipses and spinning balls constructed in steel.

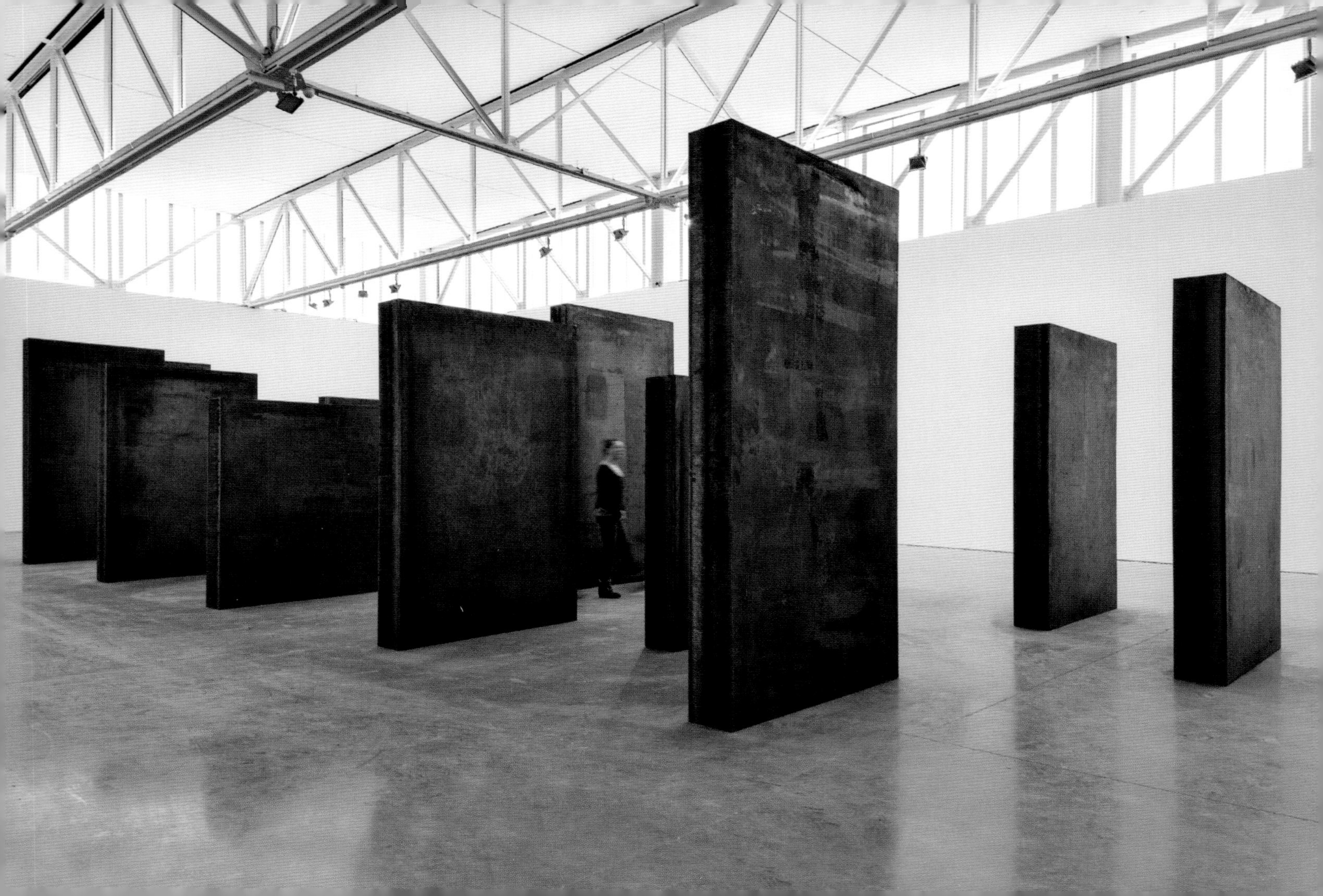

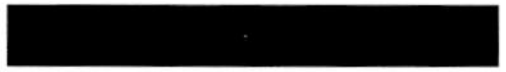

◂

Richard Serra, *Every Which Way*, 2015
weatherproof steel, sixteen slabs,
3400 x 16300 x 6400
© Richard Serra
Photo: Cristiano Mascaro

STEEL IN ART

Of all the artists who have worked with steel, two stand out. Richard Serra is known for his monumental, curving sculptures that rise vertically in slabs of rough, dirty steel – sometimes using corten steel, which is made to rust. Serra uses the material as an architect would – to shape space and sculpt interior volumes. He has said that the subject of his work is the viewer's experience of walking around and through it, an experience described by a *New Yorker* writer as 'alternating sensations of confinement and expansion... The weight of corten steel on either side makes the walk fairly frightening, but then, emerging at last into the open space at the center, you get a jolt of euphoria, space rushing away from you on all sides and the whole vast form becoming buoyant and seemingly weightless.'[12] For Serra, steel is weighty, rough, heavy, strong and monumental. The sheer technical complexity of making the sculptures (which must be moved into the gallery space by a crane), their weight and size, produce in the viewer a sense of the sublime.

For UK artist Anish Kapoor, steel is used to produce more multitudinous effects. Rough, corten steel is used in *Memory*, 2008, a work that gives the impression of a huge, steel balloon squashed into a gallery space – on one side it is possible to see into the structure and sense the acoustic and sensorial effects of staring into a dark, steel cavity. Here, Kapoor is using steel in a similar way to Serra, to shape space. But Kapoor is also known for his stainless steel works – bulbous forms, concave shapes, large discs – all of which reflect the world around them in a mirror. The quality of steel as a reflective material is explored most poetically here, in which the mirror becomes the artist's tool for exploring emptiness. With the work *Double Mirror*, 1998, Kapoor sets two concave mirrors into the walls of a corridor, opposite each other. While it is possible to see yourself in the mirror/s, it is also possible to stand at the right angle so that your reflection appears in neither. In an essay about emptiness in Kapoor's work, Homi Bhabha states: 'The spectator's relation to the object involves a process of questioning the underlying conditions through which the work becomes a visual experience in the first place: how can the conceptual void be made visible? How can the perceptual void be spoken?'[13]

PLAYING WITH STEEL IN DESIGN

A number of works in furniture, lighting and object design also use steel to create illusions, hint at nothingness or play with the qualities of the material itself. UK designer Paul Cocksedge likes to use his work to experiment and push the boundaries of our expectations and his *Poised Table*, 2013, does just that. Made from a thousand pounds of rolled steel, the table curves from floor to table top, seemingly defying gravity by not toppling over despite its limited contact with the ground. Cocksedge is even able to support the weight of himself at its edge thanks to precise engineering

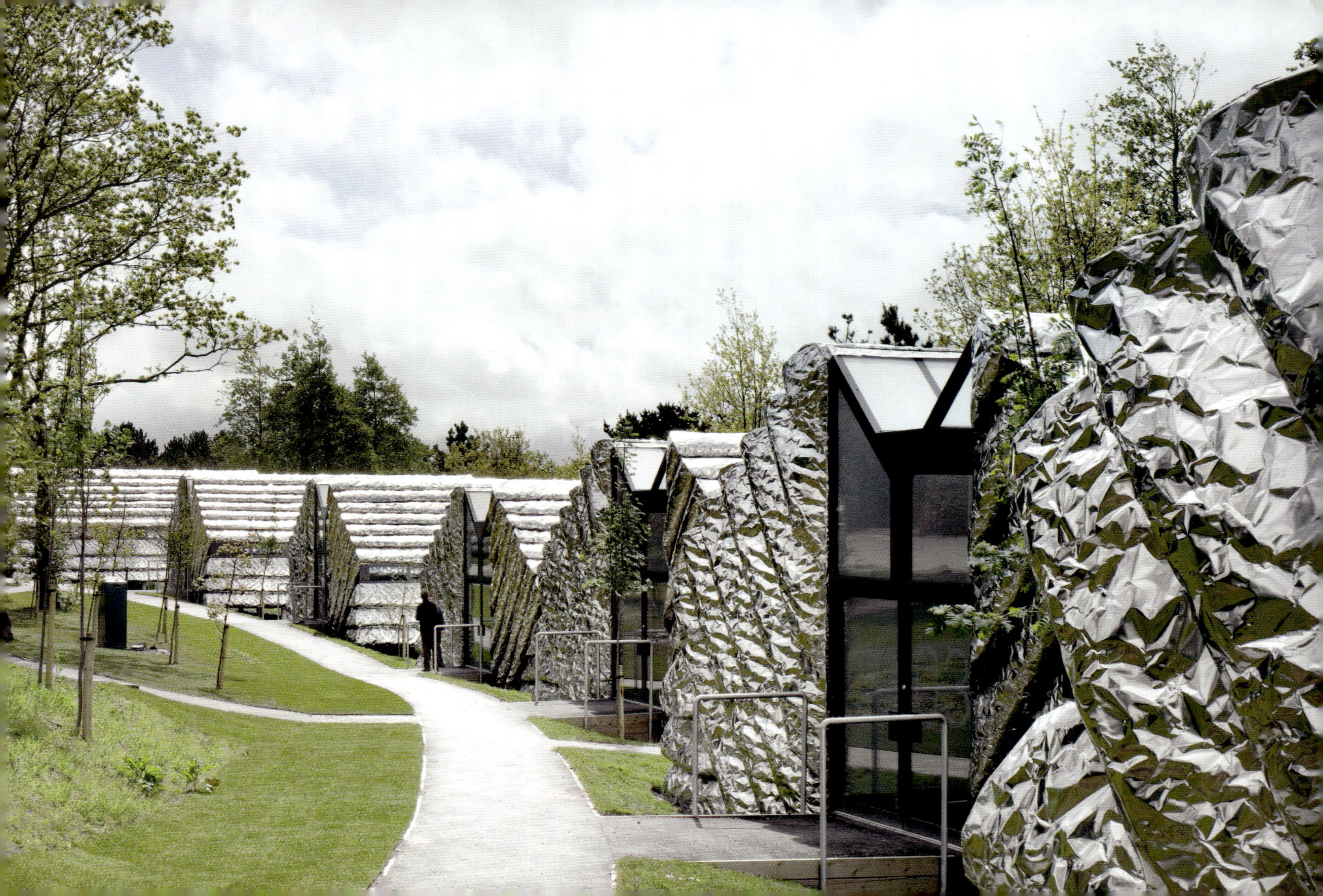

▶

Nendo company,
Softer than Steel, 2014
steel, 440 x 505 x 405
Photo: Desalto

◢

Paul Cocksedge, *Poised*, 2013
steel, 2030 x 1474 x 724,
for Friedman Benda Gallery, New York
Winner Best Contemporary design
Moet Hennessy PAD Prize
Photo: courtesy the artists

◀

Thomas Heatherwick Studio,
Aberystwyth Arts Centre, 2009
Aberystwyth, Wales
Photo: James Morris,
VIEW Pictures Ltd / Alamy Stock Photo

OVERLEAF

Mx3d Bridge, Joris Laarman Lab, 2016
Photo: Adriaan de Groot
This project is supported by the partners Autodesk, Heijmans and ArcelorMittal, the sponsors Air Liquide, ABB robotics, STV, Delcam, Lenovo, Oerlikon, UL, Plymovent, Maxibel, DEsso and the public partners TU Delft, AMS Fieldlaband the Municipality of Amsterdam.

calculations. This piece is a demonstration of the cliché that steel is strong taken to its absolute limits. Another optical illusion made with steel is the *Drawing Series*, 2014 – a chair and armchair by South Korean designer Jinil Park that look like two-dimensional drawings – so realistic it is difficult to believe the chairs are not sketches.

In contrast, Japanese designer Nendo's collection, *Softer Than Steel*, 2014, for Italian furniture brand Desalto offers another illusion – presenting folds and waves within the steel form as if they were flexible and supple. The result is a tabletop with a shape carved into it like butter, a chair with an asymmetrical bend like bent wood, shelving that seems to curve like paper and a coat stand with twisted branches. Polish designer Oskar Zieta's *Plopp* stool, 2008, for Hay also achieves a similar aim of using steel as if it were another material altogether. This time, the material mimics inflatable plastic. In order to achieve this effect, the stools are made from two hydro-formed sheets of metal welded together at the edges. This is then filled with fluid under pressure to create an effect like blowing up a balloon. Each stool is unique, the stool inflating slightly differently each time.

THE FUTURE OF STEEL

The future for steel is uncertain – technical innovations have some experts predicting that steel will be replaced by other materials such as timber, bamboo, carbon fibre or even bone. Nonetheless, research is continuing into new

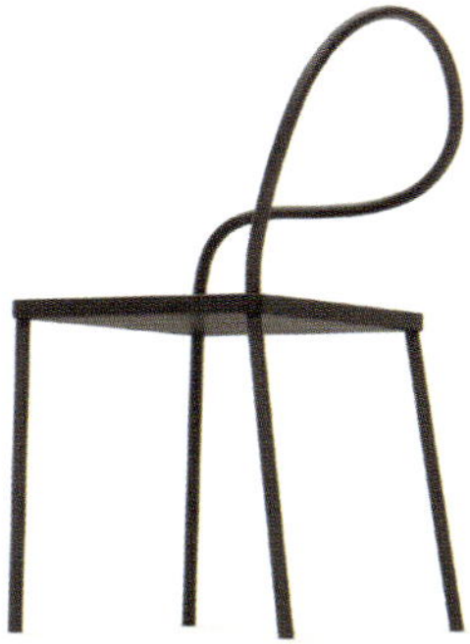

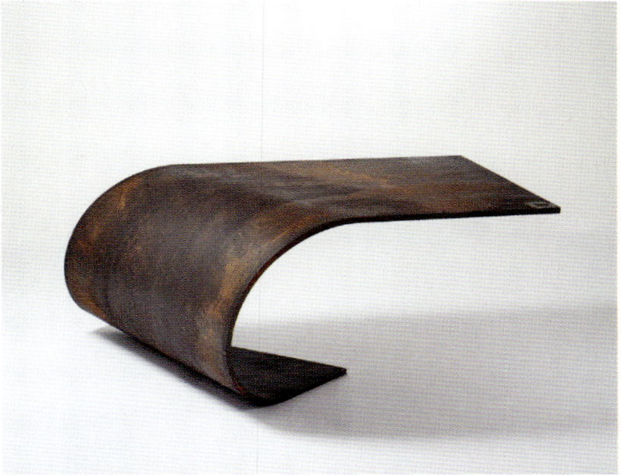

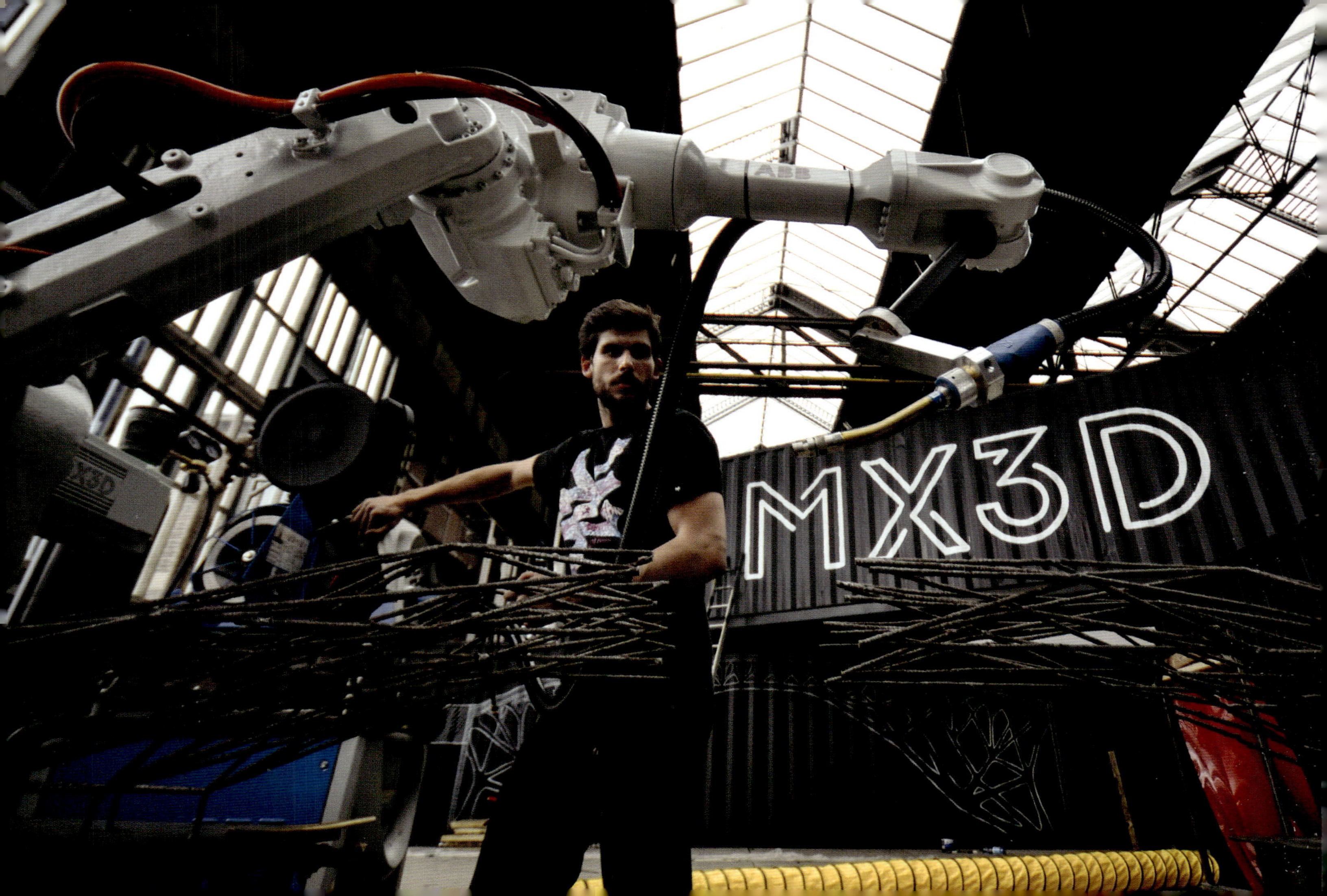
MX3D
ABB

forms of steel. Researchers at the National Institute for Materials Science in Japan have created a fibrous steel that withstands sub-zero temperatures thanks to its molecular structure.[14] Another innovation is a type of Velcro made from steel called Metaklett, a square metre of which is capable of supporting 35 tonnes at temperatures up to 800 °C, according to researchers at the Technical University of Munich, Germany.[15]

Steel is also constantly being innovated in its application. A recently finished series of low-cost facilities at the Aberystwyth Arts Centre, 2009, in Wales features an innovation in cladding. Thomas Heatherwick studio's team chose to use very thin steel – about the thickness of cooking foil – creating rigidity and thermal insulation by spraying a CFC-free insulation foam on to the back of the pre-crinkled surface. The result is an inexpensive, rigid and well-insulated cladding material with an unusual shimmering surface aesthetic.

Perhaps most impressively of all, 3D printing has seen the first steel-printed bridge that is capable of building itself with robots (2015). The project, by Dutch company MX3D, is the stuff of science fiction – if a printer is capable of printing a bridge, that's one thing – but what if a printer is capable of printing a printer? Does that point to a future with self-replicating robots? It is fitting to finish with science fiction, since steel is deeply linked aesthetically to modernism and the future in our minds. This is a material that has the power to transform – to create mega-structures, to support other materialities, to act functionally, and, in some cases, to present a gleaming, pristine perfection. ■

1 Tapon, F., *The Hidden Europe: What Eastern Europeans Can Teach Us*. SonicTrek, Inc, 2011, p. 142.

2 Walter Gropius, Ideen und Aufbau des staatlichen Bauhaus Weimar (Munich: Bauhausverlag, 1923).

3 Marcel Breuer, 'metallmöbel und moderne räumlichkeit,' (footnote 23), quoted in Werner Möller and Otakar Mácel, Ein Stuhl macht Geschichte (Munich: Prestel, 1992).

4 Antonelli, P., *Objects of Design from the Museum of Modern Art*, The Museum of Modern Art, 2003, p. 85.

5 McGrath, F., as quoted in Aitken, R., *The Garden of Ideas: Four Centuries of Australian Style*, The Miegunyah Press, 2010, p. 165.

6 Drew, P., 2006, 'Inspiration from Below: Australian Vernacular in Contemporary Architecture' in *Architectural Theory Review* Vol. 11, Iss. 1, 2006, pp. 31-32.

7 Drew, P., 2006, 'Inspiration from Below: Australian Vernacular in Contemporary Architecture' in *Architectural Theory Review* Vol. 11, Iss. 1, 2006, p. 32.

8 Pritzker Prize Jury Citation, 2002, http://www.pritzkerprize.com/2002/jury, accessed August 2016.

9 Murcutt, G., Beck, H. and Cooper, J., *Glenn Murcutt: A Singular Architectural Practice*, Images Publishing, 2002, p. 62.

10 Isenberg, B., *Conversations with Frank Gehry*, Knopf Doubleday Publishing Group, 2012, p. 138.

11 ibid

12 Tomkins, C., 'Man of steel,' in *The New Yorker*, Aug 5, 2002, Vol.78 (22), 2002, p. 52. http://www.newyorker.com/magazine/2002/08/05/man-of-steel, accessed August 2016.

13 Bhabha, H. Anish Kapoor: making emptiness. *Anish Kapoor*, 1998, pp. 11-41.

14 Marks, P., 'Fibrous' steel won't break in a cold snap', *New Scientist*, 2008, https://www.newscientist.com/article/dn13962-fibrous-steel-wont-break-in-a-cold-snap/, accessed August 2016.

15 Simonite, T., 'Extreme steel 'Velcro' takes a 35-tonne load', *New Scientist*, 2009, https://www.newscientist.com/article/dn17739-extreme-steel-velcro-takes-a-35-tonne-load/, accessed August 2016.

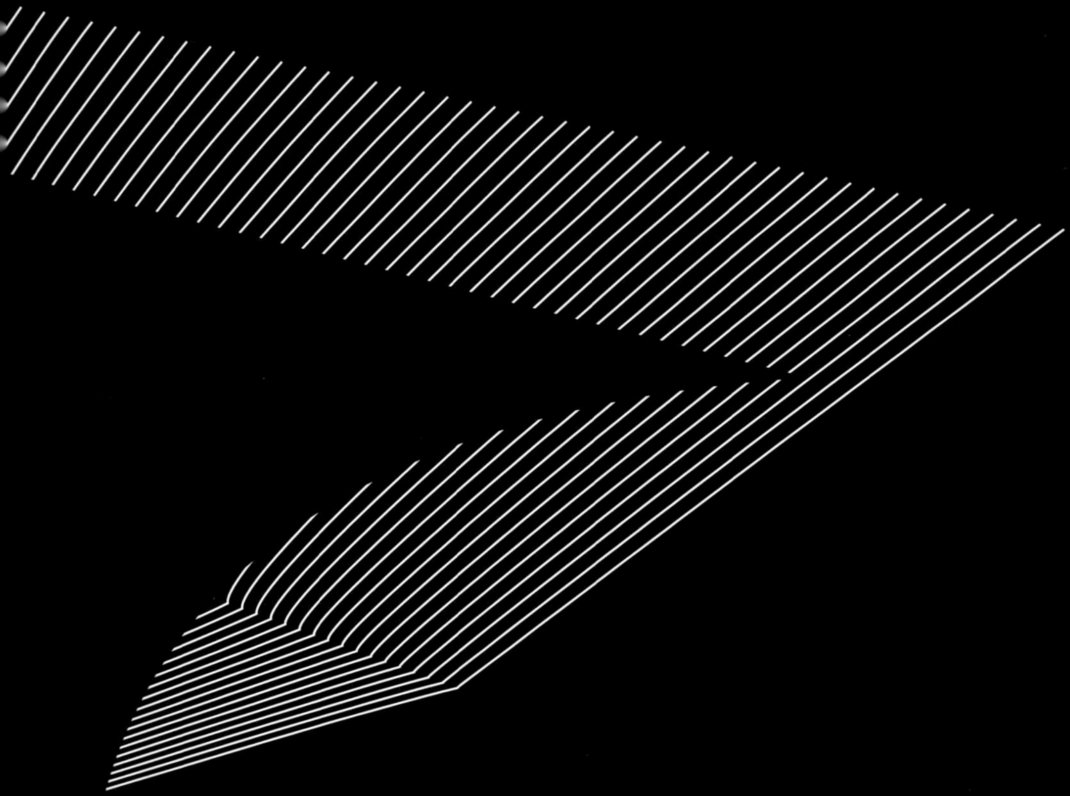

ARTISTS, DESIGNERS AND ARCHITECTS

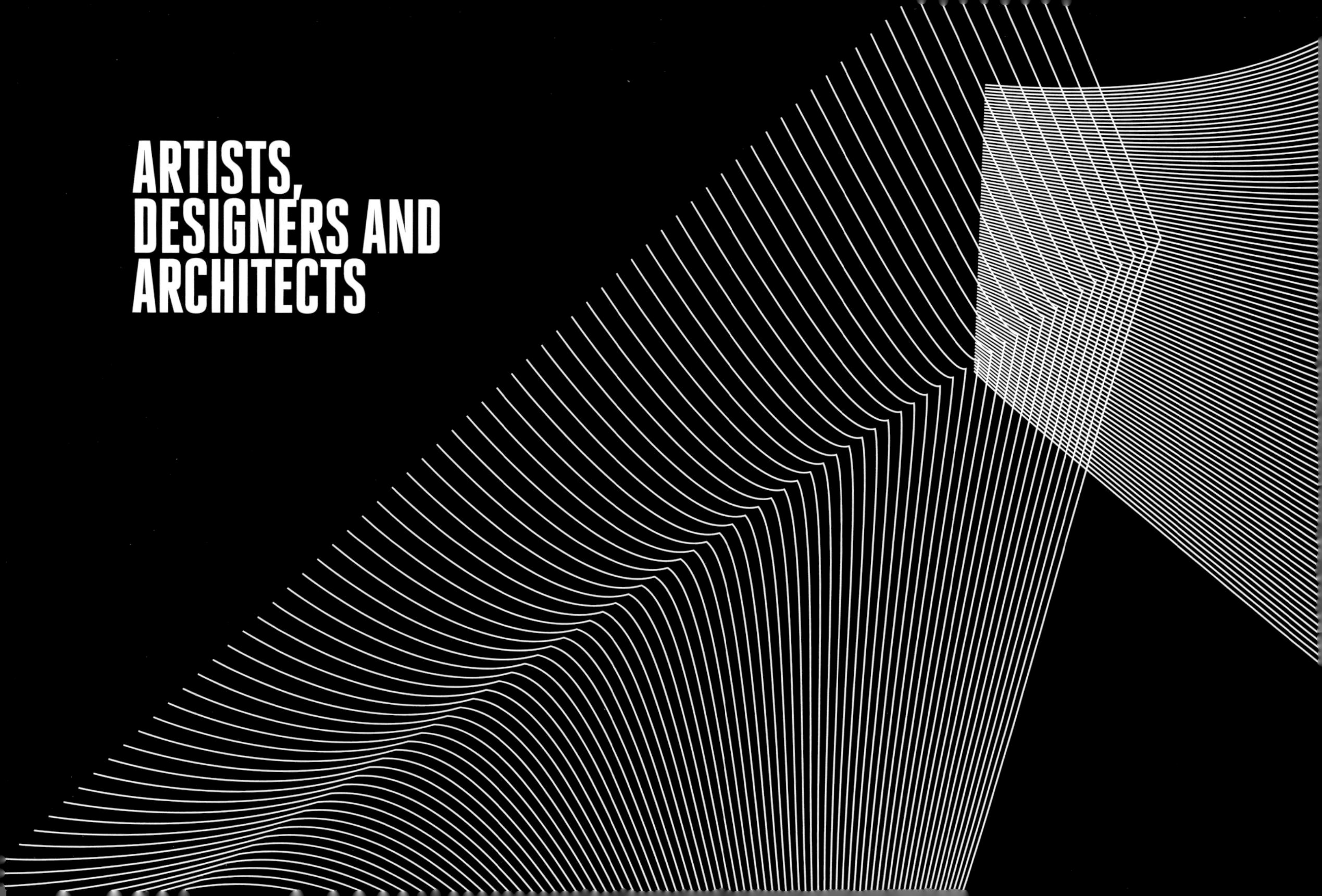

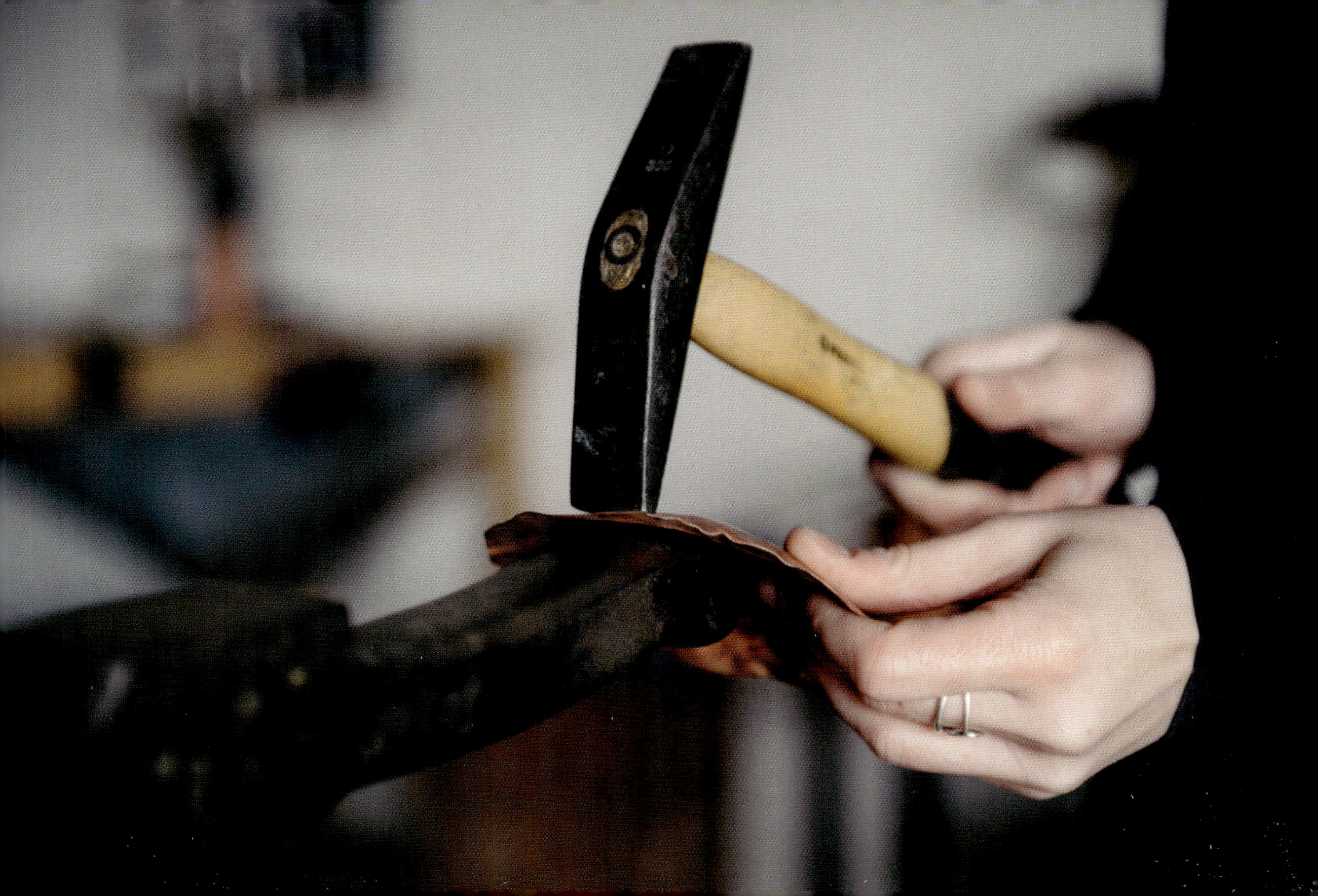

ALISON JACKSON

BORN 1986, SYDNEY, NEW SOUTH WALES
LIVES CANBERRA, AUSTRALIAN CAPITAL TERRITORY

FUNCTIONALITY is at the heart of what draws Alison Jackson to making, believing that her creations are truly appreciated when people use them as part of their everyday rituals. The expensive wedding cutlery that comes out only on special occasions is the antithesis of what Jackson seeks to create. Instead, Jackson makes elegant, pared-back designs, produced from her studio in Canberra, that have the purpose and function of a carefully considered handmade object. Recently branching into larger-scale commissions, Jackson has expanded her practice from individual handmade objects into mass production and with that comes the challenge of working on big projects. Embracing the change of pace this style of making demands, Jackson has relished the opportunity to expand her skills as a maker and in business.

Catching the bug when she was young, Jackson became enamoured with the idea of tinkering around with metal from her father's workshop, under their family home in Sydney and then progressing into jewellery making in high school. After graduating, Jackson took the leap and moved to Canberra to study at the School of Art, Australian National University where she received a Bachelor of Visual Arts (Gold and Silversmithing) with Honours.

In 2008, Jackson found the perfect space and started Pocket Studio, where she began working part-time and teaching short courses. In these first few years, while getting her own practice off the ground, Jackson was also working part-time at F!nk & Co. where she built up her skills and confidence, before committing to her practice and her studio full-time in 2013. Though relatively early in her career Jackson's distinctive style has garnered much attention, showing nationally and internationally in addition to winning a number of awards. Uniting beauty with function, Jackson has created unique designs spanning tableware, jewellery and hollowware ranges.

In the first few years, Jackson worked primarily with silver, being drawn to the simplicity of hammer on metal and the beauty of the material. Using traditional silversmith techniques (little has changed over centuries) each piece is marked with the maker's hand, or in this case, hammer. It is a labour-intensive way of making that imbues in each piece a sense of intent, to be both marked by the crafting and by its use. Many of her tableware and vessel designs are left purposefully with a rounded or imperfect base, so that they wobble, or move, inviting the user to handle and use them.

Ever curious, Jackson began to expand her practice in recent years, and in doing so she also began to use a wider range of metals. With years of making and market-stalls up her sleeve, Jackson realised that though silver is both beautiful and functional, many people still had misgivings about using it in an everyday context, its preciousness subsuming its functionality. To get around the costliness of silver, which is both labour intensive and materially expensive, Jackson branched out into stainless steel for a short-run tableware range – it has become a staple in her practice ever since.

PREVIOUS PAGE
Alison Jackson raising copper in her studio, Pocket Studio, Quenbeyan, ACT.
Photo: Christine Pobke

▶
10 Vessels 10 Days, 2015
fine silver, copper, binding wire, dimensions variable
Photo: Angela Bakker

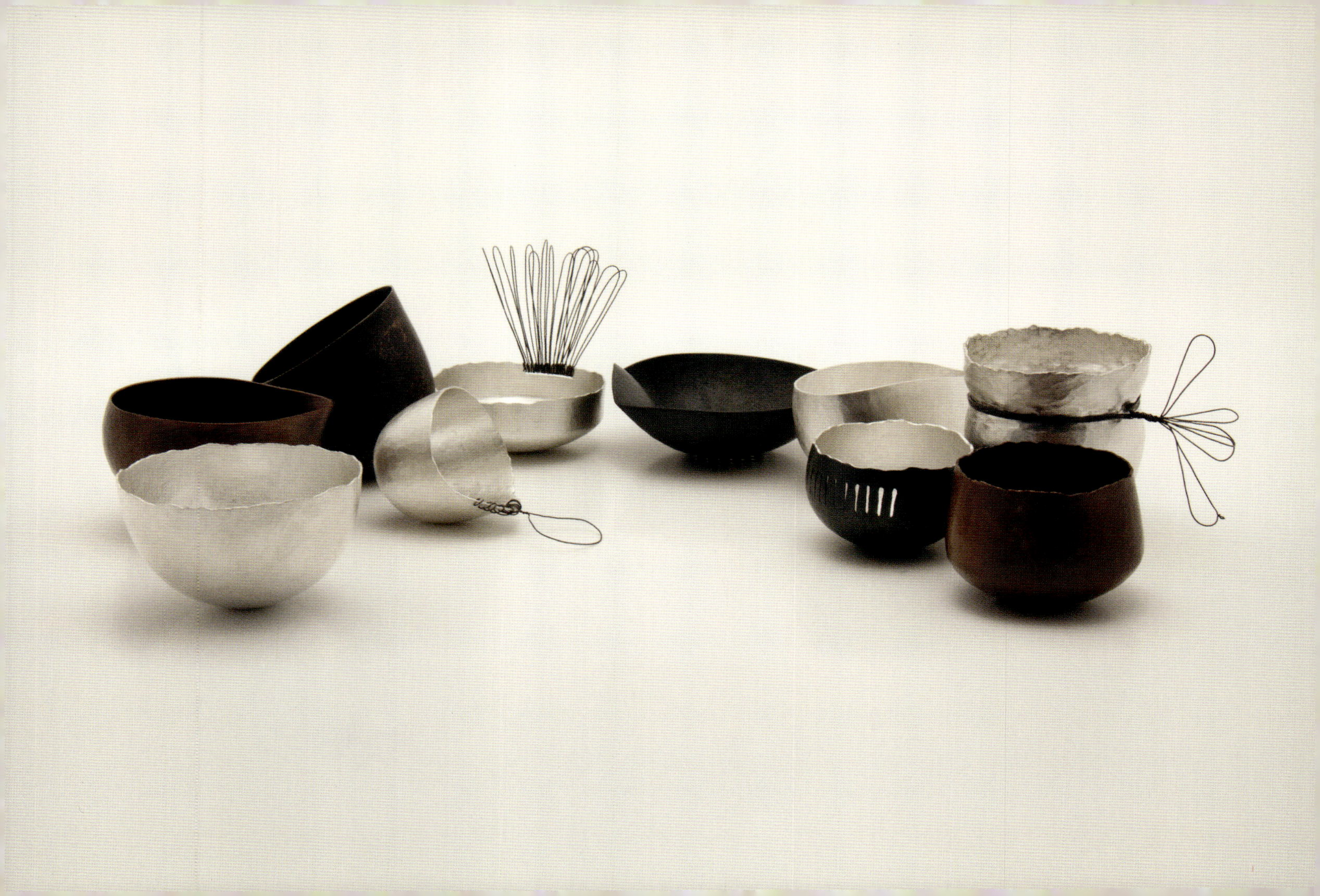

SLOWLY SLOWLY POURING POTS AND WOBBLE POTS

Embracing the change of pace that stainless steel has brought to her practice, Alison Jackson has taken advantage of the opportunity the material allows, to explore her natural curiosity and desire to keep testing her skills and ingenuity. Jackson uses paper or cardboard to sketch ideas and test prototypes to reduce the cost of working with expensive materials like silver and copper. In this way, stainless steel came with a certain freedom, but also its own challenges. The cheaper cost of the metal meant she was able to take more risks while making the object. Even though its strength meant she could no longer rely on her traditional silversmithing skills, there was greater potential for repeat production as well as increasing the longevity of the finished product.

Slowly Slowly Pouring Pots, 2015, and *Wobble Pots*, 2015, are Jackson's first one-off exhibition pieces made in stainless steel. Though stainless steel has the advantage of being easily mass-produced, the singular nature of these works created an environment of experimental freedom with different forms, playing, cutting, changing and developing the individual pieces.[1] Seeking to create sculptural pieces that were intriguing in their own right, while being playful and practical to use, these pots represent Jackson's most fully formed experiments in this material to-date.

Jackson created these works with the help of her partner Dan Lorrimer (pg 127), which led to a back and forth dialogue. Lorrimer executed the fabrication while Jackson developed the design. Lorrimer welded while Jackson restyled, imagining different joins and connections until they resolved into these deceptively simple and engaging pieces of tableware. ■

SERENA WONG

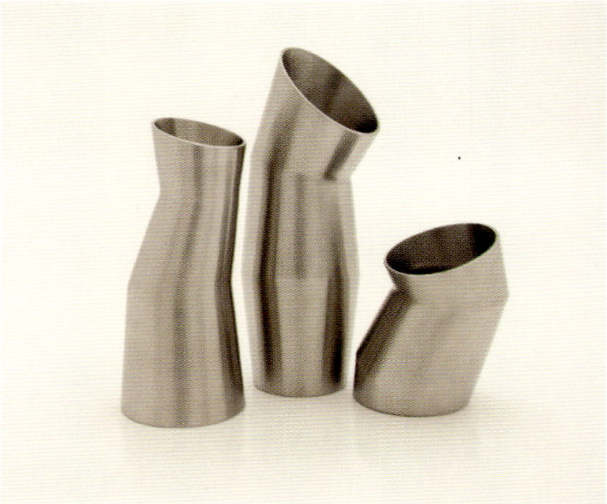

▶

Wobble Pots, 2015
stainless steel
left: 145 x 60 x 60
centre: 95 x 65 x 65
right: 180 x 70 x 60
Photo: Angela Bakker

▶▶

Slowly Slowly Pouring Pots, 2015
stainless steel
left: 80 x 75 x 55
right: 80 x 100 x 55
Photo: Angela Bakker

1 Email from Alison Jackson to the author, 4 September 2016.

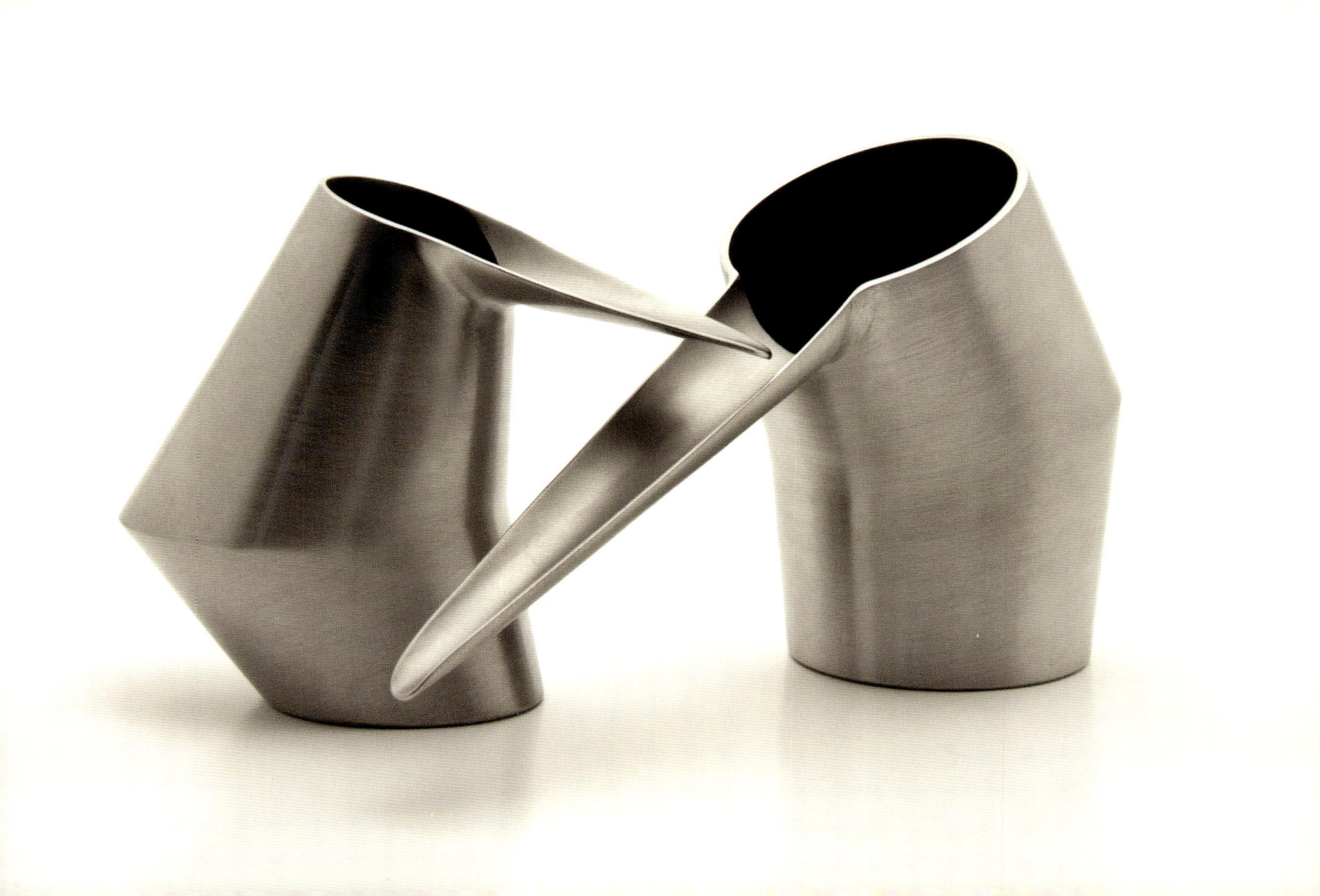

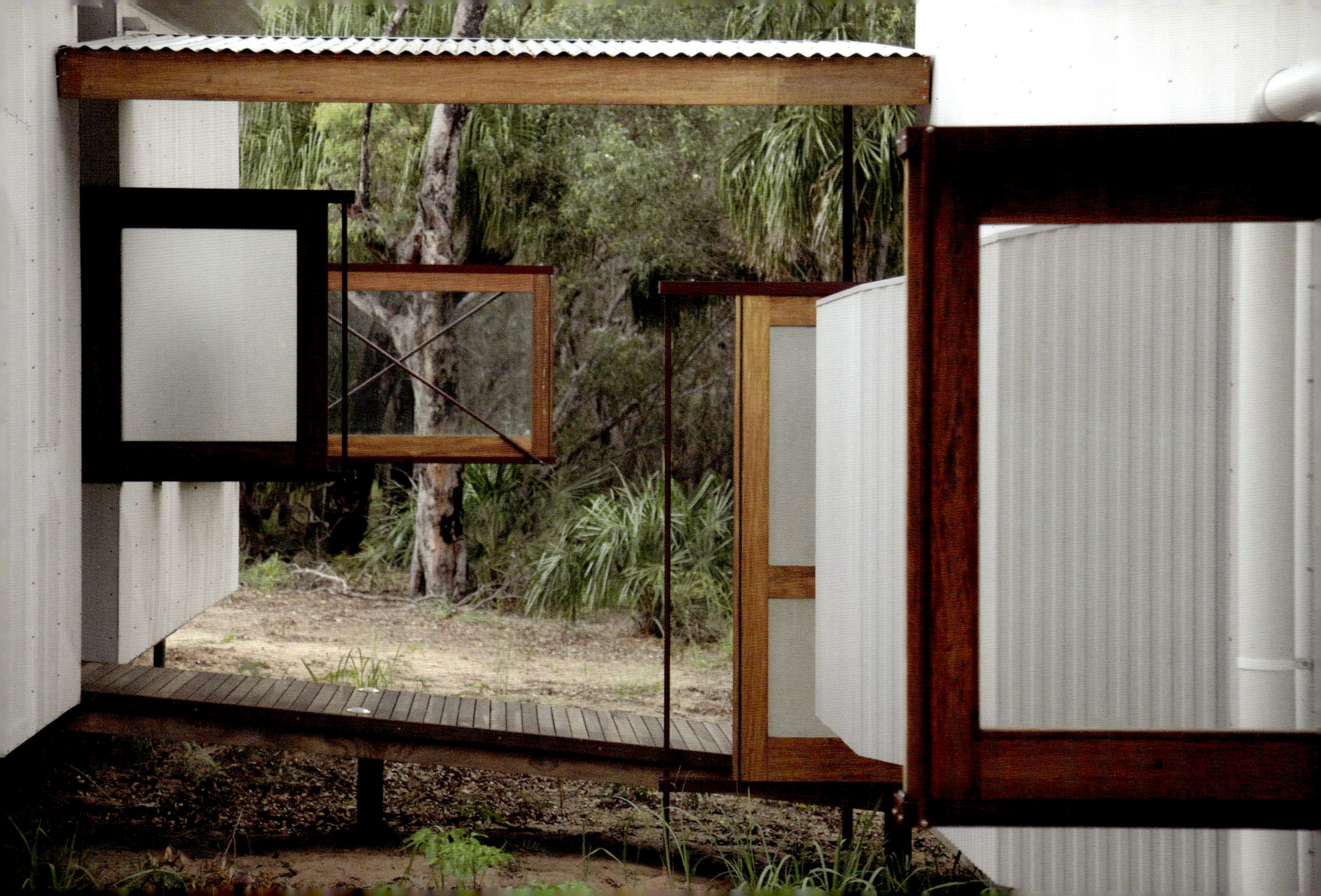

ANTHILL CONSTRUCTIONS

ESTABLISHED 1991,
EAGLE HEIGHTS, QUEENSLAND

SIMON LAWS
BORN 1966, SOUTHPORT, QUEENSLAND
LIVES HONG KONG, SAR, CHINA

HOLIDAY HOUSES are the spaces of retreat, they are a place to relax and unwind, a place to create new memories, connections and experiences whilst equally providing the opportunity to reflect nostalgically on past memories spent together. A dream holiday home allows people to come together whilst also providing the room and freedom to do as one may desire. They are a luxury and in designing holiday houses architects have the opportunity to create something fresh; they can often take the risks needed to produce something enchanting and unique for their clients. This is exactly what has occurred for the Drew Siblings Derek and Marian Drew when they worked with designer Simon Laws of Anthill Construction to produce their perfect getaway in Queensland.

Located 70km north of Bundaberg, Queensland at Seventeen Seventy, a peninsular of land bordered by the Coral Sea and Bustard Bay, the home is set back from the coast on a pristine ridge-top site, amongst the banksias, bloodwoods, casuarinas and ancient palms. Reflecting on the building and site the Drew siblings note:

What's really special about this building is it is on a piece of land that is really meaningful to us it's a place where we feel most at home and if you have any connection to land this is it for us. (MD) *We were attracted to this area for the natural forest and we wanted to build here as this would be the sort of place we would camp in.* (DD)[1]

As 15- and 16-year-olds the Drew siblings took their first unaccompanied adventures to this very spot. In the 1970s it was the kind of laid-back place that you could simply drive into, pitch a tent, and go surfing and fishing. As Derek explains 'it was sort of a magical place really this was our beach, it was first holidays away from the parents, it was a new beginning, it was something we discovered ourselves.'[2]

Wanting to capture this sense of adventure, looseness and connection to the environment – the sound and smell of the ocean, the texture of sand under one's feet – architect and builder Simon Laws of Anthill Construction was keen to create a house that was reminiscent of camping, only with more of the comforts and luxury we expect today. The result is a beautiful cluster of steel pavilions each with its own function – a living/kitchen area, two sleeping quarters and a bath house – all are connected via a series of covered walkways that culminate at the large outdoor dining area.

Nostalgia is further layered into the building through shapes and forms of the structures. On purchasing the land, the siblings took Laws to their childhood home 'Fairymede' a sugarcane mill and processing plant near Bundaberg. On arriving they found the mill was in the process of being demolished. The dramatic scale and fragmentation of the steel structure, including the boilers, cane-cutting machines and turbines informed the design language, though not conscientiously adhered to, in the resulting building.

The striking tubular living and kitchen pavilion invokes the large turbines. Formed from custom corrugated steel, its Australian hardwood timber shutters caps the circular facade and provides passive ventilation from the prevailing south-easterly wind. The breeze through the space can be regulated doing away with the need for air conditioning, a further nod to the camping experience. Speaking on the use of corrugated steel Laws notes: 'This steel is so rollable – it's like an old bangle really. It is light, and durable – you just throw it into the ute with the roller.'[3]

1 http://www.abc.net.au/tv/dreambuild/episodes/ep09.htm, accessed September 2016.

2 Ibid.

3 http://www.steel.com.au/showcase/projects/drews-house-at-sunrise, accessed September 2016.

4 http://www.abc.net.au/tv/dreambuild/episodes/ep09.htm, accessed September 2016.

5 http://www.steel.com.au/showcase/projects/drews-house-at-sunrise, accessed September 2016.

PREVIOUS PAGE
Drew House, Seventeen-Seventy, Queensland, 2010
Covered walkways connecting the living and bedroom pavilions.
Photo: Alex Chomiez

OVERLEAF
The living space is encapsulated in a steel cylinder with a louvred timber window at the end for ventilation whilst the outdoor living and dining is on timber deck under the swooping roof.
Photo: Alex Chomiez

▶
Australian hardwood timber louvers cap the circular facade of the living pavilion.
Photo: Alex Chomiez

◥◥
Bedroom and bathroom pods are constructed with fibrous cement sheeting, and connected by a timber bridge hovering above the ground.
Photo: Alex Chomiez

◢◢
Looking into the kitchen from the northern deck.
Photo: Alex Chomiez

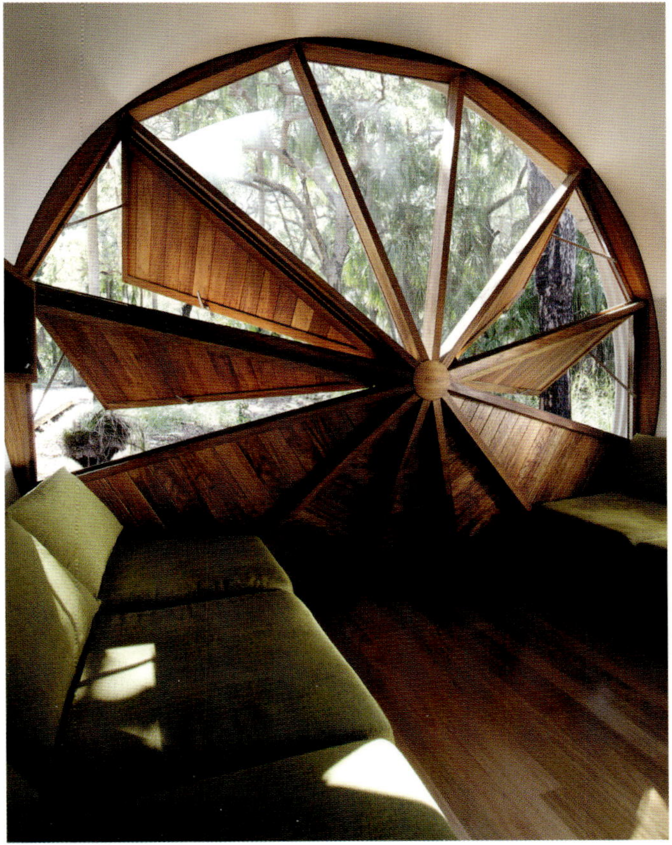

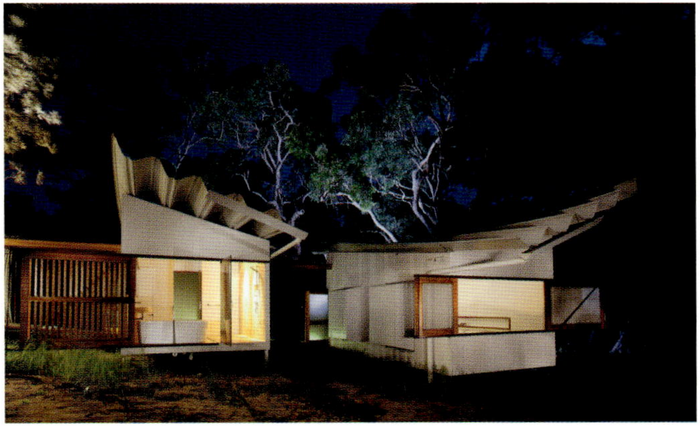

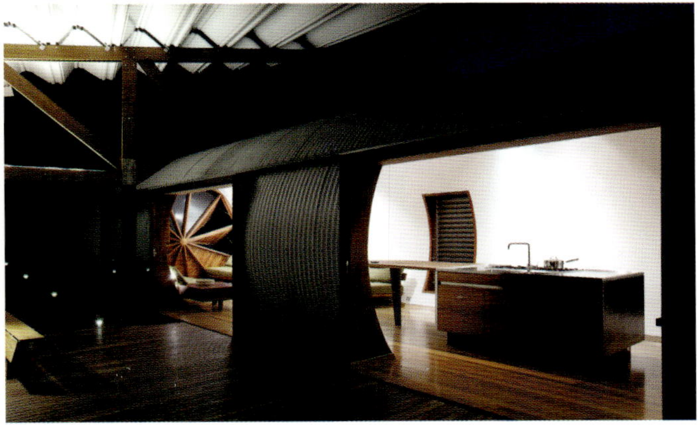

DREW HOUSE

Wishing to produce the building in Brisbane, 500km from the site, the approach to the design was always modular, with each pavilion limited to the size of a semi-trailer. Building in this manner ensured materials and fabricators were at hand and ensured less damage to the site during the construction phase. Working in a modular fashion did not compromise the scale of building as Marian Drew noted when visiting the fabricators during the build of the living and kitchen pavilion… 'the structure of galvanised hoops (the structural ribs of the building) was like a whale that you could walk into, it was the scale of a whale'.[4]

The distinctive deep V profiled Aramax roof sheeting has been used on the parabolic roofs of the outdoor dining area, sleeping quarters and bath house. As Laws notes on his choice of Aramax: 'I'd been wanting to use it on a project for some time. You can achieve these amazing cantilevers and spans in profile. It is light, durable and such good value. I love the way you can just spit out lengths of it on site.'[5] For the dining area the roof sheeting free-spans two identical, but reversed, hardwood self-braced trusses. The curve of the roof lifts off at edge, creating not only interest in the design, these soaring shapes have the practical use of improving ventilation. ■

MARGARET HANCOCK DAVIS

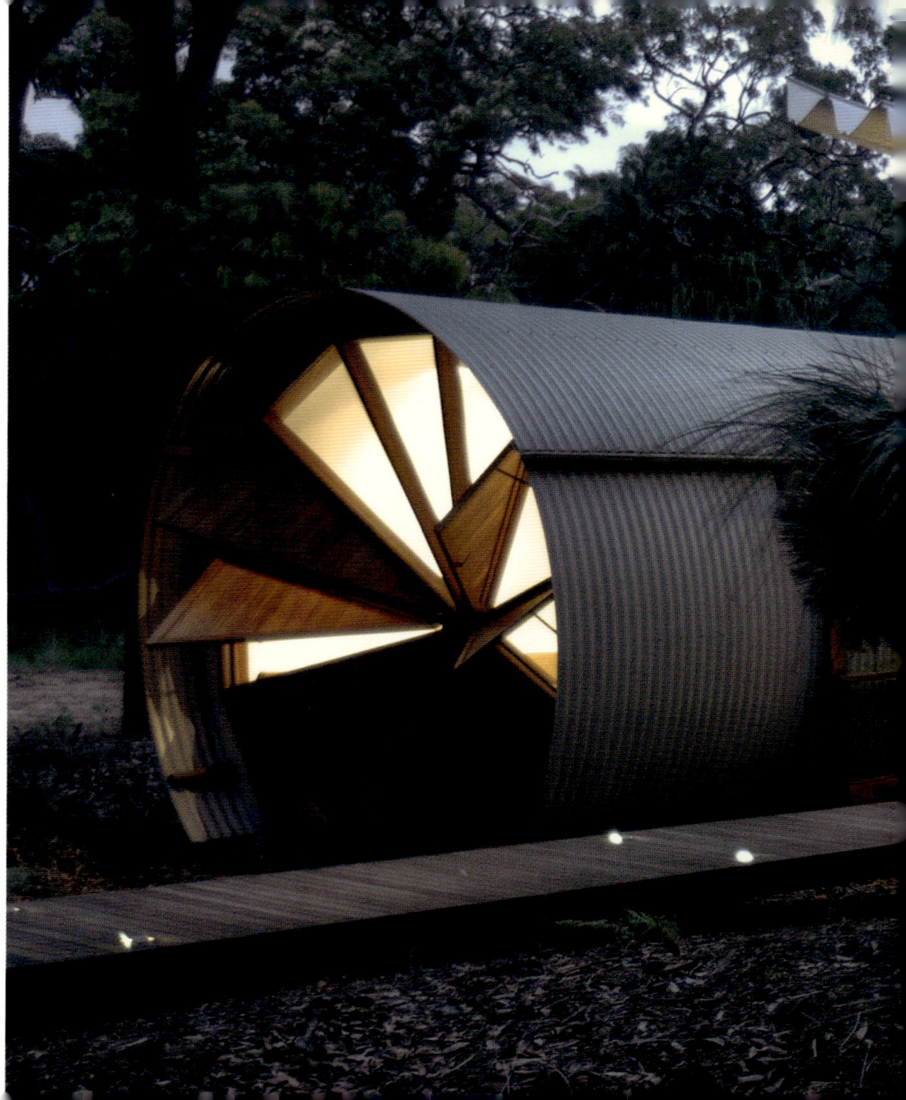

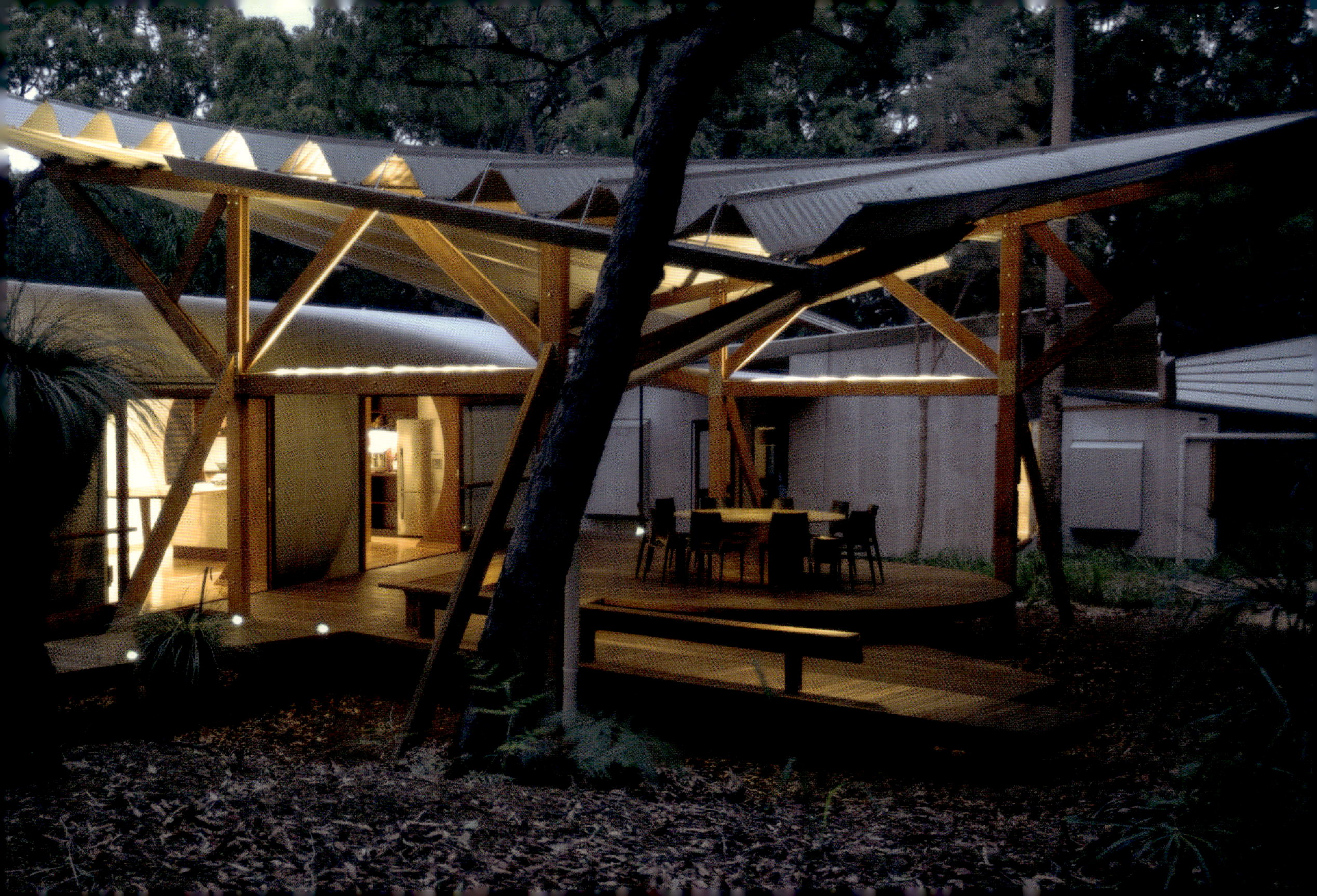

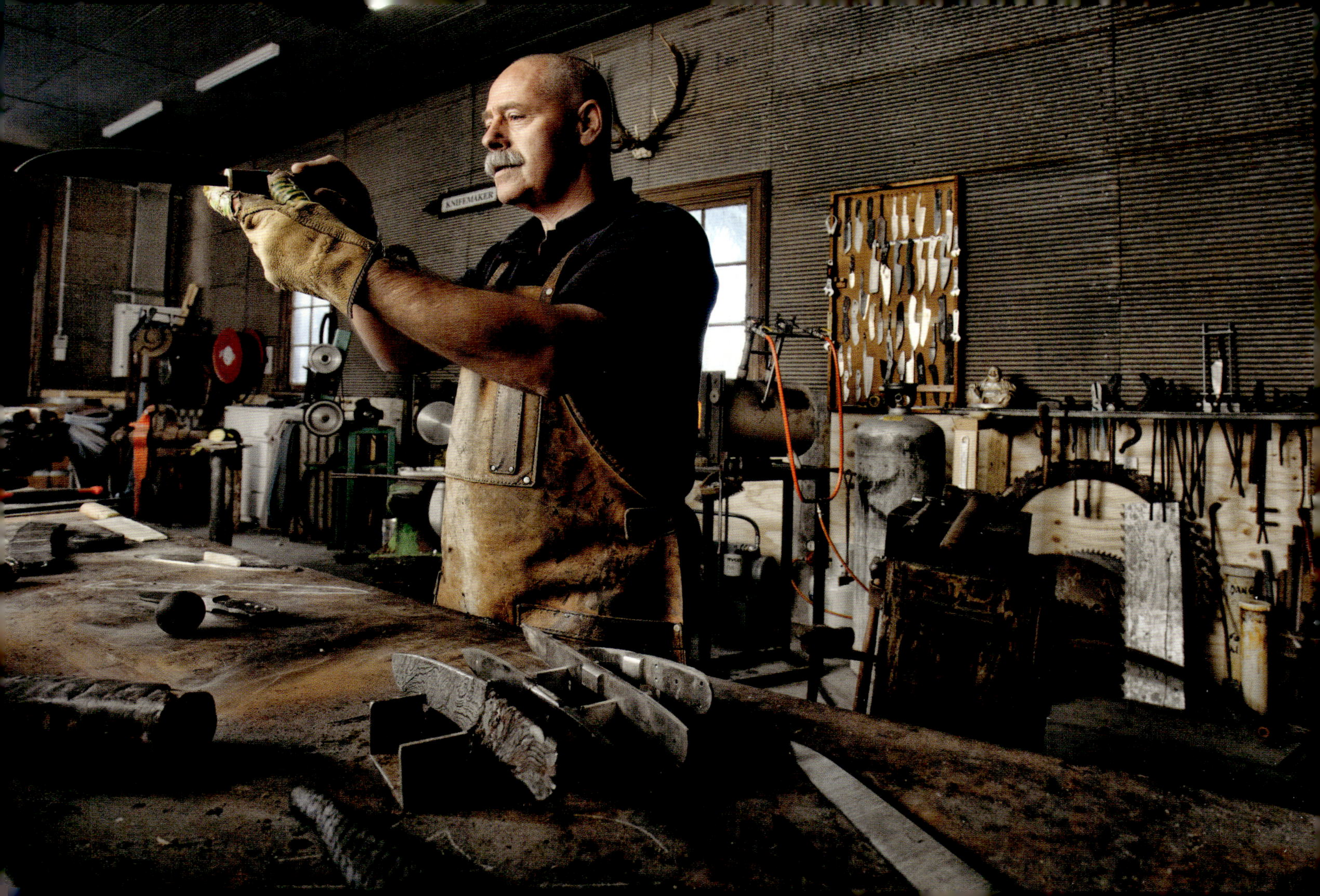
KNIFEMAKER

BARRY GARDNER

BORN 1954, TOKOROA, NEW ZEALAND
LIVES BAROSSA, SOUTH AUSTRALIA

BARRY GARDNER came to knife-making late in life. After working in road construction for 18 years, one day Gardner ended up at a gun show at the Adelaide showgrounds, and happened on a stall-holder who made his own knives. Instantly intrigued, Gardner started a conversation, that unbeknownst to him at the time, would change the course of his life.

Inspired by the encounter Gardner began to do his own research, which was followed up by endless questions to those early contacts he made from that fateful trip to the showgrounds, until finally he was ready to take the plunge and become a full-time knife maker or cutler. Learning through a process of trial and error, Gardner experimented endlessly, excited by the potential of functionality and the beauty of a well-made knife.

Gardner is also interested in recycling metal, for which he has gained somewhat of a reputation. Often, he will find steel left outside his studio – like old saws from farms in the area – which means he need never buy anything new for his craft. This suits Gardner right down to the ground. And it's not just steel that Gardner recycles, having a keen eye for reusable parts, a number of the machines in his workshop have been built through ingenious sourcing of unusual spare parts from locals.

Over the past two-and-a-half years, Gardner has run workshops where he guides people in making their own knives, which are often imbued with their own legacy. For Gardner, one of the most exciting things about working with recycled materials is that it gives people the opportunity to take an old tool from their grandfather's shed and turn it into a family heirloom. In one of his workshops, someone came in with a two-person-saw handed down from their father's father, to create five knives, one for each of his grandchildren. These stories pepper his workshops and give it not just purpose, but longevity. For the craftsman, one of the best things is to make, or help others make, something that will be appreciated, valued and most importantly, used.

Recently Gardner has noticed that he's slowing down. Now in his 60s, knife-making has begun to take a physical toll – but this has not slowed down his ability to keep creating. Driven not only by a determined work ethic, but also a list of experiments he's itching to try, Gardner says he has another lifetime worth of ideas. Recently cutting down on the number of workshops he gives, he is now taking some important time out to realise some of his own creative pursuits.

Gardner is one of the few people in South Australia to make a living as a cutler, and he is especially known for his Damascus steel blades. Gardner is also inspired by Japanese craftspeople and the traditional Japanese-style of knives like the Deba, the Usuba, the Gyutou and Nakiri. Having studied their knife-making through his personal research, he is fascinated by their simple but beautiful designs, some of which have featured in some of his own knives. Always interested in challenging himself, Gardner is looking forward to making a trip to Japan soon to delve further into their culture and knife-making ways.

PREVIOUS PAGE
Barry Gardner in his studio located at JamFactory at Seppeltsfield within the iconic Seppeltsfield winery, Seppeltsfield, South Australia.
Photo: Dragan Radocaj

▶
Grinding the edge of the knife.
Photo: Ed Halmagyi

▶▶
Working the moltern steel.
Photo: Ed Halmagyi

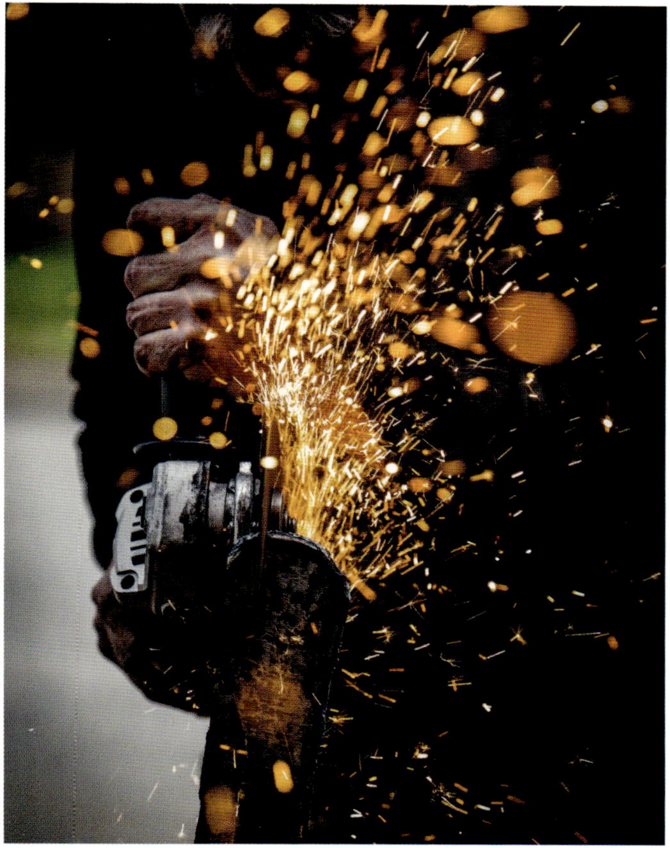

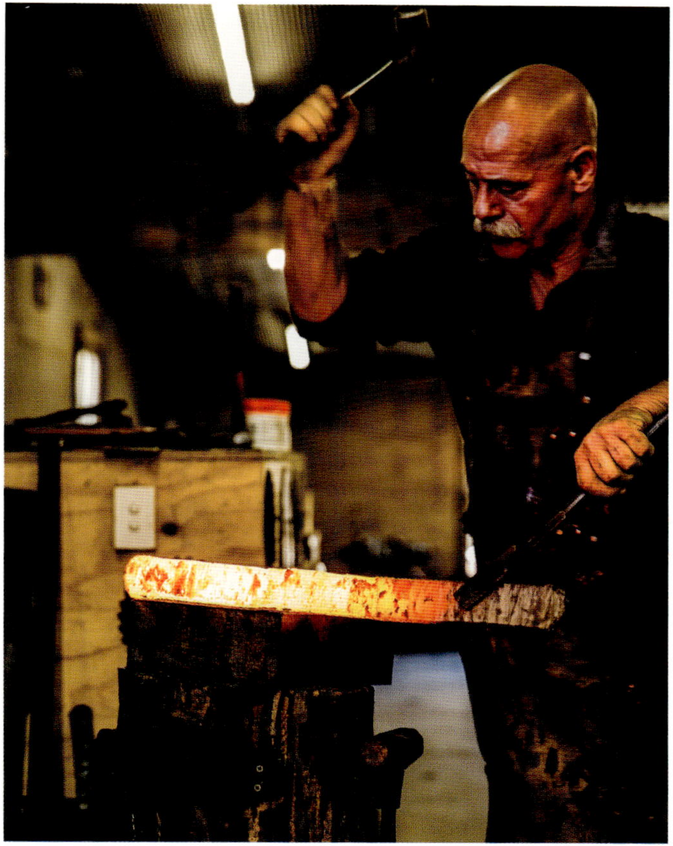

KITCHEN KNIFE AND **PERSIAN FIGHTING KNIFE**

Twenty-three years after beginning his career as a cutler, Barry Gardner is one of the biggest producers of Damascus steel in the Southern Hemisphere. The origins of Damascus steel or Wootz are not certain, but it's believed to have come from the Middle East, though this early technique thought to be lost sometime in the 16th century. Newer Damascus steel techniques forge-weld layers of different alloys together and then fold or twist them repeatedly to create a wave-like pattern that is signature to Damascus or pattern-welded steel.

The *Kitchen Knife*, 2016, is composed of 400 layers of steel, made from recycled files, forge-welded and folded repeatedly. It is a lengthy process which takes Gardner two days of heating, hammering and tempering to finish. The handle is nickel silver and has a stainless steel end-cap, with reclaimed York Gum timber from Western Australia.

The *Persian Fighting Knife*, 2016, is made from Damascus steel and is the first of its kind that Gardner has made. It comes from a mixture of carbon and nickel steel that has been fuse-welded together at extremely high temperatures. Its design comes from 150-year-old Persian style fighting-knife with a recycled Buffalo horn handle, a stainless steel guard and end-cap, and a special Mokume spacer comprised of copper and nickel fused together. ■

SERENA WONG

[redacted]

▸

Persian Fighting Knife, 2016
400 recycled files, stainless steel, mokume, buffalo horn, 370 x 65 x 20
Photo: Craig Arnold

[redacted]

▸▸

Kitchen Knife, 2016
recycled bandsaw blades, stainless steel, nickel, silver, York Gum Damascus steel, 380 x 40 x 25
Photo: Craig Arnold

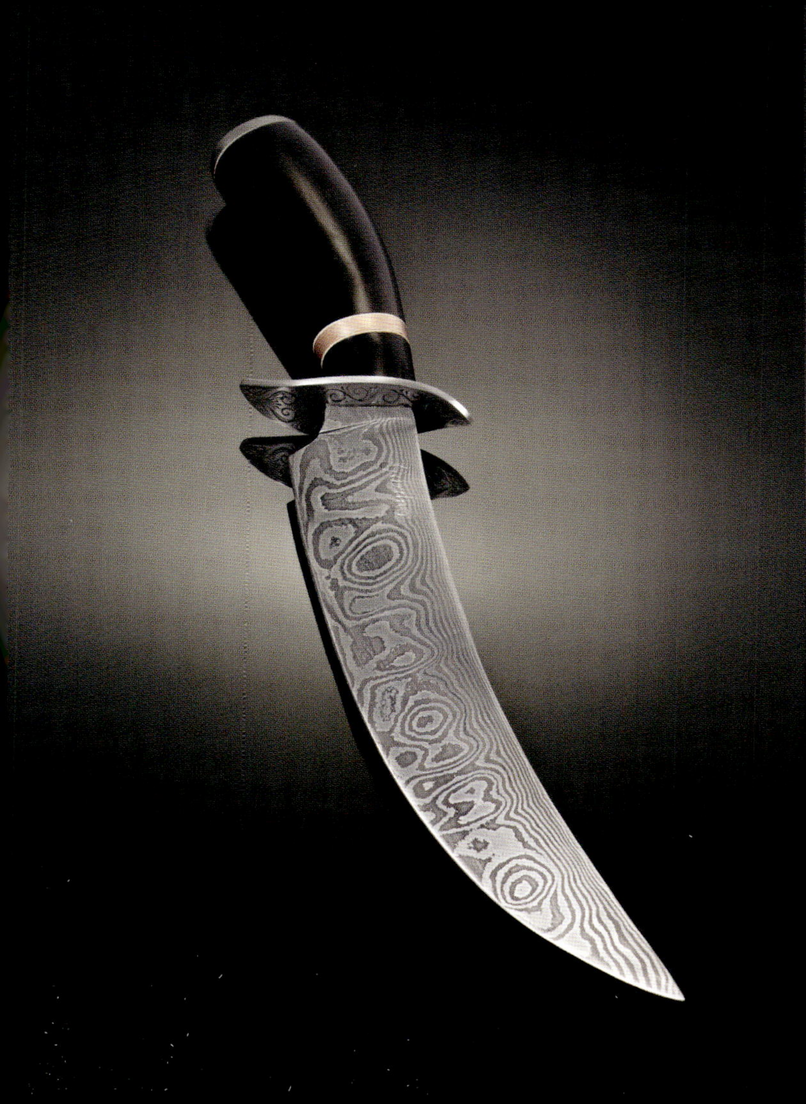

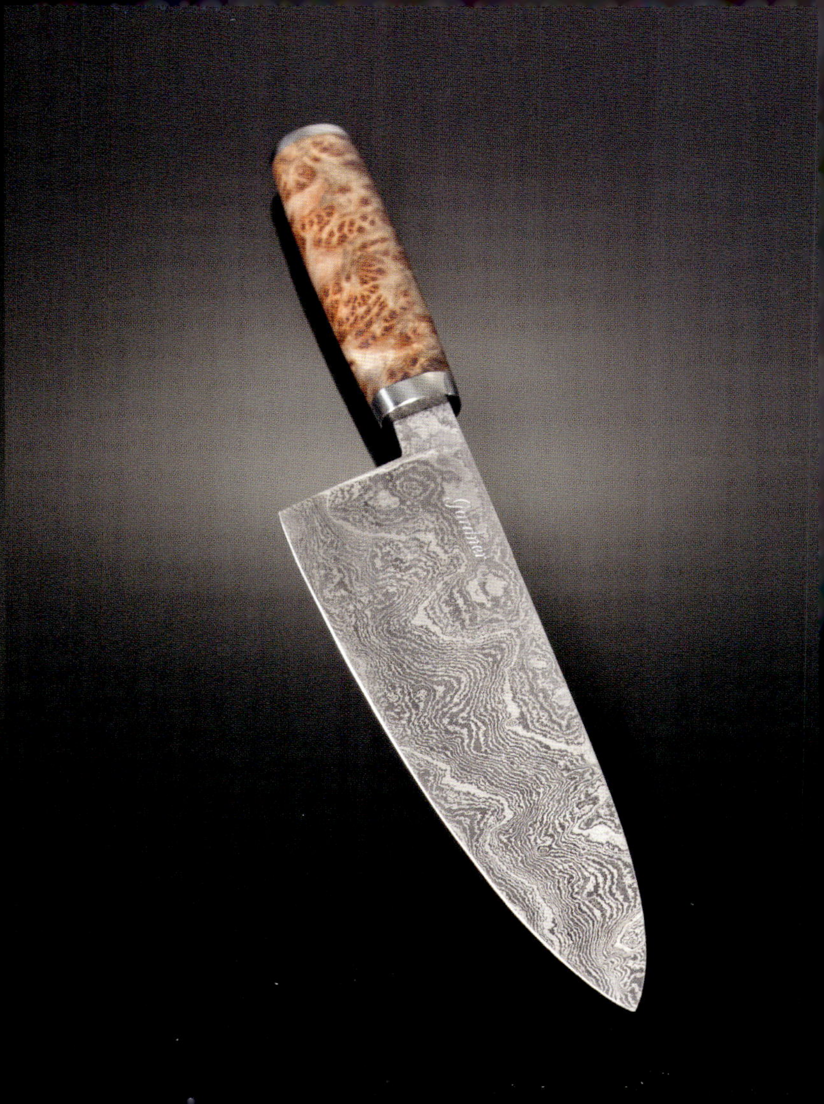

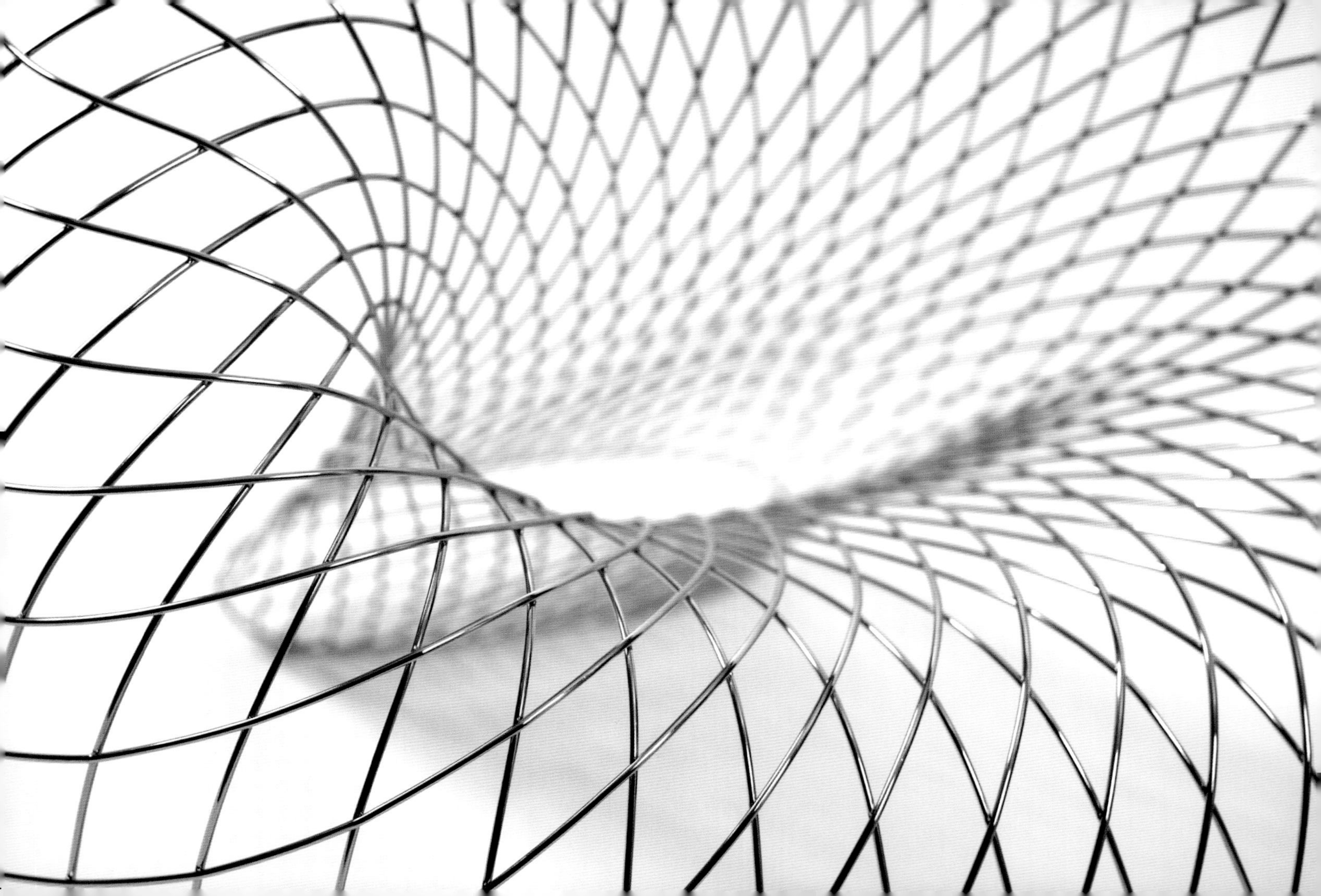

BRODIE NEILL

BORN 1979, HOBART, TASMANIA
LIVES LONDON, UNITED KINGDOM

BRODIE NEILL is inspired by expansive worlds. Be it outer galaxies or the deep sea, complex natural systems provide a wealth of scientific and mathematical principles, which the designer uses to push the boundaries of form and material in his work. 'Every design is a chance to do something new,' says Neill. 'There is creative spontaneity and romance in the process of working towards and realising a dream goal.'[1]

For more than a decade this Australian-born, London-based designer has forged a signature aesthetic by creating striking biomorphic furniture pieces. The works in his collection stand out as explorations in form and material, yet Neill is adamant that these are designs, not artworks. Aesthetically adventurous as they may be, each piece is designed to provide function. 'I always consider my editions to be design as they are the result of a design process,' notes Neill. 'They can be considered art due to their concept, but it is design that drives 'what' and 'how' I do something'.

Neill honed his designer-maker skills studying Furniture Design at the University of Tasmania. It was here that he learnt how to design in the third dimension and think like a sculptor. These formative years taught Neill the foundation of all materials – wood, metals, plastics, upholstery, glass and ceramics. 'I was a sponge, going in on Saturdays and Sundays, blagging my way into all the departments. It was important to me to learn how to express my design language in a range of materials,' says Neill.

Upon graduating, Neill set off to study a Masters Degree at the acclaimed Rhode Island School of Design in New York in 2004. While he had some early experience using digital technologies in his undergraduate degree, it was here that Neill harnessed the potential of computer-aided design in his practice.

1 All quotes in this profile were recorded by the author in an interview with Brodie Neill.

Merging advanced digital design technologies with a profound respect for material and the handmade, is a skill that has come to define the oeuvre of this furniture designer. Digital techniques afford Neill the ability to use complex mathematics to map the surface and create startlingly beautiful forms. From this, he then extracts how the hand can best be used to enhance the design. It is a delicate dance, with the digital and handmade each performing a crucial role in the creative process.

Neill entered the international design scene at Milan's Salone del Mobile in 2005 to great critical acclaim. His work caught the attention of Gregorio Spini, a founder of Italian lighting brand Kundalini, for whom he went on to develop the *Morphie Lamp*, 2006, and then the swirling, intertwined *E-turn Seat*, 2007. Later that same year he established his current studio in London's East End.

The Brodie Neill studio is prolific, producing work in a variety of scales – from the handheld to large commissions for the public realm. Works range from production pieces for design houses such as Kundalini and Riva 1920, to one-off projects for global brands such as Swarovski Crystal Palace and Alexander McQueen, to collectible edition pieces for galleries and private collectors.

In 2013, Neill founded the award-winning self-produced furniture brand 'Made in Ratio' with the aim of bringing uncompromising ideas to life by embracing experimental and boundary-pushing processes. Earlier this year, Neill cemented his position as a leading light in Australian design by being the first designer commissioned to represent Australia at the inaugural *London Design Biennale*.

PREVIOUS PAGE
Reverb Wire Chair (detail), 2010
hand formed, mirror stainless steel rods, 750 x 830 x 1000
Photo: Marzorati Ronchetti
Collection of Patrick Brillet of Patrick Brillet Fine Art Ltd.

▸
Brodie Neill, 2014
Photo: Peter Guenzel

▸▸
Reverb Chair, 2009
nickel plated aluminium
hand formed and mirror polished, 850 x 900 x 1000
Photo: Peter Whyte

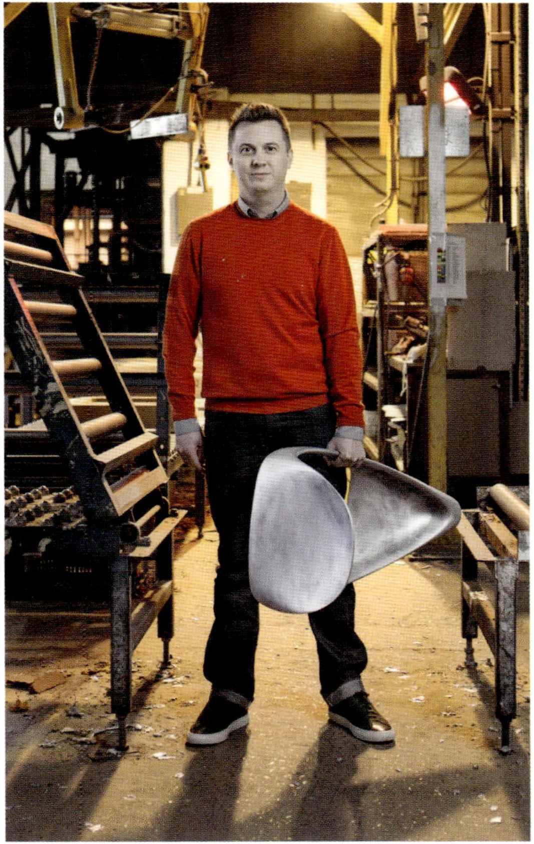

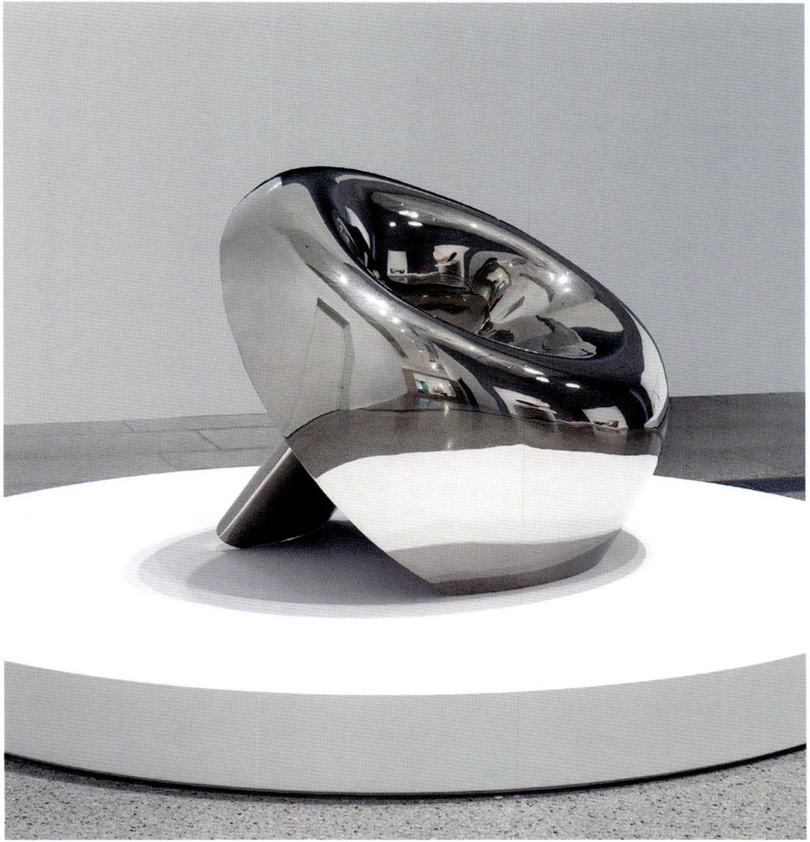

REVERB WIRE CHAIR

The *Reverb Wire Chair*, 2012, embodies volumetric presence and structural lightness. Inspired by the mathematical principles of sound reverberation, the chair comprises a networked system of handcrafted and mirror polished stainless steel rods that interlace to form a remarkable curvilinear form.

Neill was driven by the desire to create a structure using a single gesture. In 2010, the year the *Reverb Wire Chair* was designed, parametric modelling was a new digital technique creating waves in architectural fields. Adapting this digital tool to map the surface of a piece of furniture was a pioneering design approach for its time.

Each steel rod has been handmade by Italian artisans, and no two pieces are the same. The rods intersect and repeat themselves to form a rhomboidal grid with openings of different sizes. The diamond-shaped gaps are smaller in the central trunk, which blossom outward to form a curvaceous nest on which a person can sit.

The *Reverb Wire Chair* is an evolution of the *Reverb Chair*, 2009, which was crafted from solid mirror-polished aluminium. Yet while the DNA of the two chairs is the same, the process to create the *Reverb Wire Chair* was completely new. The later iteration celebrates the material properties of steel – namely its strength and malleability – to create a delightfully flamboyant stage for the everyday act of sitting. ■

DANIELLE ROBSON

▸

Reverb Wire Chair, 2010
hand formed, mirror stainless
steel rods, 750 x 830 x 1000
Photo: Marzorati Ronchetti
Collection of Patrick Brillet
of Patrick Brillet Fine Art Ltd.

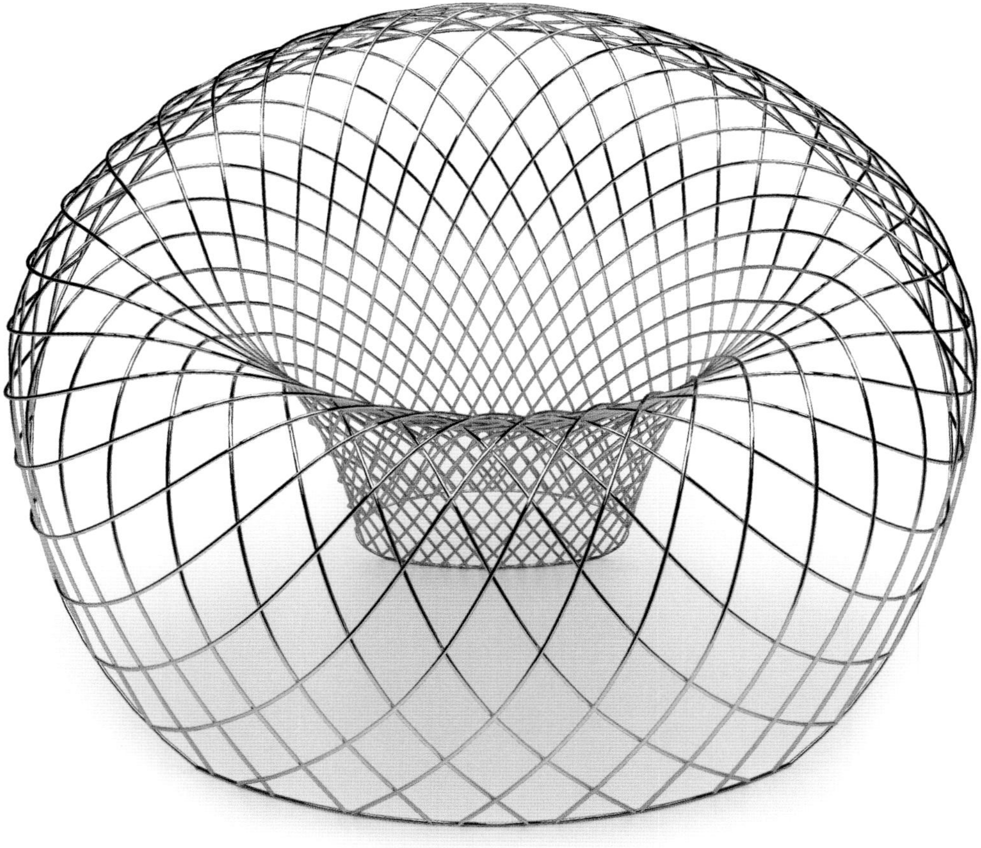

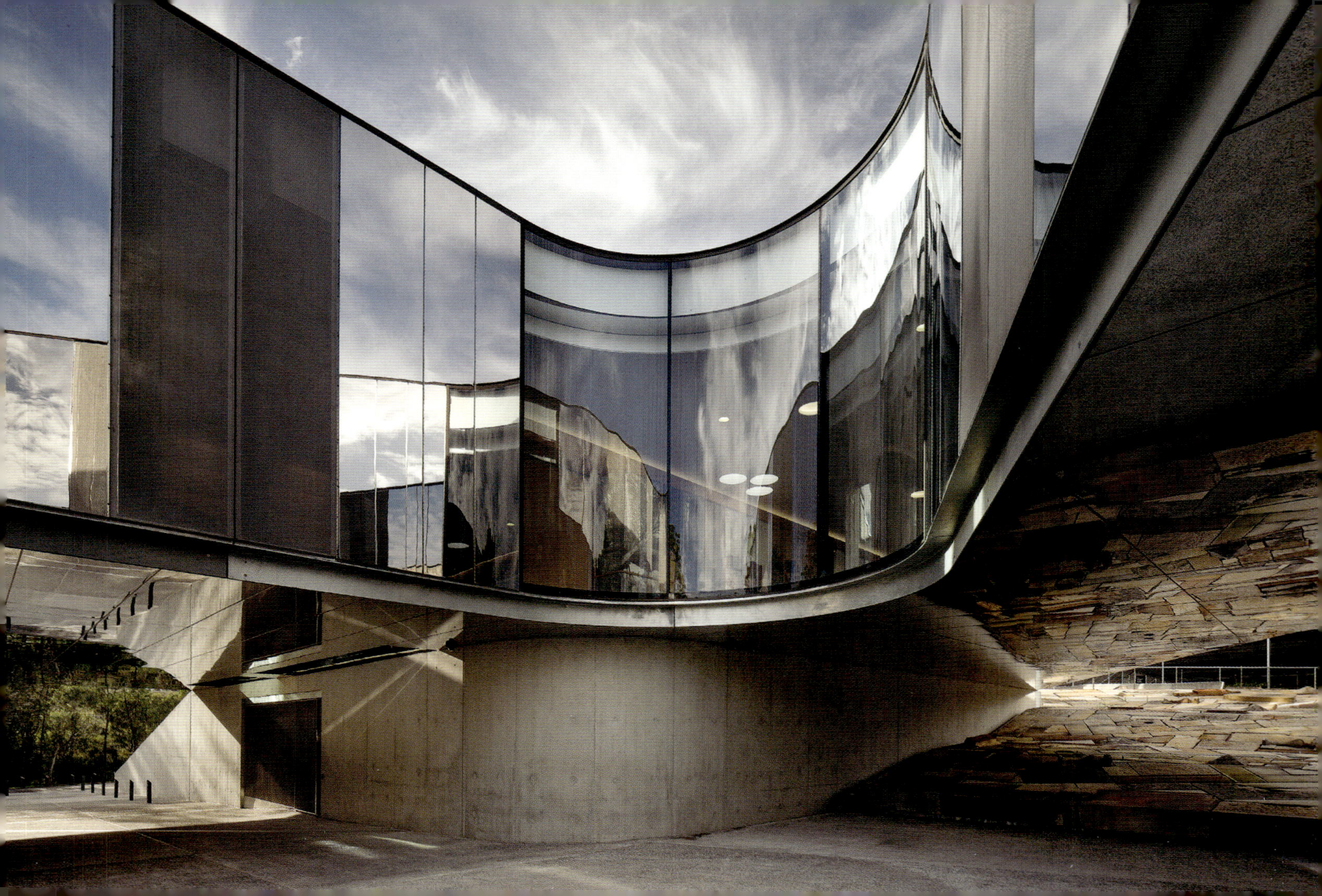

BVN

ESTABLISHED 1997,
SYDNEY, NEW SOUTH WALES

AS ONE OF AUSTRALIA'S LARGEST architectural practices, BVN[1] is widely acknowledged for award-winning design[2] across a broad and diverse portfolio in Australia and overseas. With a 90 year history and an international reputation for design leadership and innovation, this international practice has studios located in Brisbane, Sydney, Melbourne and New York, as well as project offices in Canberra and Bangkok. The practice's architectural work ranges from civic and institutional projects to office and residential design, tourism projects, industrial developments, master planning and urban design.

Celebrated for sustainable and public architecture the BVN designed Australian PlantBank, 2014, is built within the Australian Botanic Garden in Mount Annan, on the outskirts of Sydney. Part of a global network coordinated by the Royal Botanic Gardens Kew, England, known as the Millennium Seed Bank Partnership[3], The Australian PlantBank serves as a research facility and seed repository for the Royal Botanic Gardens and Domain trust.

Specialising in horticultural research and conservation of Australian native plant species (particularly from New South Wales), this repository of seeds differs from other world leading seed banks such as the Bill Gates funded, Svalbard Global Seed Vault in Norway, in that the impenetrable concrete bunkers usually associated with such projects is made accessible – revealing its inner workings to the public.

1 BVN was established in the late 1990s with the merging of Bligh Voller Architects, Lawrence Nield and Partners Australia, Grose Bradley and Pels Innes Nielson and Kosloff. Initially named Bligh Voller Nield, the company became BVN Architecture in 2009. In 2013 BVN merged with Donovan Hill to form BVN Donovan Hill, in 2014 the practice became BVN.

2 BVN has won more Sir John Sulman Medals than any other practice. The New South Wales Architects medal is sometimes referred to as the Sulman Award, and recognises excellence in public and commercial buildings.

3 The Millennium Seed Bank Project building located at Wakehurst, near London, is a vast underground storage vault. The aim is to store every plant species possible: it currently holds seed from 13 per cent of the world's wild plant species. By 2020 the goal is to reach 25 per cent, equating to 75,000 species.

4 http://www.bvn.com.au/projects/plantbank/, accessed September 2016.

5 http://architectureau.com/articles/the-australian-plantbank-garden/, accessed September 2016.

Ensuring the important ecological work of the research facility was on display throughout the building formed part of the project brief and indirectly influenced the final open plan design. As BVN describes:

The plan form allows views into the working sections of the building: from the entry through to the lobby, visitors can see researchers working within the laboratories. Beyond this they can view the incubators, cold storage facilities and the vault. The vault is the conceptual focus of the research, being the repository of seeds. The visitor heart of the building is the narrow lobby form at the junction of the research, workplace and information zones of the building. The facility has a strong educational interest and includes conference facilities for use by staff, visiting academics and the public.[4]

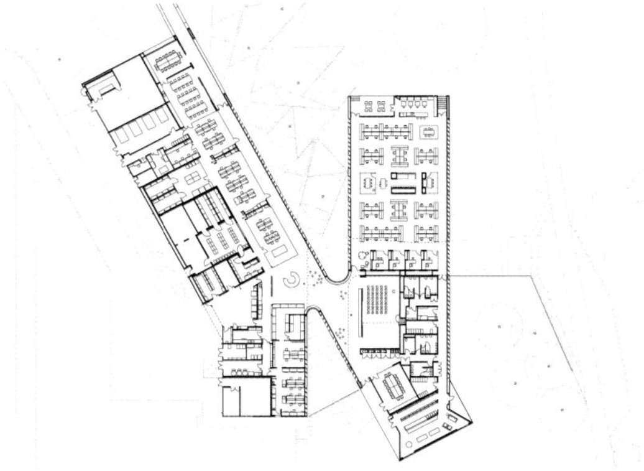

▲

A plan of the Australian Plantbank.

PREVIOUS PAGE

On exiting the mirrored tunnel under the building one arrives at the curved central point between two wings, on the right of this image, the lichen garden grows on sandstone retrieved from demolished public buildings is reflected in the mirrored ceiling.
Photo: John Gollings

▶

Glimpses of the mirrored tunnel ceiling and the view to the alternating mirror polished steel and fire resistant screen of the laboratory facade.
Photo: John Gollings

▶▶

The view from inside the curved central point of Plantbank showing the two wings embracing the courtyard and the forest beyond.
Photo: John Gollings

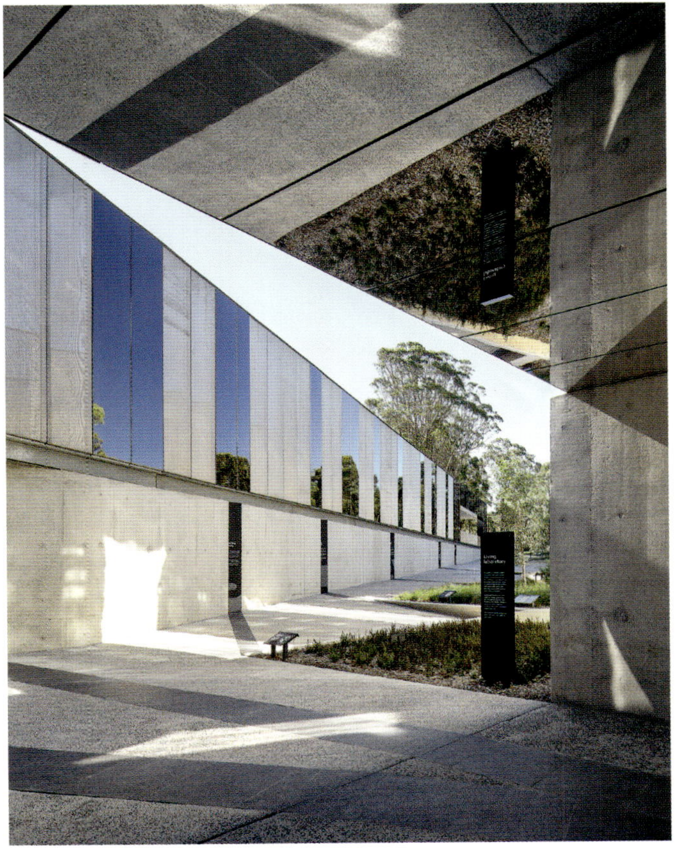

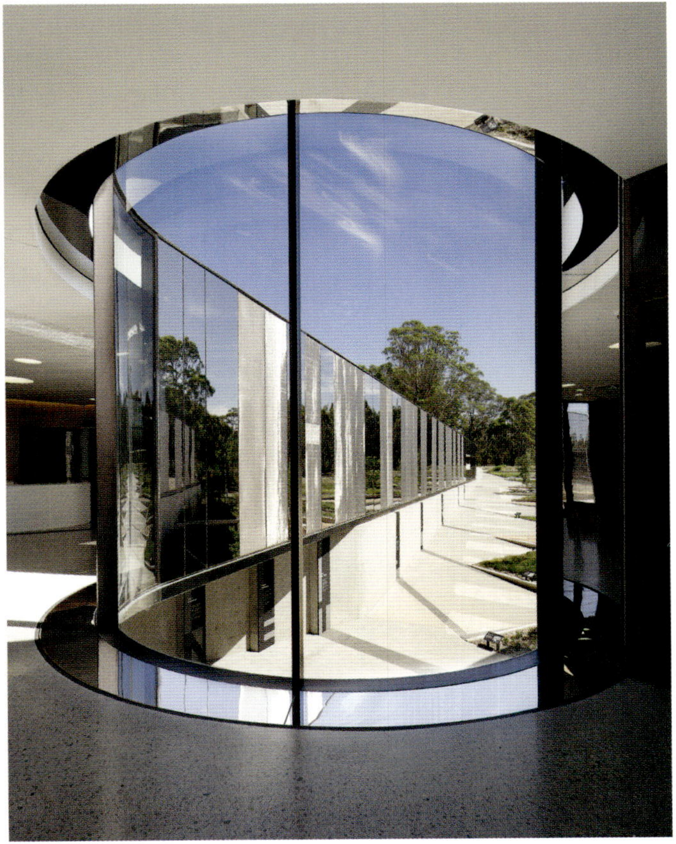

AUSTRALIAN PLANTBANK

Located in a part of the garden between a threatened and rare remnant section of Cumberland Plain Woodland and the garden's nursery that propagates species (including the famous Wollemi Pine), the Australian PlantBank, 2014, boasts two wings built at an acute angle to each other so they both embrace and reflect the woodland in its polished steel facade.

Elevated six metres from the road level, the entrance to the building is reached via an indirect ramped journey. Passing through a dark steel mirrored-roofed tunnel under the administration wing of the terrestrial concrete base, one exits out into a sun lit wedge-shaped courtyard.

The courtyard creates a luminal zone that mediates the boundary between the natural world and the man-made. Within the courtyard a series of angled garden beds scissor their way off into the surrounding landscape. 360 Degrees Landscape Architects, the lead landscape architects on the project, describe how the beds act 'as an abstracted representation of the woodland association'[5]. Original plans were to plant woodland species in the courtyard however due to fire restrictions this was not possible.

Fire codes have also led to the other great use of steel in this project. Interspersed between the polished steel surfaces, steel bushfire-resistant mesh has been used. This mesh allows large banks of louvered windows to be used within the building, creating a light-filled space that capitalises on the east-to-west passive cross ventilation, minimizing the energy consumption of the building.

Conservation and ecological concerns are further apparent in the materials chosen in the courtyard. The lichen garden comprising mosses, liverworts and lichens which are growing on Sydney sandstone, recovered from the Royal Botanic Gardens Sydney and Sydney Hospital. The details of the lichen garden are reflected in the polished steel roof, with visitors able to distinguish gate posts, statue plinths, coping stones and even a chimney flue from the two historic sites. ■

MARGARET HANCOCK DAVIS

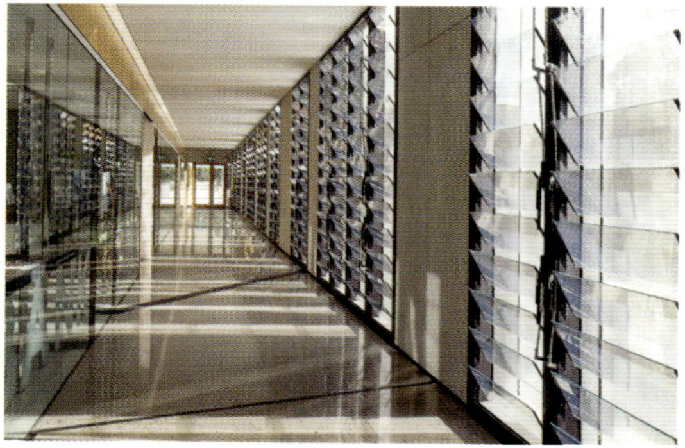

[redacted]

Banks of louvered windows provide natural ventilation.
Photo: John Gollings

A view across plant beds to the Australian Plantbank from the forest end.
Photo: John Gollings

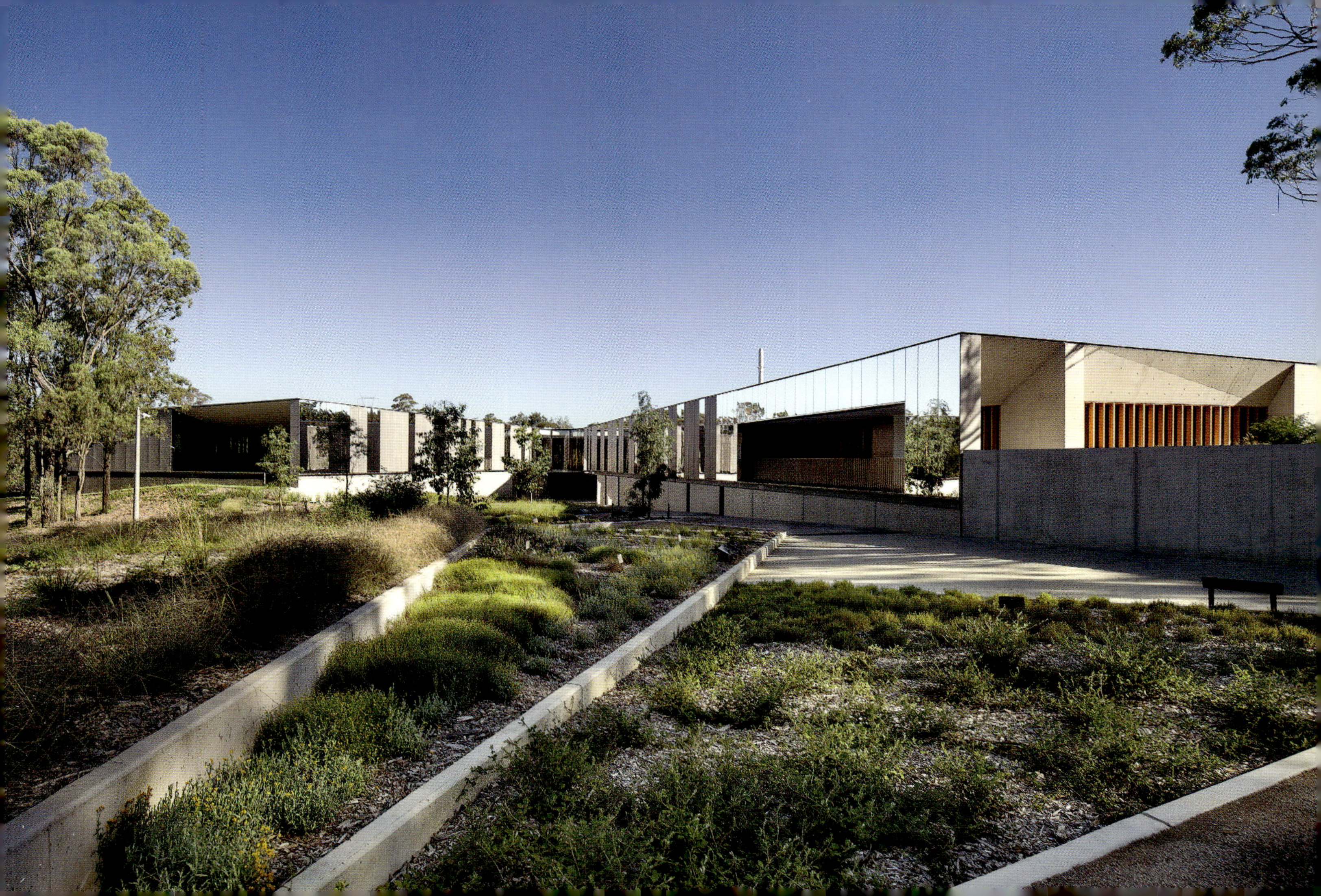

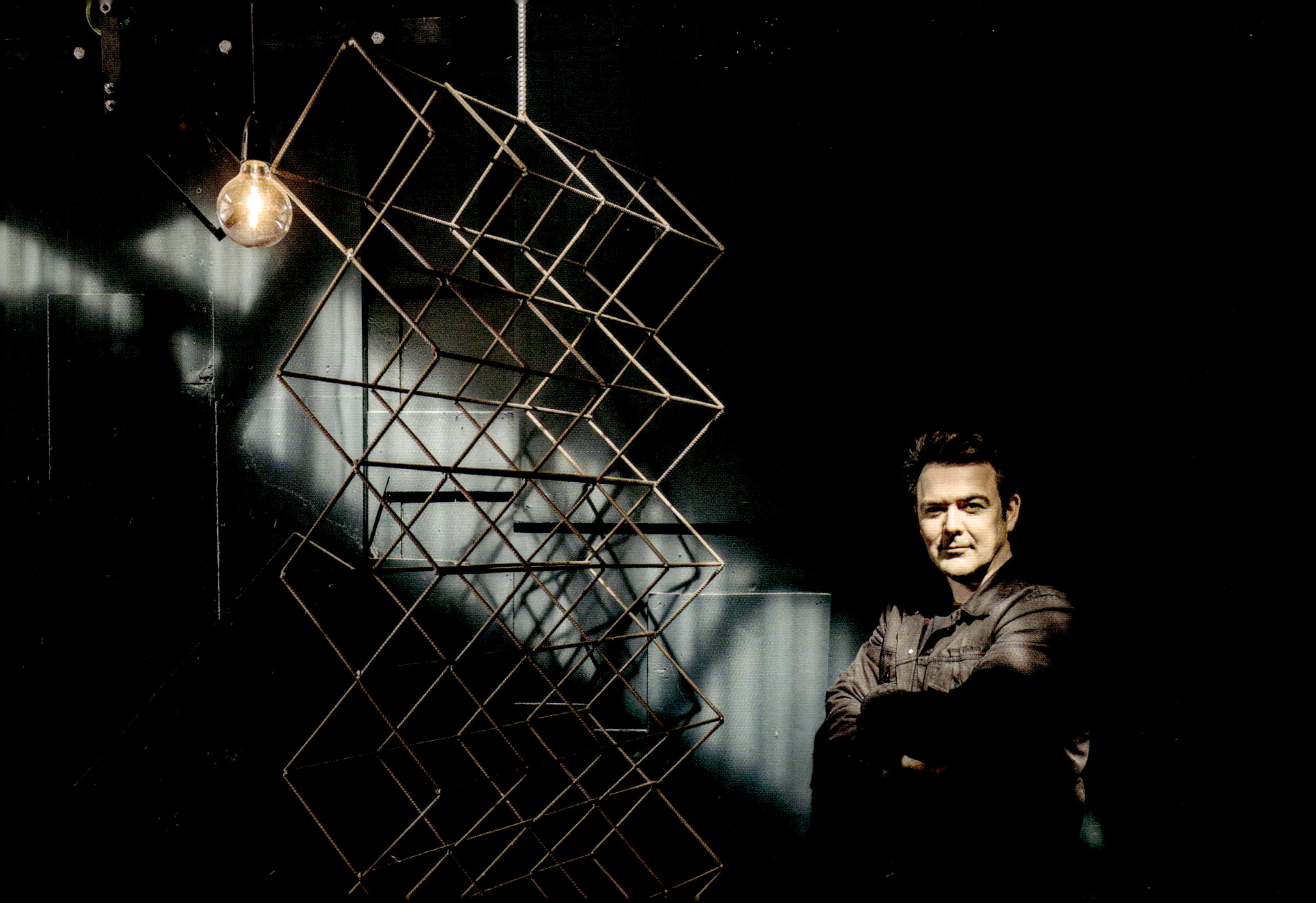

CHRISTIAN HALL

BORN 1973, SYDNEY, NEW SOUTH WALES
LIVES ADELAIDE, SOUTH AUSTRALIA

WORKING ACROSS furniture and industrial design, sculpture and jewellery, each piece Christian Hall makes is designed to inspire a moment of delight. His meticulous designs focus not only on form, but on physicality, resulting in sculptural objects which seamlessly combine hand-crafting skills with a sleek industrial-looking finish.

Graduating from Sydney College of the Arts, University of Sydney, in 1998 with a Bachelor of Visual Arts, First Class Honours, Hall began his career in jewellery and object design. Going onto complete his Masters in Visual Arts in 2003, Hall has been the Creative Director at JamFactory Metal Design Studio since 2009. An accomplished teacher and maker, Hall has exhibited widely across Australia and internationally, in addition to being the recipient of numerous awards and grants.

Inspired by transport, movement and industry, Hall's work often translates the large scale into a domestic and everyday language. In previous works, Hall scales down industrial objects, and put them in unexpected contexts. Airplanes became brooches and lamps, satellites and rockets become objects that could fit on your desk or float in a delicate complex mobile light above your head. Fascinated by the materiality of steel, particularly its ability to be lightweight and strong Hall reduces complex machines to their most basic geometric forms, drawing attention to the shape and function of the original and the recast object, while underlining the versatility of steel.

Designs are first made through a computer program, so Hall can look at it from all angles and solve any early issues. In his more recent work, this step also allows him to experiment with different viewpoints, to emphasise the repeated shapes and patterns that have become integral to his latest designs. The focus has been to create multiple viewpoints, so that his designs can be seen as flat at one point, and a formed volume at another, as a way to capture and express movement through geometry and design. Inspired by a diverse range of influences, from the microscopic to the industrial, these geometric designs are a complex web of references hidden in a clean, refined aesthetic.

Recently branching into larger sculptural works, these pieces extend his focus on playing with volume and flatness, design and pure art. They reflect his latest investigation into movement, specifically how people interacting with his work can change it by simply shifting their perspective. Moving away from a literal narrative, Hall's practice now focusses on a more abstracted investigation into flatness and voluminous, static and dynamic, designs.

His emphasis on material, not as incidental but integral to the end result, means that Hall looks closely at the unique properties of steel, not just its inherent strength but how, with the right design, it can be both lightweight and strong, and it's these, often industrial examples, which Hall draws from. In this crossover between mass-produced and hand-crafted design, Hall's work is an example of the interplay of craft and industry, not as binaries, but as complimentary practices. Through Hall's repetitive patterns and structures, notable across the breadth of his practice, he subtly and skilfully draws our attention to the overlooked beauty in our everyday structural environment.

[redacted]

▶

Cube Stand No. 1, 2015
powder coated steel,
450 x 300 x 150
Photo: Grant Hancock

PREVIOUS PAGE
Christian Hall with *TELL HENRY / RODEO Space Divider*.
Photo: Tom Roschi

[redacted]

◥◥

TELL HENRY / RODEO Space Divider, 2015
steel reinforcement mesh,
2300 x 13000 x 300
Photo: Tom Roschi

◢◢

Mesh Shelving Unit installed at Coffee Bondi Beach, 2015
mild steel, walnut,
1200 x 1600 x 300
This fitout was designed by Liam Mugavin.
Photo: Barton Taylor

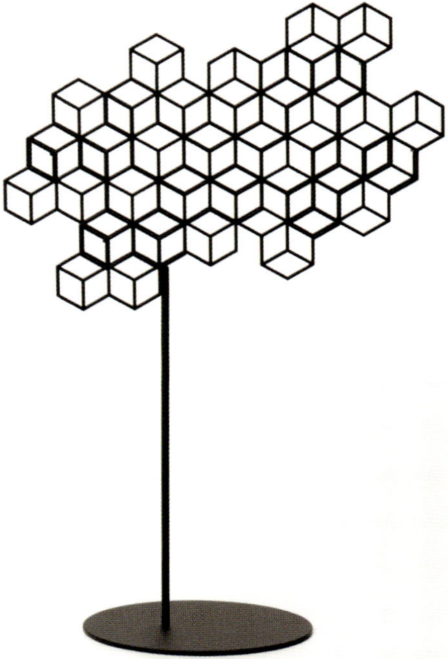

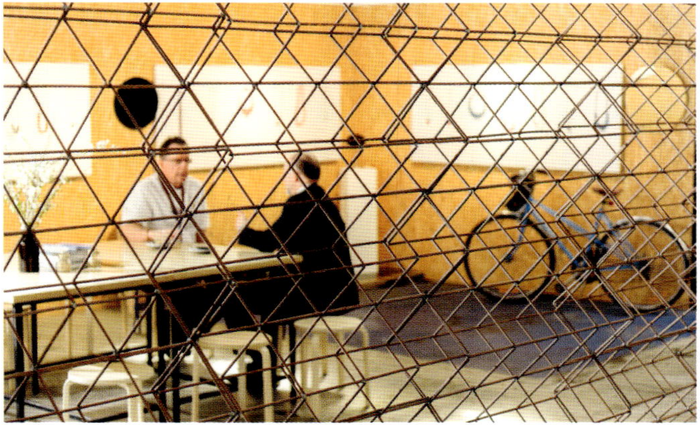

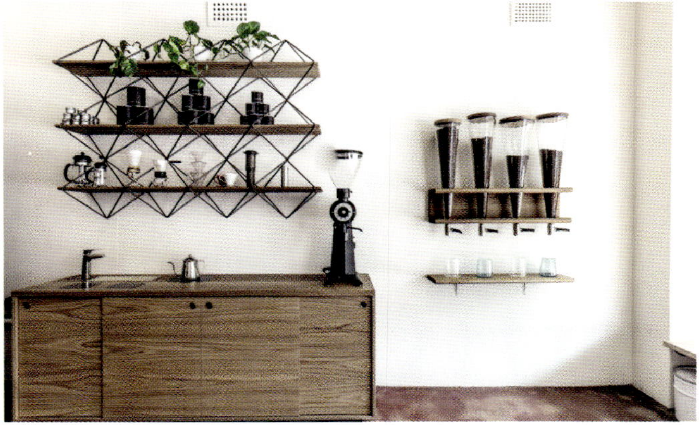

MESH ROOM DIVIDER

Mesh Room Divider, 2015, was born from a commission by a local shared space in Kent Town, Adelaide which hosts a cafe, gallery and design studio, to find a solution to separate the cafe and the design studio, without losing the sense of open space. Hall used repurposed rebar (which are the steel bars used to reinforce concrete) to create a floating room divider. Using a grid pattern based on horizontal and vertical lines, this divider proved to be the perfect solution to creating a sense of privacy and separation.

While this design was perfect for a commercial setting inside an old warehouse, Hall wanted to push the design further so it could be used in a more domestic or small-scale site. In this new version Hall opted for a powder coated mild steel, instead of rebar, while also changing the grid subtly, to diamond shaped pattern, forming a slightly softer aesthetic. This design also echoes other forms that have fascinated Hall. The molecular structure of a diamond, the hardest natural material on earth, for example shares a similar structure to the patterning in *Mesh Room Divider*, while others, more versed in industrial design, might recognise the Warren truss pattern – a structural design which allows steel to support large amounts of weight.

SERENA WONG

[redacted]

▸

Mesh Room Divider, 2015
powder coated mild steel,
2000 x 2300 x 300
Photo: Grant Hancock

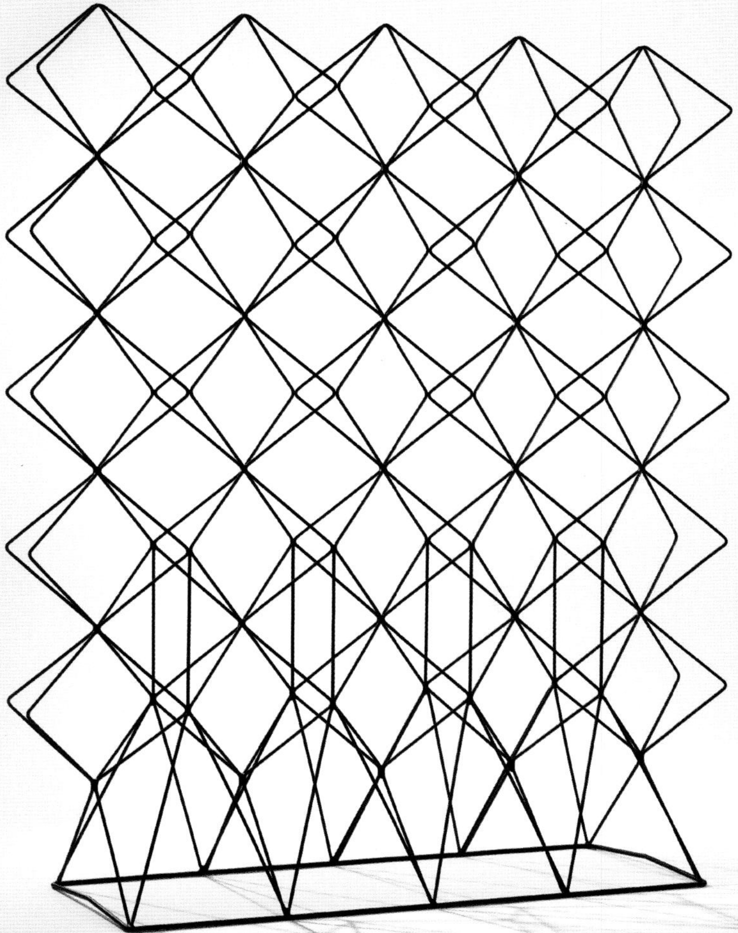

NECKPIECE IN BLACK

Both the furniture and jewellery stem from an impulse to integrate structure and ornamentation. The same material, geometry and methodology is applied to both typologies, however, the techniques, function and outcomes are divergent.

The jewellery making process combines laser cutting and micro-welding with more traditional hand-making techniques and also elements of play-like construction. Each unit is made from the same two, flat, interlocking components that are snapped together by hand to sit at right angles to each other. These singular, wire frame structures create a description of three-dimensional space that when multiplied produce works that explore an ambiguity between line and volume.

Material is kept to a minimum and steel, while perceived as heavy in fact has a specific gravity less than silver and gold, maintains a strength to weight ratio suitable to larger scale jewellery. Relieved of the necessity to overcome gravity, these steel structures are designed as light, wearable objects that tease out form from flatness and question the distinction between structure and decoration. ■

CHRISTIAN HALL

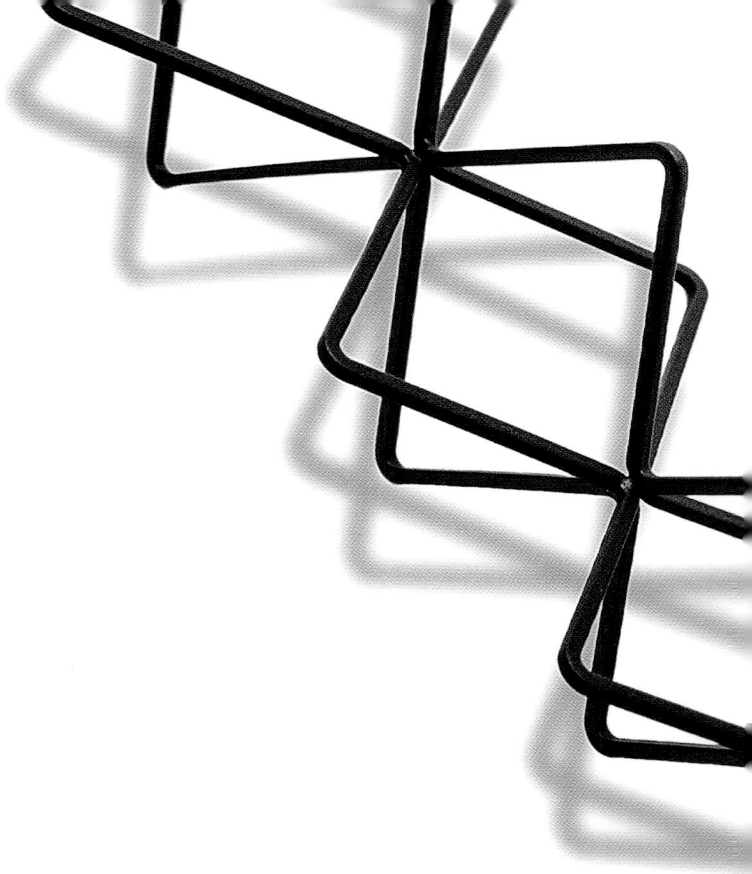

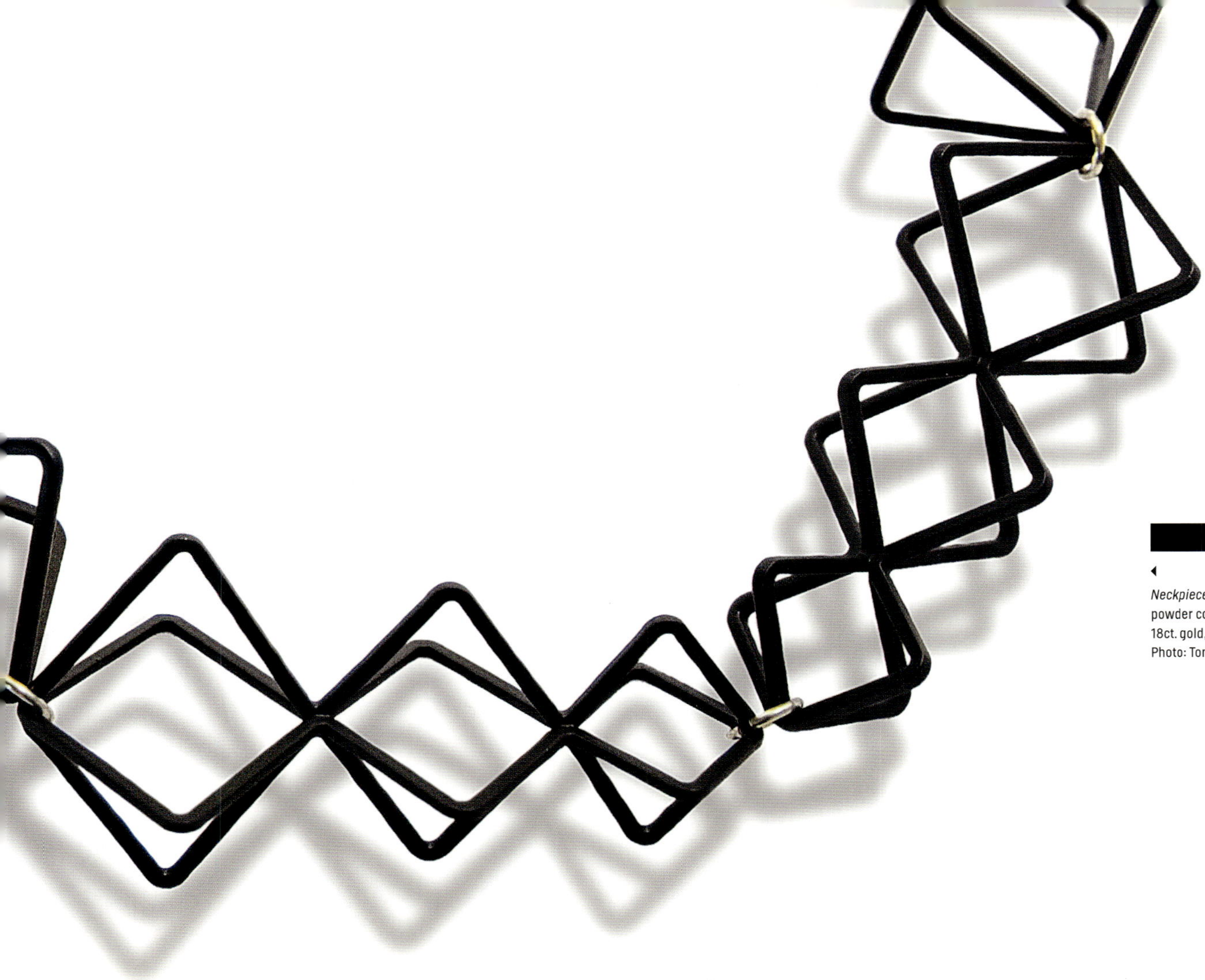

Neckpiece in Black, 2016
powder coated stainless steel,
18ct. gold, 700 x 40 x 40
Photo: Tom Roschi

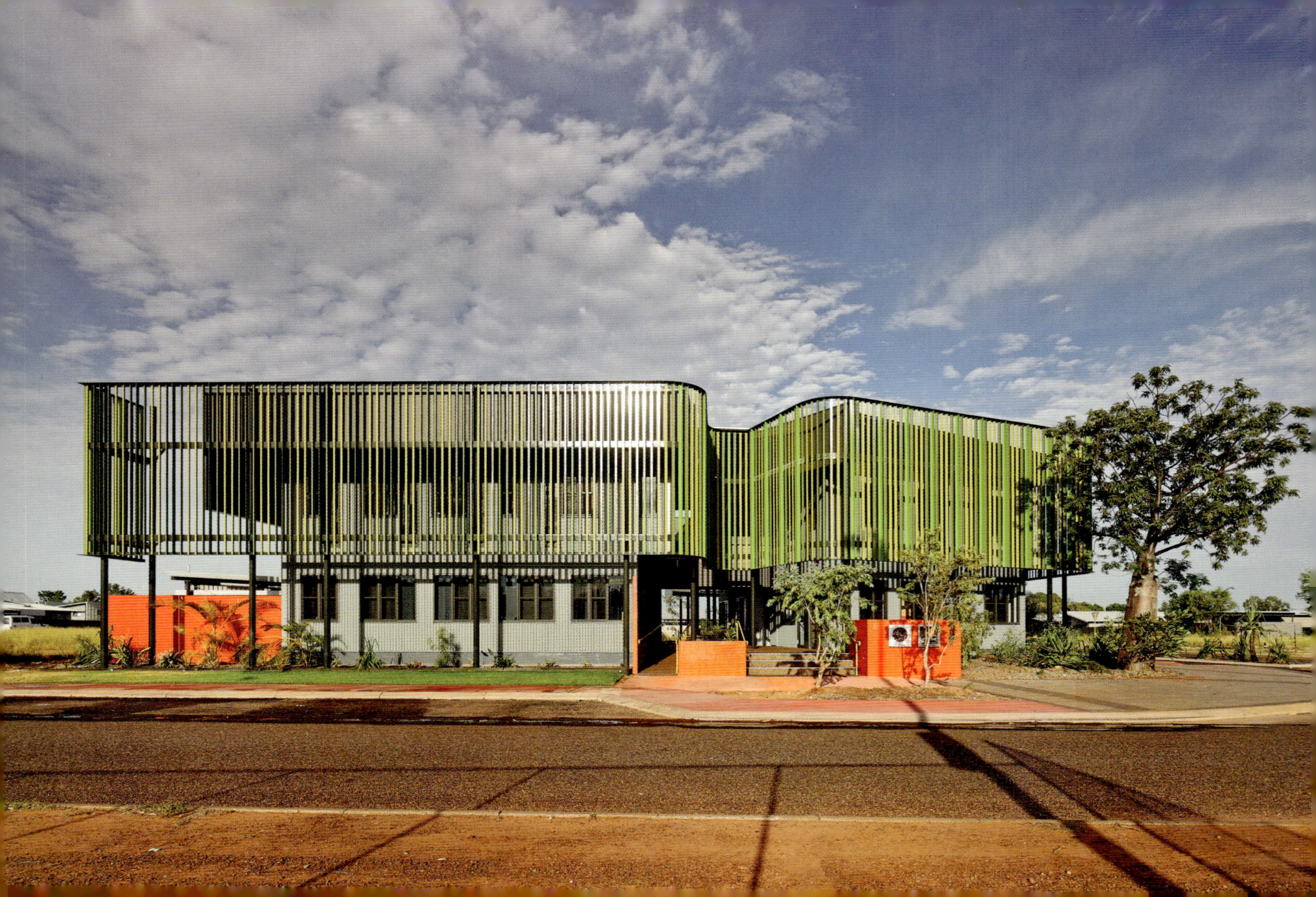

CODA STUDIO

ESTABLISHED 1997, FREMANTLE, WESTERN AUSTRALIA

EMMA WILLIAMSON
BORN 1972, PERTH, WESTERN AUSTRALIA

KIERAN WONG
BORN 1971, PERTH, WESTERN AUSTRALIA

BOTH LIVE FREMANTLE, WESTERN AUSTRALIA

CODA is a leading Western Australian boutique architectural practice and one of this country's most exciting design voices. Currently comprising a team of 13 architects and designers, the Fremantle-based studio works across a number of different sectors, from residential and commercial to hospitality and education. Its small and large-scale projects are located throughout regional and metropolitan Western Australia and are memorable for a dynamic environmental response that incorporates robust materiality and an unabashedly strong colour palette.

Co-founders Emma Williamson and Kieran Wong established the practice in the late nineteen-nineties and are still at the helm in their respective roles as Practice Director and Design Director. They managed to launch the studio at a time when the Western Australian design scene was undergoing significant change. A number of other practices were also emerging, and today, CODA and their peers (such as Iredale Pederson Hook, Gresley Abas, and Pendal and Neille) are responsible for reinventing Fremantle and Perth as two of Australia's major creative hubs.

Discussing CODA's projects often raises the subject of a particular Western Australian identity. It's an easy conversation to fall into, considering the geographical divide between the practice's base and the design hubs of the eastern states. But while a sense of place energises CODA's architecture and urban and interior design, it by no means confines or restricts the practice's outcomes.

The CODA signature is underpinned by a commitment to sustainability and the creation of cost effective, diverse and adaptable projects. This is especially evident in its urban design portfolio, where the recently awarded Broome North development[1] highlights a balance between consideration for the end user and intelligent planning. However, CODA's aesthetic is varied and adventurous, characterised by a lack of pretension, which makes it immediately appealing on so many levels.

There's joy to be found in the practice's interiors, whether due to a bright colour palette or expressive combination of materials. Williamson, Wong and the team are adept at using decorative finishes to witty effect, as seen in another recently awarded project, MLC Boarding House[2]. This project's geometric wall motifs make the living areas' seem all the more relaxed and an unexpected use of textiles in the bedrooms attest to CODA's love of playfulness and experimentation. A wonderfully restless spirit of innovation is tempered by strong architectural principles that have simple form, uncomplicated design solutions and sturdy construction at its core.

The practice's architects and designers are ultimately in the business of problem solving and their priority is meeting the client's brief. CODA is invested in collaborative working methods and its processes are very hands-on, regardless of a project's cost, scale or size. Ideas are tested through physical models and the use of collage, graphic overlays and visual documentation is commonplace during the early design stages. The objective – as always – is to create spaces that are not only visually compelling and intriguing, but are also highly functional.

While CODA projects continue to garner accolades, the practice itself has become well regarded for its role in maintaining a nationally rigorous dialogue on architecture and design. Both Williamson and Wong speak regularly at conferences and serve on juries, and Wong is regarded as a particularly authoritative voice on social housing and residential affordability. CODA may be one of Australia's greatest contemporary architectural pioneers, but its lasting legacy undeniably rests in the creation of public and private spaces that better serve the needs and enrich the lives of the end user, both individually and as part of a wider community.

1 The Broome North development won the 2010 Australian Institute of Architecture (WA) Urban Design John Septimus Roe Award.

2 The MLC Boarding House received a commendation on the 2016 Australian Interior Design Awards.

[redacted]

PREVIOUS PAGE
MG/GT Administration Building, Kununurra, Western Australia, 2012
The front elevation reveals the impressive visual impact of the building's curved steel screen.
Photo: Peter Bennetts

[redacted]

◥
The verandah spaces, shielded from the intensity of the weather by the steel screen, provides a comfortable circulation space throughout the building.
Photo: Peter Bennetts

◢
A key request was that users of the building did not feel hemmed in by their surroundings. The rear view reveals the large balcony that can be accessed from the rear of the offices, as well as the front.
Photo: Peter Bennetts

[redacted]

▸▸
The exposed entry foyer runs through the building and acts as a social meeting point for the community.
Photo: Peter Bennetts

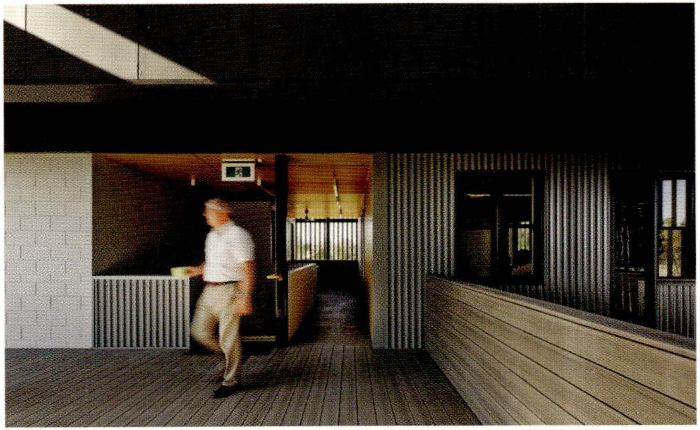

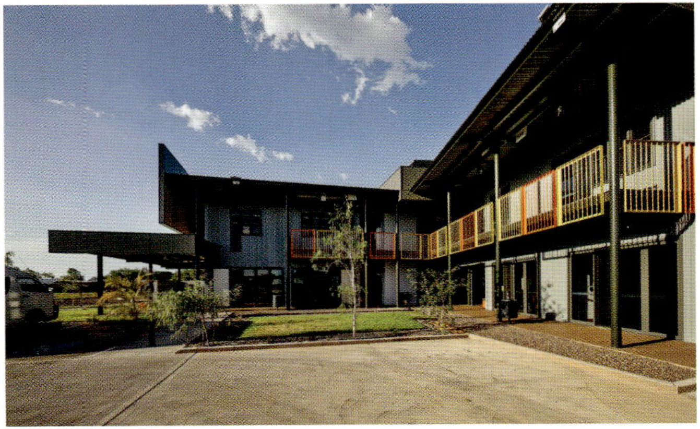

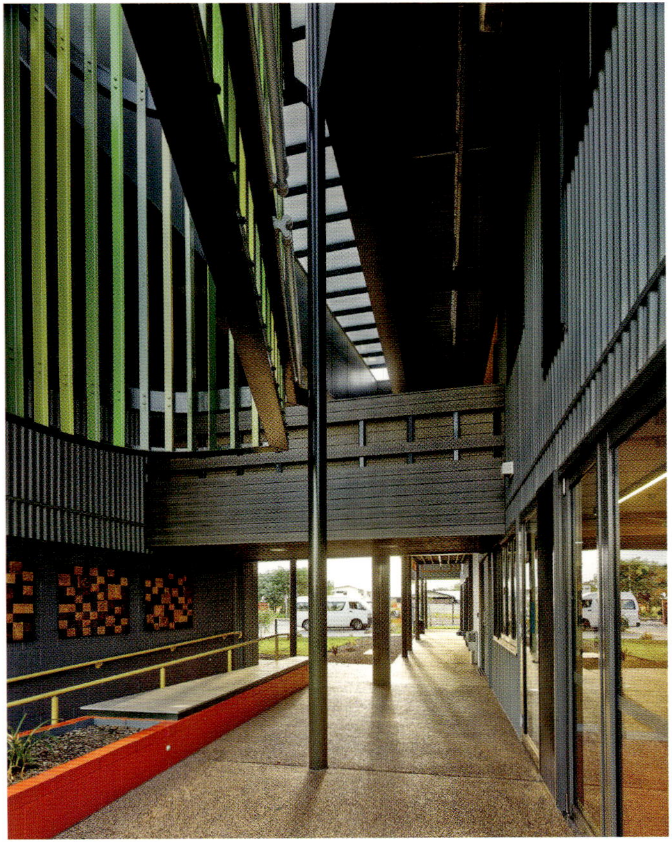

MG/GT ADMINISTRATION BUILDING

The two-storey MG/GT Administration Building, 2012, in Kununurra houses the offices of traditional eastern Kimberley landowner groups, the Miriuwung Gajerrong Corporation and Gelganyem Trust. While workspaces are positioned on the second level, an open public area dominates the ground-floor-plan. CODA's brief was to make the structure as inviting as possible and these outdoor spaces succeed in offering plentiful opportunities for community engagement and gathering.

The practice employed a robust material palette to withstand Kununurra's harsh climate. To this end the project's two volumes are formed from lightweight steel sections clad in compressed fibre cement sheeting and steel. A 'green screen' comprising vertically aligned hot rolled steel angles of differing sizes, wraps both volumes at the upper level on the street elevation, providing visual cohesion. It is the project's most dramatic design expression and also its most overtly functional, offering shade to both internal and external spaces. Along with a series of strategically placed breezeways, verandahs and walkways, this screen imbues the overall scheme with a heightened environmental response that resonates with a sense of place. The choice of bright green, orange and yellow finishes, further connects the project to its surrounding landscape and serves to soften a material palette that is resolutely industrial in aesthetic. This project won a Commercial Architecture Award at the 2013 Western Australian Architecture Awards. ■

LEANNE AMODEO

[redacted]

▸

The building, glowing at dusk.
Photo: Peter Bennetts

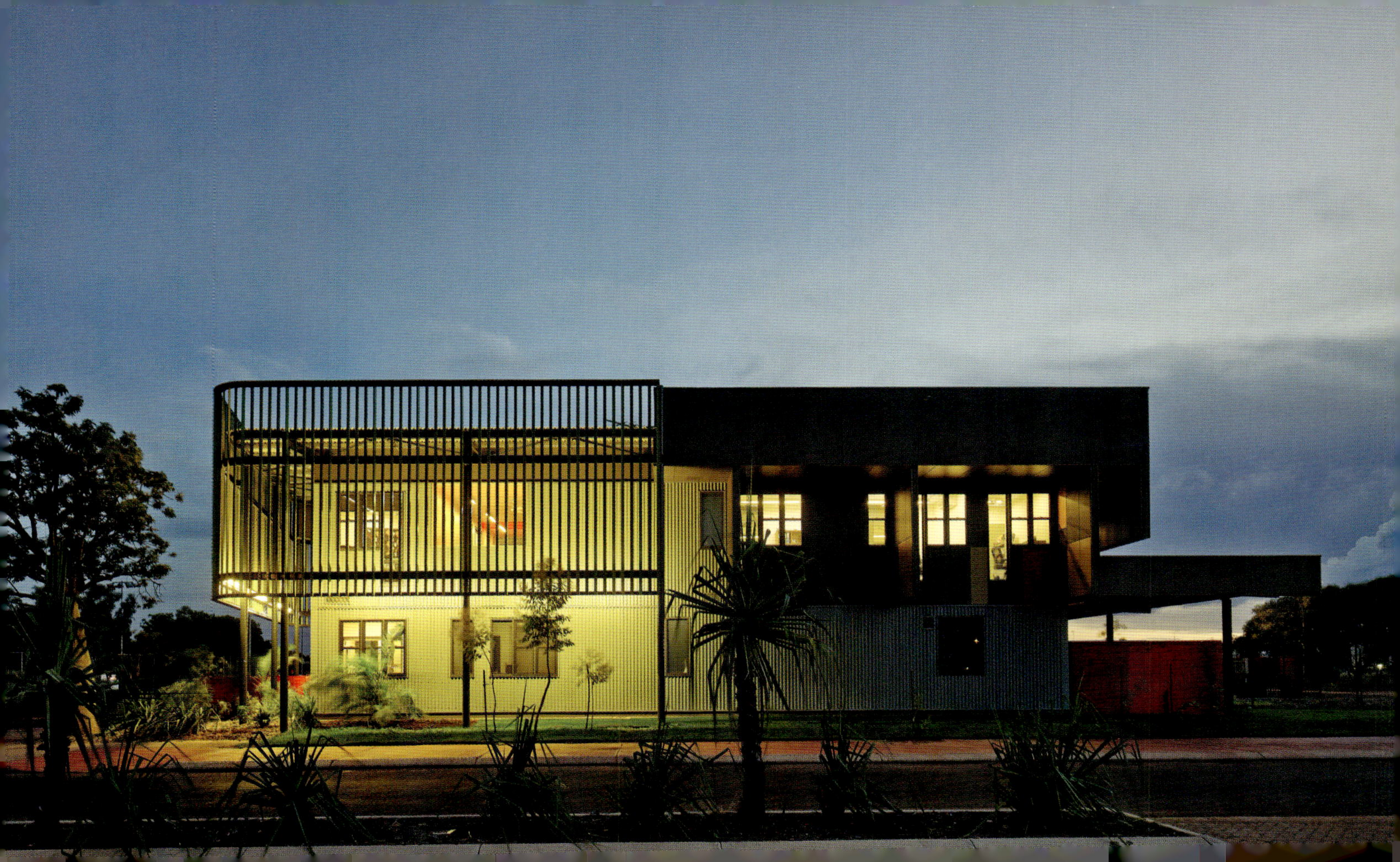

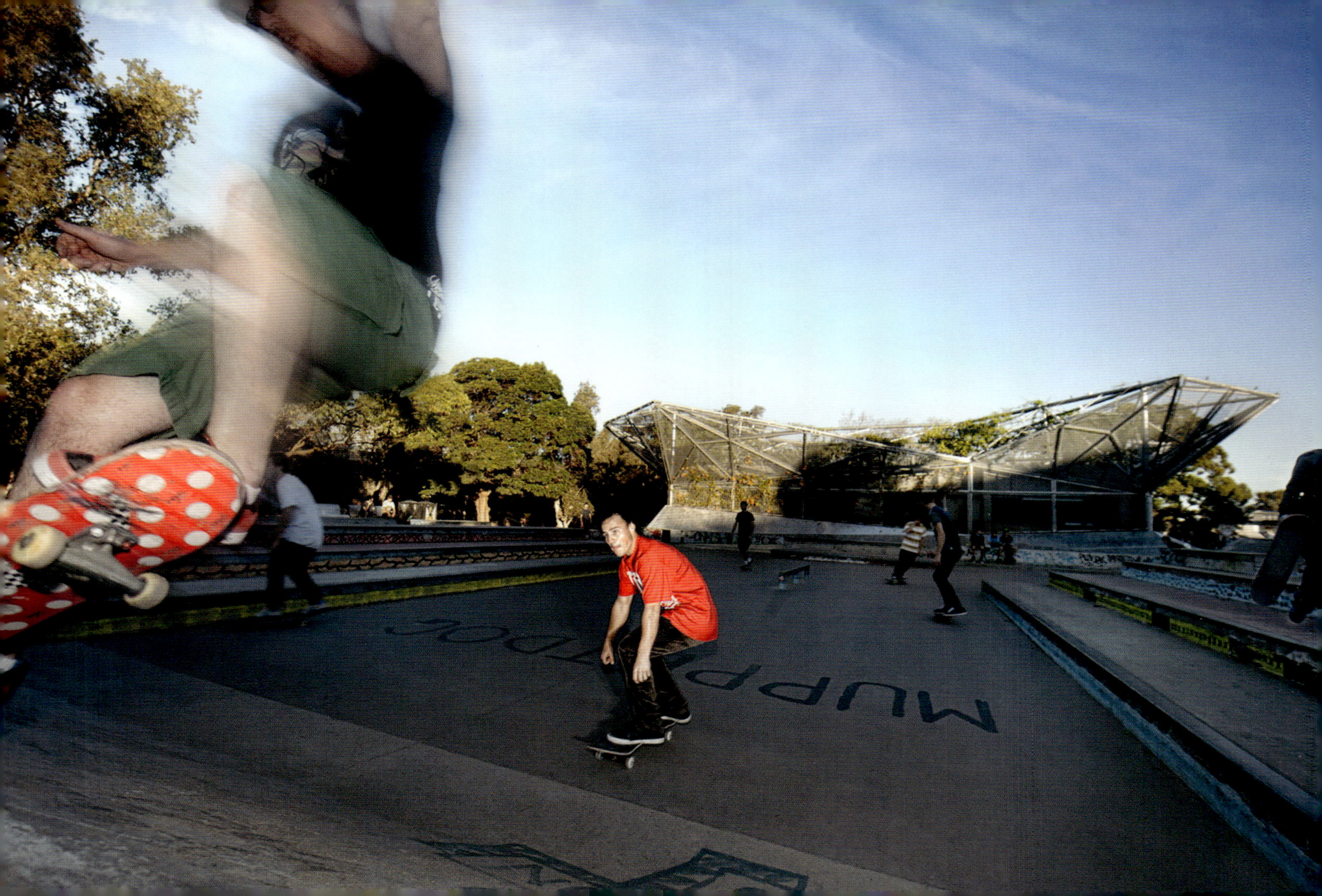

COLLINS AND TURNER

ESTABLISHED 2002, SYDNEY, NEW SOUTH WALES

PENNY COLLINS
BORN 1962, SYDNEY, NEW SOUTH WALES

HUW TURNER
BORN 1967, WALES, UNITED KINGDOM

BOTH LIVE SYDNEY, NEW SOUTH WALES

TRY TO IMAGINE what it would be like to provide services for disadvantaged and vulnerable young people, women, children and families in the South Sydney area from a dark, often vandalised, reclaimed amenities block. This was exactly what Shane Brown and his dedicated team at WEAVE[1] (Working to Educate, Advocate and Empower) had been doing for 15 years at the corner of Waterloo Park, until the City of Sydney created an invitation-only competition to redevelop the centre into a new state of the art premises. Winners of the 2008 design competition were Sydney-based Collins and Turner.

Penny Collins and Huw Turner met in 1993 whilst working at Fosters and Partner in Germany. They founded Collins and Turner, a multidisciplinary design studio, in 2002. The City of Sydney's challenging brief included a number of constraints: the building must be limited to within or minimal expansion of the existing footprint so as not to encroach into the park; it must be vandal-proof; and if possible, incorporate a green roof due to the surrounding high rises. Their response was to create a building veiled and crowned in an angular galvanised steel mesh trellis reminiscent of the Cedric Price designed Snowden Aviary at London Zoo.

Taking cues from a diversity of sources including: the adjoining skate park, grass covered iron-age forts of Celtic Wales, and the work of American naturalist John Krubsackan[2], Collins and Turner hollowed out the centre of the existing amenities building for a central courtyard. The buiding's pinwheel formation removed the need for corridors – allowing daylight and fresh air to passively refresh the building. Walls were pierced to make small expansions in available space whilst the whole building structure was encased in the trellis mesh. An independent element that is structurally separated from the more solid internal mass, the trellis cantilevers out in irregular angular ramparts beyond the roof line from four Hills-Hoist-like structures creating a private rooftop garden that has increased space for

1 WEAVE Youth & Community Services is a non-profit community organisation that has been working within the City of Sydney and South Sydney areas for over 35 years. It was formerly known as South Sydney Youth Services.

2 John Krubsack experimented with growing and grafting plants into shapes creating the first chair that was grown rather than made.

3 'Angular steel canopy covers refurbished community centre by Collins and Turner,' *Dezeen*. (27 December, 2013). http://www.dezeen.com/2013/12/27/angular-steel-canopy-covers-refurbished-community-centre-by-collins-and-turner/, accessed September 2016.

the range of programs presented by WEAVE, even creating new opportunities for the building's uses such as a rooftop vegetable garden.

In a move that may seem counter-intuitive for an organisation that supports a community often affected by violence and the impacts of incarceration, the trellis is in fact a South African prison mesh – it provides the perfect substrate to grow an array of native and introduced creeper vines that cover the building in a field of flowering green. The plantings have been done in such a manner that the blooms change with the season, in winter the orange flowers of trumpeter vine (Pyrostegia venusta) shroud the building. Whilst later in spring a cascade of white flowers of the wonga-wonga vine (Pandorea pandorana) hang from the upper rooftop garden. As the architect notes, 'as the plants mature and grow...the building will gradually merge with its park setting, becoming an abstract and sculptural green land-form that punctuates the park boundary and visually merges with the adjacent tree canopies.'[3] The trellis also has the added benefit of restricting people from scaling and/or vandalising the building.

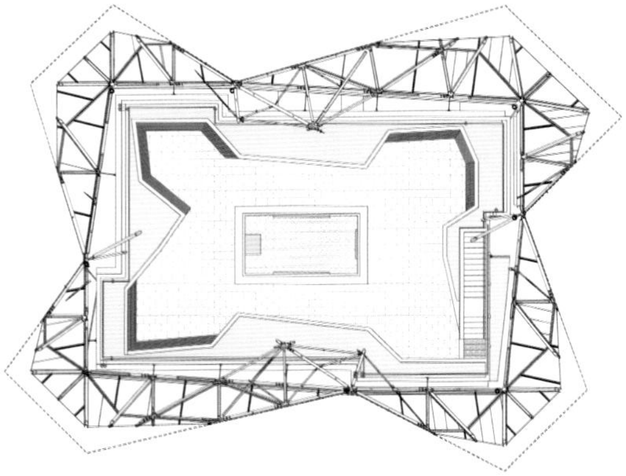

[redacted]

PREVIOUS PAGE
Waterloo Youth Centre, Waterloo, New South Wales, 2013
View of the centre across Fernside skatepark.
Photo: Josef Nalevansky

[redacted]

▲
Plan of the centre.

◥
Sketch by Huw Turner of the centre.

▶
Courtyard and open plan workspace. The artwork was carried out by young people that use the Centre.
Photo: Paul Bradshaw

▶▶
Central courtyard with view to roof top garden.
Photo: Paul Bradshaw

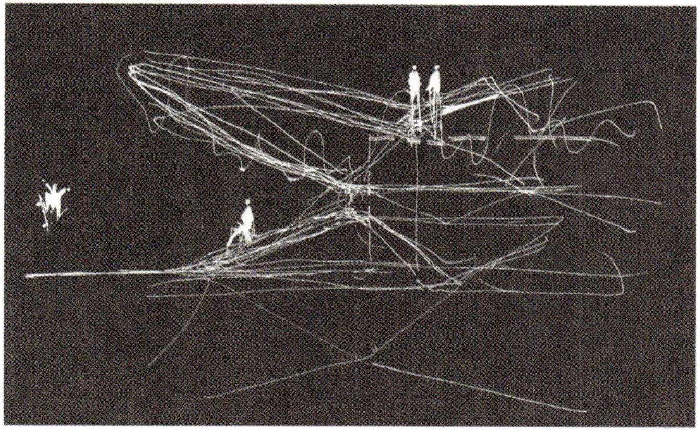

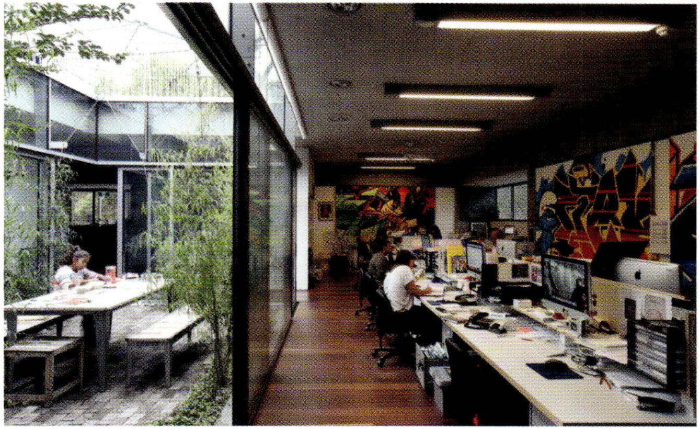

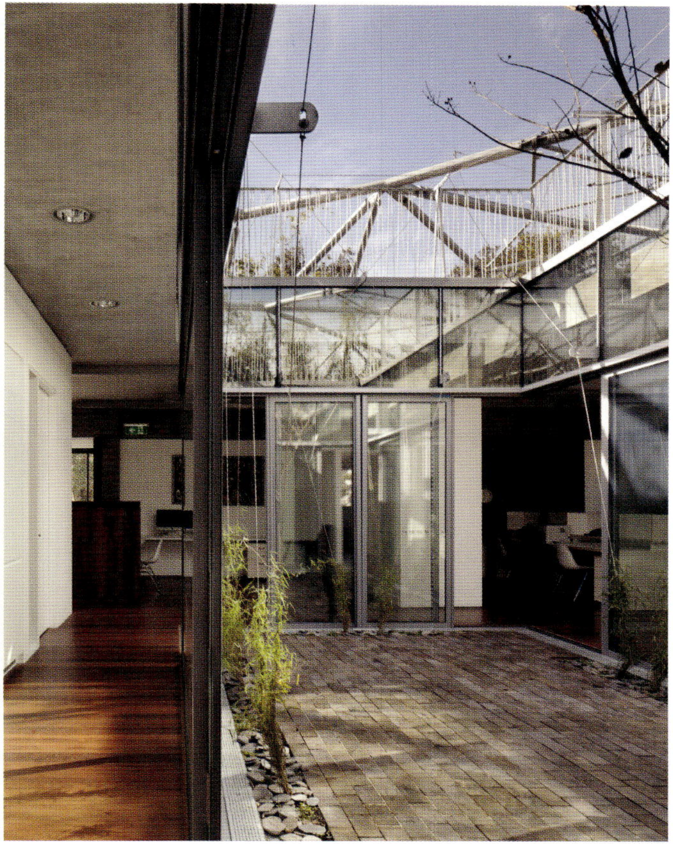

WATERLOO YOUTH CENTRE

Working with landscape architects TERRAGRAM, Collins and Turner architects have nestled the Waterloo Youth Centre, 2013, into its setting through a series of subtle adjustments in the levels of the surrounding landscape. A series of triangular galvanised steel retaining walls that echo the geometries of the building ensure the altered landscape adheres to council regulations stating that a grassed slope in a public space must not exceed a one in four gradient. These steel support structures are pierced providing further opportunities to cultivate plants. In this harsh environment pig face succulents have been planted in the perforations that spell a message in Braille.

The Waterloo Youth Centre is a multi award-winning project. In 2013 it was awarded the Australian Institute of Architects (AIA) NSW Sir John Sulman Medal for outstanding public architecture and a NSW architecture award for sustainability as well as AIA national awards for public architecture, sustainability and steel architecture. ■

MARGARET HANCOCK DAVIS

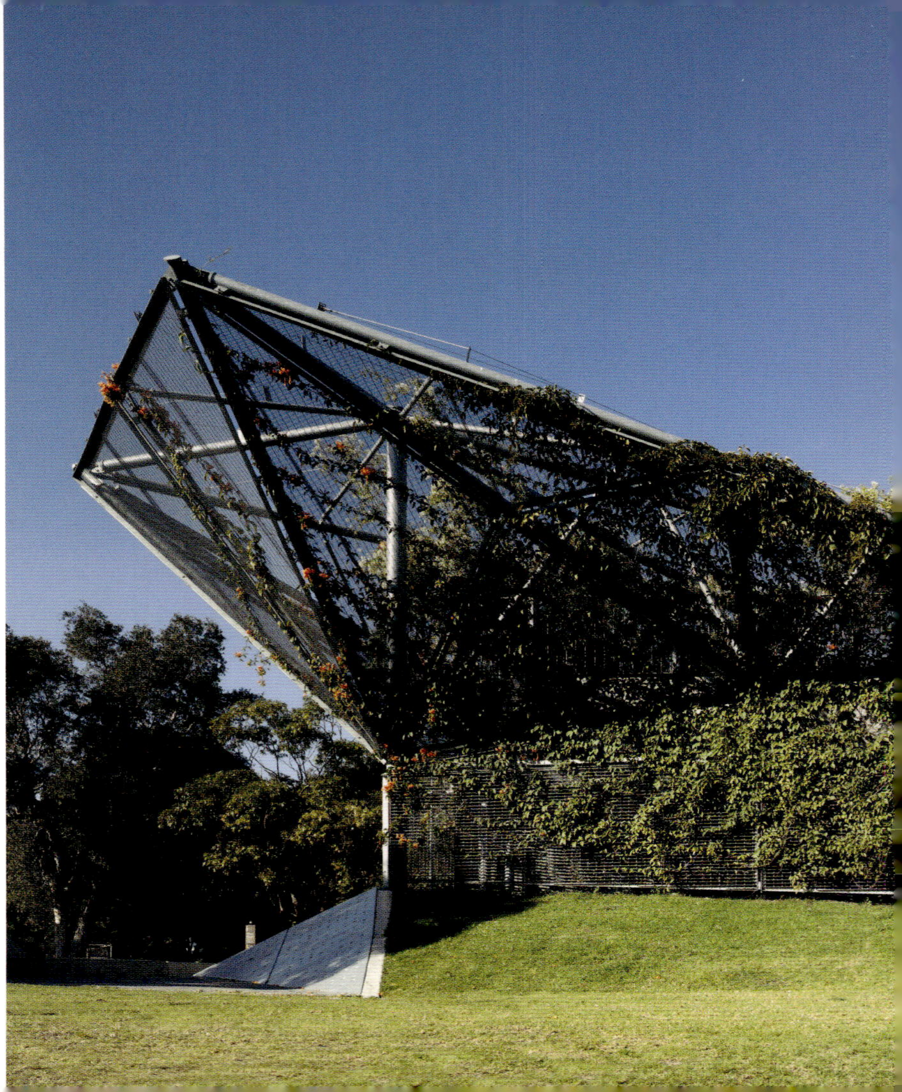

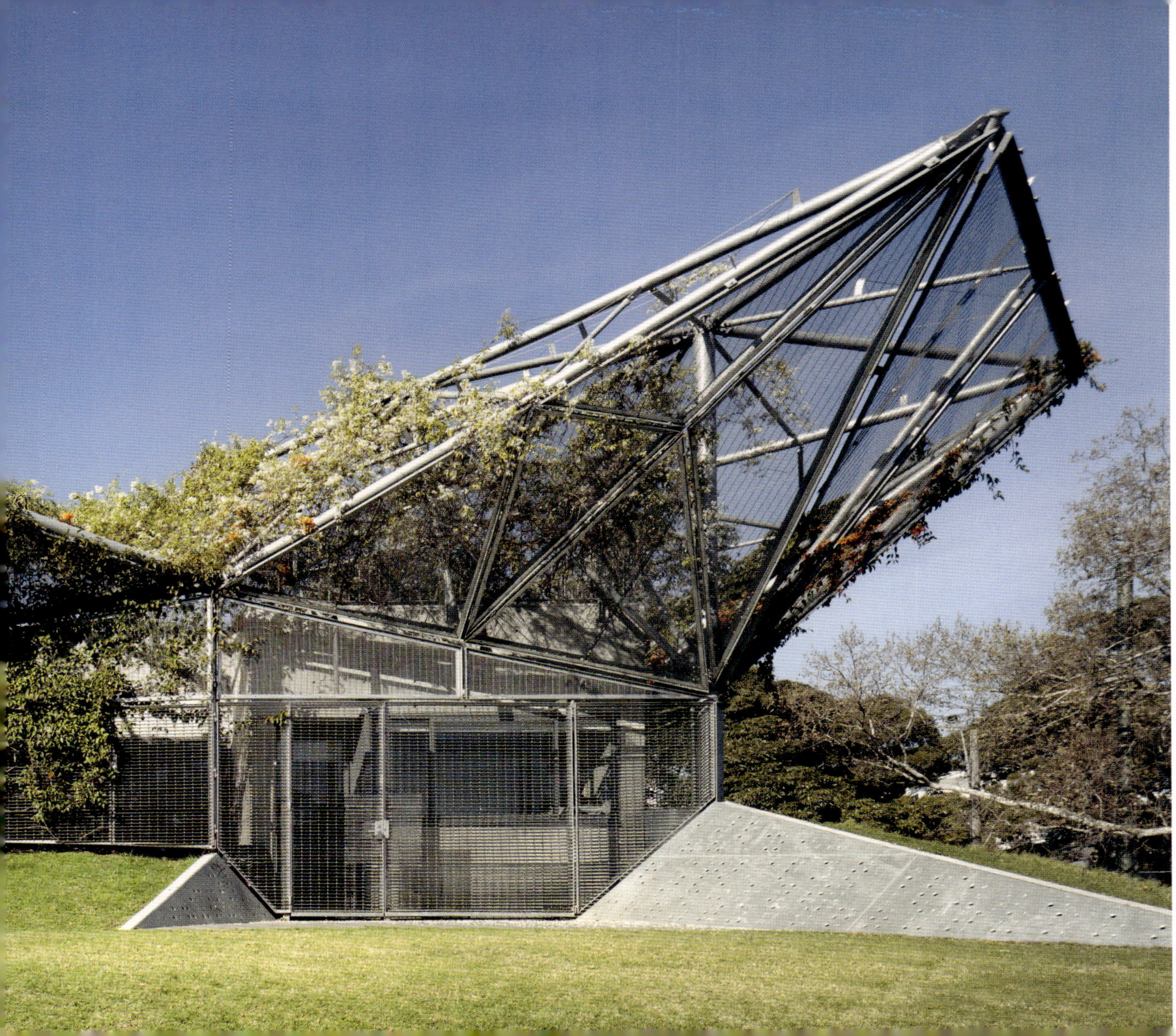

◄

West elevation
Photo: Richard Glover

OVERLEAF
Roof terrace
Photo: Richard Glover

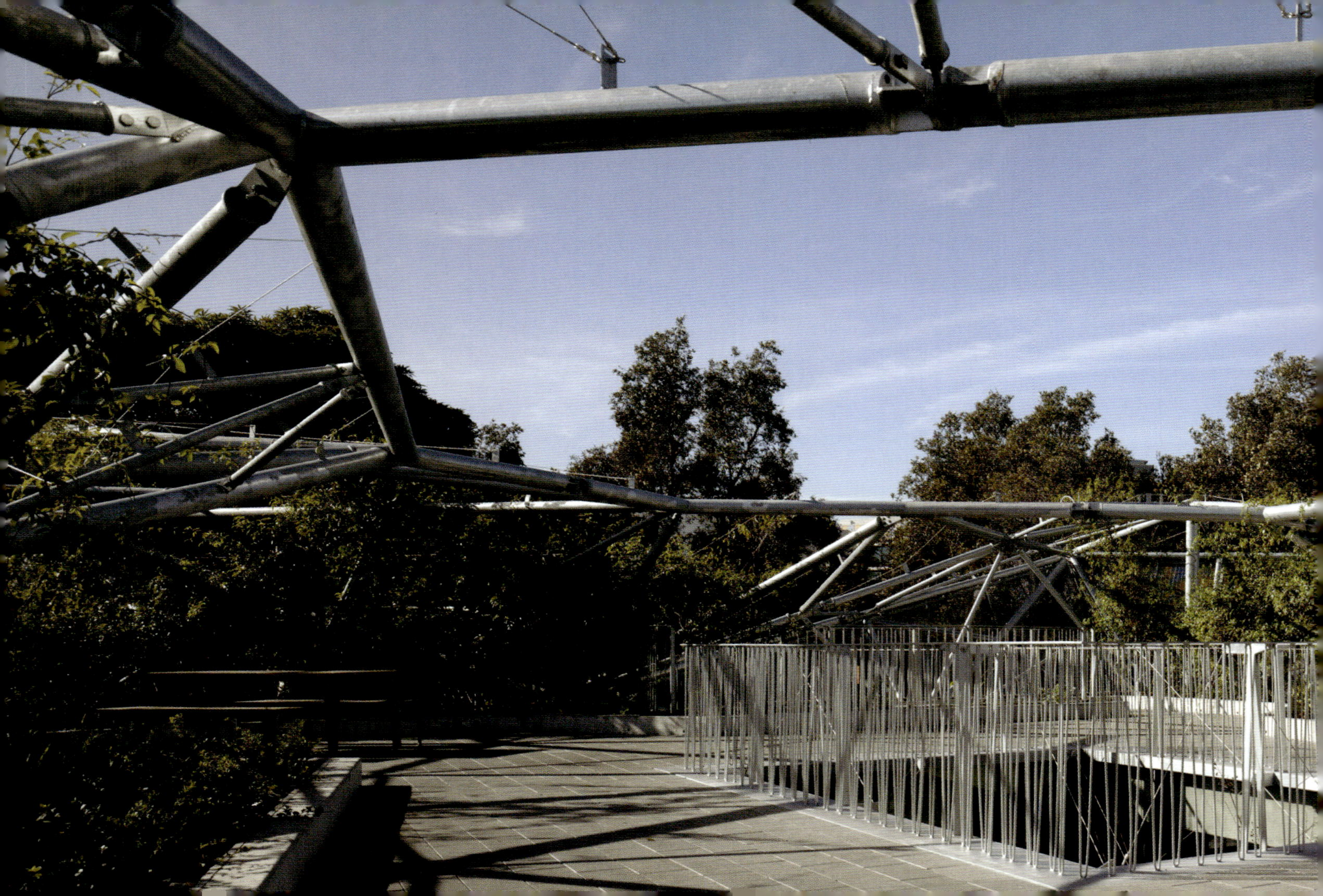

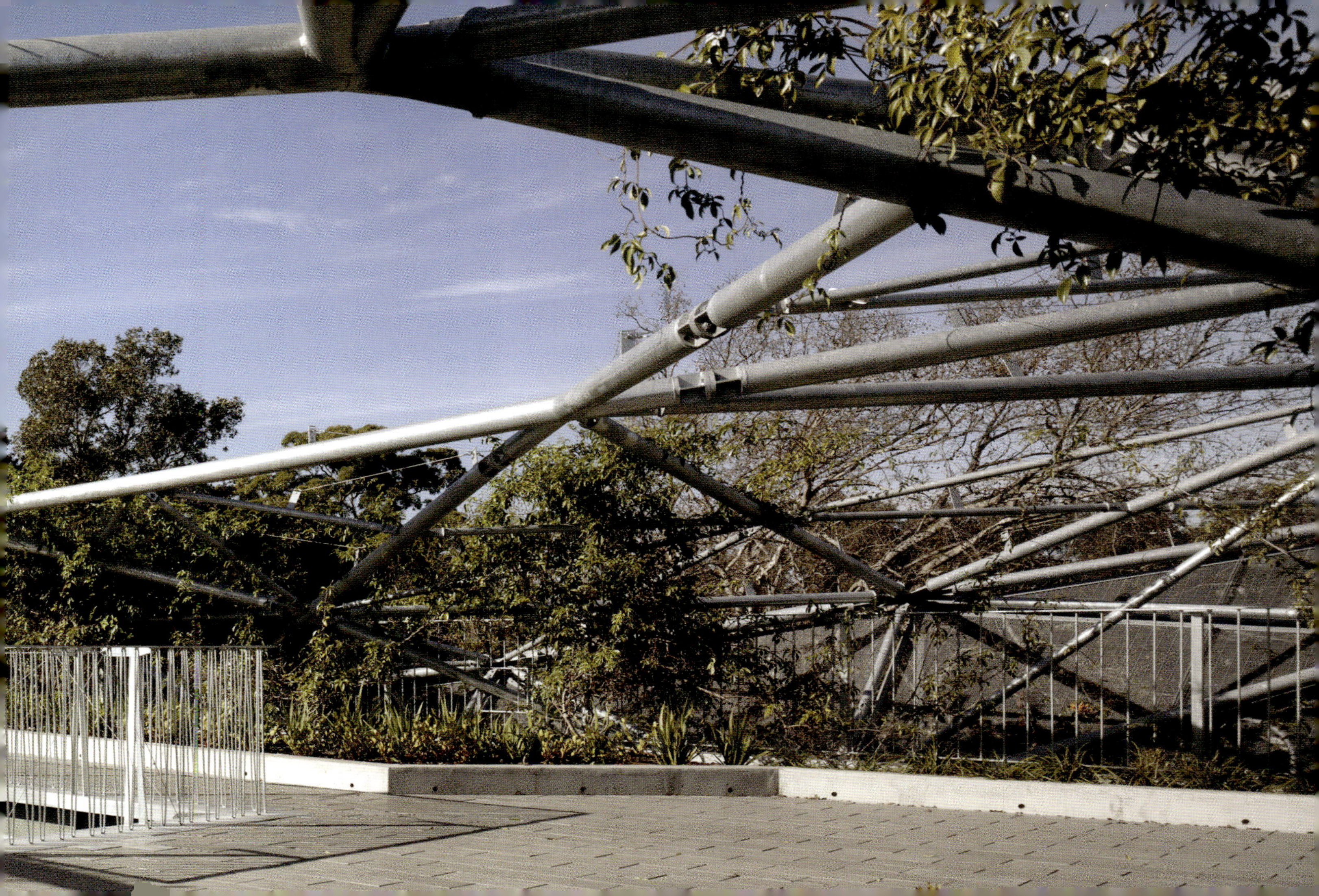

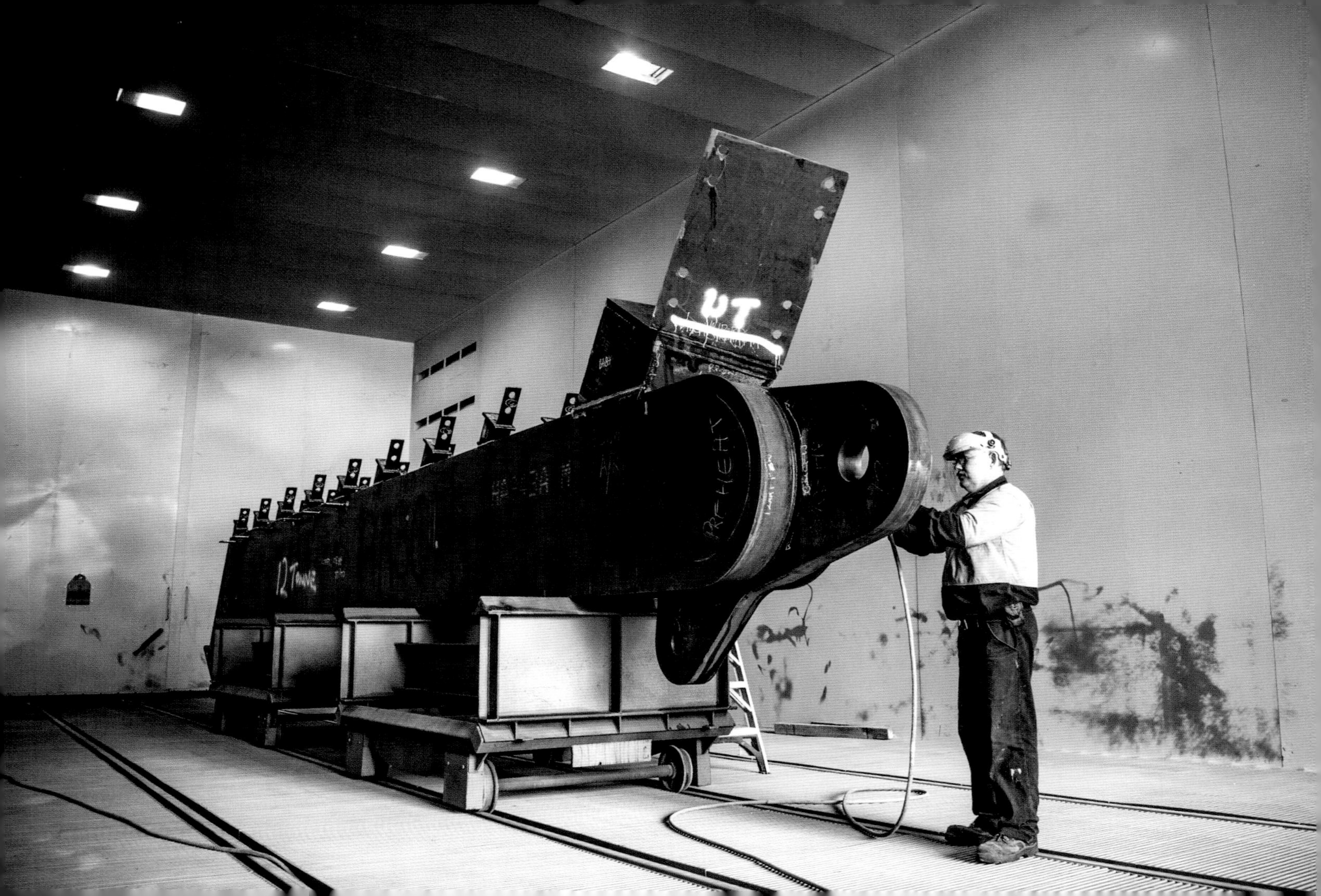
UT

COX ARCHITECTURE

**ESTABLISHED 1967,
SYDNEY, NEW SOUTH WALES**

**PHILIP COX
BORN 1939, SYDNEY,
NEW SOUTH WALES
LIVES SYDNEY,
NEW SOUTH WALES**

ONE OF THE COUNTRY'S architectural giants had its humble beginnings in 1967 when founding partner Philip Cox established his own practice in Sydney. Some 50 years later and COX Architecture operates studios in six Australian capital cities, Malaysia and the United Arab Emirates. The multi-disciplinary practice currently employs approximately 400 staff and while Cox is still engaged in the initial design stages of new projects, he's no longer involved in the day-to-day running of the business.

Each COX Architecture studio operates as a self-contained entity, although all are globally bound by an ethos that has the principals of structure, craft, art and nature at its core. This business model ensures cohesion and a consistency of detail, strengthened by a commitment to sustainability and technology, as well as an understanding of the technicalities of construction.

Cox proudly acknowledges that this studio empire developed through the invitation of major clients who had confidence in the practice's ability to deliver large-scale architectural projects. Localised openings were necessitated by major commissions in each state, such as the Australian Institute of Sport Aquatic Testing and Training Centre (AISATTC), 2004-06, in Canberra and Rod Laver Arena (formerly National Tennis Centre), 1985-88, in Melbourne. These seminal projects subsequently cemented COX Architecture's reputation for large-scale public buildings and highlighted its embrace of new material technologies. Using steel to achieve lightweight outcomes, despite the scale of these structures, has become the practice's architectural signature.

It's little wonder the architectural practice excels at sports architecture, and over the past 40 years their structural design expression has defined the form of numerous stadia and sporting buildings locally and internationally. In Australia, COX Architecture was responsible for the design and delivery of a record number of venues for the Sydney 2000 Olympic

PREVIOUS PAGE
Steel prefabrication for Adelaide Oval Redevelopment, Adelaide, South Australia, 2014.
Photo: Orange Lane

Games, and later, AAMI Park in Melbourne, 2005-10, was recognised by the World Stadium Congress as the World's Most Iconic and Culturally Significant Stadium in 2012. This project is not only notable for its highly functional seating bowl, but also for its effective relationship with its context, providing a dynamically strong visual connection to Melbourne's CBD, the Yarra River and surrounding parklands.

COX Architecture is also highly regarded in redevelopment and refurbishment of existing major sporting facilities and since 2002, it's been responsible for upgrading three of the country's major ovals – Melbourne Cricket Ground, Sydney Cricket Ground and Adelaide Oval. The practice's design process employs both manual and technological tools to consider a project's impact at a macro level and to determine its form and function at a micro level. Regardless of the emphasis based on computer-generated methodologies, each studio still simultaneously constructs physical models of projects, reinforcing Cox's belief that the 'poetry and craft' of architecture is just as important as the science.

Many of COX Architecture's directors and associates are involved with the Australian Institute of Architects as committee members or award judges, while others hold teaching positions or sit on advisory panels. A positive workplace culture has long encouraged staff to give back to the architecture industry and Cox himself received the Order of Australia for services to architecture in 1988 and is a Fellow of the Australian Academy of the Humanities. He undoubtedly set the standard for a level of professionalism and service, and one which continues to grow. As do the practice's portfolio of projects that are as visually impressive as they are conceptually well-considered.

▸
Aerial shot of Adelaide Oval Redevelopment, the Oval is located in the historic parklands of Adelaide.
Photo: John Gollings

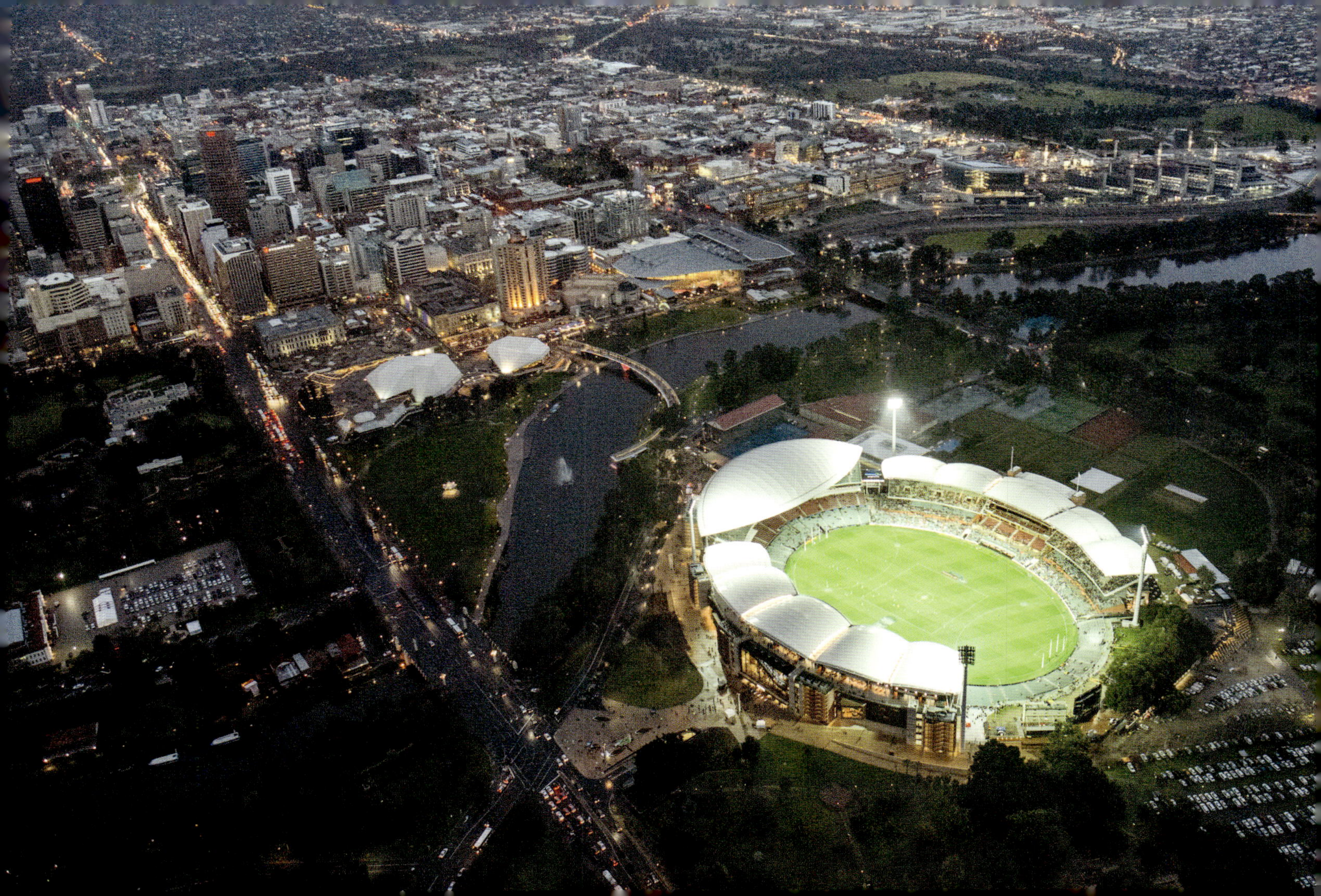

ADELAIDE OVAL REDEVELOPMENT

The redevelopment of Adelaide Oval by COX Architecture (in association with Hames Sharley and Walter Brooke) was an ambitious $535 million undertaking completed in 2014. It involved construction of new southern and eastern stands and public plazas, as well as reimaging the northern mound and ensuring the preservation of the heritage scoreboard. COX Architecture conceived the project as a series of three pavilions that project from the northern end, retaining the scoreboard and conserving the large existing Moreton Bay fig trees.

It is an innovative scheme that prevents the redevelopment from appearing as an impenetrable monolith. Instead, the resulting three-part roof structure resembles a horseshoe in shape, with a gap at the northern end, encouraging views of the site's surrounding parklands and historic St Peters Cathedral. Not only does the redevelopment elevate Adelaide Oval to a world-class sporting venue, it also serves as an instrument of activation in a precinct that was previously under utilised.

The roof structure's curved form is dynamic in expression, heightened by a white finish that makes its presence felt even more so against the Adelaide skyline. Approximately 450 tonnes of steel and 14,000 bolts were used to construct the Southern stand in what was a complex erection methodology involving a number of 30-metre-high tower supports. Adelaide Oval's history dates back to 1871 and COX Architecture succeeds in maintaining its heritage while positioning the venue as an important host for future international sporting events. Among the project's many accolades is the Australian Institute of Architects 2015 National Award for Public Architecture. ■

LEANNE AMODEO

OVERLEAF
The three pavillions of the redevloped oval.
Photo: Orange Lane

▸
The steel structure is complimented by the use of bronze that embeds the stand within the parkland surrounds.
Photo: John Gollings

▸▸
South Stand roof structure.
Photo: Orange Lane

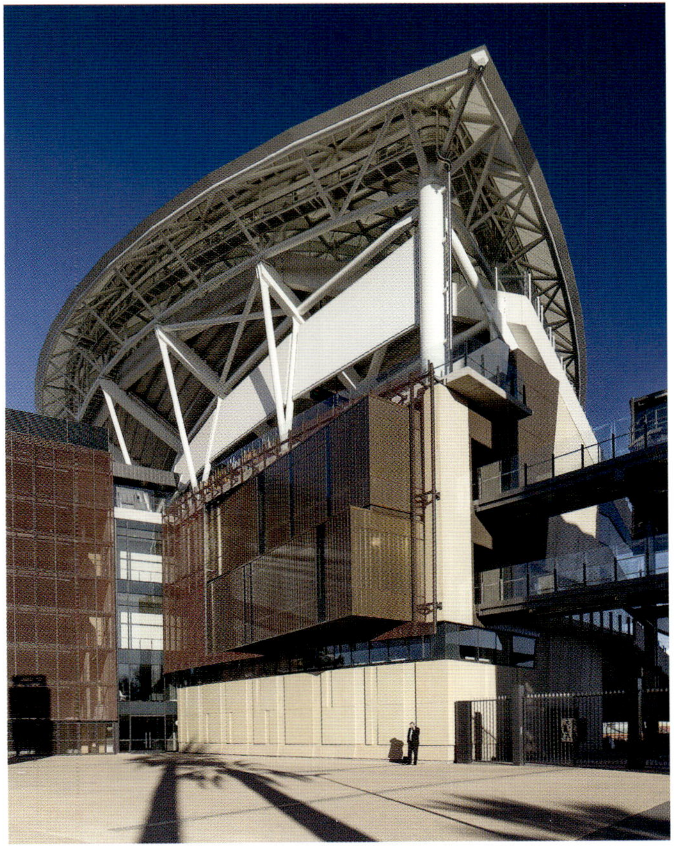

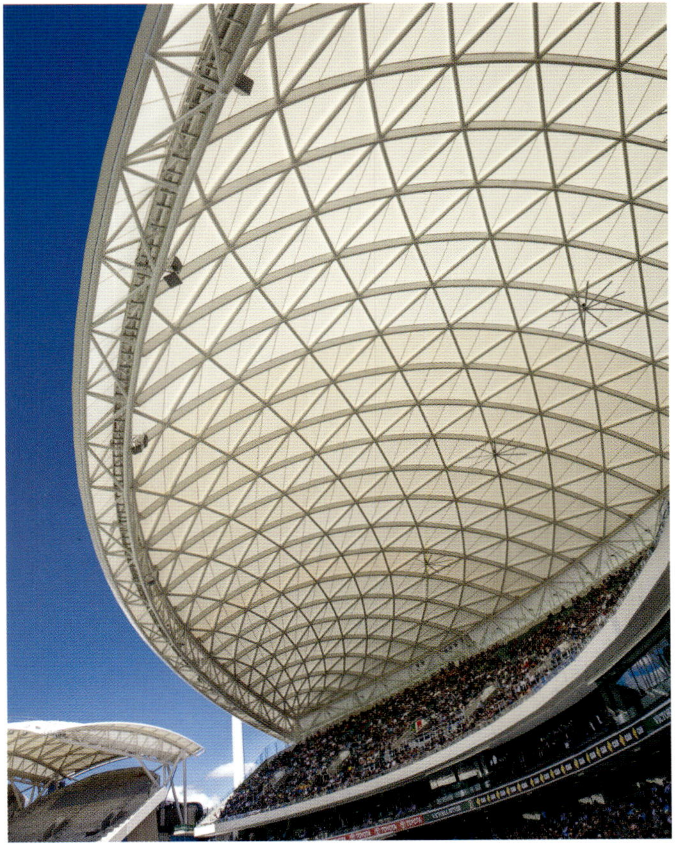

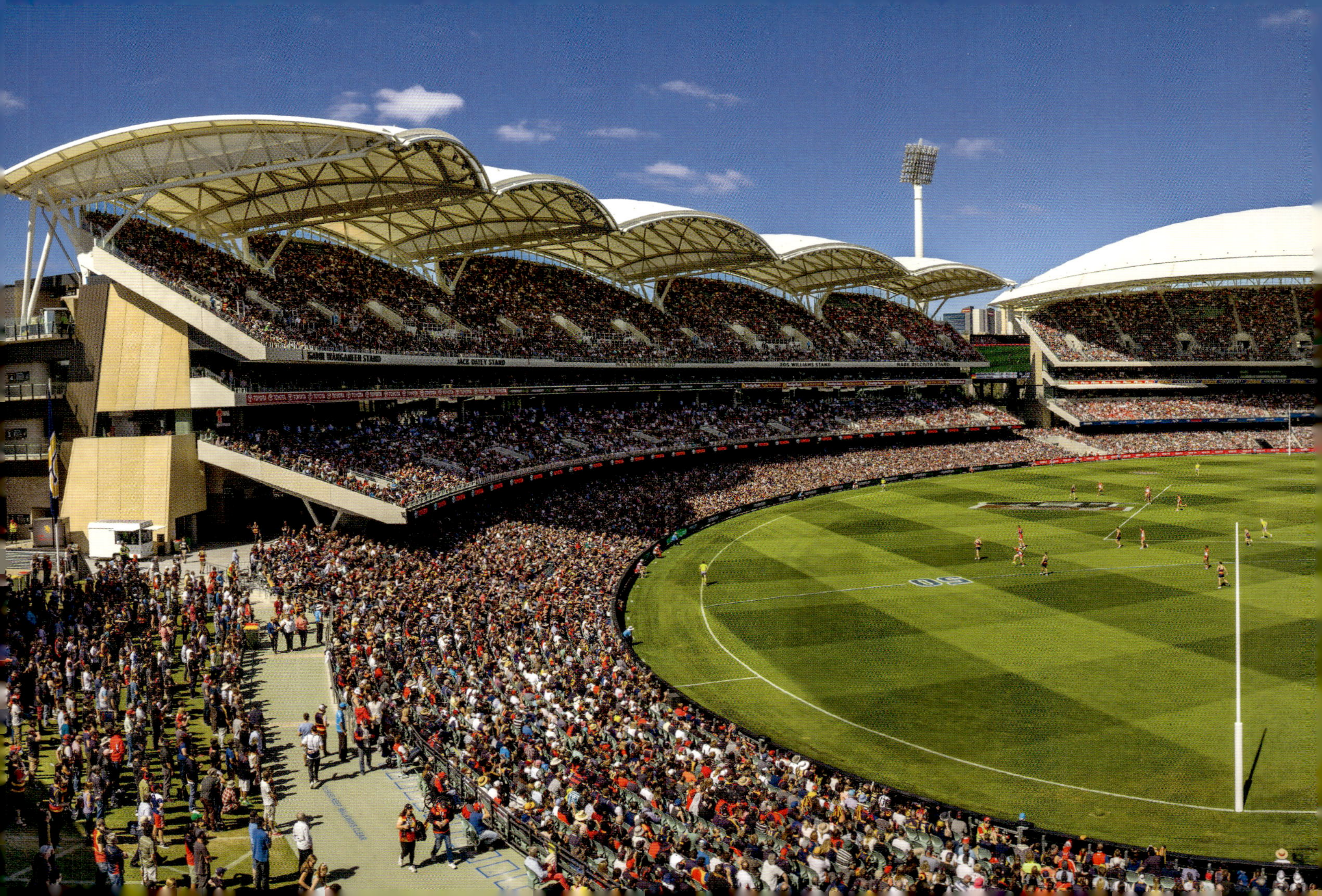
JACK OATEY STAND
FOS WILLIAMS STAND
MARK RICCIUTO STAND

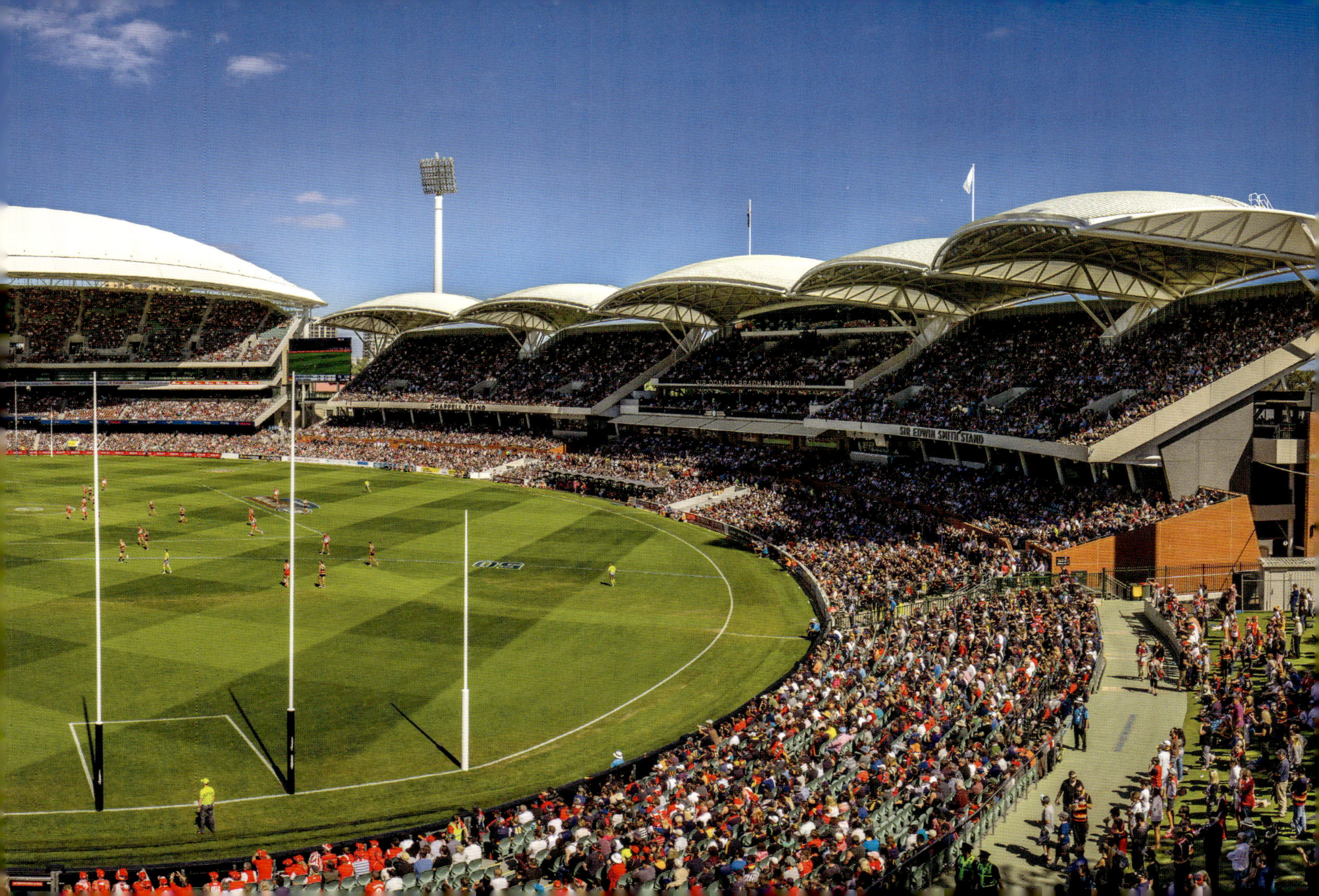
SIR DONALD BRADMAN PAVILION
CHAPPELL STAND
SIR EDWIN SMITH STAND

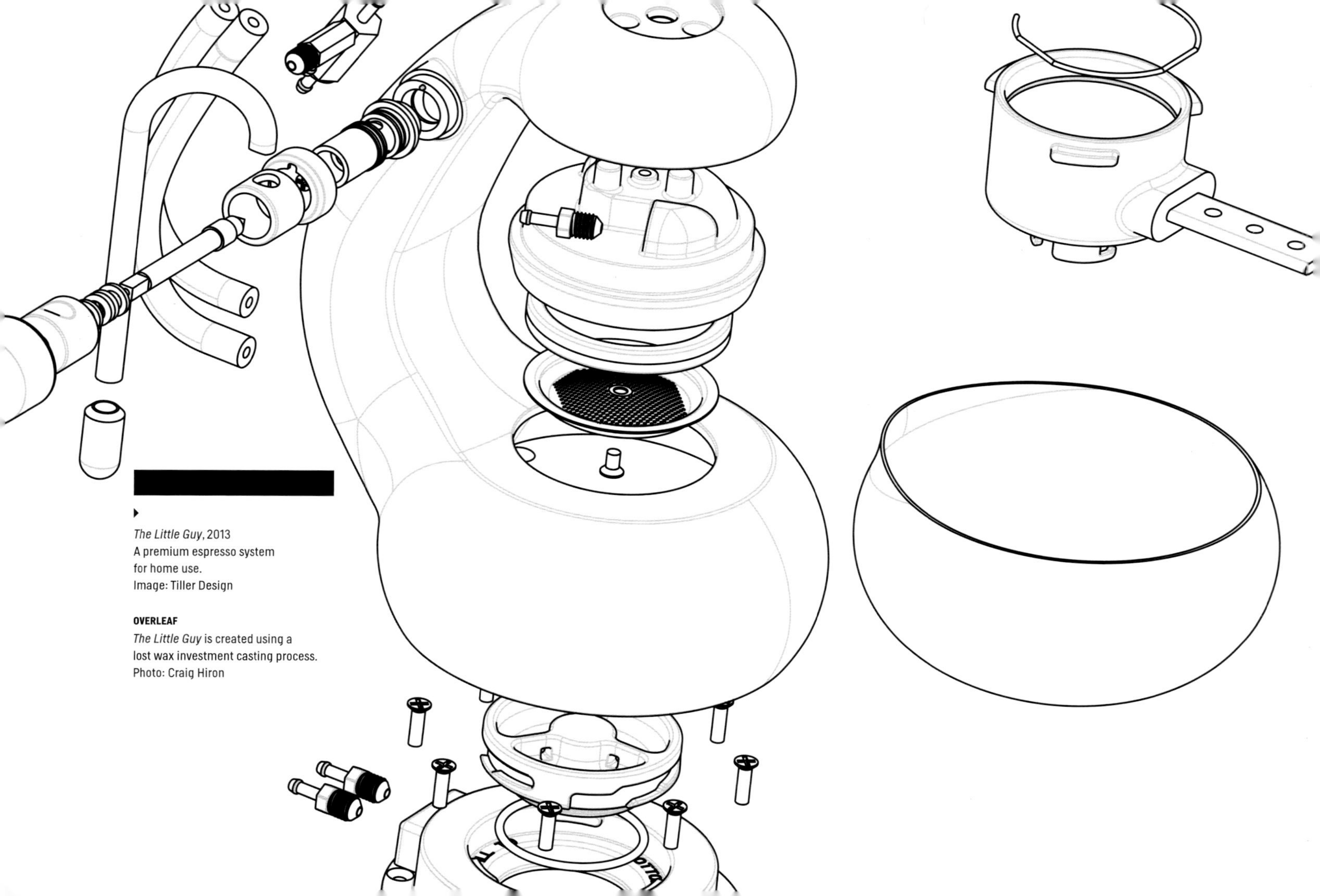

The Little Guy, 2013
A premium espresso system
for home use.
Image: Tiller Design

OVERLEAF
The Little Guy is created using a
lost wax investment casting process.
Photo: Craig Hiron

CRAIG HIRON

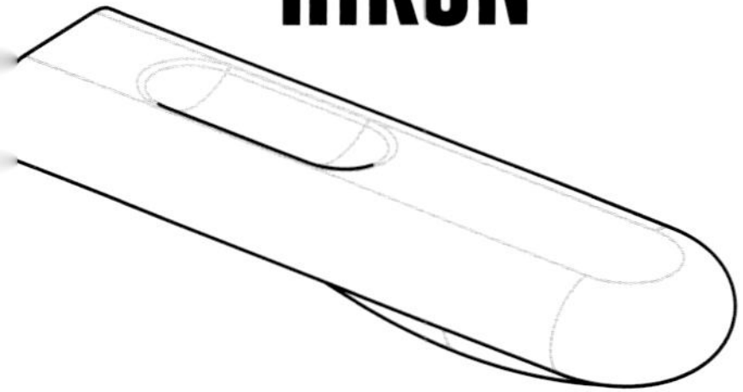

BORN 1971, SYDNEY, NEW SOUTH WALES
LIVES SYDNEY, NEW SOUTH WALES

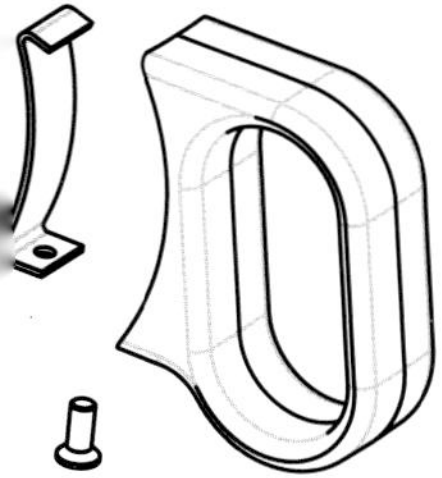

IN 2005, tradie-turned-entrepreneur Craig Hiron set himself the task of creating a product that could deliver cafe-grade espresso coffee in the home. Inspired by Giordano Robiatti's 1947 design classic the *Atomic*, Hiron saw an opportunity to marry the convenience of a stovetop coffee machine with the quality of espresso.

Coffee is measured in terms of total dissolved solids (TDS), which indicates the concentration of coffee in the water. Simply put, the higher the percentage of TDS, the stronger the flavour. Drip-filter coffee typically measures 2.5%, stovetop methods produce 5%, with espresso coffee measuring around 13%. With espresso as his benchmark and clean intuitive design as his inspiration, Hiron enlisted a team of experts to help him realise his ambition. The team included award-winning industrial designers, Tiller Design, professor of thermal dynamics Dr Allan Wallace, mechanical specialists, engineers and a manufacturing agent. After four years of research, development, design, tooling and production, *The Little Guy*, 2013, espresso maker was born.

Bringing *The Little Guy* into the world was an exercise in dogged determination. Twelve months into the design process, it became apparent that the single-unit internal shape of *The Little Guy* was hindering its ability to achieve espresso-grade extraction. In order to maintain Hiron's insistence that there would be no external part lines visible on the body of the machine, the internal mechanics had to be completely re-engineered. This juncture led to the breakthrough patented design by Dr Allan Wallace which divided the internal workings of the machine, so that the head and boiler could heat independently. This was the moment when Hiron's initial idea became a workable reality.

This was also the moment that dictated *The Little Guy* be crafted from stainless steel. Steel is the only material that provided the thermal stability required for precise espresso extraction.

Sustainability is an important thread in the story of *The Little Guy*. The stainless steel used to cast each unit is recycled scrap material that has been collected and melted for the casting process. The product has also been designed with no moveable parts, meaning that there is no wear and tear – *The Little Guy* is a product that has been designed to last many lifetimes.

Despite committing over a decade to the creation and promotion of *The Little Guy*, Hiron recently made the decision to suspend production of his stove-top espresso maker. Although warmly embraced by the design and coffee aficionado communities in Australia, recent inroads into the international market have not led to the kind of traction to ensure business is sustainable. Hiron's commitment to design and coffee excellence – in equal measure – saw the idea for *The Little Guy* come to fruition, despite countless obstacles. The uncompromising manufacturing methods used will ensure that the machines currently in existence will be used and loved for generations.

The Little Guy has received many accolades, including winning the Australian International Design Mark in 2008, being a finalist in the International Design Excellence Awards in 2009, winning The Chicago Athenaeum's Good Design Award in 2011, and being nominated for the prestigious German Design Awards in 2013.

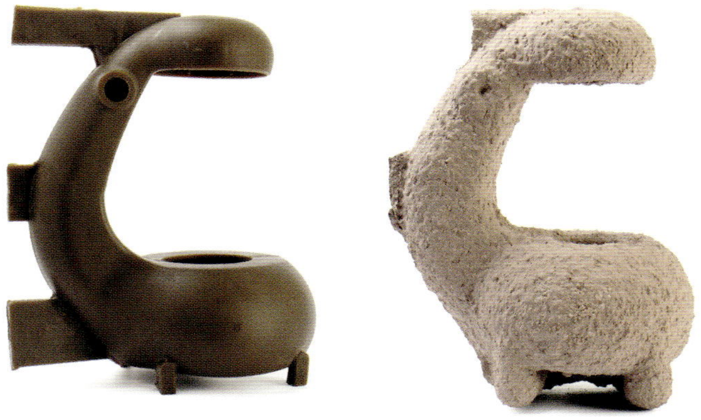

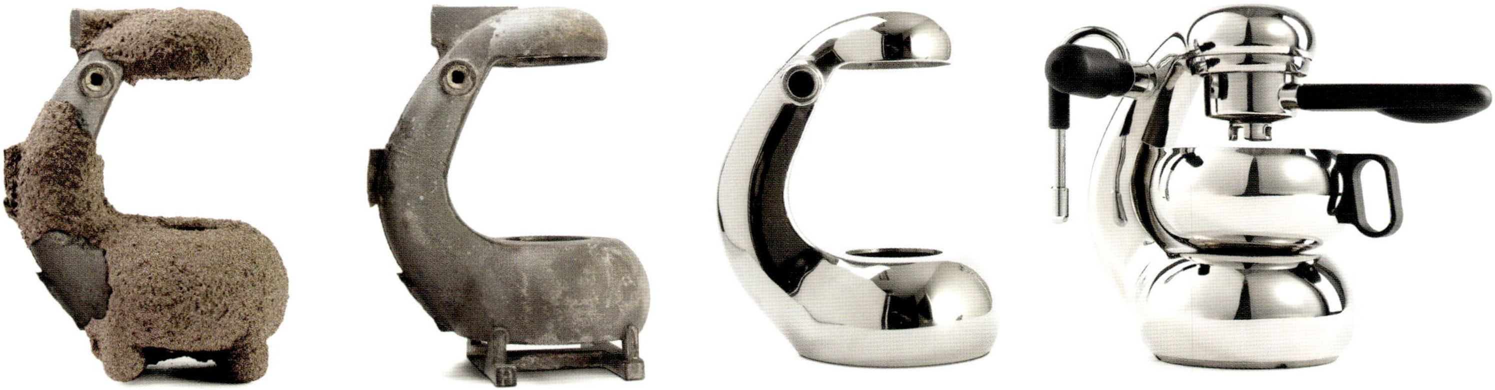

THE LITTLE GUY

The smooth mirror polished stainless steel surface of *The Little Guy*, 2013, instantly conjures parallels with Giordano Robiatti's iconic stovetop coffee machine, the *Atomic*. Yet minimal embellishments and sultry curves are where the similarities between these two machines end. The clean lines of its exterior belie the complexity and sophistication of the internal design of *The Little Guy*. It is here, that Hiron's fastidious attention to detail is most keenly felt.

Stainless steel offered thermal stability to *The Little Guy*, allowing the head and base of the machine to heat and operate independently. It is precisely this separation that meant Hiron was able to achieve his ambition of producing cafe-grade espresso coffee and milk from a stovetop unit for the home. Without the material properties of steel, this would be impossible.

The steel body, boiler, boiler cap, head and group cup of *The Little Guy* are created using a lost-wax investment casting process, a technique that was first used in the Chalcolithic Age more than 5,700 years ago. Each part is hand-polished for three to four hours to achieve the surface lustre. *The Little Guy* combines a respect for material, a commitment to process, and the pursuit of perfection. Together, these attributes create a machine designed to stand the tests of time. ■

DANIELLE ROBSON

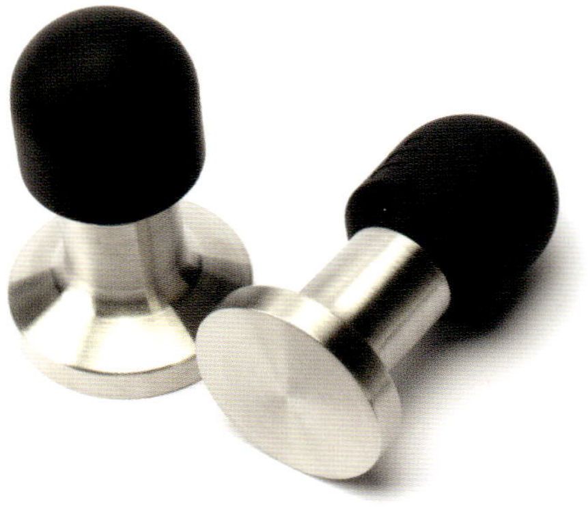

▲ Stainless steel and nylon tampers.
Photo: Nick Bowers

▶ *The Little Guy*'s mirror polished stainless steel provide the correct thermal dynamics to produce a cafe style espresso at home.
Photo: Nick Bowers

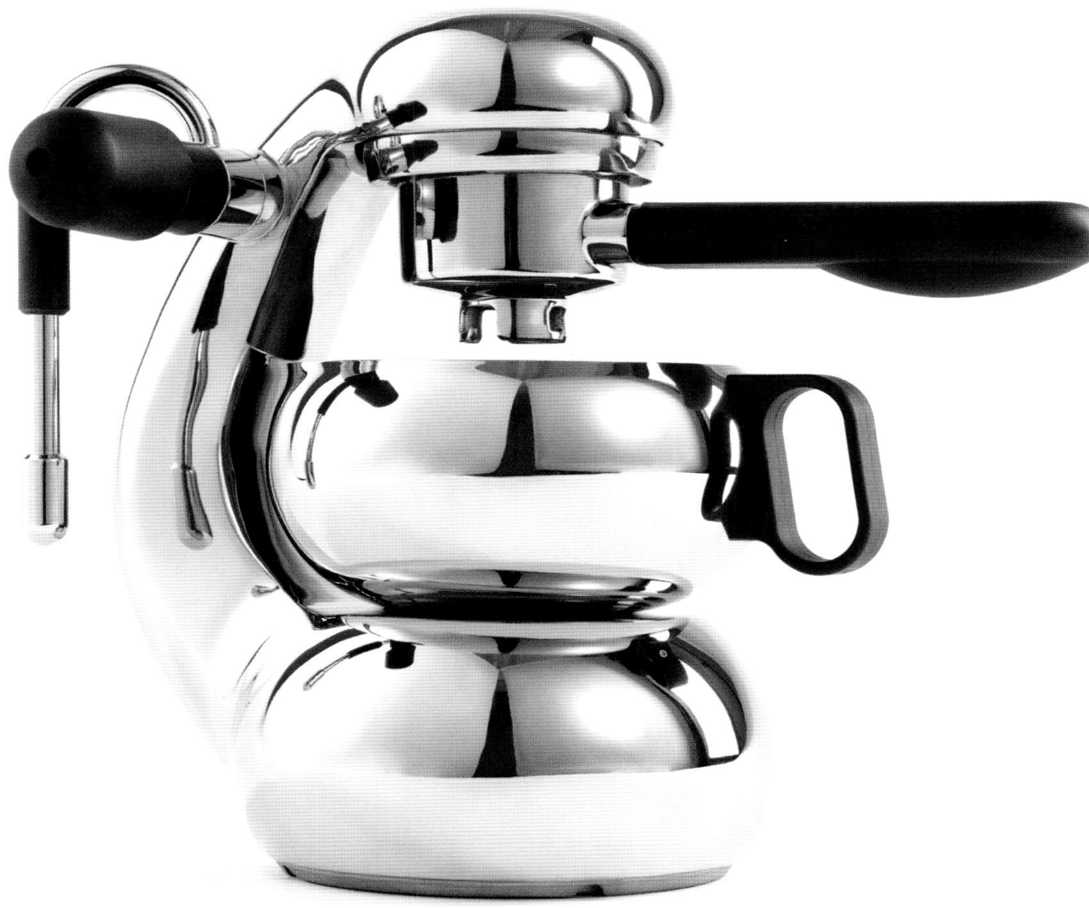

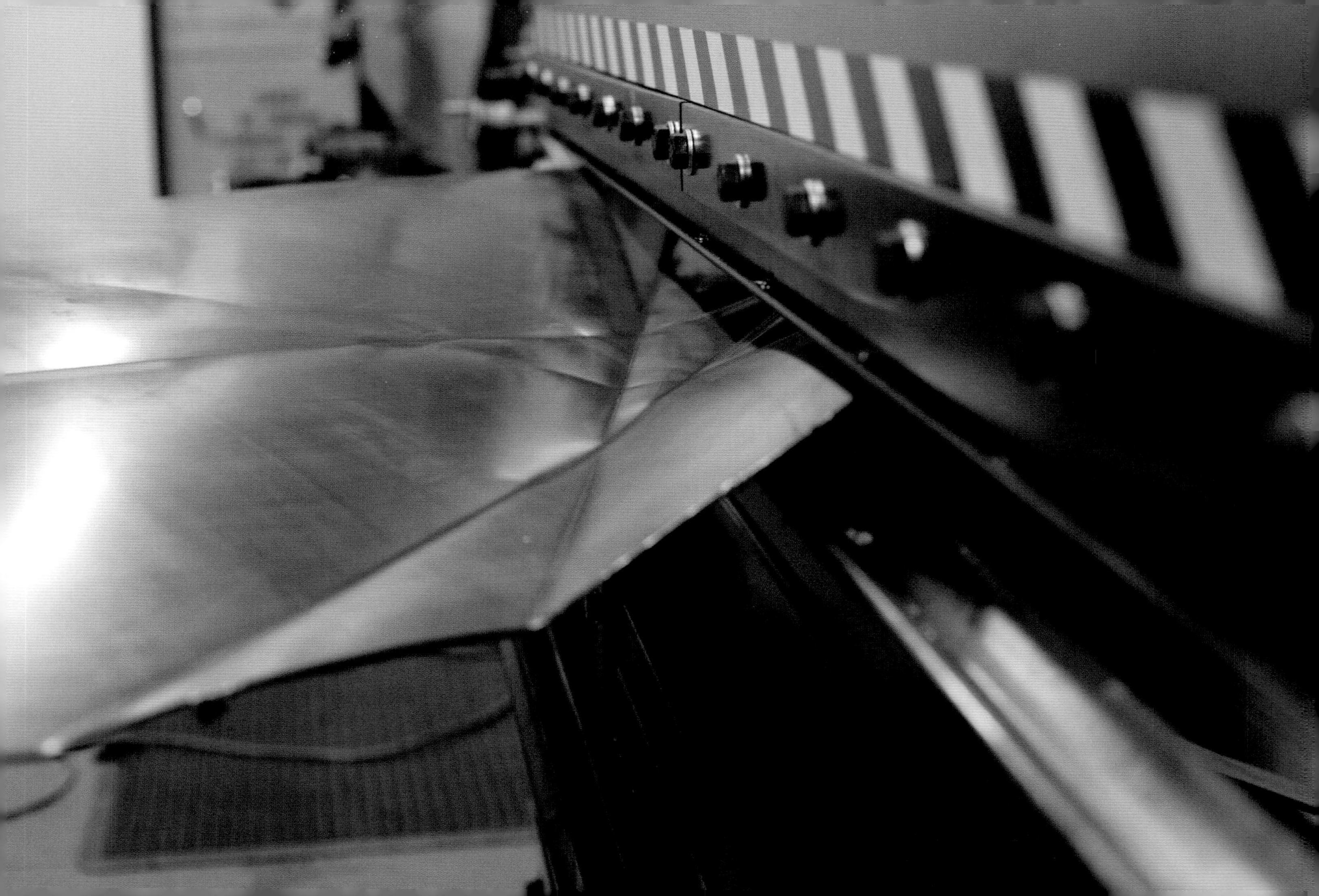

DAN LORRIMER

BORN 1987, SYDNEY, NEW SOUTH WALES
LIVES CANBERRA, AUSTRALIAN CAPITAL TERRITORY

DAN LORRIMER'S work has both the material and materiality, or the *idea* of the material, at the very centre of its design. The artist appears to be challenging the form and the form's reputation – attempting to make steel behave like a far more manageable substance. To be folded, for example, like paper.

Says the artist:
The work explores the way in which steel sheet is transformed through a process of repeated folding and manipulation under hydraulic pressure, this process creates forms that mimic both liquid and solid rock. These forms are highly kinetic simulating the movements of tectonic plates crushing together, the shaping of human-led intervention or the erosion of water flowing over the land creating waterways and intricate contours in the earth.[1]

Lorrimer's work began attracting attention not long after finalising his study at the School of Art, Australian National University in 2009. Working alongside some of the capital's leading makers, including Richard Whitley, Mathew Curtis and Robert Forster's iconic F!NK & Co. studios clearly assisted Lorrimer's quick progress. In 2011 the writer and curator Yolande Norris was already calling Lorrimer's work 'terrifyingly strong' and the artist as 'a deadly serious contender'[2].

His practice mixes sculpture with product design. *The Griffin Blueprint Dish* (in collaboration with Mitchell Brooks under their MAKEOUT banner) was selected as one of the five winning entries in the *Centenary of Canberra – a legacy of Good Design* competition in 2013. Lorrimer collaborates widely, informing his sculptural practice with work in furniture and homewares. MAKEOUT both custom-make their products and construct much of the machinery they use to fabricate these pieces themselves, including the etching tank used to detail the plans of Canberra first dreamt up by the Griffins.

1 All quotes in this profile were recorded by the author in an interview with Dan Lorrimer.

2 https://yolandenorris.com.au/2011/02/15/digital-ether-dan-lorrimer/, accessed September, 2016.

3 Artist Profile: Dan Lorrimer, *BMA Magazine*, September 2014, http://www.bmamag.com/articles/artist-profile/20140908-dan-lorrimer/

[redacted]

PREVIOUS PAGE
Dan Lorrimer works the surafce of his sculptures like paper, folding and creasing it with hydraulic presses.
Photo: Dominic Lorrimer

Speaking to *BMA Magazine* in 2014, Lorrimer detailed his path toward this practice.

I've always had a passion for making things and understanding how they work. From a young age I experimented with the usual backyard materials, making billy karts, skateboards and weapons. This developed into a fascination for metal and different ways of working with it.[3]

Like his fellow Canberran Kensuke Todo (pg 153), Lorrimer's lines possess a refined elegance – a tangible grace impressed upon a hard substance. *Triple Junction*, 2016, and *Lineal Divide*, 2016, both pieces that form part of his ongoing *Fragment* series, create intrigue through the inference of steel's raw strength, and the processes impressed upon to create another sense of stress and fragility:

The work I create is driven by a deep understanding of materials, industrial processes and a keen sense of exploration through making. The common themes I try to explore are movement, energy, solidity and illusion within minimalist sculptural forms. I try to locate the work between the artificial and natural world, as if it has been naturally created.

Other works in Lorrimer's already rich catalogue continue these themes of fragility and the testing of a material's capabilities. In *Surface Tension, 2009,* a metal structure manipulates lycra, activated via sensors triggered by the audience. *Point of Contact*, 2011, takes equally measured components and assembles each in various ways, creating a startling sense of kinetic movement and pace. And in those collected under the Fragment banner, Lorrimer has created an affecting suite of works that stresses the fragility of the hardest objects. Lorrimer's work articulates a fascinating and attractive duality in a form, and in doing so creates a humanistic narrative in this most mechanised of materials.

GLEN MARTIN

[redacted]

◥◢
Dan Lorrimer working in his studio.
Photo: Dominic Lorrimer

▸▸
Fragment A3, 2012
blackened steel, 350 x 280 x 100
Photo: courtesy the artist

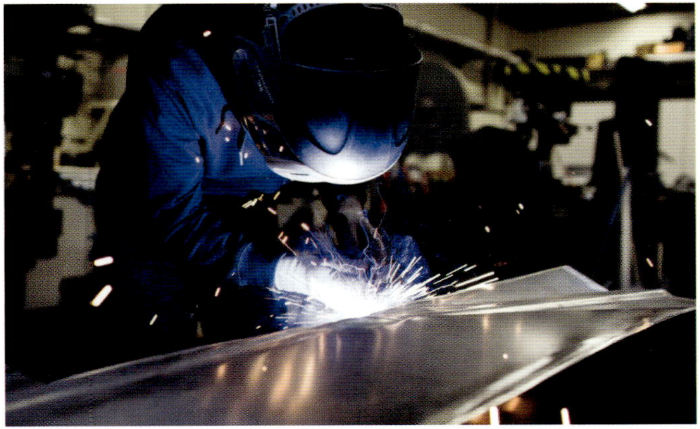

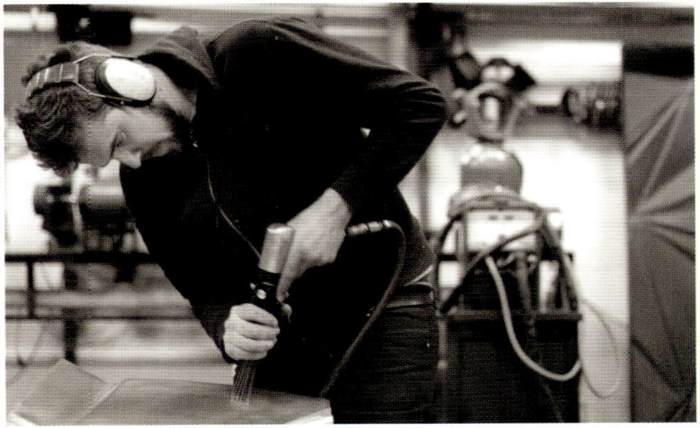

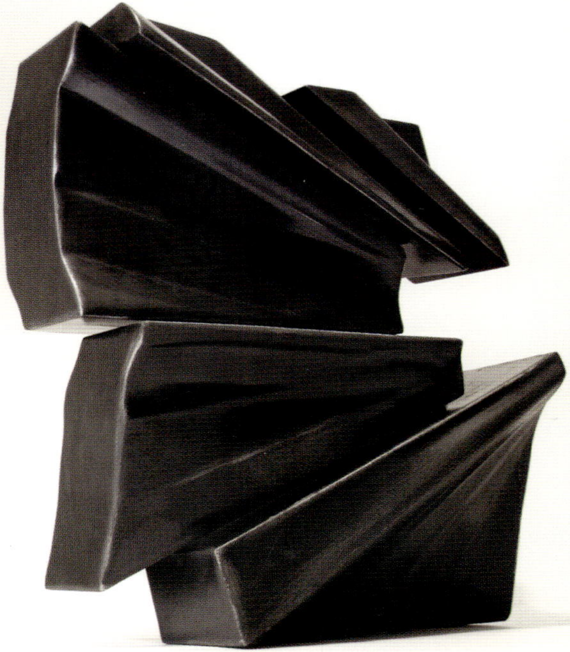

TRIPLE JUNCTION AND LINEAL DIVIDE

'*Triple Junction*, 2016, and *Lineal Divide*, 2016, are both from a series called *Fragment*. The work explores the way in which steel sheet is transformed through a process of repeated folding and manipulation under hydraulic pressure, this process creates forms that mimic both liquid and solid rock. These forms are highly kinetic, simulating the movements of tectonic plates crushing together, the shaping of human-led intervention or the erosion of water flowing over the land creating waterways and intricate contours in the earth.

Fragment is an ongoing series of work that aims to explore the relationship between paper and steel through a process of repeatedly folding, cutting and working sheet metal with hydraulic pressure. The material then begins to take on the same characteristics of its paper counterpart, beginning to stress, crumple, tear and finally fragment. Through this process the work begins to explore the possibilities of form whilst highlighting the beauty of the raw materials from which the work is constructed.

My practice incorporates sculpture and object design. I have been making things most of my life, it's an obsession!' ■

DAN LORRIMER

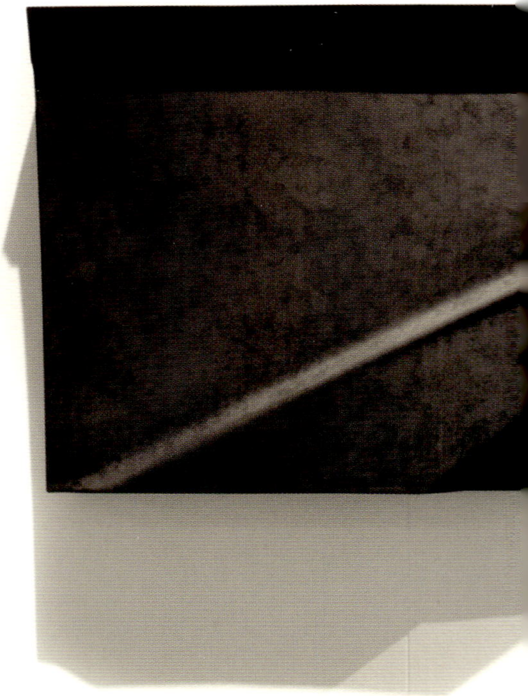

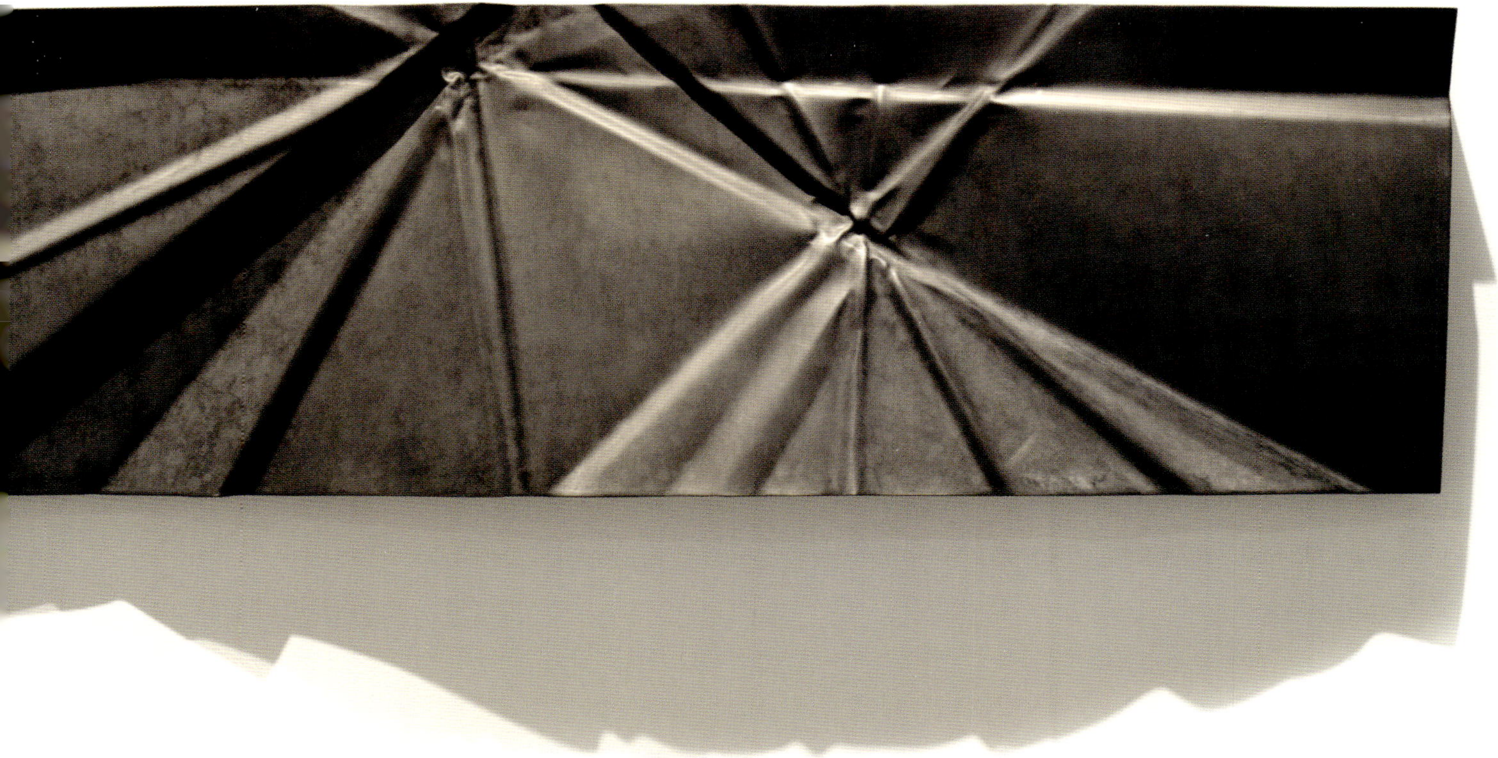

PREVIOUS PAGE
Lineal Divide, 2016
stainless steel, 450 x 1800 x 150
Photo: Mitchell Brooks

▸

Triple Junction, 2016
rusted steel, 350 x 1800 x 150
Photo: Mitchell Brooks

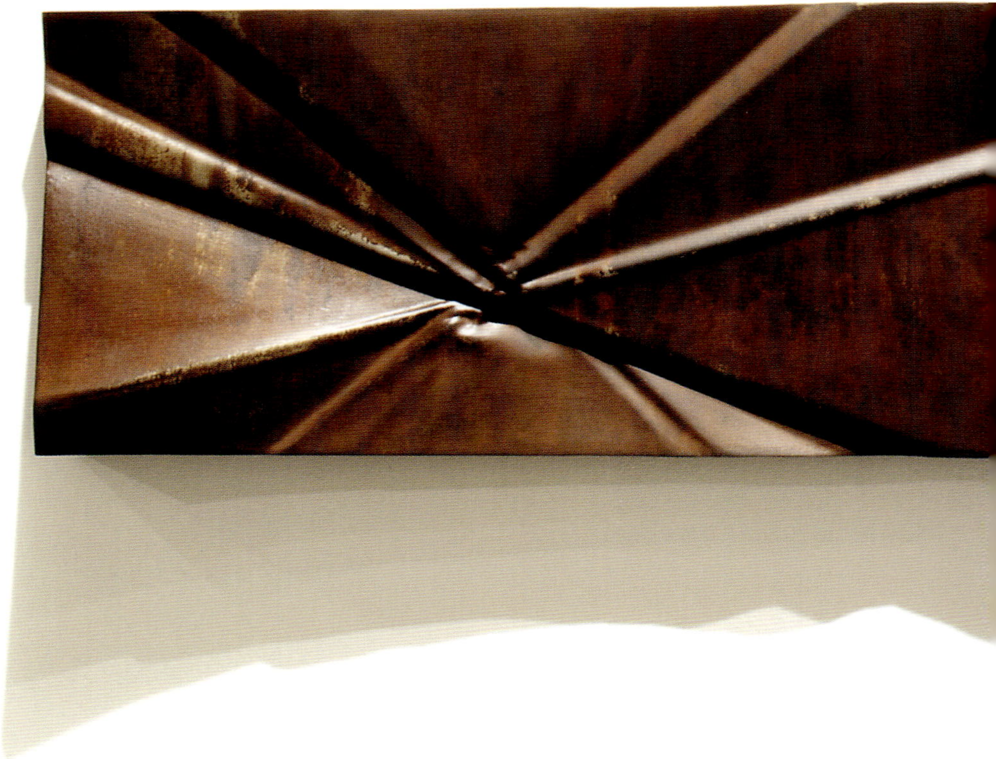

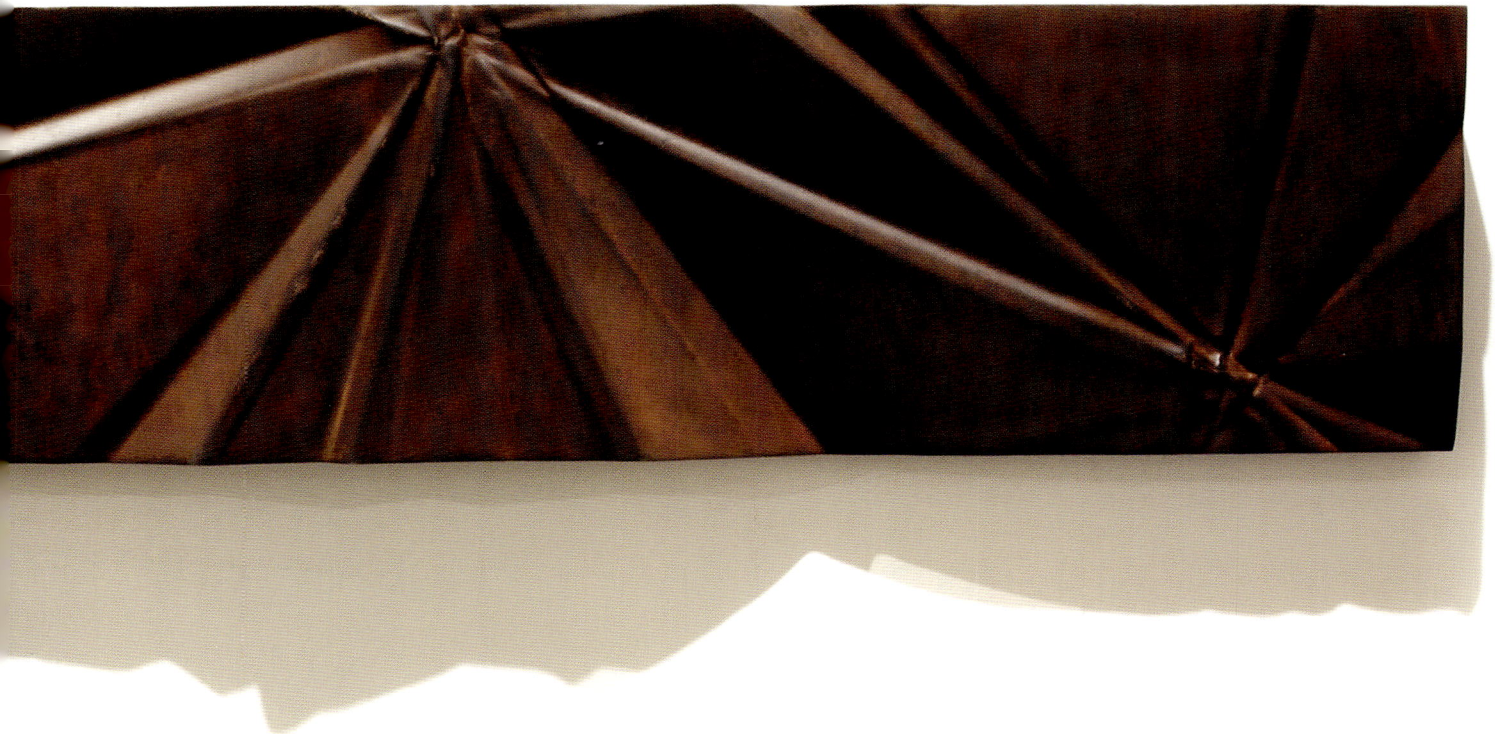

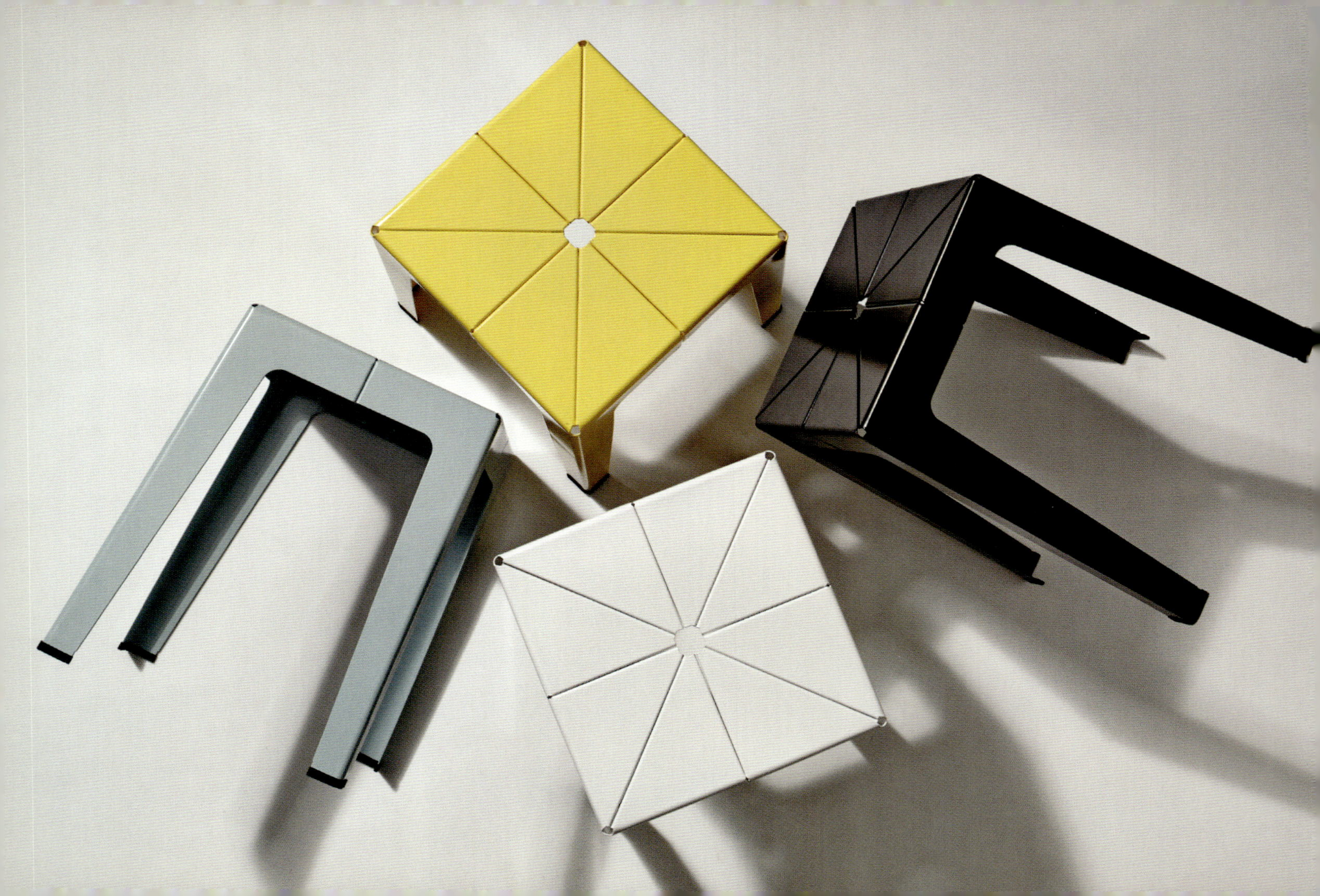

DESIGN BY THEM

ESTABLISHED 2007, SYDNEY, NEW SOUTH WALES

SARAH GIBSON BORN 1982, SYDNEY, NEW SOUTH WALES

NICK KARLOVASITIS BORN 1984, SYDNEY

BOTH LIVE SYDNEY, NEW SOUTH WALES

LIKE MANY bourgeoning industrial designers in Australia, Sarah Gibson and Nick Karlovasitis were nearing the end of their studies and found themselves beleaguered by the tough conditions of staying local and forging a design career. While many young graduates head overseas in pursuit of work and opportunities, Gibson and Karlovasitis resolved to stay put and build the option that they felt was missing in Australia. And so in 2007, DesignByThem was born.

DesignByThem is a furniture and object design house that develops and represents the work of Australian design talent. As well as creating products themselves, DesignByThem counts the likes of Stefan Lie, Trent Jansen (pg 253) and Jon Goulder among their stable of collaborators. The DesignByThem collection is a careful balance of fun and function. Products must be innovative, but not forced; useful, yet enjoyable; contain personality, but also humility. The result is a body of work that explores process, shape and material with marked respect, adding pops of colour and hints of whimsy with a deft touch.

In the near-decade they have been collaborating, Gibson and Karlovasitis have refined and honed their aesthetic, pursuing a 'form follows function' approach. As noted by Gibson, 'We love nothing more than taking out a detail. It's about minimalism, and personality, and reducing the form to a point where it satisfies both.'[1] The *Dial Hose Hanger*, 2014, is a recent standout product for the pair, and a perfect example of this pursuit. Comprising a simple circular shape in flat, block colour, this garden-hose-concealer is an ingenious reinvention of an Aussie backyard staple. It's also a reflection of how their work has changed: 'We wouldn't have designed a garden hose hanger in that way when we were starting out,' says Gibson.

Understanding their customer, their expectations and what they value has also shaped their design practice. 'We've become much more comfortable designing for the customer, rather than trying to impress our peers,' notes Gibson. 'We value what people love to buy and own in their home. If someone with no preconceived notion of design sees our products and loves them, then we're happy and we know we've nailed something intuitive'.

An in-house workshop is further evidence of their acute attention to detail. Assembling, inspecting and dispatching every item they sell is par for the course for DesignByThem. A perfectly executed finished product is just as important as a thoughtfully and carefully conceived concept.

DesignByThem has also had to balance the commercial realities of wanting to support local manufacturers and produce their wares in Australia, with their mandate to support Australian designers, which in turn means being accessible to their customers. This ever-present tension led the duo to concede that sometimes it is in the best interests of the designer and the customer to manufacture products overseas. This means the company can invest more in the materials and processes used. However, a commitment to local manufacture remains important, and DesignByThem offer the option of locally-manufactured versions of their products to their customers.

DesignByThem is a member of the Design Institute of Australia. Karlovasitis is a DIA fellow and is involved heavily in their events around Australia. Both Gibson and Karlovasitis studied Industrial Design at the University of Technology, Sydney, graduating in 2006.

TUCK SERIES

Named after the contained neatness of the folds of steel, the *Tuck*, 2013-15, series of chairs and tables are an exercise in restraint. The hero of each piece is the complicated fold pattern, which brings both strength and embellishment to the design.

'We were inspired by the structural patterns found in children's paper fortune-tellers. What transpired next were explorations in material folding that would go on to inform the stool's functional and playful aesthetic,' notes Gibson.

The *Tuck* series of objects are made from sheet metal steel, which are folded to form a single leg section. Four legs are then used to create a complete stool or table base, which are then connected using the underside folds.

Early prototypes in the *Tuck* series used thicker steel, making the final product incredibly heavy. Through a testing and refinement process, the designers realised that they were not taking advantage of the durability provided by the material and folds. As such, each item in the *Tuck* series uses a thin, lightweight sheet of steel.

As with all DesignByThem products, the *Tuck* series marries material with form, function and personality. They honour the qualities of steel, celebrating the natural proclivities of the material.

1 All quotes in this profile were recorded by the author in an interview with Sarah Gibson.

PREVIOUS PAGE
Tuck Stools, 2013
powder coated steel,
440 x 310 x 310
Photo: Pete Daly

▸

Tuck Stools and *Tuck Table*, 2013
powder coated steel,
stool: 440 x 310 x 310
table: 720 x 800 x 800
Photo: Pete Daly

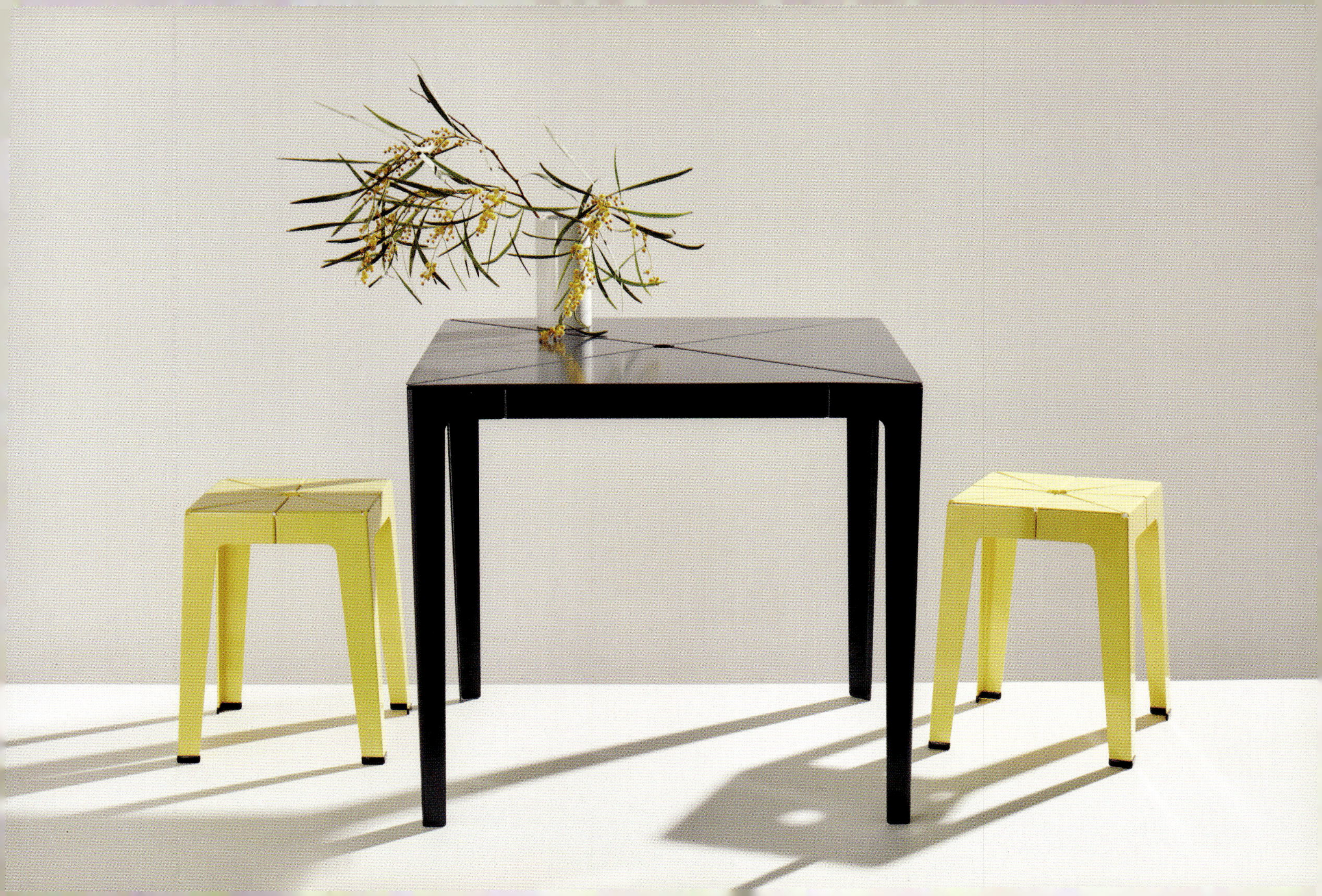

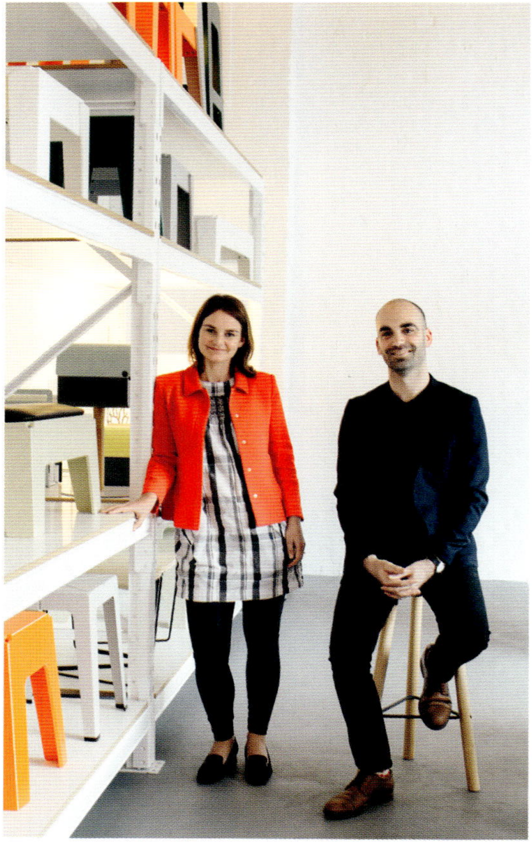

▶

Sarah Gibson and Nick Karlovasitis in the DesignByThem showroom and workshop, Chippendale, New South Wales.
Photo: DesignByThem

▶▶

Corro Bowl, 2009
stainless steel, 85 x 350 x 280
Photo: Pete Daly

CORRO BOWL

Inspired by corrugated roofs, *Corro Bowl*, 2009, is an ode to the Australian landscape. Made from rolled corrugated mirror-polished stainless steel, the designers sought to showcase steel's inherent strength and malleability, recontextualising this industrial material in a high-end design object.

Gibson and Karlovasitis were determined to produce their bowl using the manufacturing processes available in Australia at the time. Upon deciding to use corrugated sheet steel, they embarked on a rigorous research and experimentation phase in order to understand the manufacturing processes, and the aesthetic options they afforded. This meant countless conversations and tests with roofing and rainwater tank manufacturers who found the determination of these two product designers intriguing.

The final design is the product of six processes: sourcing material not normally used for roofing, corrugating, and then rolling the sheet metal by the roofing manufacturer, being cut to shape by a robotic laser cutter, hand-polishing the steel to achieve the mirror finish and finally, etching the DesignByThem brand onto the underside of the bowl. The result is a celebration of material and Australian aesthetics, with a dollop of humour for good measure. ■

DANIELLE ROBSON

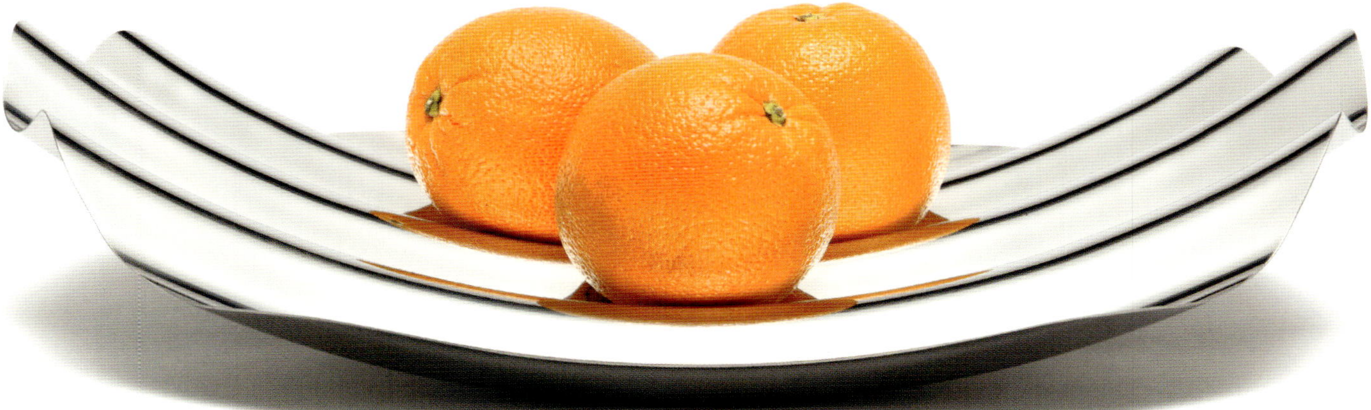

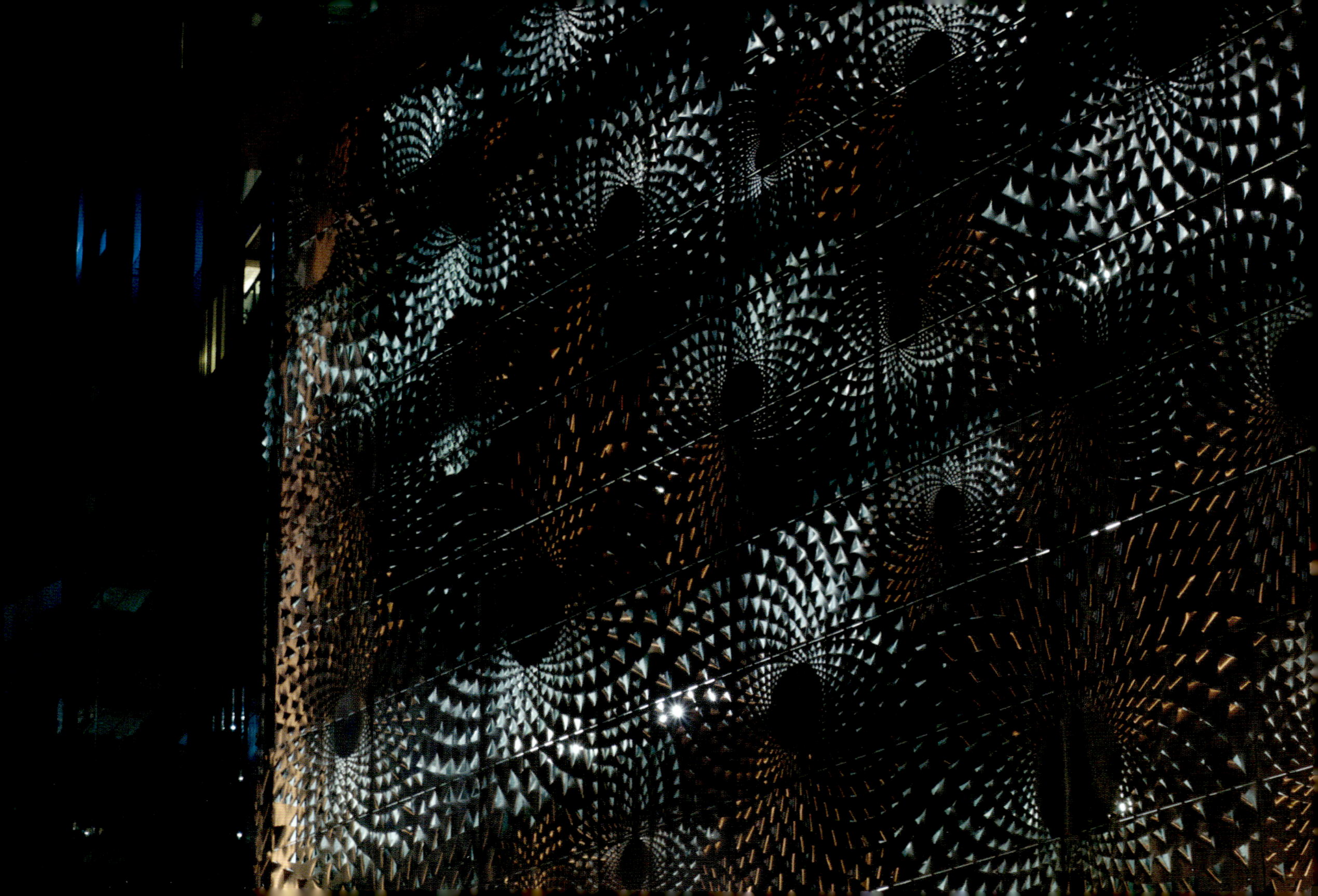

GEOFF NEES

BORN 1970, MELBOURNE, VICTORIA
LIVES MELBOURNE, VICTORIA

KNOWN PRIMARILY as a paper artist, Geoff Nees' expanded practice in steel poses an interesting question of materiality. His collaborations with architects and engineers make us question in what ways seemingly opposite materials can be similar. Interdisciplinary in approach, Nees works as an artist/curator/DJ and it is in part this ability to think laterally that has driven his ability to transform studio-based paper practice into large-scale architectural works.

Graduating from RMIT University in 1995 with a Bachelor in Visual Arts, Nees majored in sculpture, and his resulting practice follows an unexpected line of sculptural enquiry. In creating patterns through cutting and folding paper, Nees changes what would traditionally be considered a flat form, into work that considers and sculpts negative and positive space. Some years later, seeing the potential of his work, Nees was commissioned to design the facade for the Australian Pavilion for the 2005 World Expo held in Japan. This commission gave Nees the taste for working in large-scale architecture, which has formed an ongoing part of his practice.

Architecture, after all, has had a long relationship with paper, from detailed building plans to simple sketches, but Nees extends this relationship further. Describing the materiality between paper and steel as surprisingly similar, the challenge in translating his works from paper to steel has been largely in keeping the element of the hand-made or crafted.

Though Nees' designs are based on an extrapolated isometric grid, giving them the appearance of order through repetition, there is a very deliberate, but subtle emphasis on imperfection. Nees' choice to execute the designs by hand, means that there is the occasional crooked line or wonky fold. These variations are important to Nees in creating quiet moments of questioning by viewers, where they can perceive imperfection without identifying it. These are the instances which give both his paper and steel work, a certain character and beauty that wouldn't exist in a perfect execution. Likening the flaws in his work to the imperfections created by the human hand in any endeavour (the beauty of music for instance, isn't in a perfect execution but the way in which it's executed) Nees deliberately plays with the tension of human and mechanical making.

The opportunity to upscale his work has also meant that Nees can create pieces that are not just art for art's sake. Getting it out of institutions where audiences are limited or self-selecting, and putting his works in the public sphere, has meant that his practice becomes part of people's everyday encounters and language, changing the way they interact with his work. Though riskier, and a more drawn-out and abstracted process, being able to see his work in this new light has led Nees to ongoing architectural collaborations that emphasise sustainability and economy married with good design. While the gamble is much greater on this scale, so are the rewards, and for downtime, Nees still has his studio.

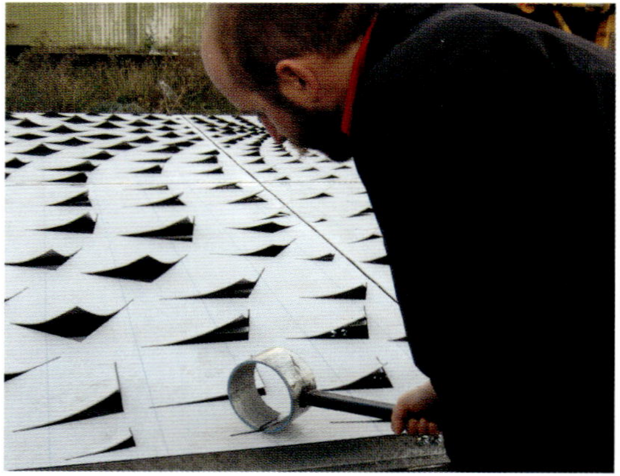

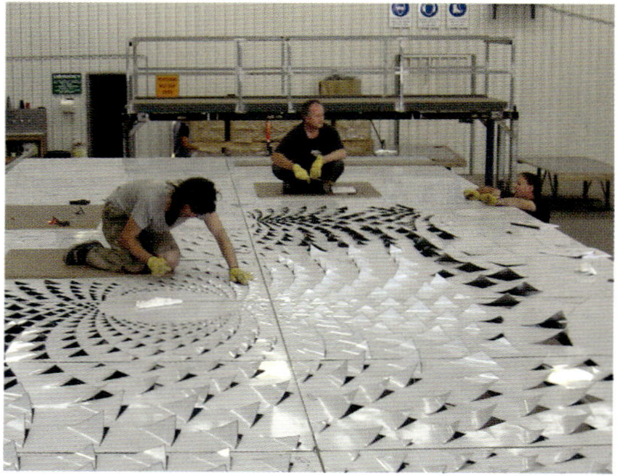

PREVIOUS PAGE
Royal Domain Tower St Kilda Road, Melbourne, 2006, at night.
Photo: Dirk Zimmermann

▶

The art facade is made up of a series of stainless steel sheets with intricate laser cut petals hand folded outwards.
Photo: courtesy the artist

▶▶

The panels are lifted into place.
Photo: courtesy the artist

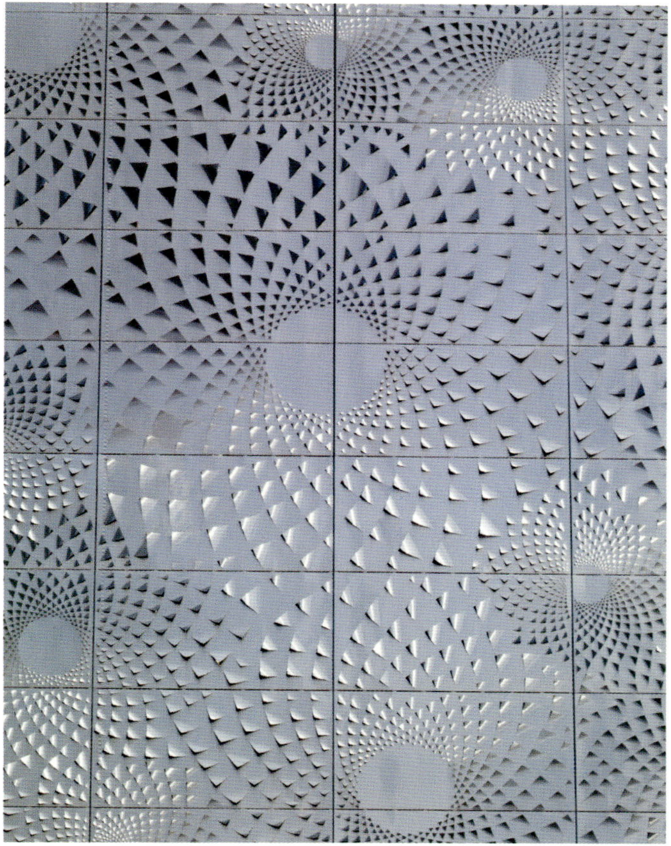

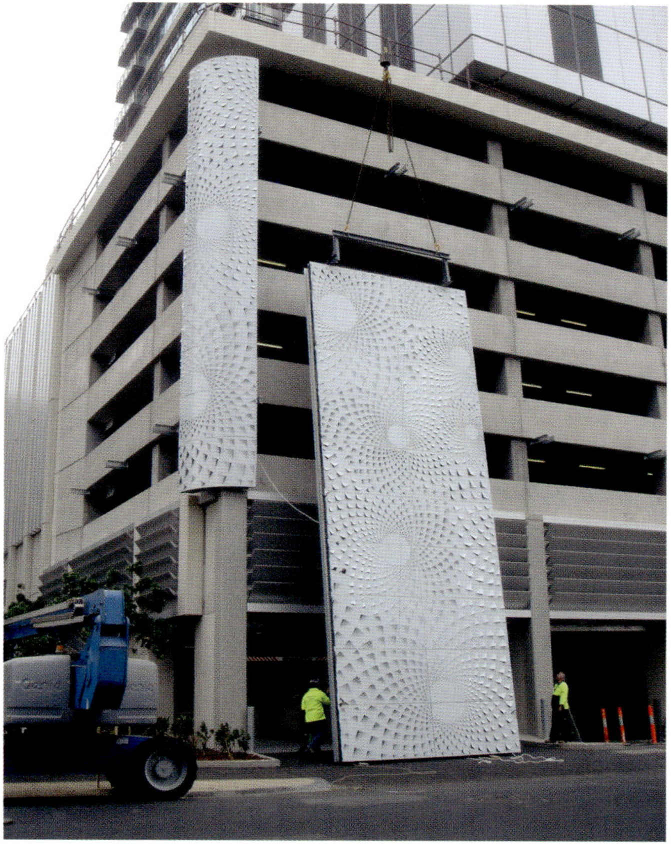

THE ROYAL DOMAIN TOWER ART FACADE

Completed in 2006, The Royal Domain Tower Art Facade is among Geoff Nees' earliest architectural pieces. Created in collaboration with studio505, this facade is an addition to the Royal Domain Residential Tower on St Kilda Road, Melbourne and was awarded Best Contribution to Urban Art by the City of Port Philip in 2007.

Made from stainless steel, this piece is approximately 450m^2 with 25,000 individual laser-cut folds. Nees' commitment to maintaining a hand-crafted design, even at such a scale, meant that it took three weeks in the workshop to finish the design by hand, folding every element of cut steel. As a cladding for the Tower's five-storey car park, the work serves as an aesthetic solution while incorporating smart design.

The open folds provide an essential natural ventilation, while the combination of stainless steel and the textured pattern, allow the work to become a light feature without the cost or infrastructure of any additional lighting. During the day, the steel facade captures and reflects the light, becoming luminescent, its swirling patterned surface showing to full effect, displaying a spectrum of greys and silvers, as the undulating surface catches the light at different angles. When night falls, it's the negative space that shines, with the artificial lights from inside the structure, shining out against the dark unlit steel. ■

SERENA WONG

▸
Stainless steel car park screen
Royal Domain Tower St Kilda Road,
Melbourne, 2006.
laser cut hand folded
stainless steel, 17000 x 52000
Produced in collaboration
with studio505 Melbourne
Photo: Dirk Zimmermann

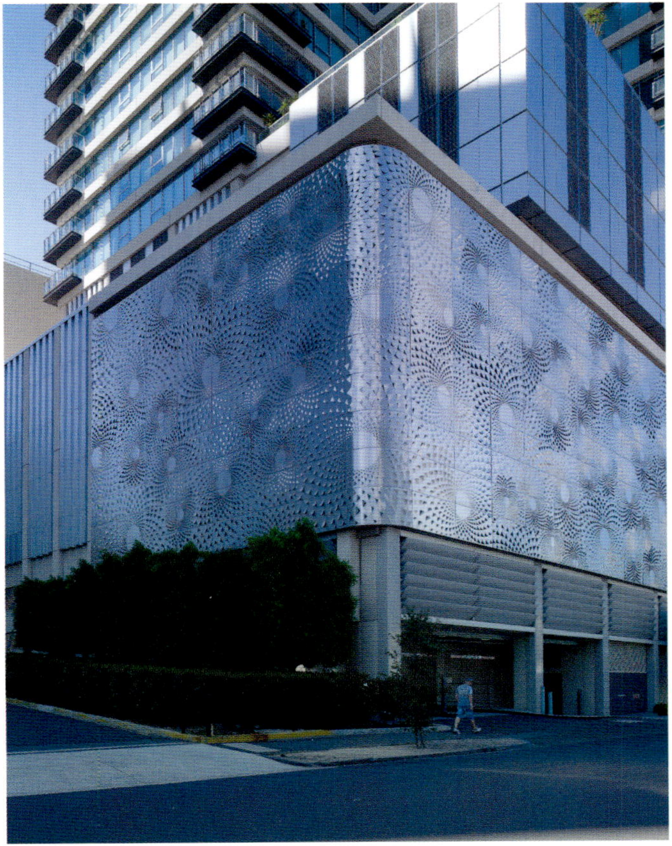

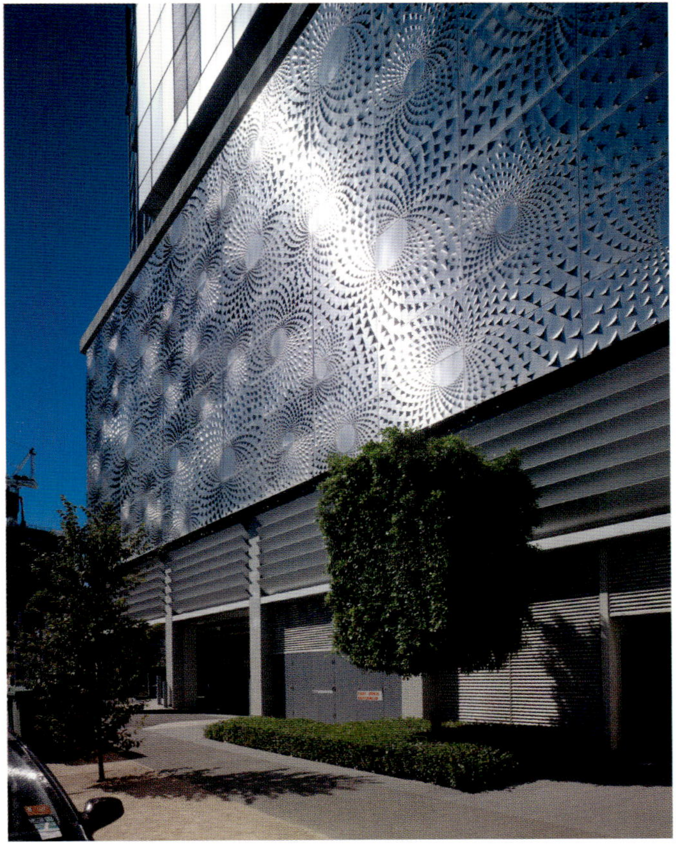

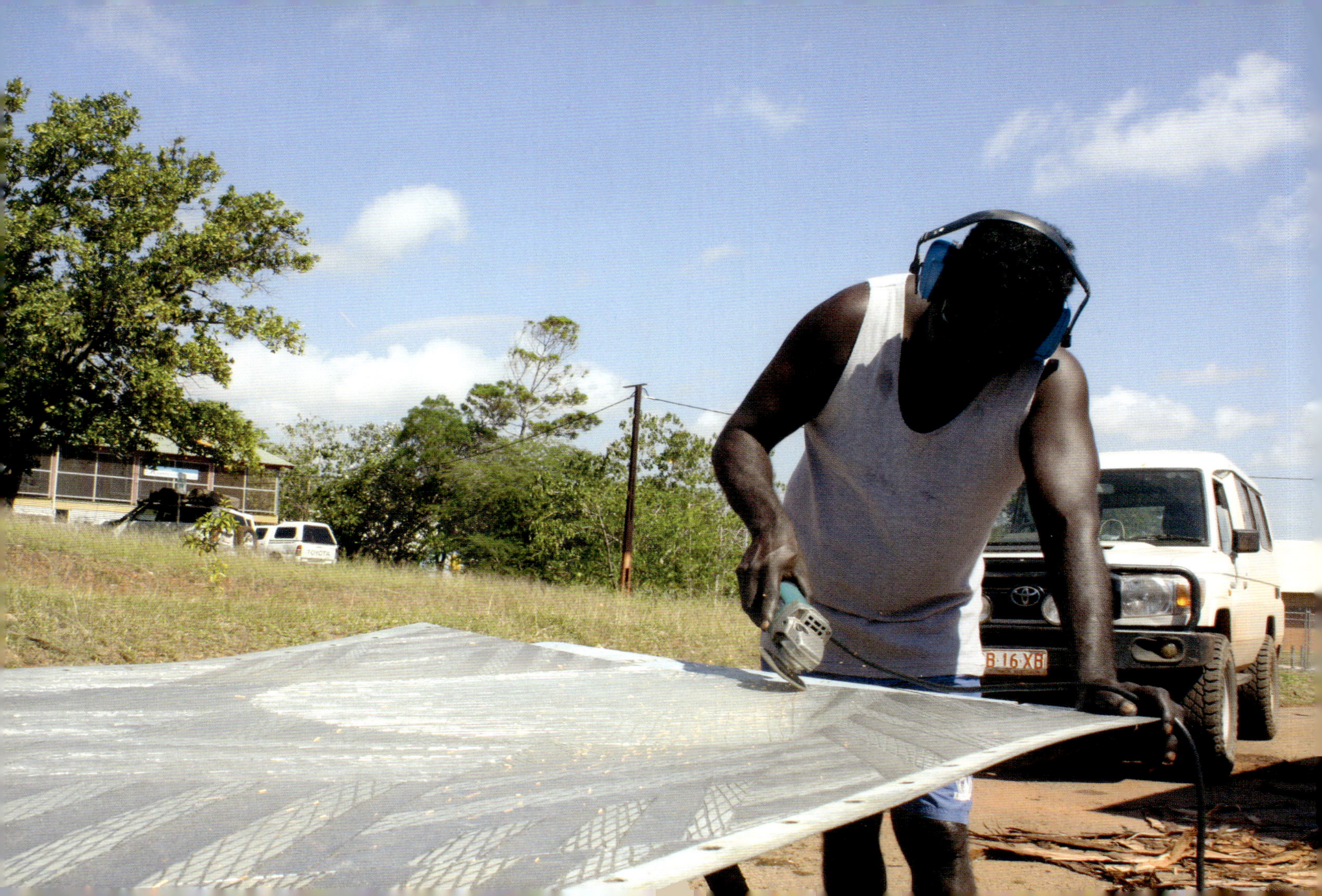
B·16·XB

GUNYBI GANAMBARR

BORN 1973, YIRRKALA, NORTHERN TERRITORY
LIVES GANGAN, NORTHERN TERRITORY

MY ARTS are according to the songs, it is what they are singing.[1]

Acclaimed artist Gunybi Ganambarr creates with steel like no other Yolngu artist has before and revolutionising the way that his culture is being creatively expressed. Moving beyond the boundaries of bark painting or the Larrakitj poles (hollow log coffins) to working with steel and found object this practice resides somewhere between, embodying the traditions of Yolgnu art making and expressing it in a completely new way, resonating just as powerfully as the work of the elders who have taught him.

Gunybi[2] is of the Dhuwa moiety and the Ngaymil clan of North East Arnhem Land. Mentored by many of the master artists of the region Gunybi began his artistic career in painting on bark and the Larrakitj. Since these beginnings he has pushed his making in exploratory new directions. Transforming both mediums in completely new ways to his predecessors, Gunybi's practice has also gone on to take new forms in found objects including galvanised water-tank, plastic piping, rubber and insulation panels, discarded across his lands.

The works of Gunybi are layered with the stories of his people and his cultural being as a Yolngu man. The meticulous designs carved into the remnants of old water tanks or the cut out flowing lines in sheet metal embody the master hand of his Yolngu aesthetic and represent the systems of knowledge and art traditions that have been present for many thousands of years. The re-invention of the found media, (particularly steel, perhaps) is also an influence of Gunybi's time building houses in his homelands for over a decade, applying the craftsmanship of building and using new materials in his artwork through innovative re-purposing. The incising and cutting of designs into steel communicates his intrinsic connection to culture and its continuity, expanding the ever-developing dynamism of Yolngu art traditions.

The stories of Gunybi's Ngaymil clan are carved into the steel, a harsh, heavy material which he inscribes with delicate ancestral stories such as the Gudurrku (Brolga) dance and of Djanda the sacred goanna whose movement amongst the totemic Darra (waterweed) leaves flowing herringbone pattern across the Gudalmirri, the deep water. The power totem to his clan Ngaymil is Warrukay or Murrukula, the Barracuda that also features in the steel cut-outs of Gunybi's work. The stories in his creations are of the ancestral beings of the Yolngu, of cycles of season and of law. These themes are carried across his art, not only depicting culture but are also a statement – that there will always be new forms of telling and passing on old ways. The works are not only contemporary manifestations of cultural practice they assert that the chain of generational knowledge will never be broken. He says: 'My thought is different from what they were thinking when the old people were painting. I try and bring the Yolngu law (madayin) into reality. That is what is in my mind. To show what is already there.'[3]

NGAYMIL

The large-scale carved steel work, *Ngaymil*, 2012, represents an area called Ngalkan, on Ngaymil land and sea, which is the clan of artist Gunybi Ganambarr. Ngalkan is an area between the Cato and Gurrumurru Rivers that run into Arnhem Bay, which has a watercourse that takes you to a sacred fresh water Milngurr (spring) with special qualities called Balawurru. At the Milngurr there are many sacred animals to the Yolngu and it is where the Gudurrku (Brolga) dance and where Djanda the sacred goannas make swirling movements in the water as they swim through the Darra (waterweed). The meeting and motion of where the saltwater meets the freshwater and where animals are swimming and dancing can be seen in this work – the herringbone pattern carved to represent the weed that Djanda the goanna swim through and the circular motion alluding to the movement of the waters.

1 Ganambarr, G. in Gilchrist, S. *Gunybi Ganambarr, unDisclosed 2nd National Indigenous Art Triennial*, National Gallery of Australia.

2 As a Yorta Yorta curator and writer Kimberley Moulten's methodology is to refer to people she is writing about by their first names.

3 Ibid.

[redacted]

PREVIOUS PAGE
Gunybi Gunambarr working steel with an angle grinder.
Photo: Buku-Larrnggay Mulka Centre

Ngaymil, 2012
corrugated steel
2290 x 940
Photo: Tom Roschi
Collection of Ross Bonthorne

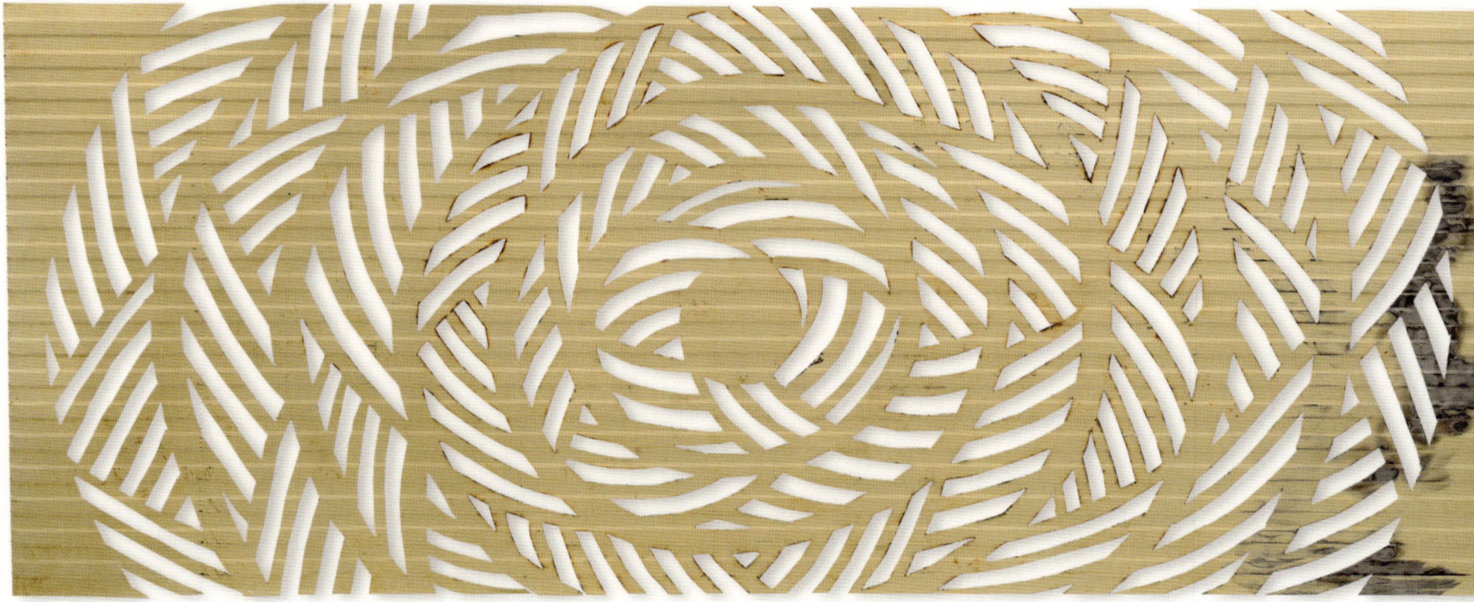

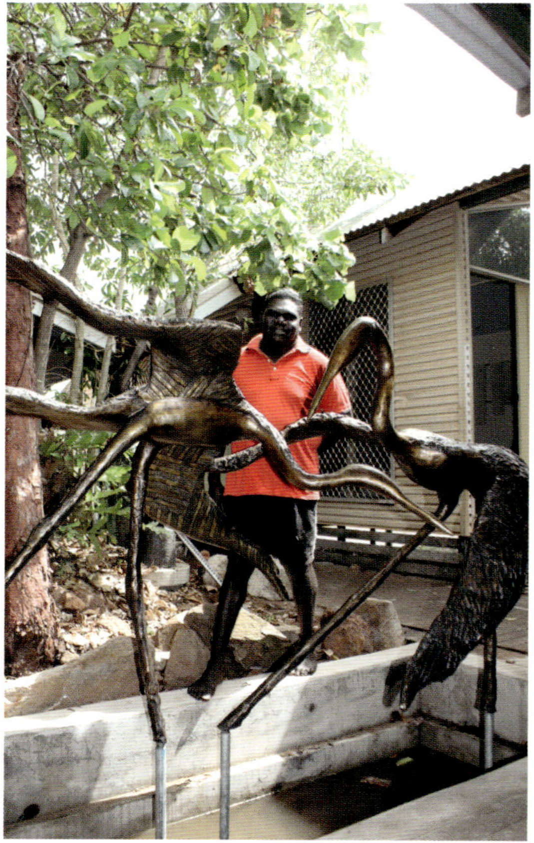

▸
Gunybi Gunambarr
with brolga sculptures.
Photo: Buku-Larrnggay Mulka Centre

▸▸
Ngalkan, 2013
etched water tank, 1800 x 1200
Photo: Tom Roschi
Collection of Ross Bonthorne

NGALKAN

Ngalkan, 2013, is also referencing this area on Ngaymil land, the galvanised iron from a watertank collected by Gunybi at Gangan where he lives, has been heavily incised with the designs of his heartlands. The works of Gunybi carry his clan markings however the material itself is integral to the message: caring for country is just as important as caring for culture, they are but one and the same. In recycling the steel and scrap-metals discarded across his homelands, Gunybi is also making a strong statement about caring for environment while at the same time, carrying the art traditions of the Yolngu into the future. ■

KIMBERLEY MOULTON

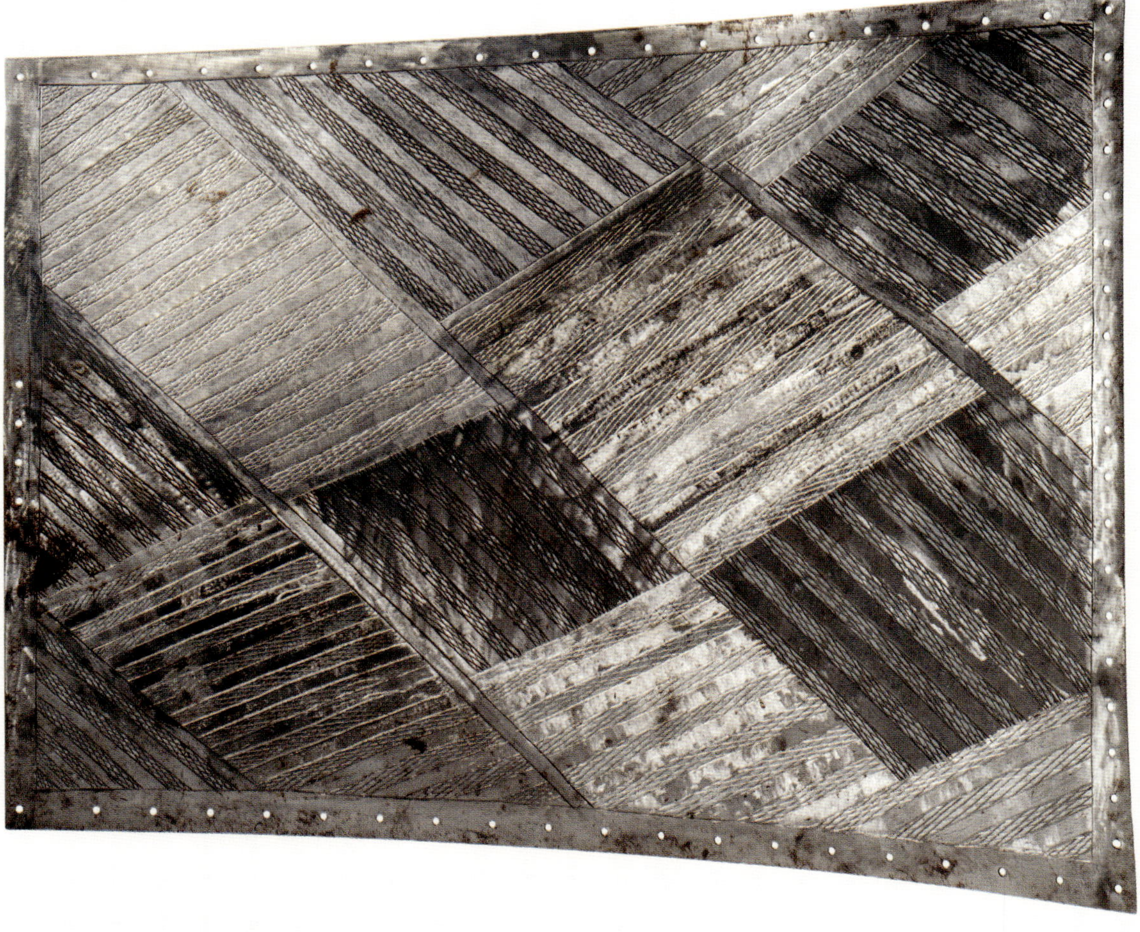

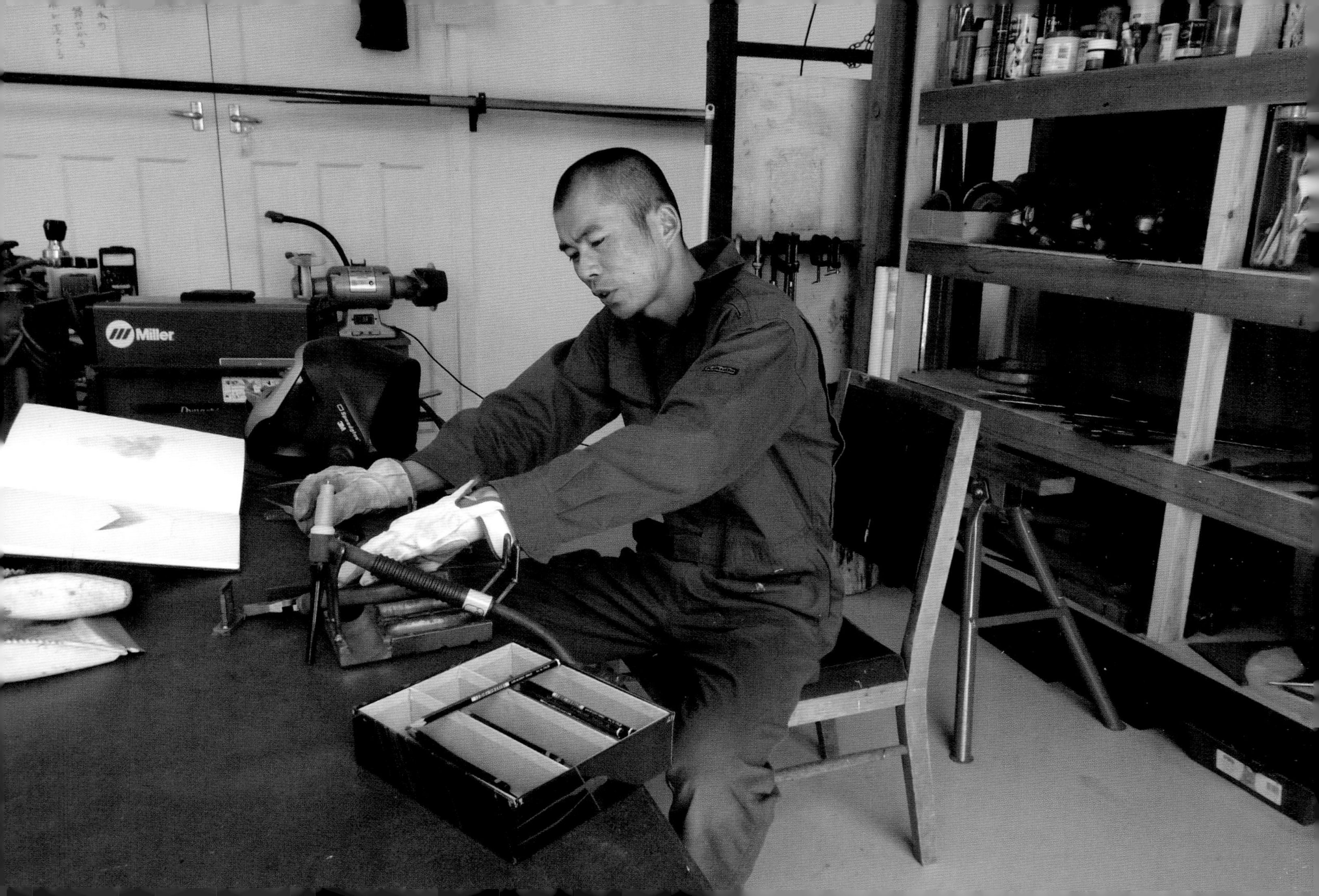
Miller

KENSUKI TODO

BORN 1975, KYOTO, JAPAN
LIVES CANBERRA, AUSTRALIAN CAPITAL TERRITORY

RECENTLY I NOTICED quite an important thing – ever since I was a student, there's always rectangular form coming into my work,' says Kensuke Todo. 'It's always there, always (as part of a) question of why we live this way, in this society.'[1]

Todo's work uses steel to examine the strangeness of possessing a human body in an industrialised landscape. The rectangles, and the variations imposed upon them, form a discussion of what it means to be alive in the cities we have constructed. His work plays with the idea of the hard object against an intimate, soft form – a way to reflect this intrigue between the softness of the body and the hardness of this mechanised world we have created and inhabit.

Growing up in Japan and moving to Canberra to study, Todo found that his physical dislocation from home and from his history provided the perspective to create, and to view his place in the world with a fresh set of eyes.

When I'm in Australia I look at my culture or my background with a more objective view. Living in Australia definitely encouraged me to explore this. Australia was my first overseas trip, and coming here from Japan was totally different. I feel more encouraged to make sculpture when I'm in Australia than when I'm in Japan.

I feel like I can be more true to myself in Australia. In Japan I feel that I must fulfil my expectations, social expectations. When I'm here, people already know that I'm from a different background. How I behave is based on who I am. When you do this in Japan it can be seen as strange, sometimes unacceptable.

His adopted city has embraced him and his work, with the Canberra critics circle and the *City News* magazine naming Todo the 2014 Canberra artist of the year. Examples of his work

1 The quotes in this profile were recorded by the author in an interview with Kensuke Todo

are seen through the city in places as diverse as the ACT Legislative Assembly and the Commonwealth Club, and he has exhibited in a similarly eclectic range of spaces including Canberra's Drill Hall Gallery, Sydney's King Street Gallery on William and the Cowra Regional Art Gallery to name a few.

Todo is interested in steel as a way to embody a dialogue about what it is to be human in modern life, alongside the continuation of an examination of one's physical and emotional place.

I was interested in using a hard material in a soft form. All the individual hammer marks create different aspects to the material; it's a bit like being a panel beater really. I was looking at the futon form as a representation of emotion or the body, and the rectangle as the society, or the environment we live in. We're supposed to be animals. We have soft skin, very complex forms. We're supposed to live in nature, but we live in this, consisted of the rectangular forms, vertical and horizontal axes.

As clear and as beautifully articulated as Todo's pieces are, his work and his desires are in no way didactic. Given that the human experience is a key theme of his practice, Todo expresses a desire for a human response to the work:

I would like the audience to have their own interpretation – I don't believe in the artist telling them what the work is about. It doesn't need to be about the 100% truth. It is for the audience to decide.

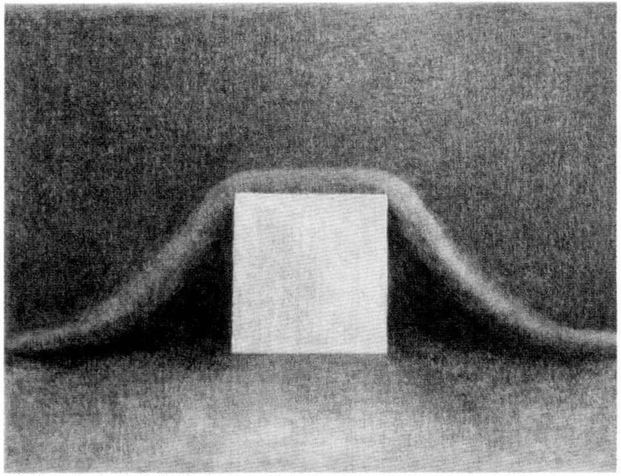

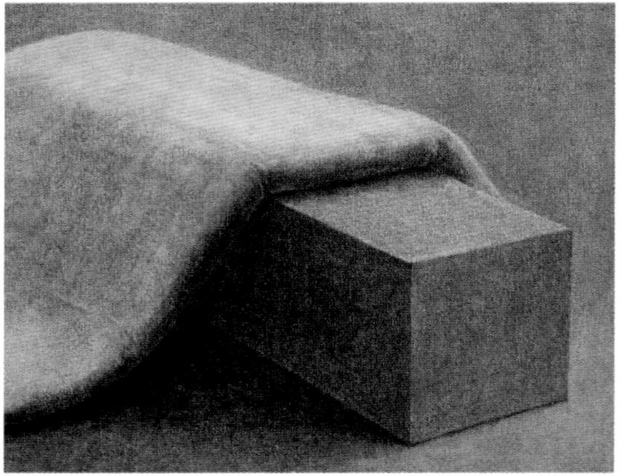

PREVIOUS PAGE
Kensuke Todo in his studio, Canberra, Australian Capital Territory, 2014
Photo Kim Johnston

◥◢

Studies for *Insufficient*, 2012
charcoal on paper,
top: 591 x 750
bottom: 420 x 595
Photo: David Paterson

▸▸

Insufficient, 2013
mild steel, 280 x 950 x 4550
Photo: David Paterson

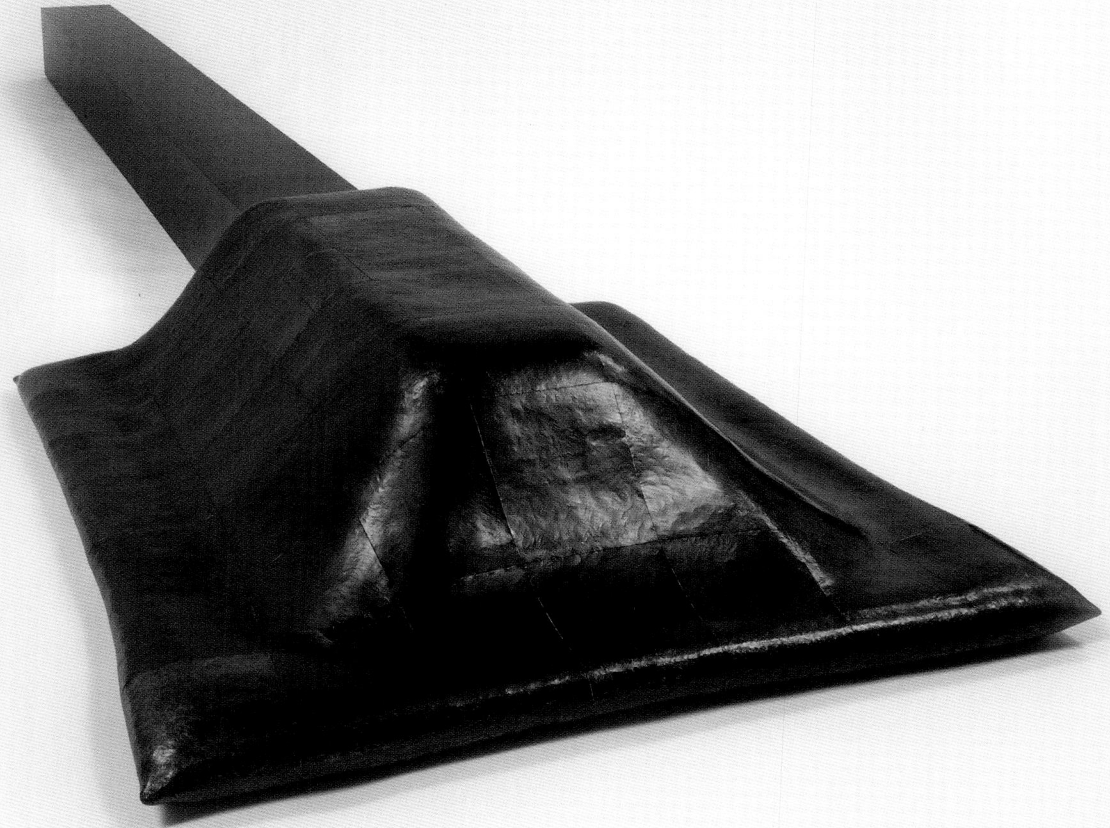

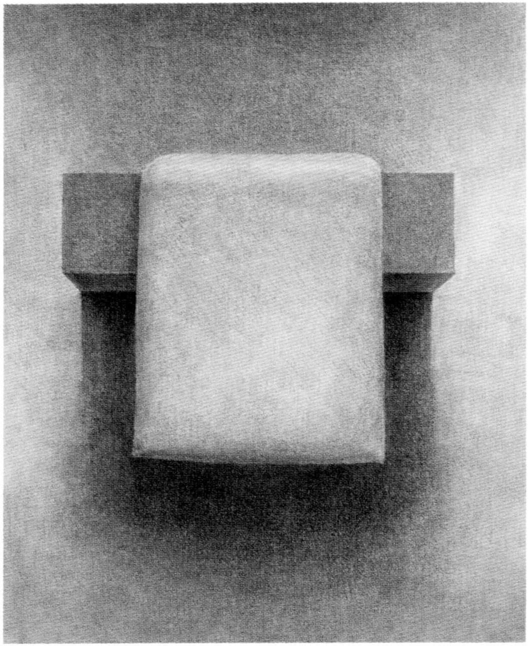

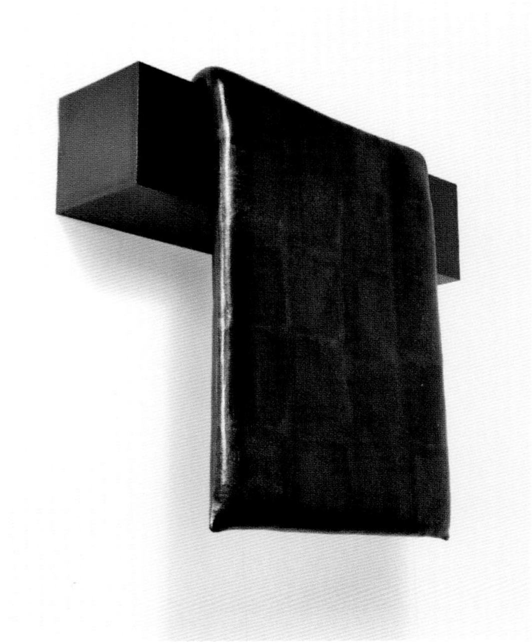

▶

Study for *Drape*, 2012
charcoal on paper, 751 x 595
Photo: David Paterson

▶▶

Drape, 2013
mild steel, 765 x 823 x 250
Photo: David Paterson

▶▶▶

Envelop, 2013
mild steel, 285 x 290 x 1950
Photo: David Paterson

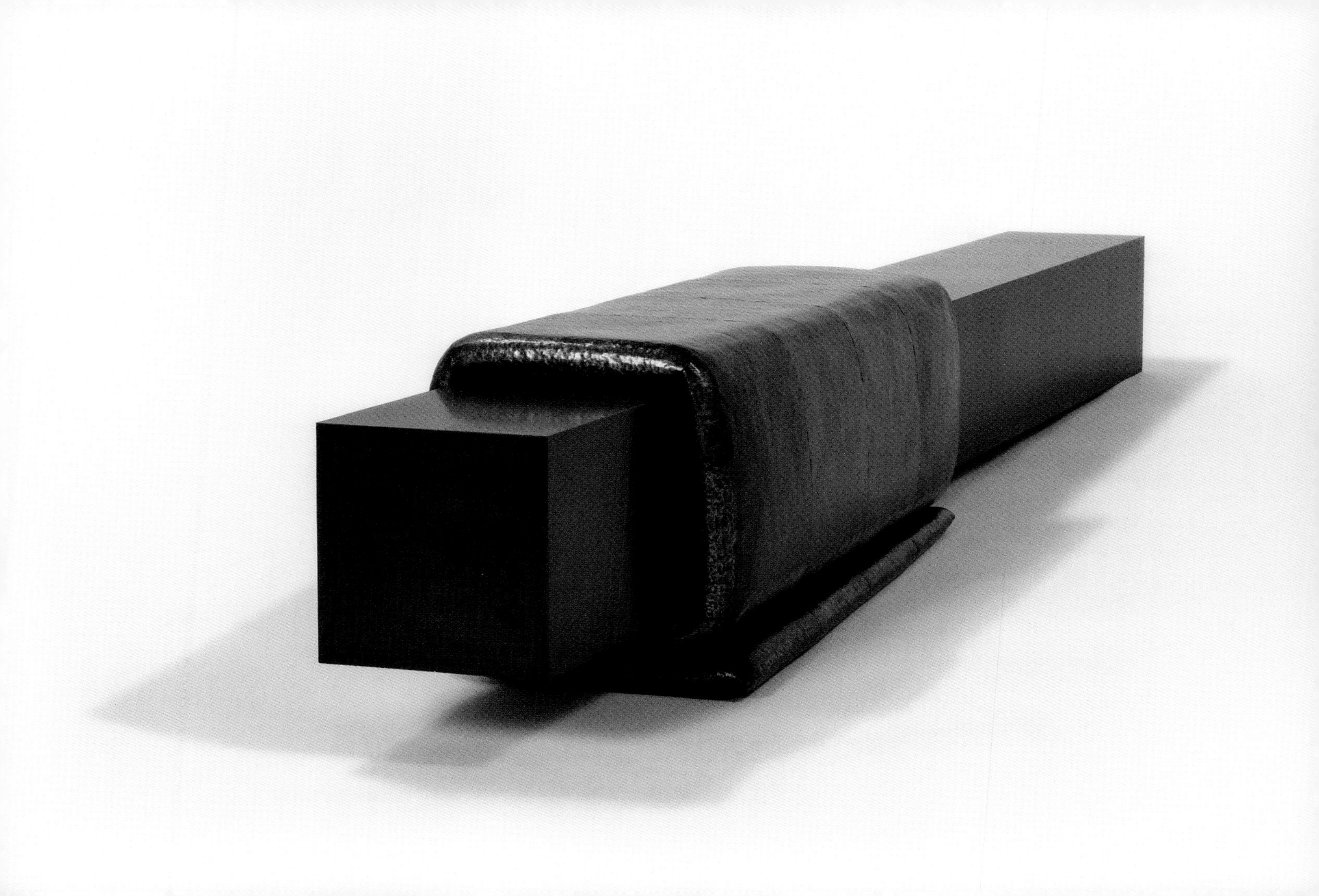

FUTON FALLING

The futon form carries a large amount of symbolic weight, a most intimate and private object. Here, through a painstaking application of rare abilities, a visual illusion of softness is created through the forging and striking of steel. The work speaks to several human essences – of warmth and coldness, of the fleshy, vulnerable human form and its place within the defined mechanics of vertical and horizontal axes, and also of home. In Japan, the futon is familiar. In Australia, it is less ubiquitous. The artist is looking at his homeland from afar, but somewhere in the process of leaving home and establishing a new life elsewhere he has become permanently displaced – home is now a memory more than a physical place, and with this a sense of critical distance is created. *Futon Falling*, 2014, exists within worlds – animal and mechanical – the home of memory and the physical place one creates a life within. It asks the viewer to consider the work with all the senses, including the inference of steel on the skin in a place recognisable as a structure of rest and intimacy. ■

GLEN MARTIN

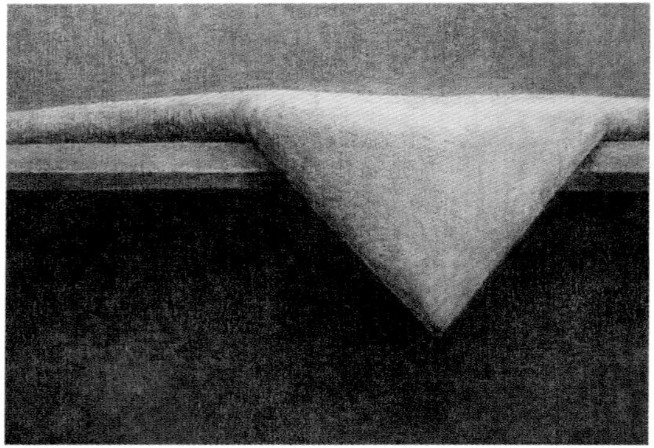

▲
Study for *Corner*, 2012
charcoal on paper,
420 x 595
Photo: David Paterson

◥
Futon Falling, 2014
mild steel,
futon: 380 x 205 x 15
rectangle: 855 x 780 x 80
Photo: David Paterson

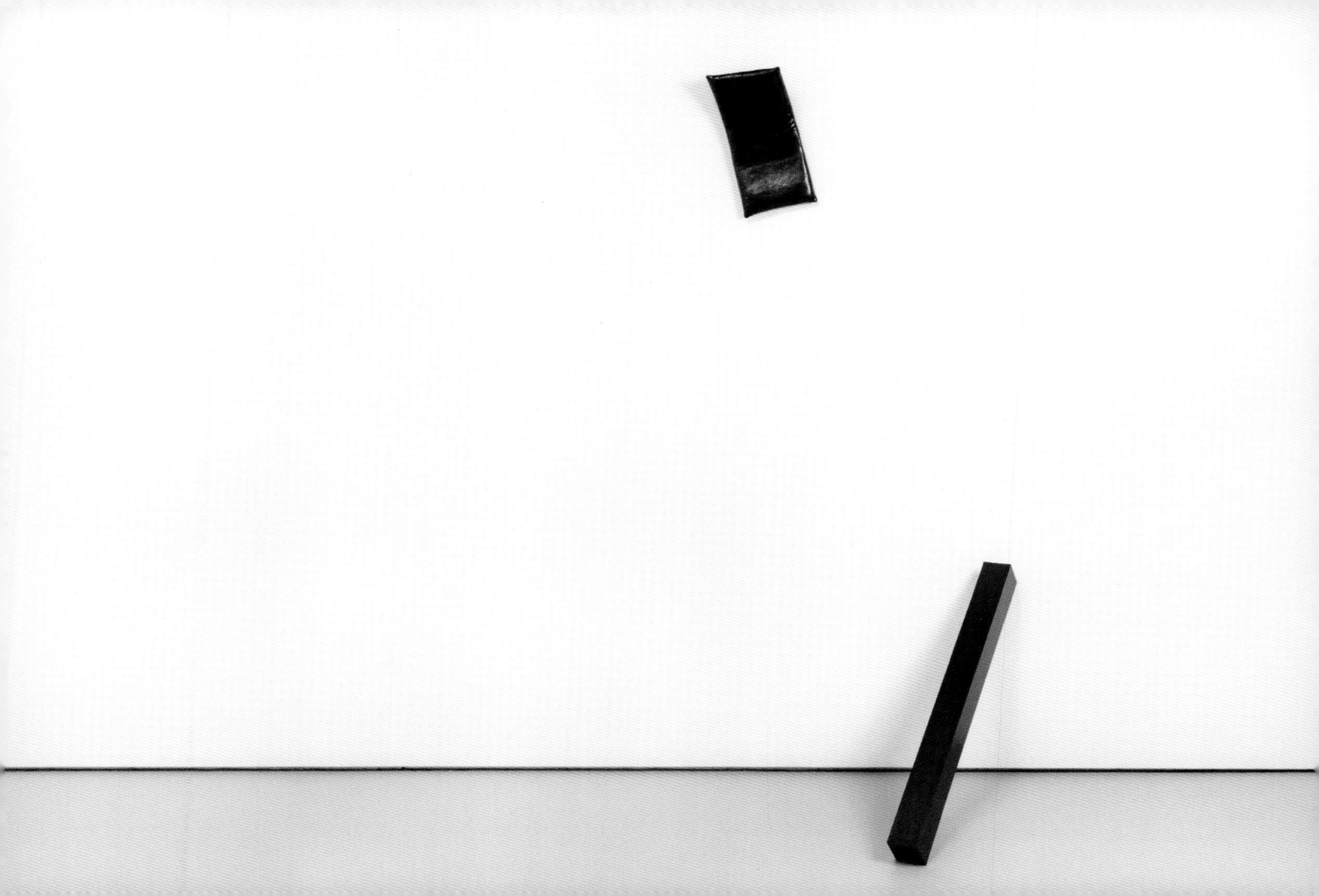

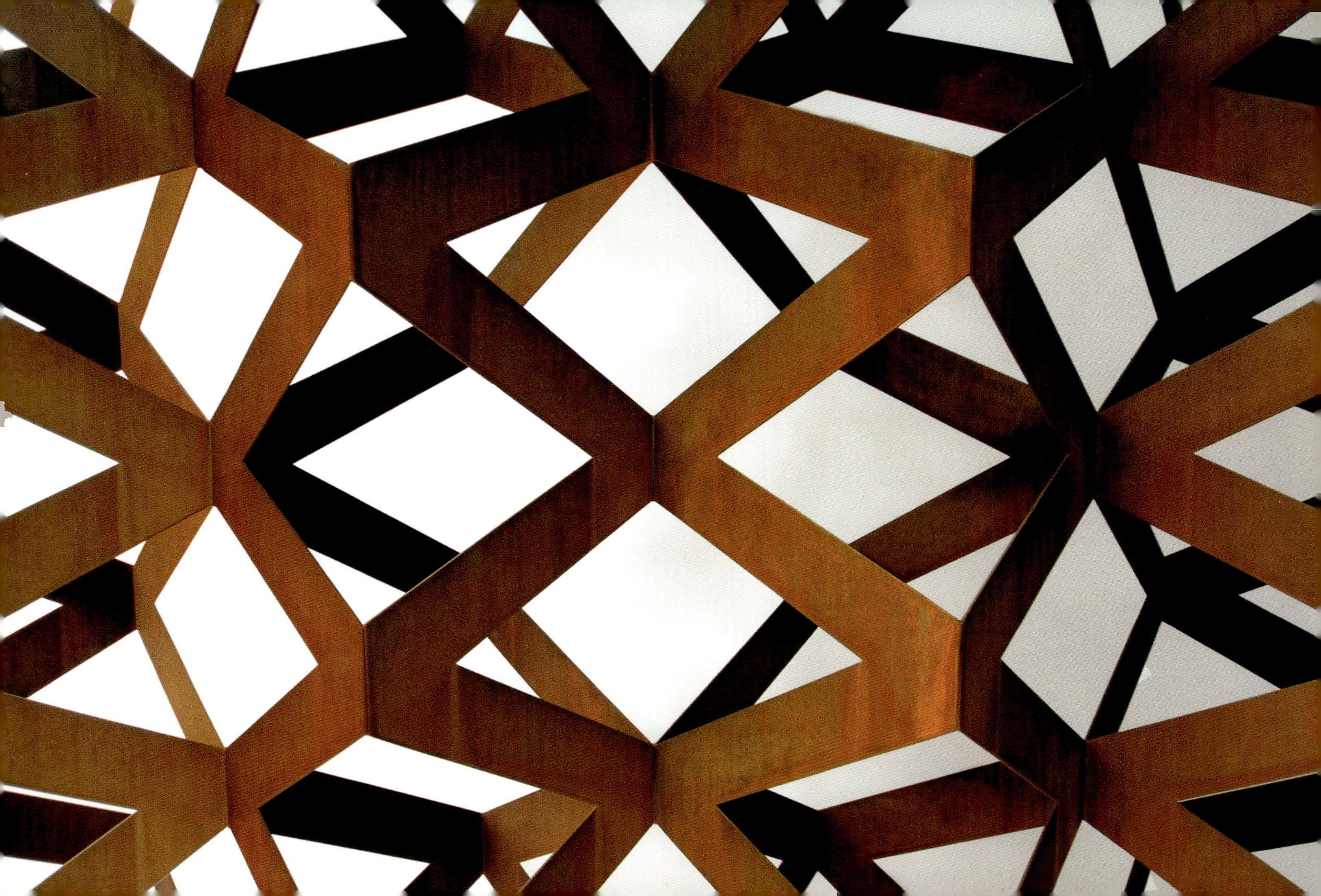

KORBAN/ FLAUBERT

ESTABLISHED 1993, STUTTGART, GERMANY

STEFANIE FLAUBERT BORN 1965, LONDON, UNITED KINGDOM

JANOS KORBAN BORN 1961, PORT AUGUSTA, SOUTH AUSTRALIA

BOTH LIVE SYDNEY, NEW SOUTH WALES

METAL IS TREASURE from the Earth...it should be treated like treasure from the Earth, something special should come from it. We are trying to make something rare and valuable out of dirt... since it is a finite resource, we do not want to waste it, we want to do something interesting and special with it.[1]

The directness and confidence in the work of korban/flaubert has evolved through a dedicated and involved material investigation. Pushing the limits of metal's physical and expressive potential whilst challenging their making capabilities, the creative team of Janos Korban and Stefanie Flaubert have created a distinctive practice that spans furniture design and sculpture. They have developed both a national and international reputation for their works in both stainless and corten steel.

As Flaubert notes:

We love the ductility and lustre of metal. Janos has spent 20 years wrangling metal: testing and manipulating it. He has developed pretty amazing technical skills but metal is always a challenge. The stresses in metal can be like heightened stresses in a living human or animal body: creases, muscles, fluidity. Metal can express emotion this way too. The energy and motion of something animal. Contained energy, ready to spring or run or attack or recoil.[2]

On graduating from university in Adelaide, Flaubert in architecture, Korban in arts majoring in psychology and genetics, the pair worked in Melbourne for a few years before heading off overseas. Settling in Stuttgart, Germany, facade specialist Flaubert worked for the German lightweight structures architect Gunter Behnisch, whilst Korban worked across projects at first as a model-maker for exhibitions and theatre before working in a specialist metal workshop, K.M. Hardwork. Here, Korban was seduced by the material.

His fascination was infectious leading the pair to spend weekends designing and experimenting.

In 1994 korban/flaubert launched their inaugural collaborative works, a series of experimental chaise longues in an exhibition in Stuttgart. Returning to Australia in 1995 they opened their first studio and workshop in Newtown, New South Wales, then in Alexandria in 2001. The pair's two skill sets marry well.

Wishing to create works that have a sense of fluidity, energy and motion Flaubert spends hours creating models in the studio. The unforced and expressive nature of these models are further interpreted by Korban in the workshop where he utilising his impressive making capabilities bringing the models to life in metal. Flaubert describes the process as such:

We treat design as a process of discovery and we use both spaces to generate and develop ideas and forms. In the studio we generally start by developing a three-dimensional phenomenon or effect using simple model-making techniques. The workshop operates as a laboratory for form, with model making, experimenting with materials and prototyping central to our methodology.[3]

Recent works including, *Iron in the Soul*, 2015, explore the idea of metal objects as artefacts. The works have an appearance of something dug up: broken, truncated, a sense of history, memory or loss. This loss or reflection on the past finds analogy with the pairs concern for the Australian manufacturing industry, in which precious making and technical skills are being lost in Australia, as production is shifted overseas. In 2016 korban/flaubert moved their studio to Paddington.

MARGARET HANCOCK DAVIS

1 http://www.ngv.vic.gov.au/multimedia/41842/, accessed September 2016.

2 http://www.habitusliving.com/products/site-specific-art-korbanflaubert, accessed September 2016.

3 http://www.powerhousemuseum.com/collection/database/?irn=342880, accessed September 2016.

[redacted]

PREVIOUS PAGE
Crystal screen, 2011
corten steel, 2100 x 2050 x 420
Photo: Stefanie Flaubert

[redacted]

▸
Refuge, 2015
stainless steel, 1500 x 2800 x 1500

Tetrasphere, 2002
stainless steel, 400 x 600 x 500
Photo: Stefanie Flaubert

▸▸
Iron in the Soul, 2015
corten steel, 1100 x 3400 x 2300
Photo: Stefanie Flaubert

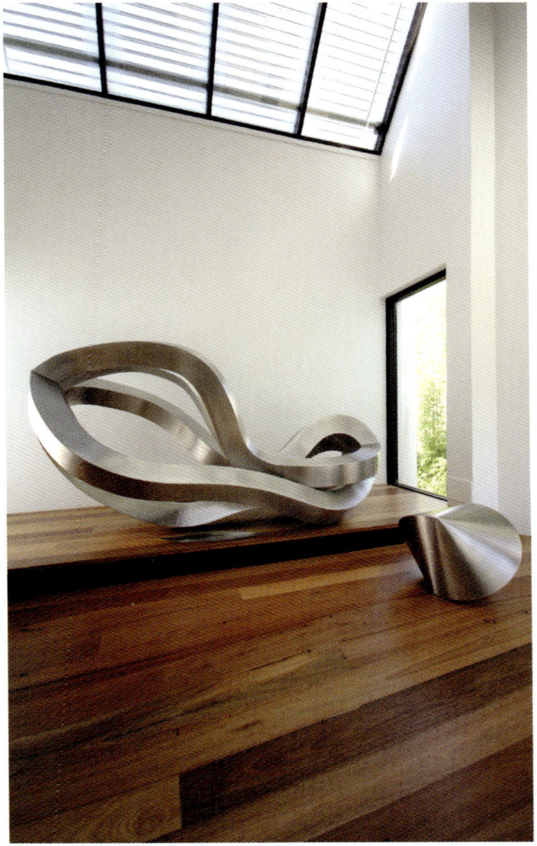

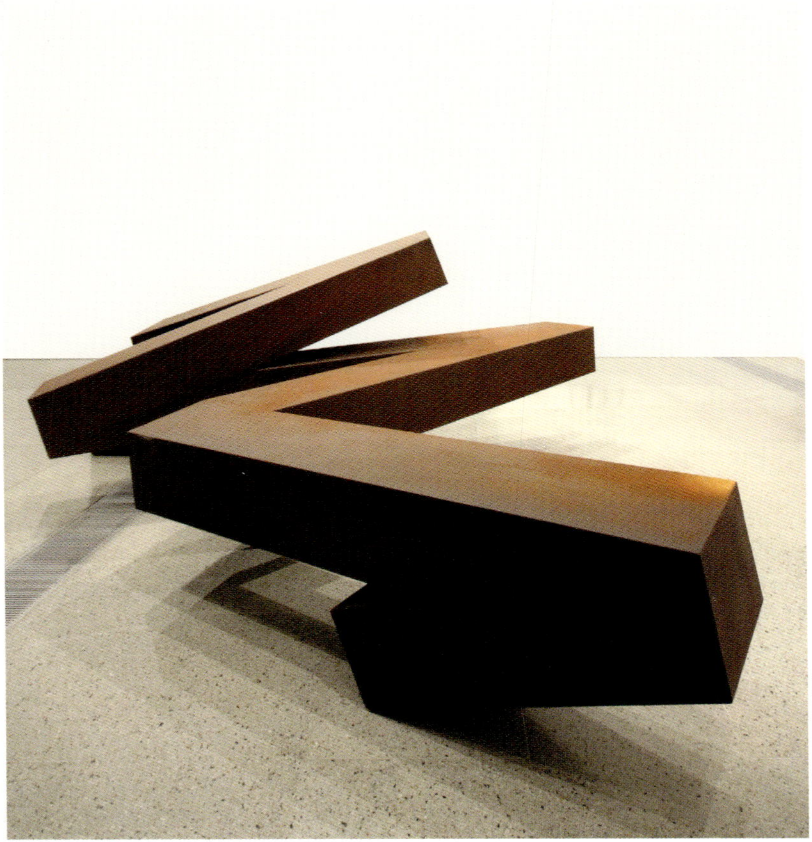

ARMOUR SCREEN

'We have produced several screens over the years, based on pattern, repetition and sequence. These screens explore the sculptural possibilities of folded mathematical structures.

Armour Screen, 2012, explores the solidity and lustre of stainless steel: solid stainless steel plates fold into each other to form a rhythmic and chunky screen. Armour plates protect: the fortified form is constructed by diagonal translations of a repeated module. The blocky modelling of the screen is enhanced by the stainless steel picking up light from different directions. Apertures are like metal helmets, facing both directions.'

STEFANIE FLAUBERT

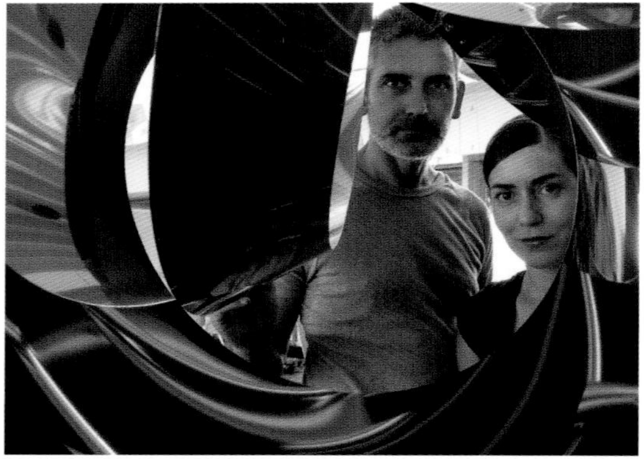

▲ Janos Korban and Stefanie Flaubert.
Photo: Sharrin Rees

▶ *Armour Screen*, 2012
stainless steel, 1850 x 2100 x 400
Photo: Stefanie Flaubert
Collection of Cafe Sydney

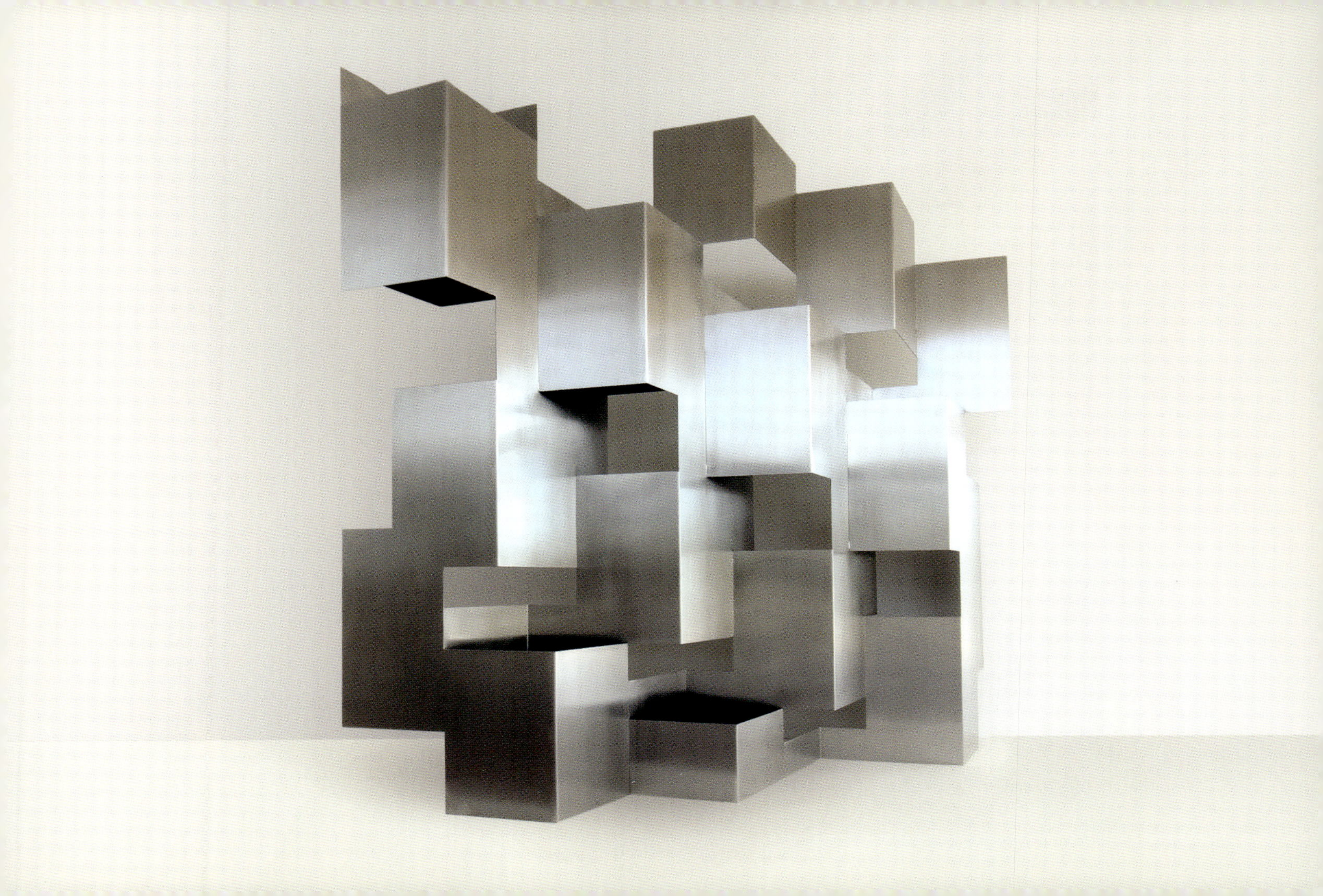

INVOLUTE

'*Involute*, 2009, is one of a series of our projects exploring motion and continuity, instability and equilibrium.

An endless loop spirals conically around and in on itself, an involute position, protective, constantly enfolding and refolding the space within. The tight geometric flow traces the double loop infinity symbol and draws it into a renewing three-dimensional envelope. The two sides flow together in an involved constant equilibrium, balanced but endless... slow, sculptural, perpetual.' ■

STEFANIE FLAUBERT

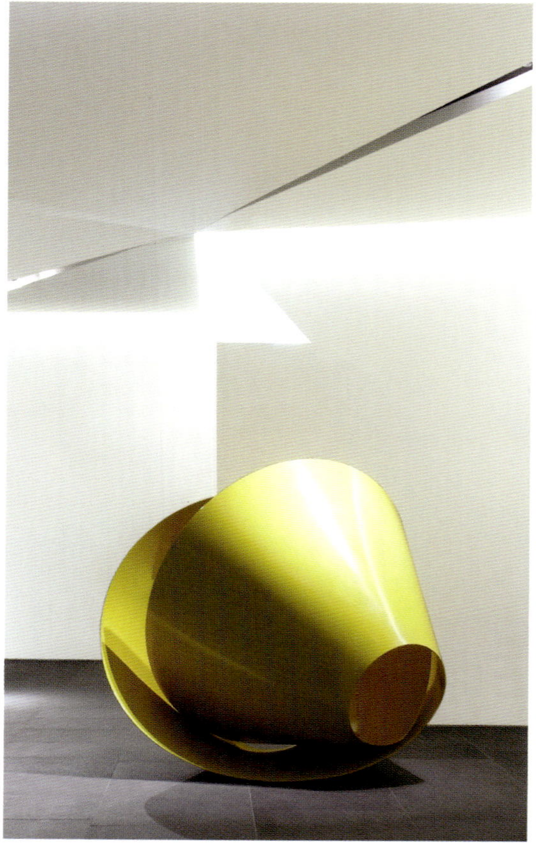

▸

Maquette for Involute, 2009
stainless steel,
500 x 550 x 550
Photo: Stefanie Flaubert

◂

Involute, 60 Clarence St, Sydney, New South Wales, 2009
powder coated steel,
1500 x 1500 x 1500
Photo: Sharrin Rees

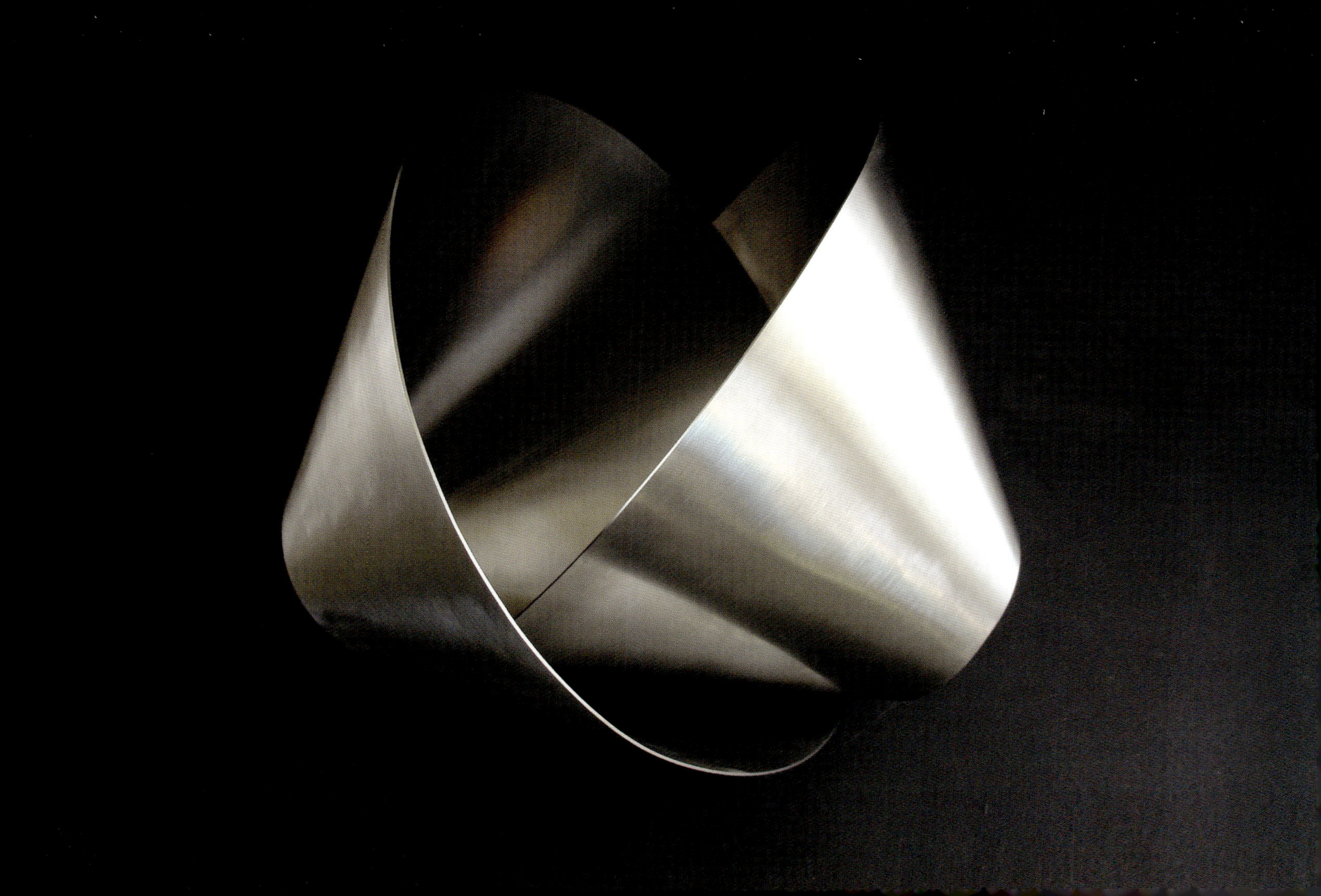

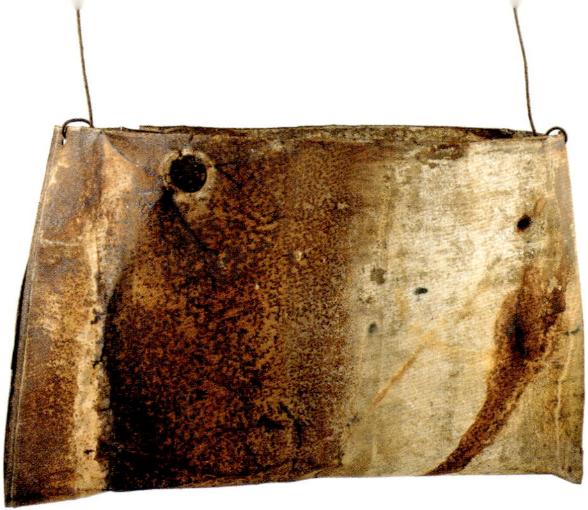

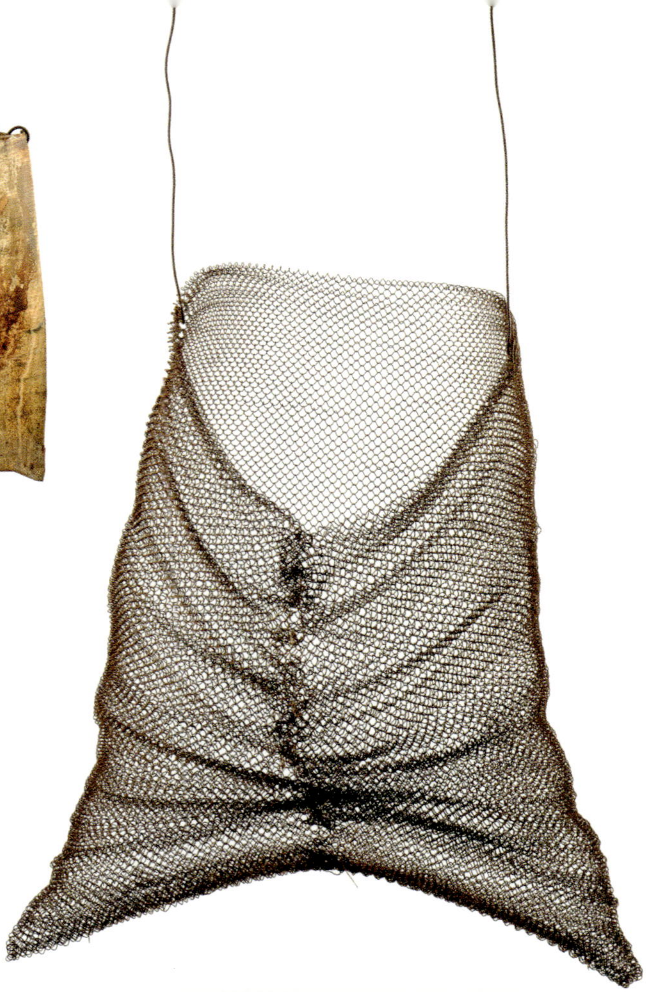

▲

Narrbong (fibre bags), 2009
rusted, galvanised iron with fencing wire 1610 x 910 x 230
Gift of Susan Armitage through the Art Gallery of South Australia Foundation 2015. Donated through the Australian Governments cultural gifts program. Collection of the ArtGallery of South Australia, Adelaide.

▶

Narrbong (fibre bags), 2009
bed base wire, fencing wire, 1780 x 890 x 660
Gift of Susan Armitage through the Art Gallery of South Australia Foundation 2015. Donated through the Australian Governments cultural gifts program. Collection of the Art Gallery of South Australia, Adelaide.

LORRAINE CONNELLY-NORTHEY

BORN 1962, SWAN HILL, VICTORIA
LIVES COROWA, NEW SOUTH WALES

THE SCULPTURAL WORKS of Lorraine Connelly-Northey entwine a poetry that speaks to the land, our colonial settler history and of a culture that is ever-present. The twisted wire and found objects – including iron and scrap metal – form cultural vessels that carry the duality of the many generations of her Waradgerie (Wiradjuri) and Irish ancestry, and her innovative approach to telling culture through this media has cemented her as one of Australia's most acclaimed Indigenous artists. The works have a gracefulness to their presence whilst embodying the harshness of a colonial legacy so heavily current in the landscape – wire and steel used to both fence First Peoples out and also to keep them in.

Cultural material such as canoes, baskets, koolimans (coolamon/ bush bowl), and narrbongs (fibre bags) that were made from the natural environment are molded out of wire and steel and take new form that represent Lorraine's[1] lived experience as a Waradgerie woman. Born in Swan Hill, Victoria in 1962 Lorraine grew up making and connecting to the concept of using found material. Working closely with her mother, learning to use her hands to create, Lorraine also had her foundations solidly placed in the environment. This was nurtured by her father, a farmer, who would share his knowledge about the landscape and the many thousands of years of Aboriginal connection to and occupation of the country. 'Dad would take me out bush and teach me what he had learnt about Mum's culture and about the bush. He taught me about the river, its tributaries, lake systems, Aboriginal sites and artefacts, nature, animals and plants, how to read rain clouds'[2].

Respect for the land and the Murray River informs her practice, as does the history of gathering, both in the sense of her Waradgerie ancestors who gathered to weave and provide food for community but also in the physicality of gathering rusted wire and metal from the landscape, collecting the 'dead' metal waste left on country and turning the material into inspired creations imbued with meaning and life.

1 As a Yorta Yorta curator and writer Kimberley Moulten's methodology is to refer to people she is writing about by their first names.

2 Connelly-Northey, L. In Munro, K essay. *unDisclosed 2nd Indigenous Art Triennial*, NGA. http://nga.gov.au/exhibition/undisclosed/Default.

The memory of stories told by her mother and the knowledge of the narrbongs that were made from local fibres by the loving, knowing hands of her ancestors are strong conceptual elements in Lorraine's work. It is this passing on of the matriarchal tradition that has been handed through thousands of generations that now sits with the artist. Extending these cultural traditions to the found and forgotten steel of the frontier was an inspired progression from her initial works in weaving, going on to make her first intricate wire narrbong in 2002. Over the years the scale and vision for the works have grown to develop into large-scale sculptural forms that have extended to steel monuments of possum skin cloaks, baskets and narrbongs. The woven creations of Lorraine's ancestors and the sculptured, twisted barbed-wire and steel of her works are but one in the same, they are her family's influence and her Waradgerie culture. Lorraine's works are instilled with the tradition of the old, however, instead of carrying the food from the land and river they carry memory and serve to honour this history, they are strong statements of the ongoing presence of culture. The life and materiality of the found wire and steel represent not only the imposition of the colonial settler and the ongoing desecration of the environment but is a manifestation of resilience ensuring the continuity of cultural practice while powerfully pushing the boundaries of contemporary Indigenous cultural expression and art making.

[redacted]

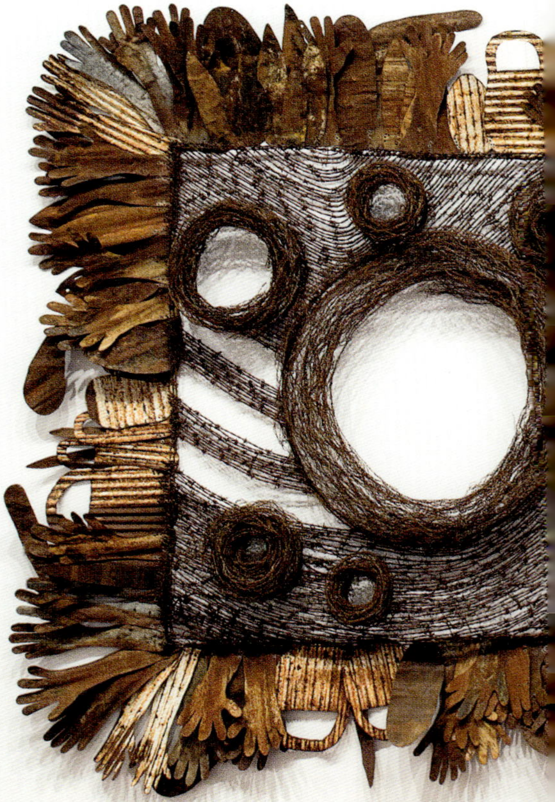

▸
Possum-skin cloak: Blackfella road, 2011-13
rusted iron and tin, fencing and barbed wire, wire, 2685 7030,
National Gallery of Victoria, Melbourne, purchased by NGV Supporters of Indigenous Art, 2014
© Lorraine Connelly-Northey

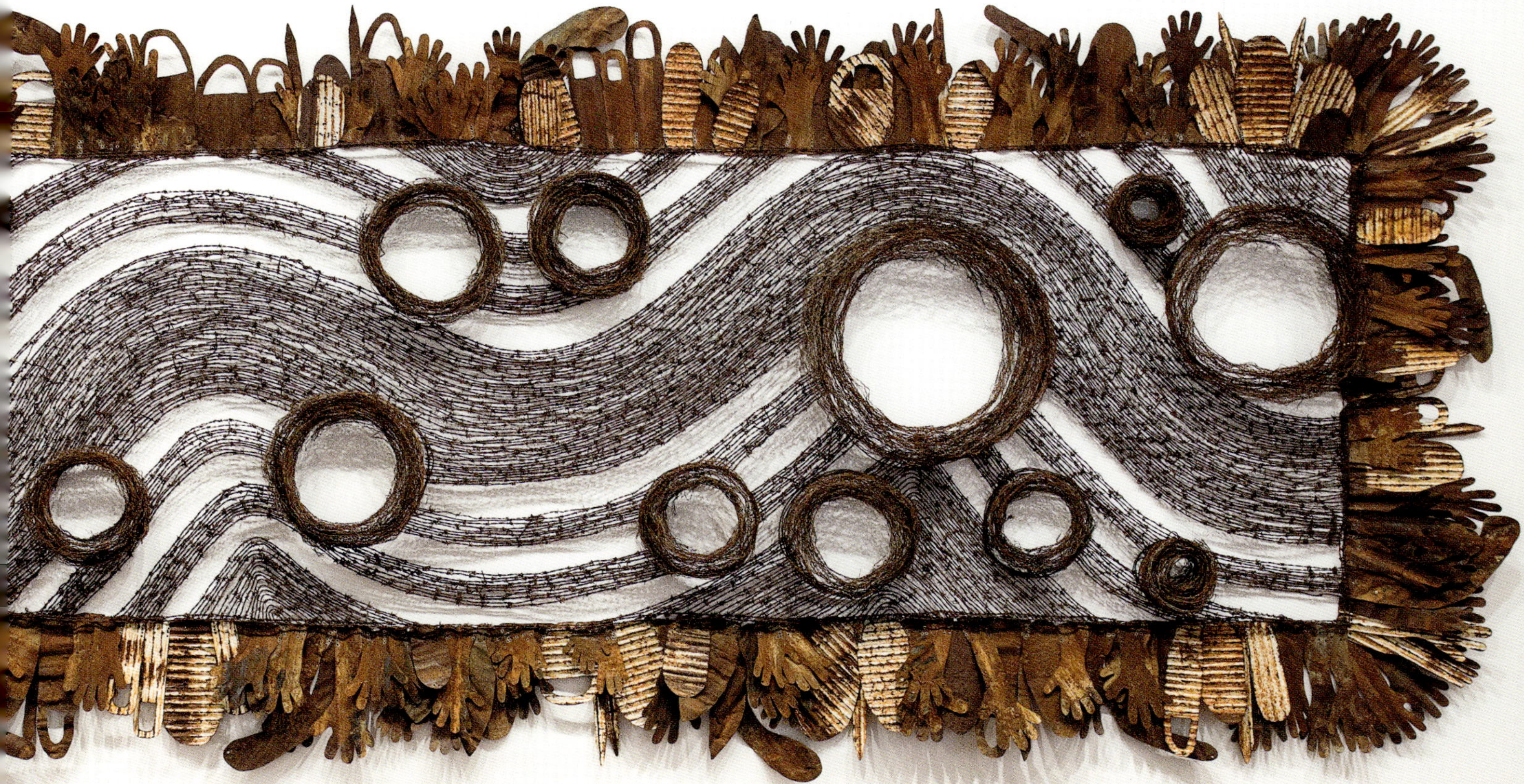

NARRBONG, **KOOLIMANS** AND **DIGGING STICK**

The works, *Narrbong (fibre bags)*, *Koolimans (coolamon/ bush bowl)* and *digging stick* of Lorraine Connelly-Northey reference the gathering of food and resources for thousands of generations by her Ancestors. This practice is also embedded in her own artistic development, ardently collecting found materials and reenvisaging them into sculptural forms of narrbongs and koolimans dishes used for collecting, cradling and winnowing. Making use of what is available from the landscape has shifted to what has been left and discarded, gathering barbed wire and sheets of metal, the rough rusted remnants are recycled and transformed into vessels speaking to the old ways and catapulting them to the present. The re-imaging of these materials into cultural forms speak of the past yet also explore Lorraine's Waradgerie culture in the here and now. The sculptural works are elegant reflections of what can continue to be achieved by honouring history and cultural practice of the old people, they are statements of sovereignty and Lorraine's connection to the land and are powerful guides of culture for generations to come. ■

KIMBERLEY MOULTON

[redacted]

▸

Narrbong (fibre bags),
Koolimans (coolamon/bush bowl)
and *digging stick*, 2016
rusted iron and pipe,
dimensions variable
Photo: Tom Roschi

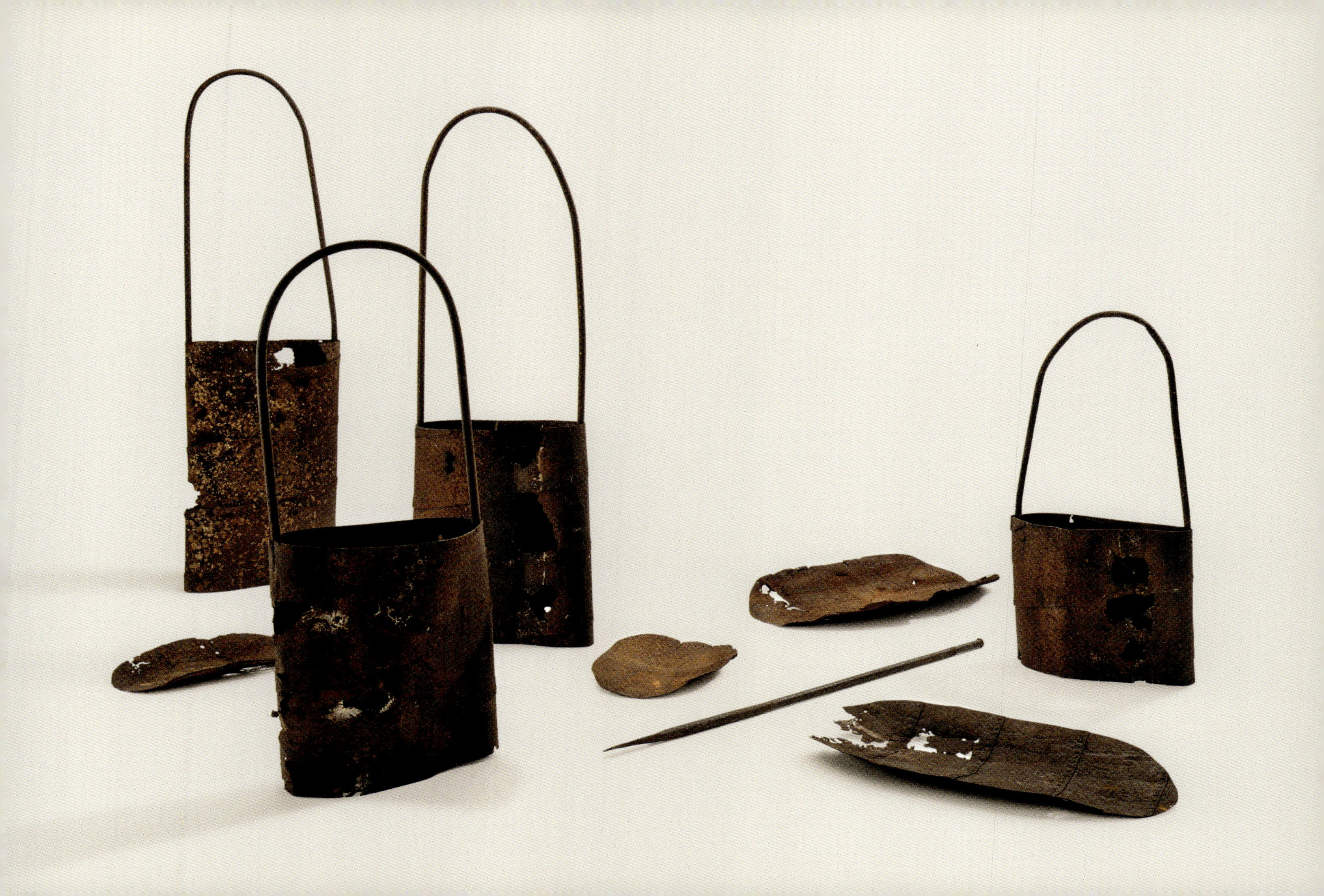

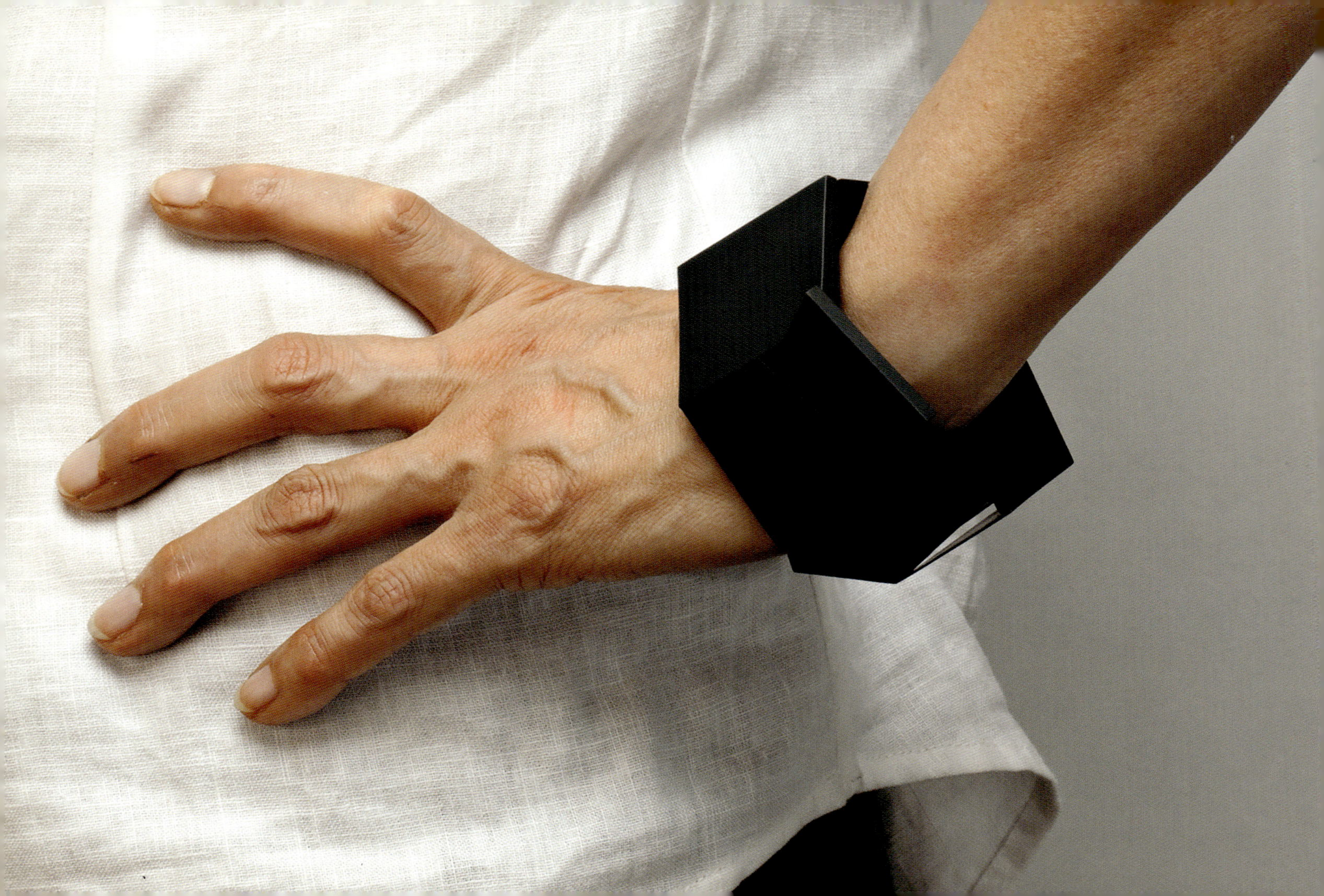

MARI FUNAKI

BORN 1950, MATSUE, JAPAN
DIED 2010, MELBOURNE, VICTORIA

MARI FUNAKI nearly always worked in gold and mild steel. In artist statements she wrote:

I have been dominantly using gold and mild steel. I am attracted to gold for being soft, having a rich colour and conveying a sense of purity; mild steel I like for being hard and sharp, conveying somberness and austerity, yet at the same time maintaining softness, warmth and purity...

It also creates a beautiful black, which adds depth to the shadows and delicate structures. Subtle shadows create a sense of mystery.[1]

Funaki's decisive choices speak to a distinctive vision, forged from Japanese culture and upbringing, and unleashed by Australian education and life in Melbourne. Profoundly intelligent and self-aware, Funaki understood that in every sense – as a woman, as an artist, as a cultural force in her adopted country – coming to Australia in 1979 made her. As she said:

People often find my work very Japanese in aesthetic. If I had remained in Japan, I would never have been doing what I am doing now. In Australia I learnt freedom to express myself and to build my own identity.[2]

Funaki trained in painting, then jewellery and metalsmithing at RMIT University in Melbourne. As a jeweller, she made splendidly angular rings, brooches, cuffs, and containers that owed a great deal to ceaseless drawing. In the last decade of her life, Funaki explored larger sculptural forms, eventually translating several into major public works, notably *Twilight*, 2010, now in the garden at the National Gallery of Australia in Canberra, Australian Capital Territory. These forms are drawn from an extensive group of exquisite sculptural objects that started, conceptually, as containers.

Funaki noted:

Packaging is one of the most recognisable characteristics in Japanese culture. The box is not just to contain something, but it is used to present something, to treat it with respect and add an air of anticipation.[3]

These rapidly developed a life of their own, for though firmly rooted in Japanese ways of seeing, Funaki's approach to making was always intuitive. And, while visiting her family in Japan, she had encountered the inspiration for her mature work:

It was spring and she was walking in a local park with her nephew who was interested in insects. He picked up a beetle. As Mari recalled, 'it was so beautiful and I held it in my hand and studied it, moving it around in my fingers'. This was, she felt, 'the three dimensional world, and I suddenly saw it so differently. It was a secret little world. There was so much expression, intricacy and unusual form in the beetle'.[4]

At first these riffs on containers sheltered actual hidden spaces, the kernel of the objects, but over time the forms became freer, more experimental, with internal spaces discernible only through close observation, and with new shapes added that suggested the built environment.

Alongside her practice, Funaki created Australia's most important private platform for exhibiting and supporting contemporary jewellery. Passionate in her commitment to art and design, Funaki saw that Australia's exceptional jewellers needed a showcase and in 1995 she opened Gallery Funaki, off the top end of Melbourne's Bourke Street. The tiny bolt-hole quickly became one of the world's best addresses for the finest contemporary jewellery, and continues today under the directorship of Katie Scott.

PREVIOUS PAGE
Mari Funaki wearing *Bracelet*, 2008
mild steel, heat coloured
Photo: Jeremy Dillon,
courtesy of the Estate of Mari Funaki

▸

Bracelet, 2006
mild steel, heat coloured,
80 x 76 x 47, private collection
Photo: Jeremy Dillon,
courtesy of the Estate of Mari Funaki

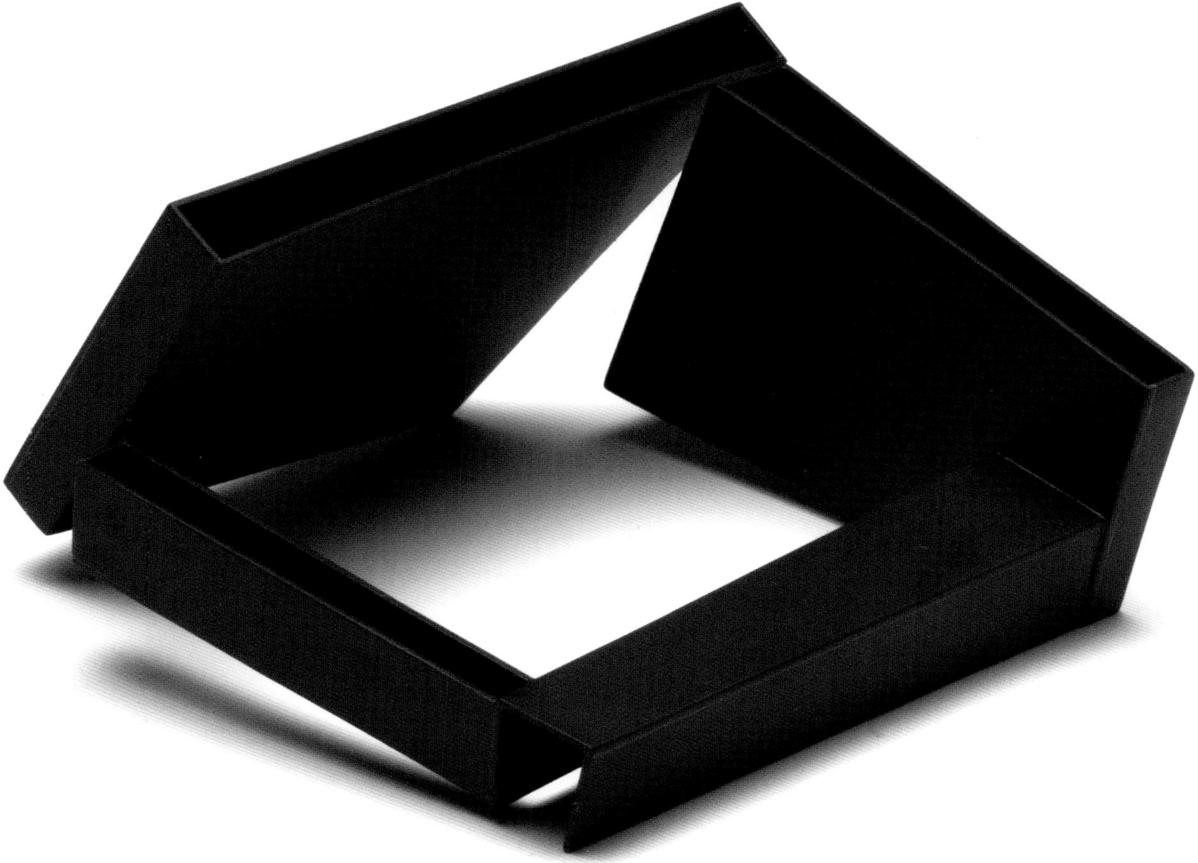

OBJECT

Mari Funaki subjected everything she made to intense scrutiny. I watched her considering her works, lined up on the kitchen table, from every angle: physically, conceptually, in their emotional impact. The small 'containers', in particular, were an evolved amalgam of many sources and life experiences. Here only two from the series *Object*, 2009, show vestiges of their origins as containers: they carry delicate coffin shapes atop spiky legs. Or are these the abdomens of peculiarly evolved creatures? In the end, no defining reference suffices. The sprightly shapes sometimes resemble insects, leaves, or other natural forms, but very often they are simply analogues of physical forces and principles, always beautifully resolved, often miraculously poised – the balance seems improbable, even deliciously precarious. The gently implied peril of Funaki's balancing act was captured by the distinguished Swiss jeweller Otto Künzli:

A stringent aesthetic imparts the dark, injured, fragmented and finally finely skilled, built and erected on a wilful beauty – an unwieldy elegance. Is this architecture, sculpture or three-dimensional cubist calligraphy? [5]

Working with a personal vocabulary, Funaki prized the affective aspects of each piece, the way it could suggest emotional states or stir memories. Refined, elegant, impeccable, her work distilled a lifetime of close observation into small moments of great beauty. ■

JULIE EWINGTON

1 Mari Funaki's artist statements, Gallery Funaki, Melbourne; the first is undated; the second is dated 2005.

2 Ibid.

3 Mari Funaki, artist statement, Gallery Funaki, 2010.

4 Cook, R. Art Gallery of Western Australia, May 2010, http://www.artgallery.wa.gov.au/about_us/Mari-Funaki.asp, accessed September 2016.

5 Künzli, O. (Translated by Johannes Hartfuss), *Cubist Calligraphy? Mari Funaki*, Gallery Funaki, 2007, p. 5.

OVERLEAF
left to right:
Object, 2009
heat coloured mild steel,
410 x 50 x 45

Object, 2009
heat coloured mild steel,
287 x 440 x 287

Object, 2009
heat coloured mild steel,
220 x 179 x 106

Object, 2009
heat coloured mild steel,
75 x 140 x 48

Private collection,
courtesy of Sotheby's Australia
Photo: Jeremy Dillon, courtesy of the National Gallery of Victoria and the Estate of Mari Funaki

▶
Object, 2009
heat coloured mild steel,
287 x 432 x 244
Private collection,
courtesy of Sotheby's Australia
Photo: Jeremy Dillon, courtesy of the National Gallery of Victoria and the Estate of Mari Funaki

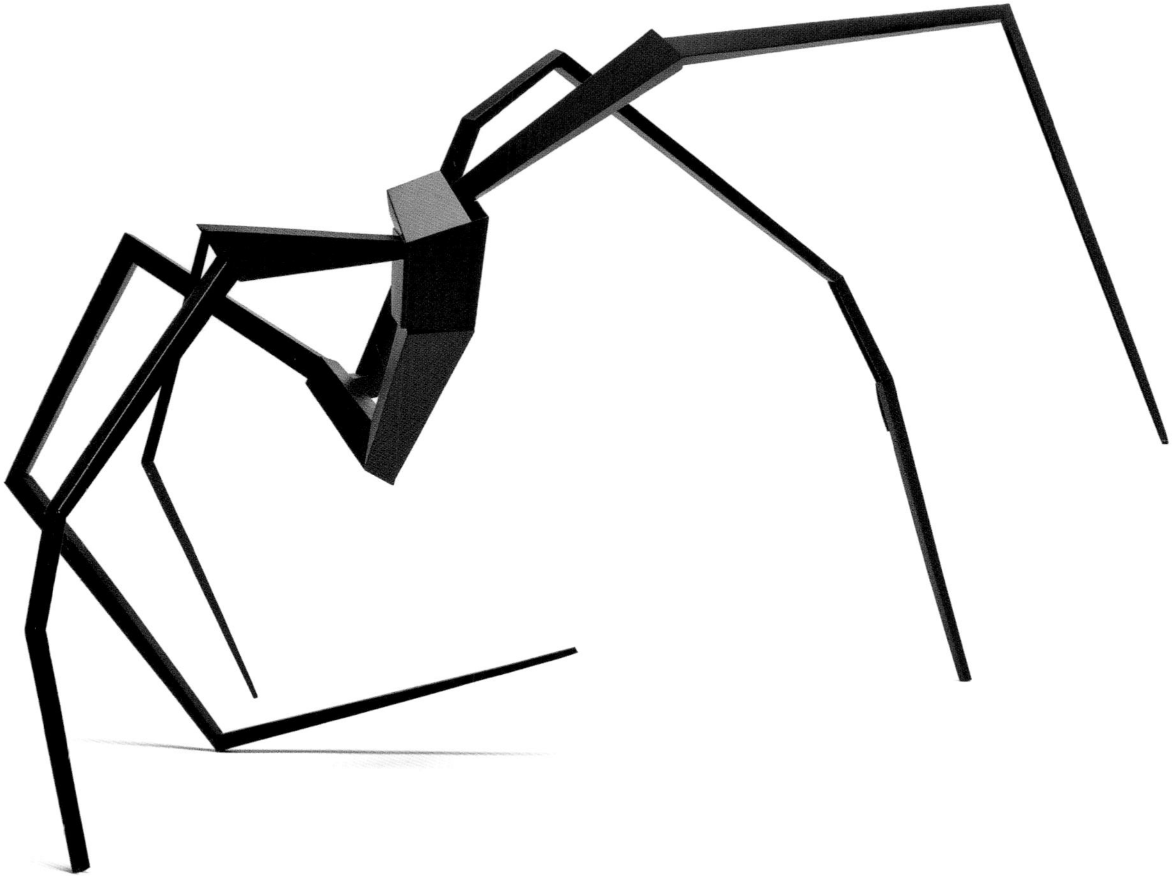

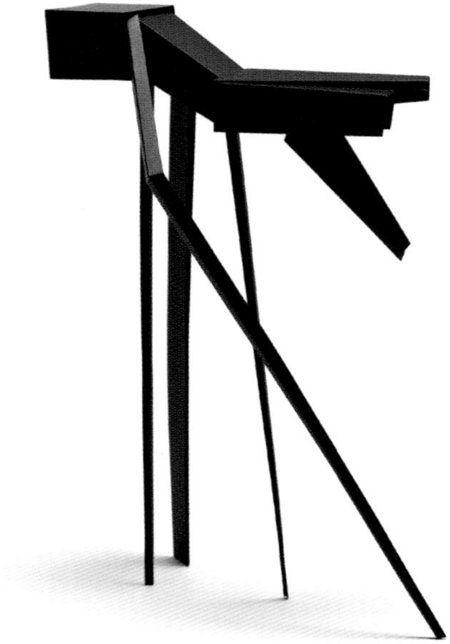

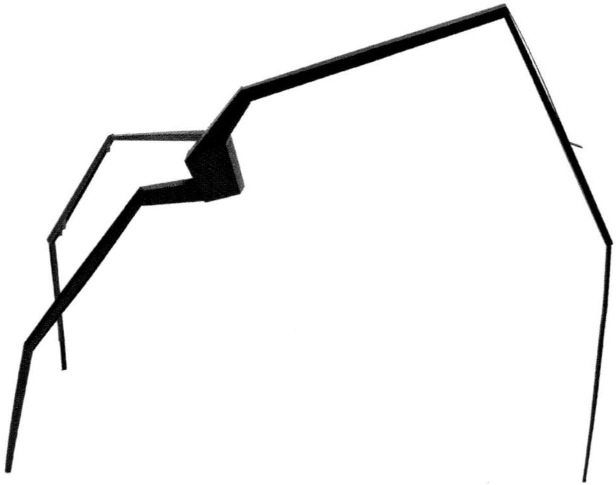

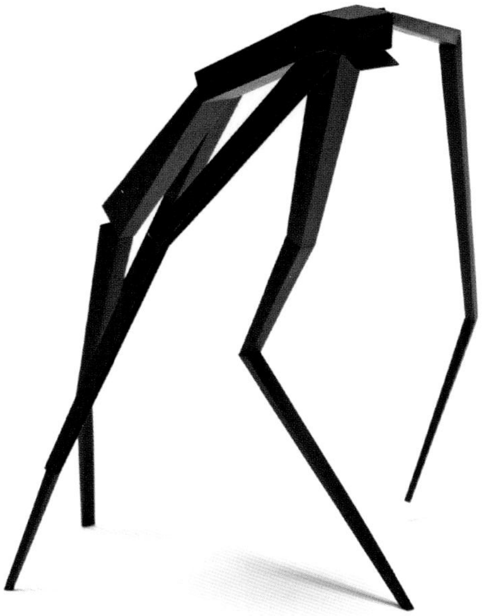

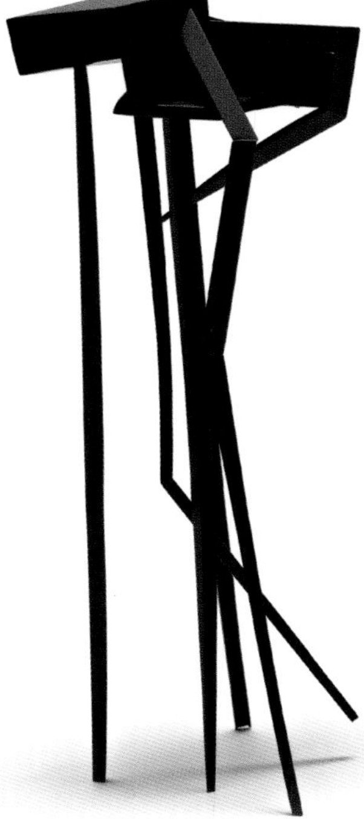

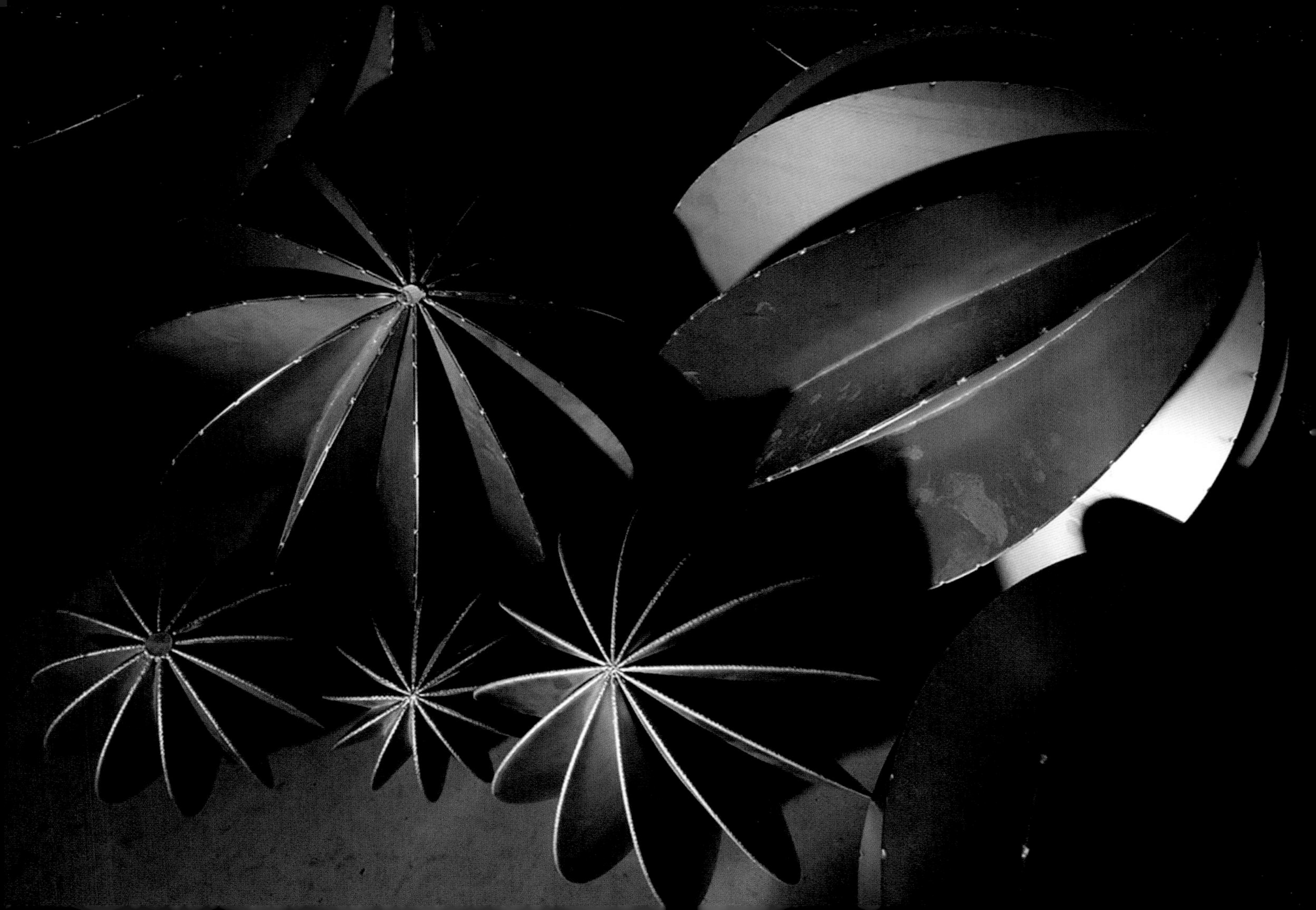

MATTHEW HARDING

BORN 1964, SYDNEY, NEW SOUTH WALES
LIVES TRENTHAM, VICTORIA

MATTHEW HARDING grew up watching his father manipulate material with his hands. A builder by day, Harding's father spent his free time shaping boats, a passion that forever instilled in Harding a love of, and respect for, the creative potential of raw materials.

Following in his father's footsteps, Harding originally trained as a carpenter. However, on the day he completed his apprenticeship, he promptly left and enrolled at the Hunter Street School of Art and Design in Newcastle (now the Newcastle TAFE) to pursue a career as an artist. He originally focused on painting, not equating 'art' with the material skills he had left behind in carpentry. It didn't take long for Harding to find his way into sculpture, with carving his technique of choice: 'Carving is a way of thinking that is distinct from other art practices. Most processes are constructive, additive, where you model a shape to take form. To carve is to reduce. It requires a different sense of visualisation, and I fell in love with that process.'[1]

The idea that a form emerges almost organically from a material, underpins much of Harding's work. He is a maker of forms, above all else. While much of his career has been spent creating permanent works for the public realm, Harding has adamantly held on to his need to work intuitively. 'I start off with a thought, with the material in hand. I look at it, and go with it. I try to maintain as much plasticity in the process as possible'.

Harding went on to study Furniture Design at the School of Art, Australian National University in 1992. He describes this experience as the pivotal moment where he was able to reconcile himself as both an artist and builder, '...because design bridges that. It removes all the divides between artist and artisan, between art and craft, art and design. As pure aspiration of form, art is design and design is art. They are both processes that are seeking to express an outcome.'

1 The quotes in this profile were recorded by the author in an interview with Matthew Harding.

Harding produces innovative art and design pieces, which utilise his unique sculptural sensibility and refined craftsmanship. Whether creating large-scale public art, sculpture pieces or design objects, Harding's tenacity and hunger to push the boundaries of what is possible are ever-apparent.

While diverse in materials and processes, Harding's works demonstrate a common theme and investigation into the experiential aspect of form and materiality. He creates objects to be interacted with, touched, and sat on. His are objects that reflect and morph; objects that have a vital and poetic relationship to their surrounding environment and the people who interact with them.

In a stellar career spanning almost three decades, Harding is renowned for his steel forms, both stainless steel and corten. His thorough understanding of material, and boundary-busting approaches has seen him reap countless accolades, and exhibit in group and solo shows across the globe, with his work held in public and private collections around both locally and internationally.

Alongside his art practice Harding has guest-lectured and taught in various higher education institutions across the country, including the Australian National University and the University of Tasmania. Cross-cultural collaboration and skill-sharing and transference has also been a particular area of interest for Harding, and he has actively participated in many cultural exchange platforms in Australia and abroad including symposia, collaborations and residencies.

[redacted]

PREVIOUS PAGE
Seeds of Thought, 2015
weathering steel, dimensions variable
Photo: Fred Kroh

[redacted]

▸
Matt Harding finishing sculptures in his studio, Trentham, Victoria.
Photo: Fred Kroh

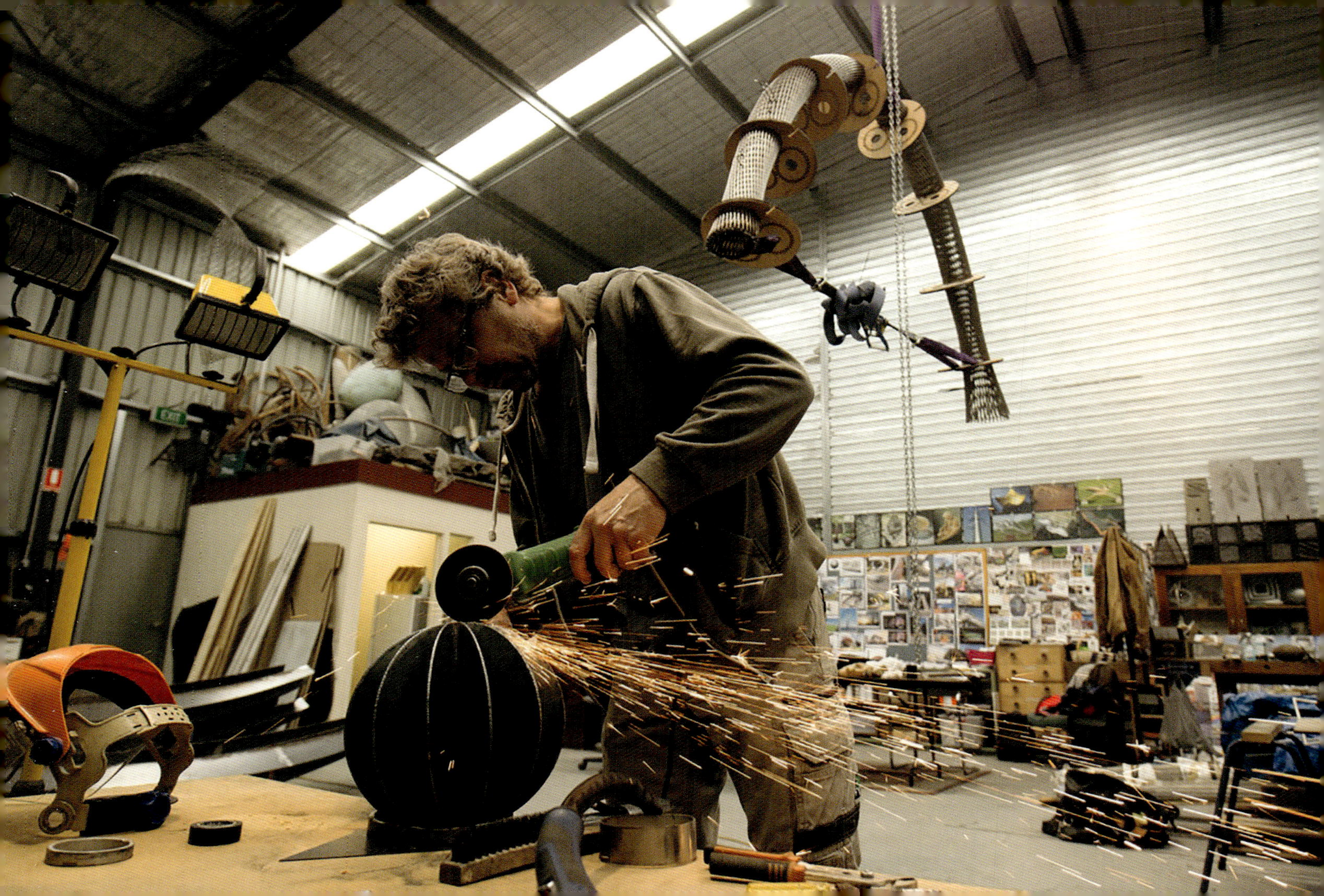

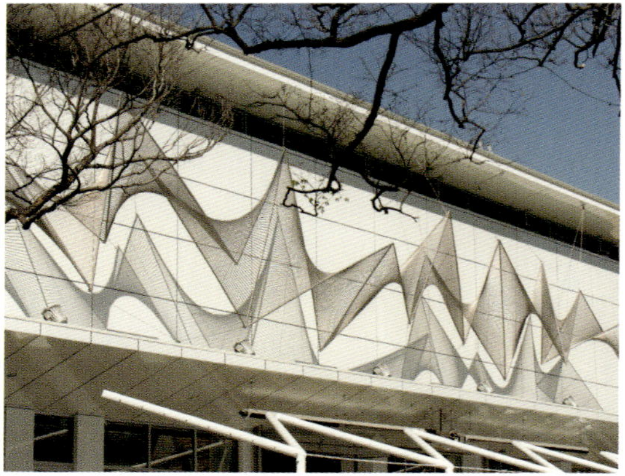

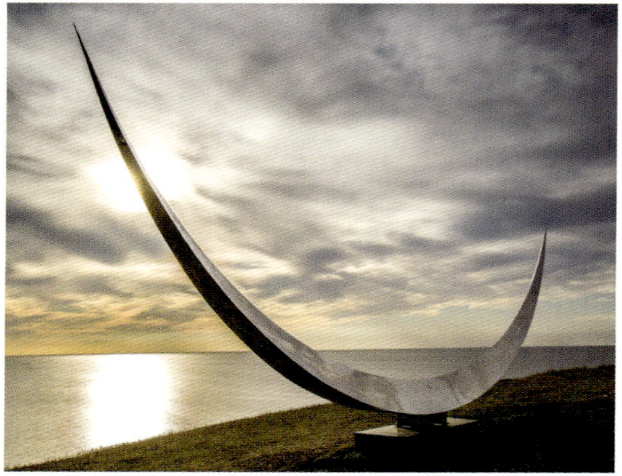

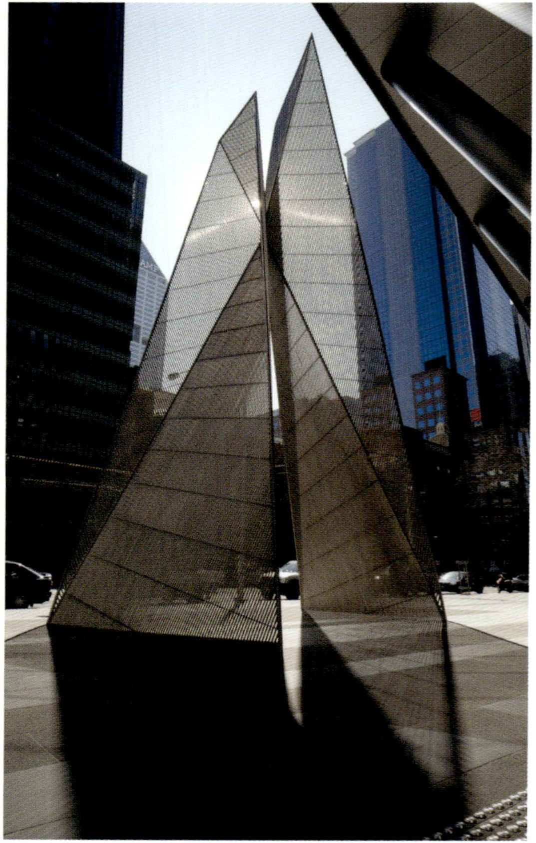

[redacted]

▸

Pipe Dreams, Pipemakers Park, Maribrynong, Victoria 2016
stainless steel, LED lighting, 12000 x 8000 dia
Photo: courtesy the artist

[redacted]

◤◤

Degrees of Separation, MAMA Gallery, Albury, New South Wales, 2015
stainless steel, LED/DMX lighting, 4000 x 30000 x 1500
Photo: Fred Kroh

◣◣

The Cheshire's Grin, Sculpture by the Sea, Bondi, New South Wales, 2013
stainless steel, 2400 x 6200 x 400
Photo: Gareth Carr

◂

567 Collins St, Melbourne Victoria, 2015
stainless steel, 14000 x 9000 x 4000
Photo: Fred Kroh

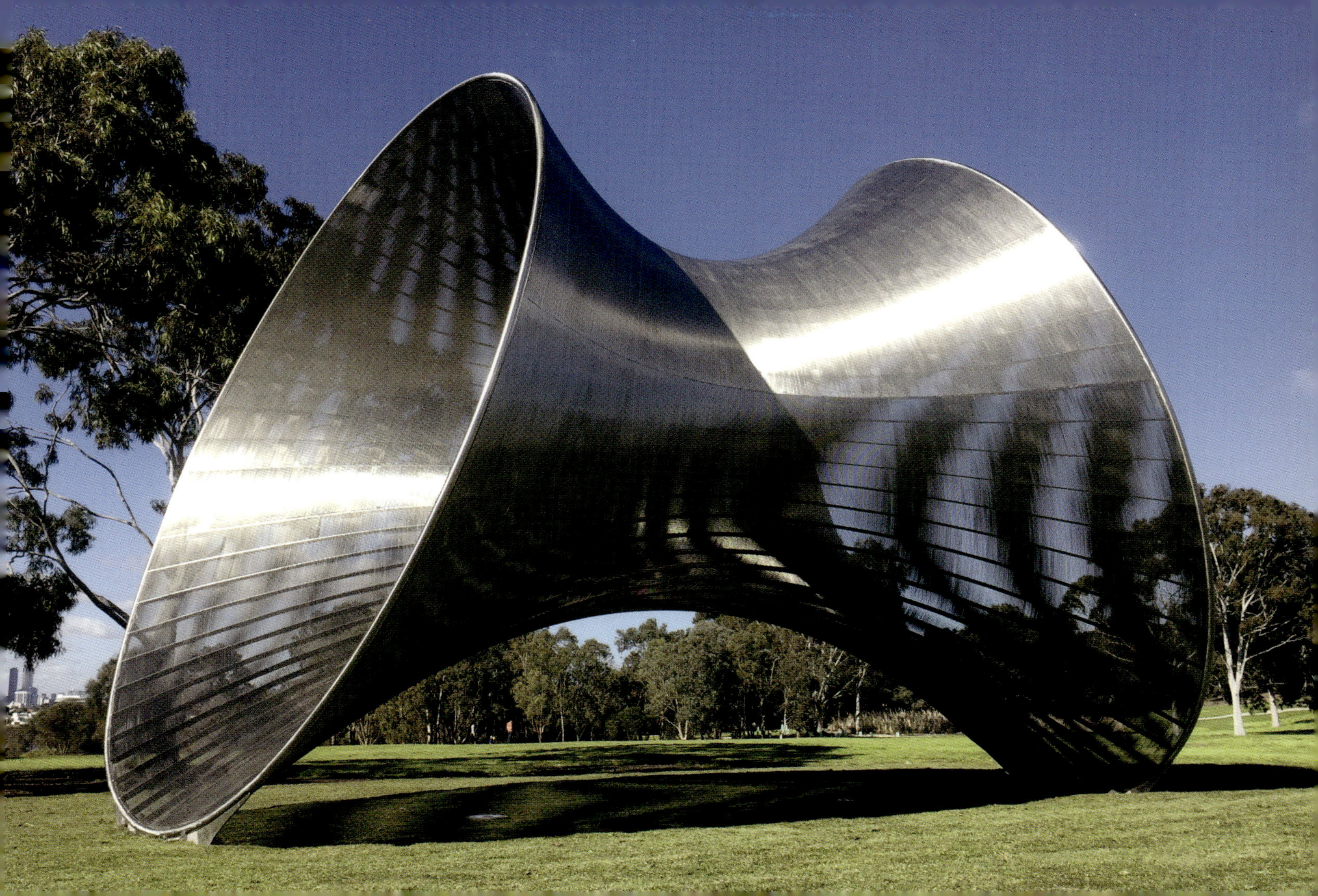

SEEDS OF THOUGHT

Taking inspiration from the shape of a seedpod, *Seeds of Thought*, 2015, continues Harding's interest in binary relationships, including growth and decay, strength and fragility, nature and humanity. The sculptures have been crafted from corten, which is a steel alloy that was originally developed for the building industry. Corten eliminates the need for painting, as a stable rust-like coating forms on the surface of the steel when exposed to weather conditions. As an artistic medium, the material embodies both man-made industry and the science of the natural world – a binary relationship central to the work of Harding.

'I first started creating seed forms in 2003 when the Canberra bushfires occurred. I was fascinated by the latent potential held within seeds and the regenerative abilities of the Australian bush,' says Harding. 'I am inspired by the process of growth, from germination to decay and regeneration. *Seeds of Thought* represents the poetics and transience of life cycles. I have utilised a number of metals in the production of these works: bronze, stainless steel and corten. I enjoy the contrast of material to subject – this is an organic form produced in a medium which cannot decay.' ■

DANIELLE ROBSON

[redacted]

▸

Seeds of Thought, 2015
weathering steel, dimensions variable
Photo: Fred Kroh

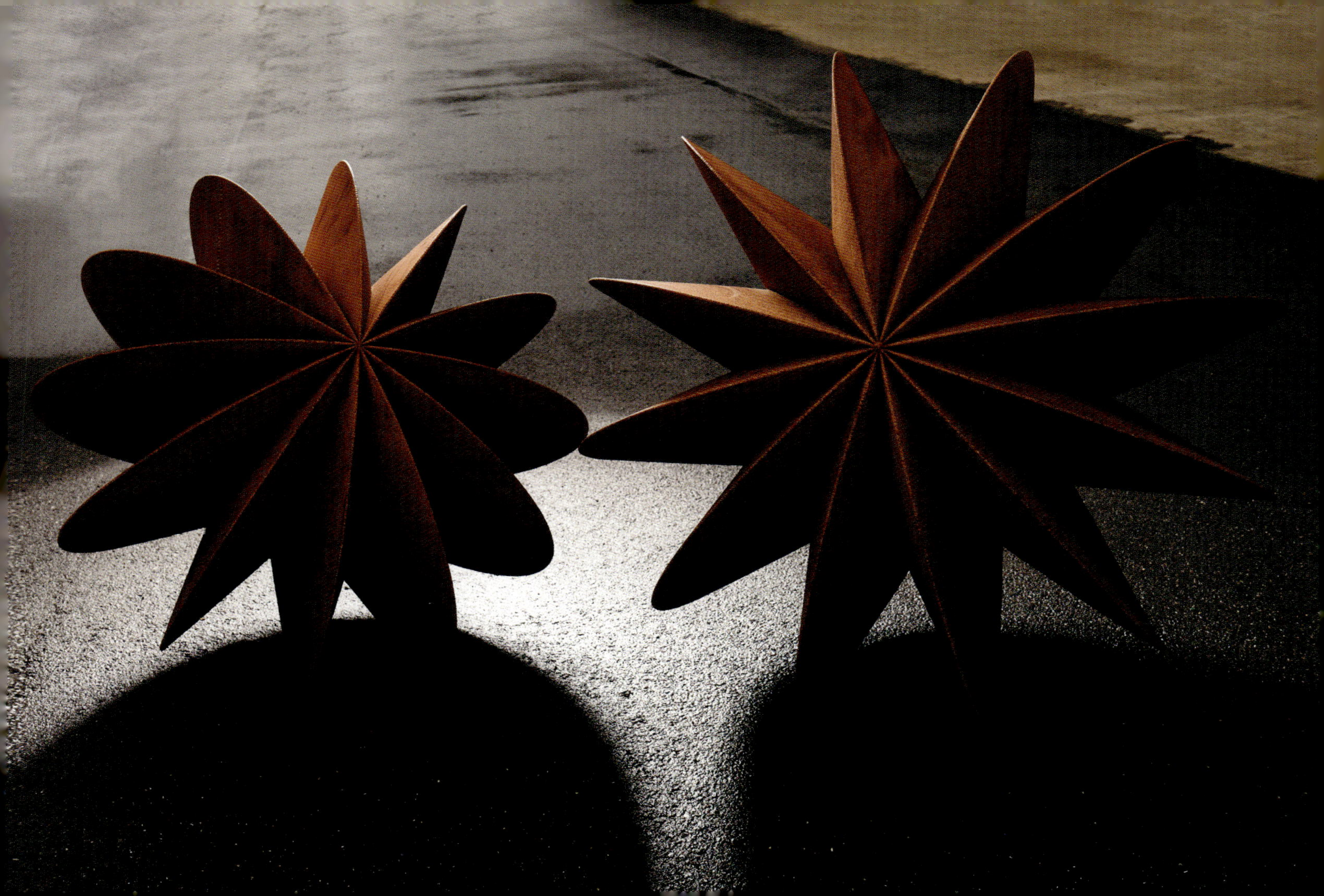

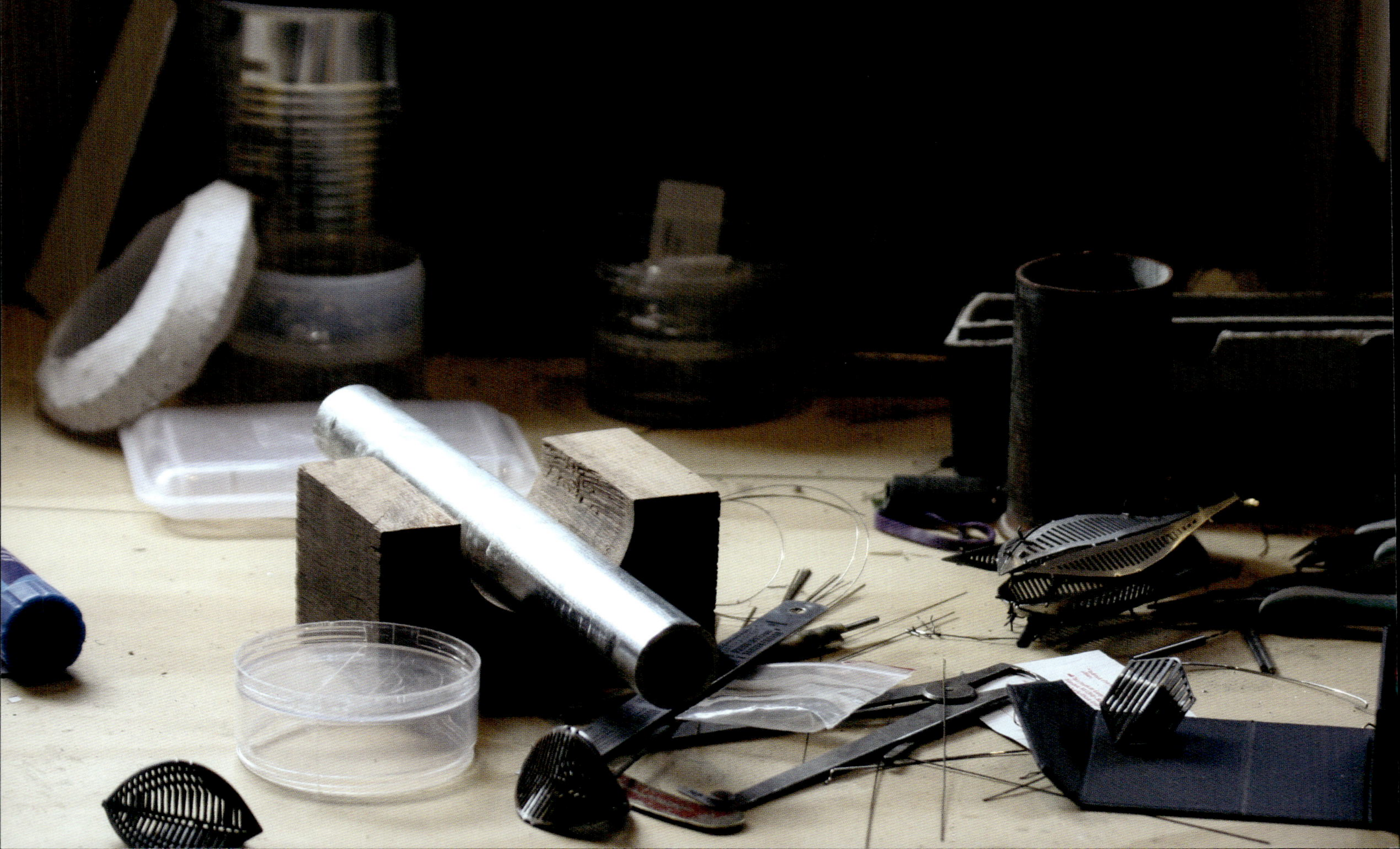

MAUREEN FAYE-CHAUHAN

BORN 1969, MELBOURNE, VICTORIA
LIVES MELBOURNE, VICTORIA

AT FIRST it may come as a surprise that the work of Maureen Faye-Chauhan is inspired by the natural world. Her jewellery formed with fine laser-cut steel components welded together seemingly hold a visual affinity closer to complex mathematical problems or possible designs for futuristic architectural projects, compared to the more sinuous lines and organic forms we usually equate with nature. However, Faye-Chauhan derives inspiration from her deep-seated and ongoing fascination for the way plants and other organic forms grow, develop and manifest themselves in the environment. As you delve into the forms of Faye-Chauhan's jewellery and investigate the world she inhabits, links to natural world abound.

Located in a semi-rural property an hour from Melbourne, Faye-Chauhan's studio and mud brick home are surrounded by dry bushland scrub. Its subdued palette of greys, greens and sand rewards the conscientious observer as the dappled light plays across the surfaces of gums, rocks and shrubs to create an ever-shifting landscape of subtle differences. This trick of the light, finds expression in Faye-Chauhan's jewellery. Generated with fine steel planes perforated with holes accentuating the form, Faye-Chauhan's jewellery creates optical effects that reflect her fascination with moiré patterns and the play of light. These patterns are further expressed when the brooches, necklaces or earrings are worn, as the movement of the wearer's body further enlivens the angles and planes.

Walking through her local environment Faye-Chauhan's trained eye looks to the varying growth patterns in nature. Returning to the studio, Faye-Chauhan has created a quiet contemplative space that allows her to strip back the world, and to focus closely on the fundamental geometric patterns, nature's building blocks. This idea of building is analogous to her own creative process as she describes 'for an artist, part of the creative process is bringing forth something from nothing, ideas develop, a drawn line closes and becomes a shape, and through the manipulation of space, that shape becomes a form.'[1]

Having the neurological condition 'aphantasia' Faye-Chauhan is unable to visualise mental images. So what does that mean for a maker? This has led her to work more readily with three-dimensional computer programs for the realisation of her forms and jewellery, and likely explains her extensive use of paper models. Starting with a concept she wishes to interrogate, her mode of working with these programs is more akin to a traditional jeweller's method of material investigation. She jumps from one platform to the next pushing each program to the edge of her knowledge, just as one may manipulate a material to its extremes.

Faye-Chauhan studied at Monash University under the tutelage of respected Australian jewellers Marian Hoskings and Mascha Moje, completing a Master of Fine Art in 2008. Her work has been exhibited at leading internationally events including Schmuck Munich in Germany and SOFA New York in the United States. In 2015 Faye-Chauhan was awarded the Australian Decorative and Fine Art Societies Emerging Artist Award at The BUDA Contemporary Australian Silver and Metalwork Awards for her *Concurrence*, 2015, and *Shell*, 2015, brooches.

PREVIOUS PAGE
Maureen Faye-Chauhan studio located in bushland outside of Melbourne.
Photo: Janak Chauhan

▸

Expansion and Contraction brooches
from the *Cluster* series, 2008
heat coloured mild steel,
left: 85 x 55 x 40,
right: 60 x 40 x 40
Photo: Janak Chauhan

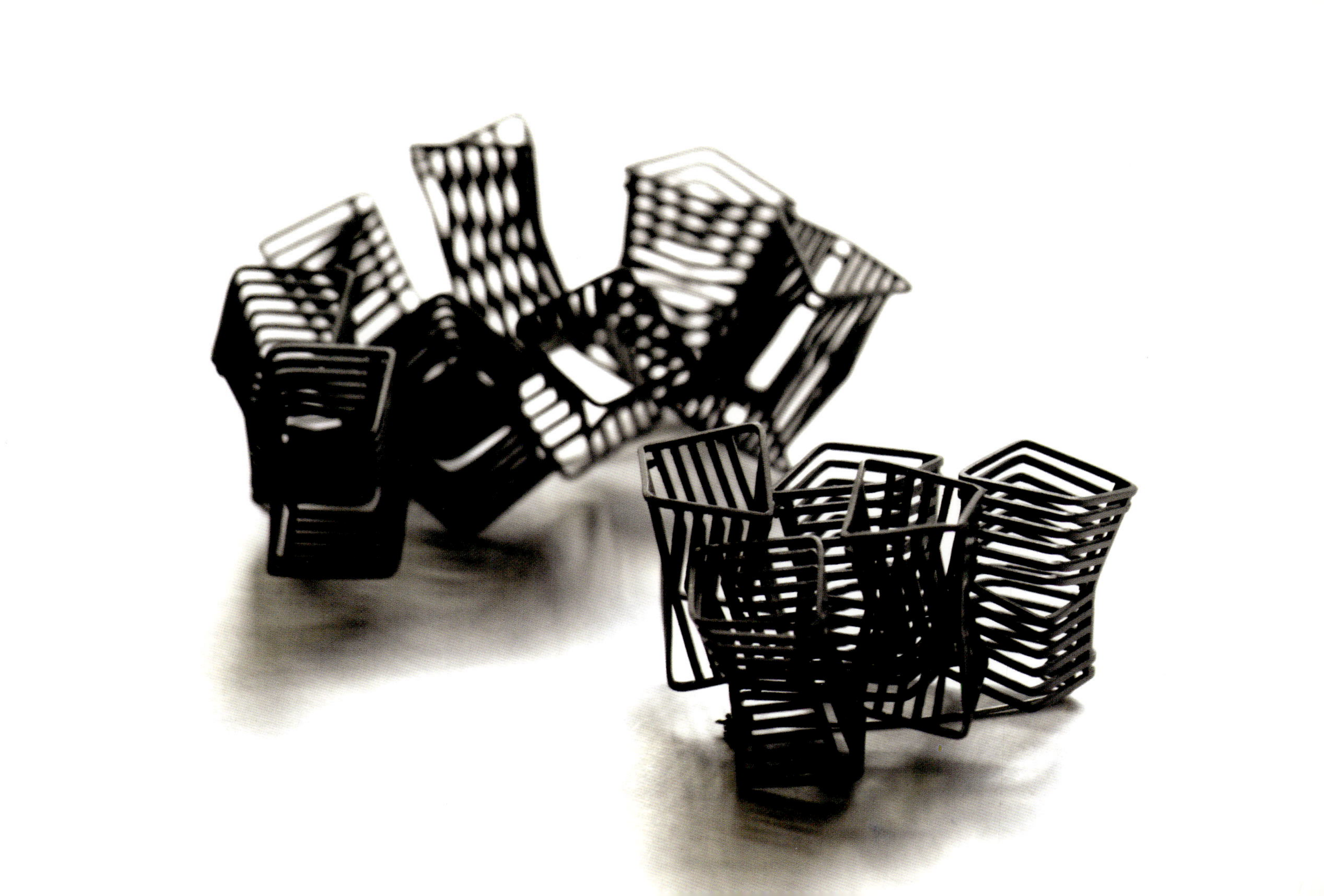

1 http://www.mfayechauhan.com/, accessed July 2016

2 https://artjewelryforum.org/artists/maureen-faye-Faye-Chauhan-concurrence, accessed July 2016

BROOCHES 2008-2016

Working across computer-aided design platforms such as Rhino and Grasshopper, Faye-Chauhan describes her process of making as such:

I might use a technique from one application to do one thing and then move on to another application for the next part, and then head back to the original platform for the next. This is probably not the simplest way of doing things, but perhaps this technique adds to the vitality of the finished works.

I also bring the unfolded forms out of the computer halfway through this process to get a feel of them in the material world. I make numerous paper models, which is a little tedious but necessary, for to work well in context with the body it is crucial to understand how the actual shape and volume of a piece actually feels in the hand. At a later stage I also construct black and white printed acetate models, which is essential for understanding the play of light, pattern, and interaction between both positive and negative space within certain forms.

When the artwork design process is completed, they are laser cut and once back in the studio I start re-forming them using my TIG welder. Some parts come together fluidly and some require brute force. I learned early on that stainless steel doesn't always fold together as easily as paper.[2] ■

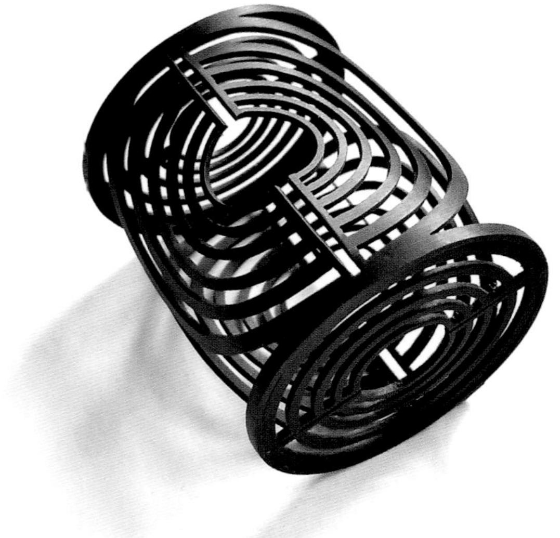

▸ left to right:
En-trance, 2006
heat coloured mild steel,
48 x 40 x 40
Photo: Janak Chauhan

Cellular brooches
from the *Cluster* series, 2008
heat coloured mild steel,
left: 85 x 80 x45,
right: 70 x 40 x 30
Photo: Janeck Chauhan

Basket brooch, 2013
heat coloured mild steel,
105 x 50 x 40
Photo: Jeremy Dillon

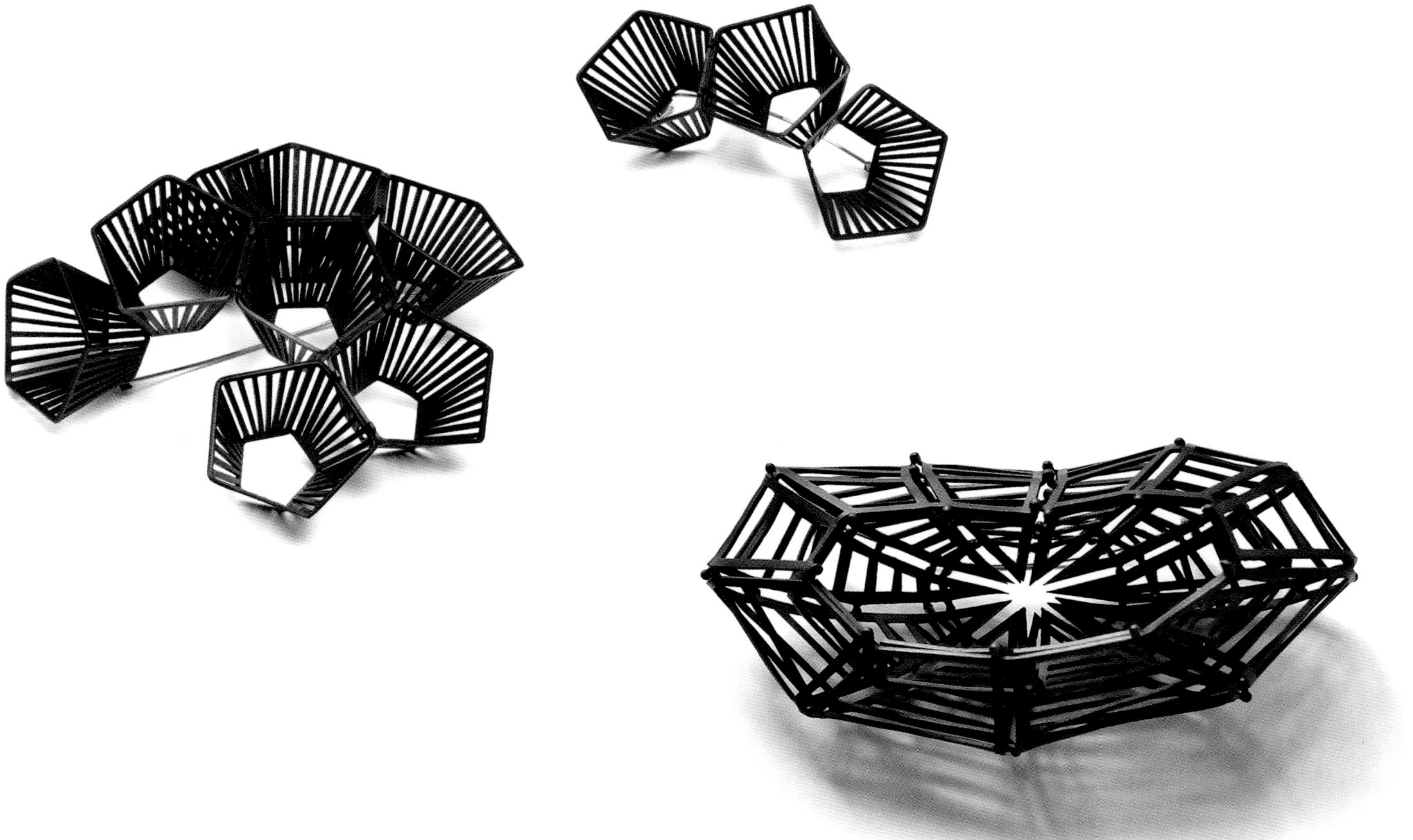

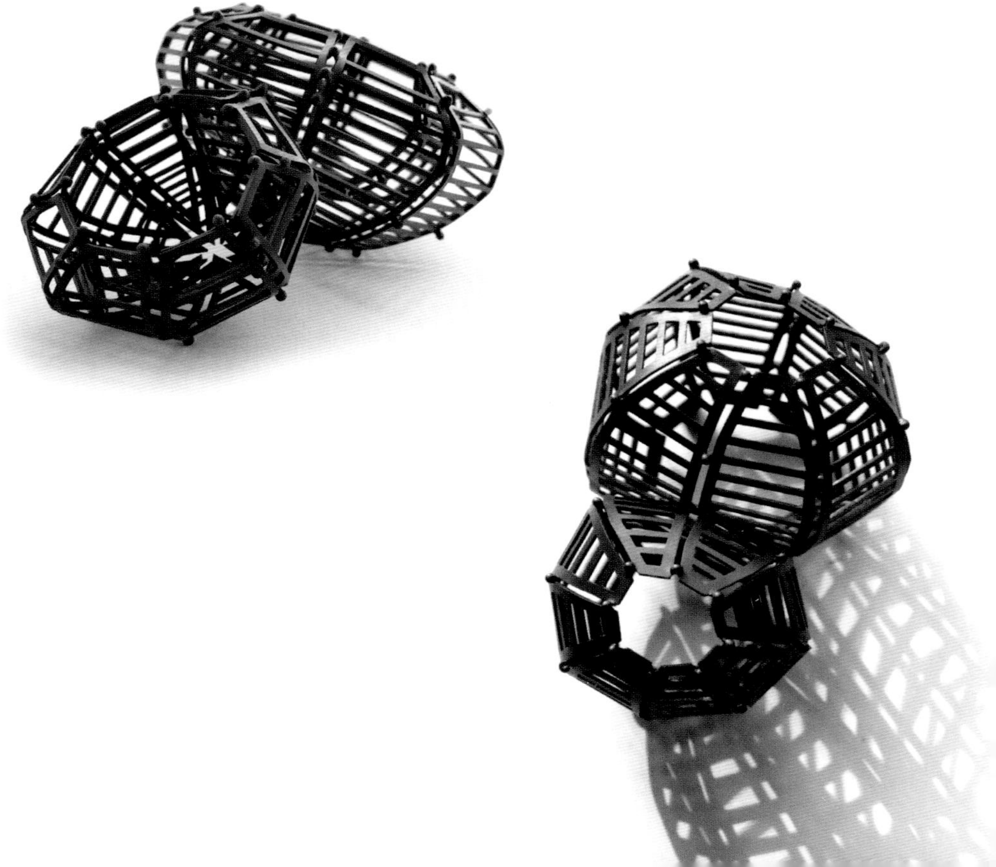

left to right:
Two cups brooch, 2013
heat coloured mild steel,
105 x 60 x 60
Photo: Janeck Chauhan

Duo brooch, 2015
heat coloured mild steel,
80 x 55 x 55
Photo: Janeck Chauhan

Concurrence brooch, 2015
heat coloured mild steel,
80 x 80 x 15
Photo: Janeck Chauhan

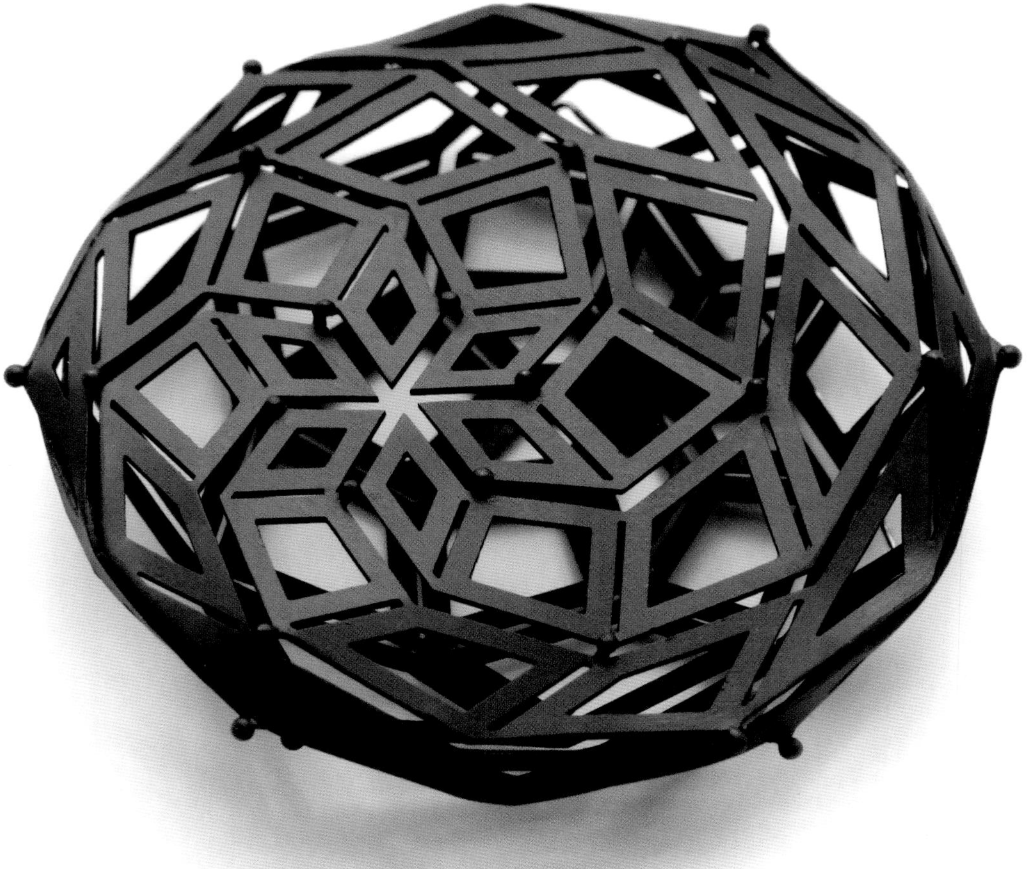

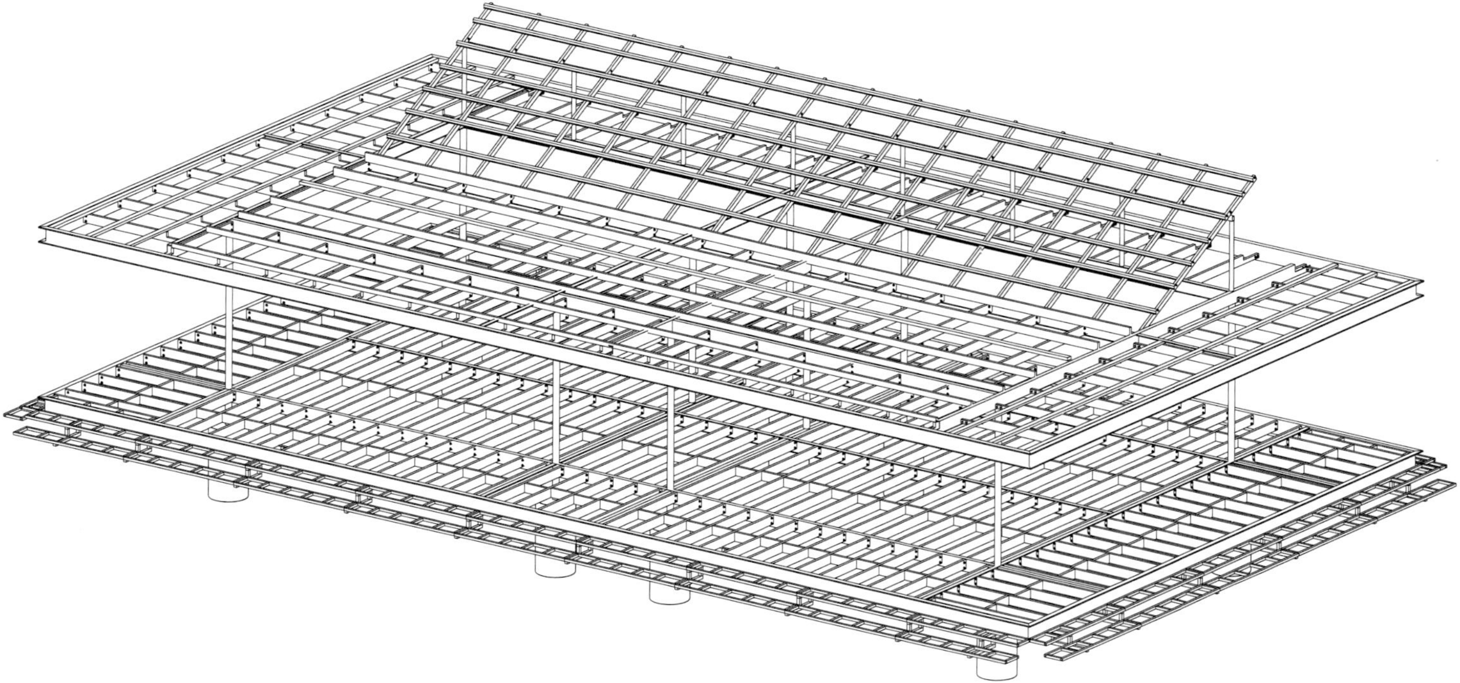

MISHO + ASSOCIATES

ESTABLISHED 1991, SYDNEY, NEW SOUTH WALES

MISHO VASILJEVICH
BORN 1964, LEVIN, NEW ZEALAND
LIVES HUONVILLE, TASMANIA

MISHO + ASSOCIATES is an Australian architectural practice that works across both commercial and residential design and architecture. Misho + Associates' director, Misho Vasiljevich's philosophy towards the built environment is 'that while architectural form must be exciting and visually stimulating, it should always be pragmatic and functional.'[1] From large-scale projects such as the proposed new zoo in western Sydney and the redevelopment of Hobart International Airport, through to modest homes, this pragmatism for good design can be achieved, as Vasiljevich states, by cleverly responding to the site and the climate in which the building is to be sited.

After many years working and living in Sydney, Vasiljevich made the decision to move his home and practice to the beautiful Huonville, south of Hobart in Tasmania. His 2005 move was in many ways driven by his desire to practice what he preached in terms of energy efficiency and sustainability – issues he could not adequately address whilst living in apartments under body corporate restrictions in the city.

Located on a steep block of reclaimed farming land with sweeping views across the Huon Valley, his home and studio have become working laboratories for his ideals. Initially living and working from a converted 80 square metre shed, Vasiljevich took time to engage with the seasons, prevailing winds and light on property before deciding where best to position his future home.

Thinking about what could be the most efficient home for him and his partner jeweller Linda van Niekerk, the resultant 36-square-metre 'box' cantilevers out from the hill. The structure has an external walkway shielded on three sides with galvanised steel screens. For Vasiljevich, the use of steel was an obvious choice. 'Galvanised steel embodies one third of the energy of aluminium and is structurally more efficient than timber, which is why it was chosen for the external facade skin. The other facade skin is thin steel, which heats up and cools down faster due to its thinness. This prevents the internal skin from taking the heat load and keeps the internal space at a comfortable temperature.'[2]

In a nod to his playful nature Vasiljevich planted a ring of callistemon circling his studio. Not only do they attract the local wildlife Vasiljevich notes that he is be able to easily locate his property on Google Earth when they are in bloom.

In 2010, Vasiljevich was able to revisit his home design. As part of Victoria's State of Design Festival green magazine developed an exhibition that questioned the trajectory over last the 50 years of the ever expanding Australian home. In an attempt to shift the mindset from 'bigger is better to smaller is smarter', the magazine invited selected architects to respond to a sustainable housing brief. The brief asked architects for a modest but highly liveable home for a family of four, that used sustainable materials and demonstrated thermal and energy efficiency. The resultant exhibition *Scale vs. Status* presented an array of alternatives or propositions about how the built environment can be handled.

This brief was well suited to Vasiljevich who bemoaned the 'McMansions popping up in Australian capital cities – "hideous developments", he insists, "inappropriate for the landscape, with paper-thin walls and no insulation"'[3] and the ever growing excess leading to demands on our finite resources. His submission was a 78-square-metre house based on the principles he had employed on his own home designs. Again using the structure of a box within a box, the design takes the 36-square-metre envelope of Vasiljevich's home, the 'box', and places a second 36-square-metre box side-by-side. These boxes are then separated by a wet area down the centre of the building.

The DNA for the Premaydena House was formed.

1 http://www.misho.com.au/misho.html, accessed August 2016.

2 Kennedy, S., *Huon Valley Box*, green magazine, 2009.

3 Zamiatin, L., *Building Blocks*, McGrath The Weekly Magazine, 22 April, 2006.

4 Eichbatt, S., *Into the wild*, Dwell – at home in the modern world. Small Spaces, November 2015.

5 McGillick, P., *Paradise Found*, Steel Profile, #120, May 2015.

[redacted]

PREVIOUS PAGE
CAD drawings of the Premaydena House, Premaydena, Tasmania, 2013.

[redacted]

◥
The colours of the sliding screens are matched to the fiery lichen ubiquitous to the local beaches.
Photo: Peter Whyte

◢
The house is located on the site to make the most of the beautiful views in southern Tasmania.
Photo: Misho + Associates

▸▸
The house is a steel frame construction.
Photo: courtesy of the artists
Photo: Misho + Associates

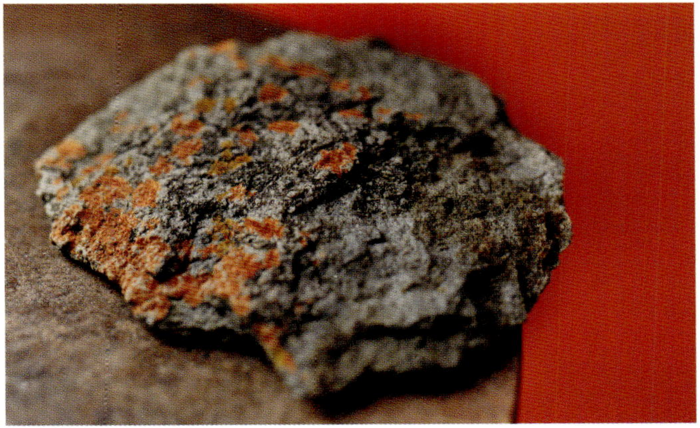

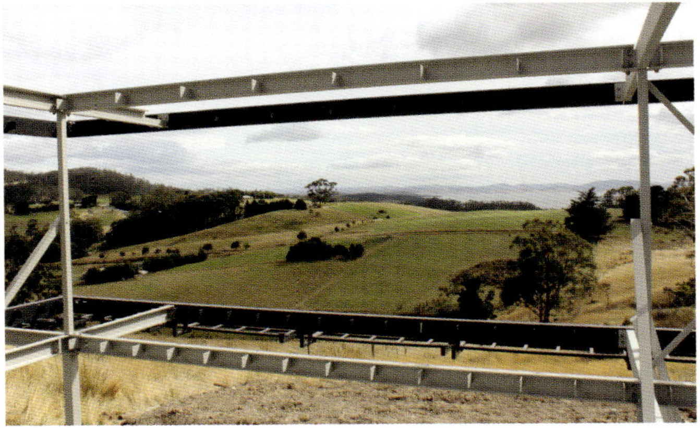

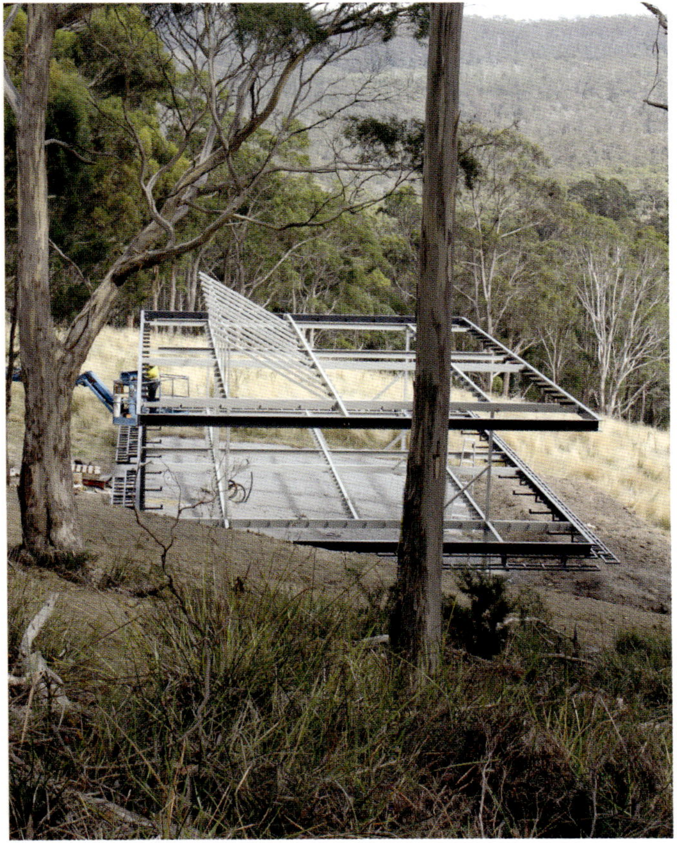

PREMAYDENA HOUSE

The remote Tasman Peninsula of Southern Tasmania is a wild and pristine landscape, its rugged terrain calls for exciting and environmentally-conscious self-sufficient housing design that provides suitable protection from the elements. Premaydena House, 2013, is one such low impact home. Built on a site weathered by both the icy-cold winds from the Southern Ocean and salty, wet winds from the north east, the home is sited half way up a rocky escarpment where a stand of eucalyptus buffers the southerly whilst the brightly-coloured steel screens surrounding the verandah of the home can be completely shuttered or left open as the weather dictates. The screens also provide a unique solution for security as Vasiljevich notes 'the house has been designed so you can basically shut it down and walk away'.[4]

Facing north overlooking Norfolk Bay this box within a box is raised upon a podium and is aptly described by Paul McGillick as 'a subtle re-purposing and a thoroughly appropriate application of the Japanese aesthetic in a distinctly different climate and landscape using contemporary materials, notably, steel.'[5] Due to the isolation of the site the building's structure of steel was prefabricated in Launceston decreasing impact on the site during construction and availing the frame to be erected in two days. ■

MARGARET HANCOCK DAVIS

[redacted]

▶

The house is highly visible due to the external red and orange galvanized steel screens.
Photo: Lucas Allen

OVERLEAF
To address the issue of cold, salty wind, the house is 'a box within a box'. Sliding steel screens allow the house to be opened up or inversely closed down depending on the conditions.
Photos: Peter Whyte

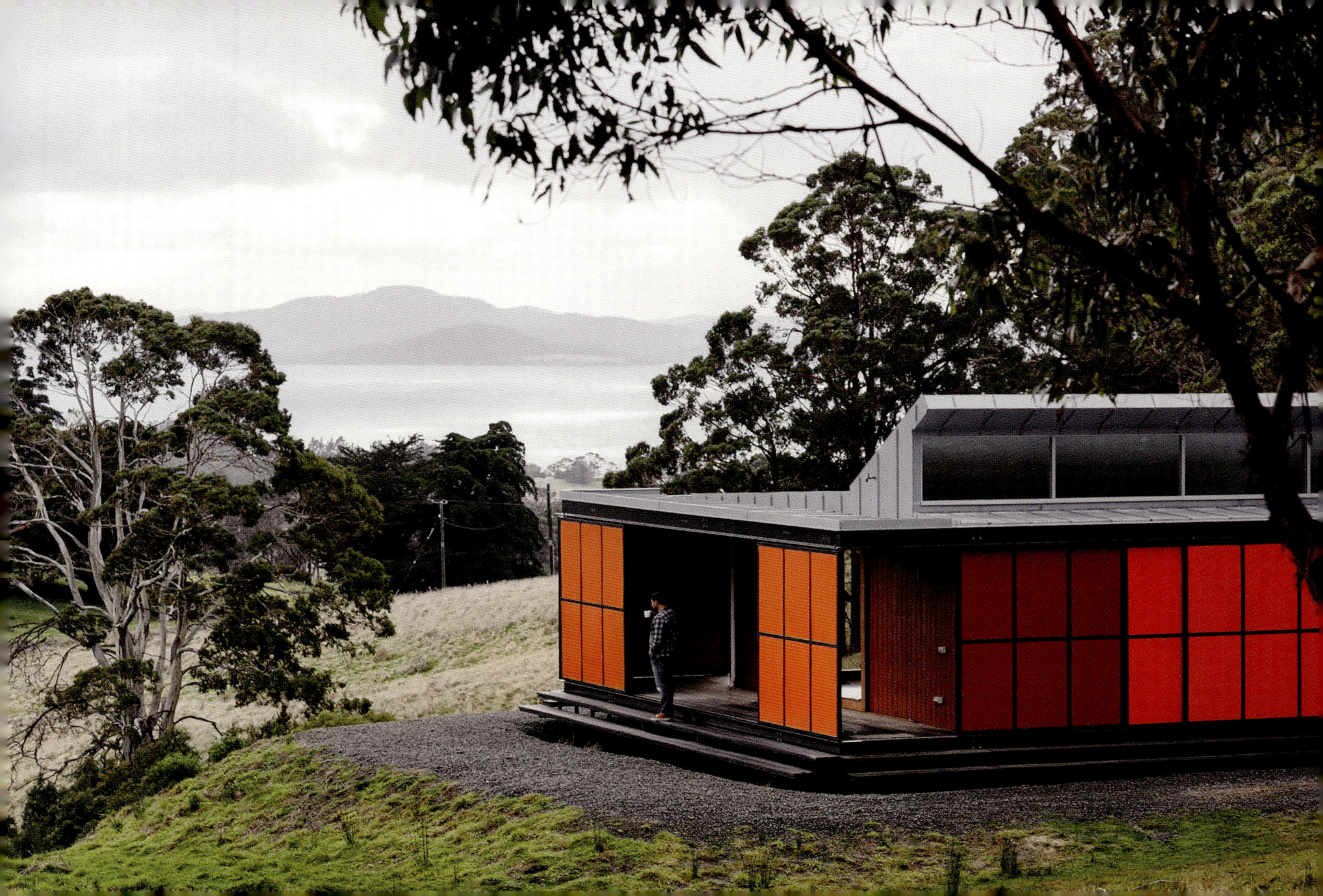

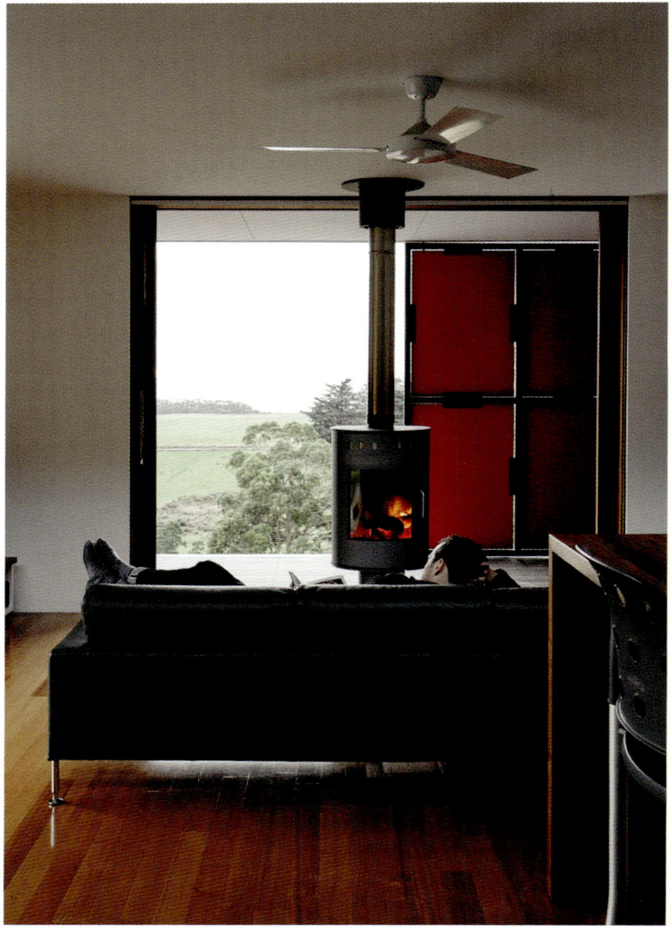

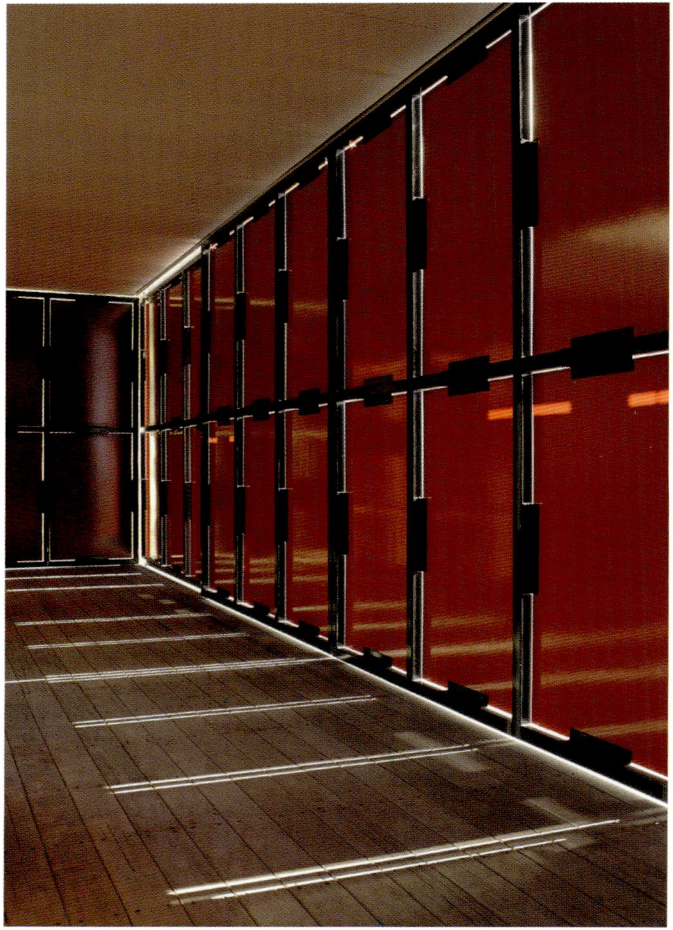

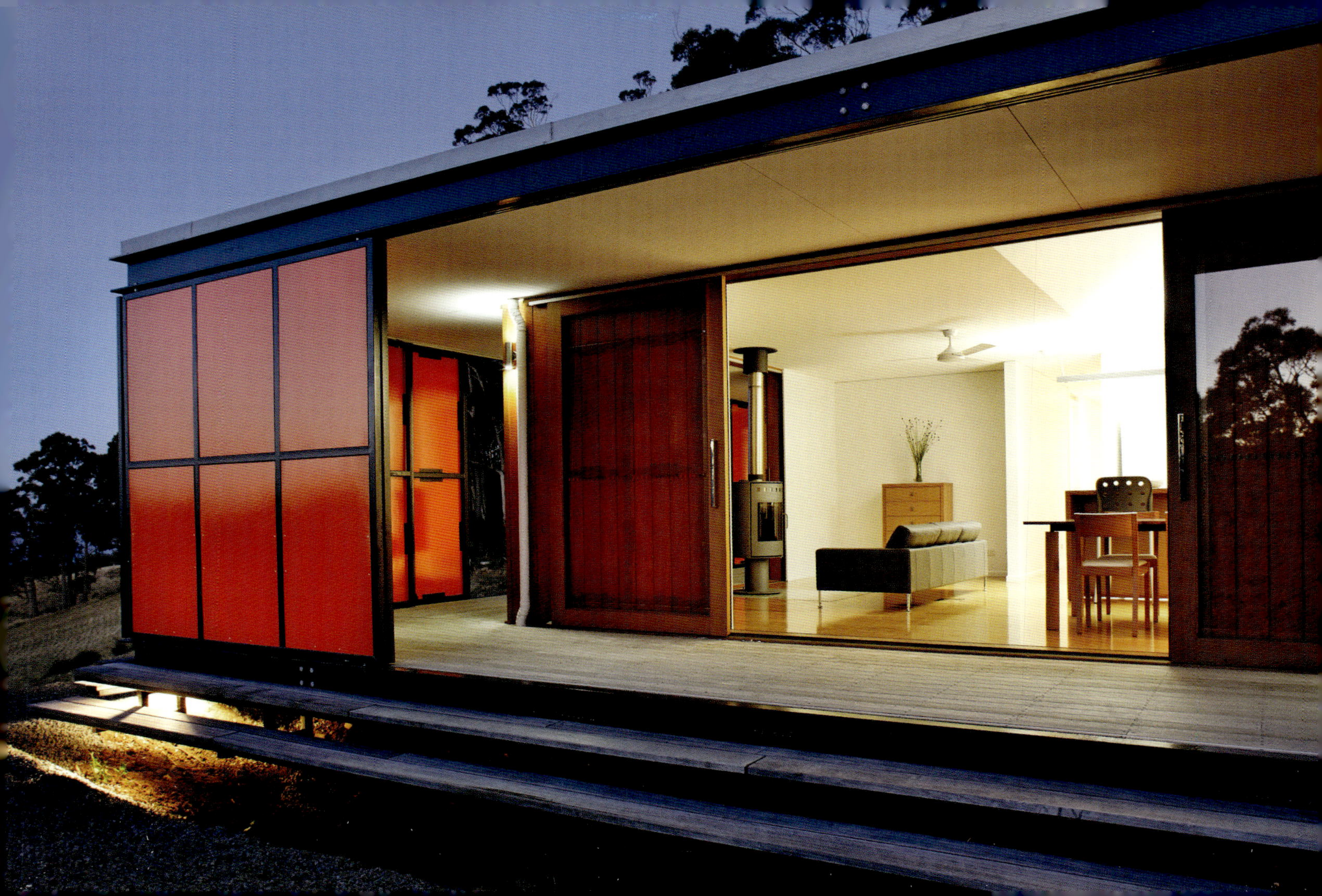

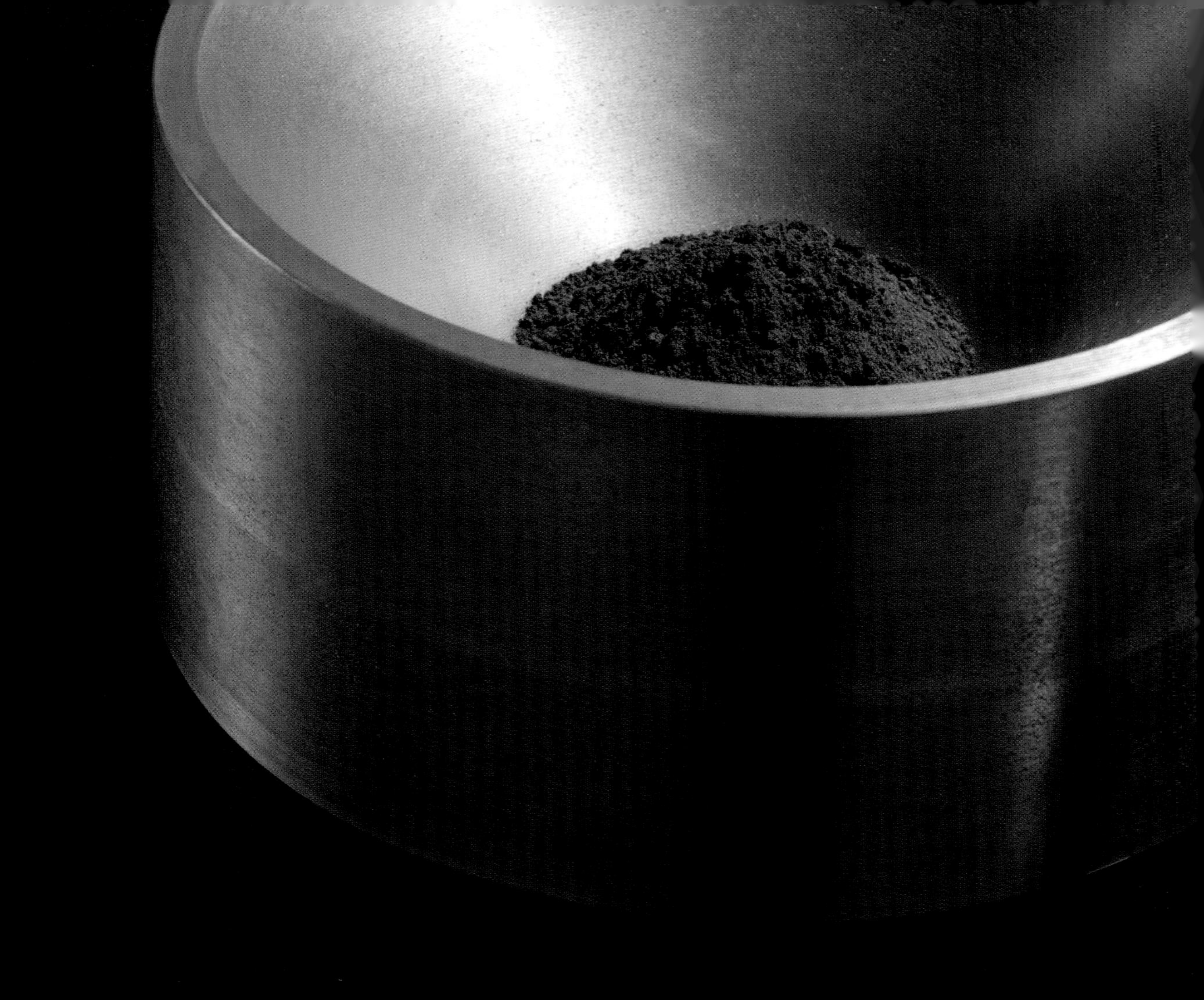

OLIVER SMITH

BORN 1974, SYDNEY, NEW SOUTH WALES
LIVES CANBERRA, AUSTRALIAN CAPITAL TERRITORY

OLIVER SMITH has a long and storied history with steel, completing his Bachelors at the Sydney College of the Arts, University of Sydney Jewellery & Object Studio in 1995 before embarking on an extended tour of New Zealand, Mexico, Germany and England, where he worked with silversmiths and metalworkers in an ongoing period of apprenticeship.

He returned to study at the School of Art, Australian National University obtaining a Masters of Philosophy in 2003 and since then has combined practice and theory, assembling a long list of honours while acting as the Head of Contemporary Art at the Sydney College of the Arts' Jewellery & Object Studio.

For Smith, the cultural and social history of steel is central to his process.

The work … is informed by my background in silversmithing, an area of practice in which steel is the vehicle to impart energy and transform other softer metals. The hammer, the tongs and the anvil, all made of ferrous alloys, are utilised in shaping the silver. In this way iron is the extension of the human will or intent and the point of contact. As Kipling wrote:

'Gold is for the mistress — silver for the maid —
Copper for the craftsman cunning at his trade.'
'Good!' said the Baron, sitting in his hall,
'But Iron — Cold Iron — is master of them all.'[1]

Further, as a silversmith I'm familiar with mixing pure elements to make alloys and thus am mindful of the crystalline structures of metals and their working properties. Another aspect of my creative thinking regarding steel grows out of my extensive

1 Kipling, R. 'Cold Iron' (poem) in *Rewards and Fairies*, 1910.

2 The quotes in this profile were recorded by the author in an interview with Oliver Smith.

engagement with designing and making cutlery and tableware. Drawing on all of this Razorback, *2016,* Field of Wings, *2016, and* Divine Ratio, *2016, are a graphic and sculptural expression of my metallic understanding.*[2]

Smith's two layered sheet metal wall pieces mounted alongside a sculptural centrepiece, are an examination not only of the material's historical and cultural significance, but also of a more essential discussion of what steel actually is.

As a material steel is in essence a combination of iron and carbon. The many and varied steel alloys have this in common. The ratio of carbon to iron is very important and to create the desired qualities and characteristics of specific specialised steel alloys this ratio is extremely nuanced and further complicated by the addition of other elements and highly controlled methods of manufacture. In very, very simple terms steel is predominantly made from Iron (Fe) and around 1% to 2% Carbon (C). Too much carbon and it is no longer considered steel. Too little carbon and it is a soft iron material without the strength and toughness we associate with steel.

The sculptural representation of this simplified 98:2 ratio is made up of a cast iron bowl and pure graphite or carbon. The sculpture becomes a physical embodiment of the two separate elemental constituents of steel in ratio. For me this leads to a reverie on the smelting of iron and the creation of steel. To understand the importance of the ratio you need to investigate the internal structure of the material itself.

The essential compositional nature of the material and its usages over time, as reflected through both human hands and the signifiers of animal motifs – iron horse, horse power, pig iron, razorback – form Smith's total exploration of the very nature of material and its relationship to the world.

I'm motivated to enliven our reading of steel, what it is and what it can do!

GLEN MARTIN

[redacted]

PREVIOUS PAGE
Divine Ratio, 2016
cast iron, graphite, 110 x 225
Photo: Greg Piper

[redacted]

▸
Razorback, 2016
mild steel, circular saw blade, brass, 50 x 450
Photo: Greg Piper

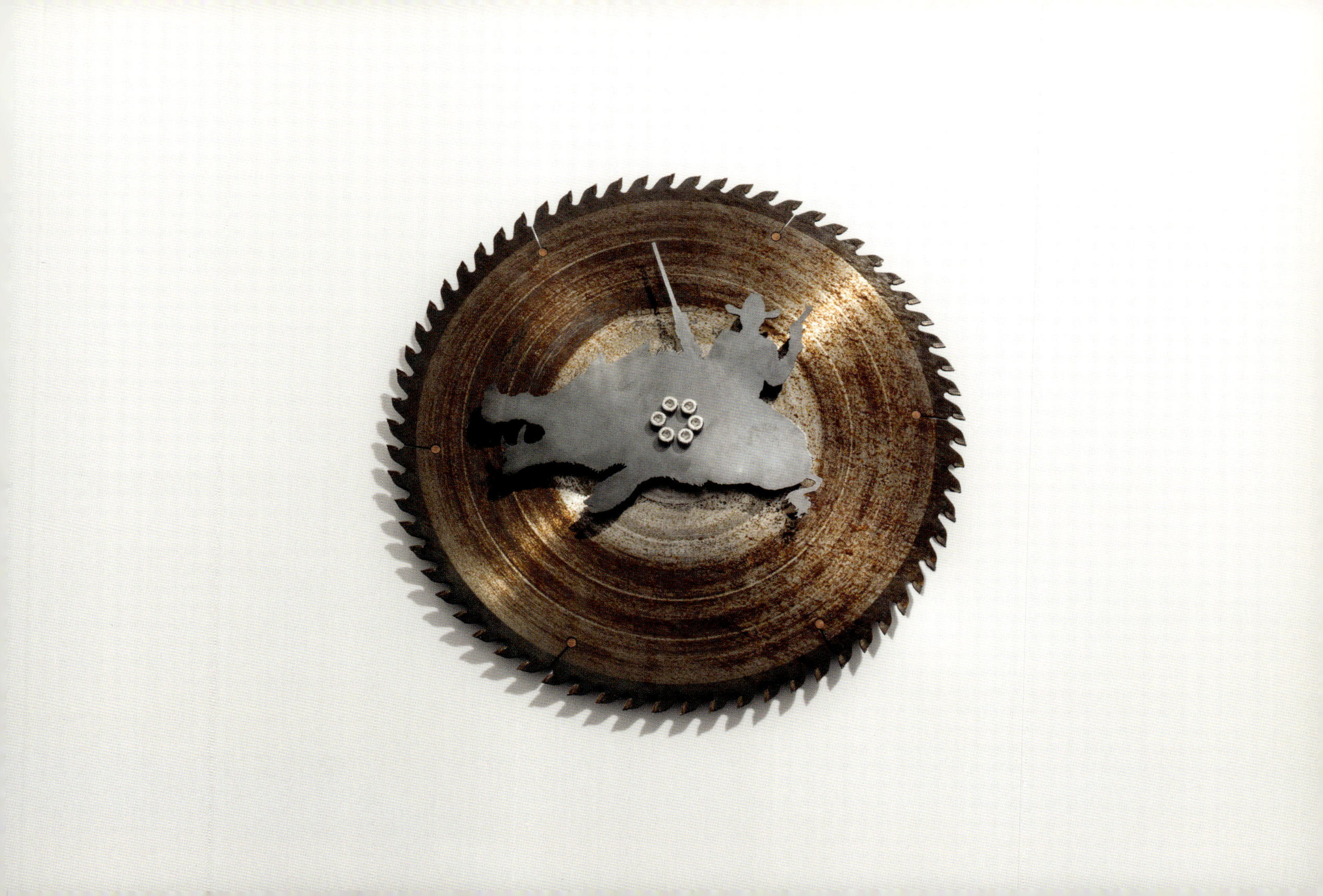

RAZORBACK*, *FIELD OF WINGS* AND *DIVINE RATIO

'The wall pieces and sculpture are concerned with the elemental nature of steel and the importance of ferrous metals in human culture. As a material, steel is in essence a combination of iron and carbon. Too much carbon and it is no longer considered steel. Too little carbon and it is a soft iron material without the strength and toughness we associate with steel. So the proportion of carbon to iron is very important and the ratio quite specific. To understand the importance of the ratio you need to also investigate the internal structure of the material itself.

Razorback, 2016, employs porcine symbolism. From pig iron to the legend of the Calydonian Boar, the wild pig embodies raw, terranean power. The vanquished pig is a brutal representation of our mastery over the natural environment. Steel enables this dominance, and when considered in light of the Anthropocene we heighten our awareness of the destructive potential of this material.

Field of Wings, 2016, has an equine theme. This references the iron horse, horsepower, the internal combustion engine, the mythology of movement and mobility and the ubiquity of petroleum as a fuel.

Divine Ratio, 2016, harnesses a machine aesthetic and is a sculptural expression of my metallic understanding of the ratio of carbon and iron that makes steel. In combination the three works are an investigation into totemic animal symbolism and the role of material agency and technology in cultural history.' ■

OLIVER SMITH

[redacted]

▶

Field of Wings, 2016
stainless steel, 44 gallon drum lid, silver, 40 x 600
Photo: Greg Piper

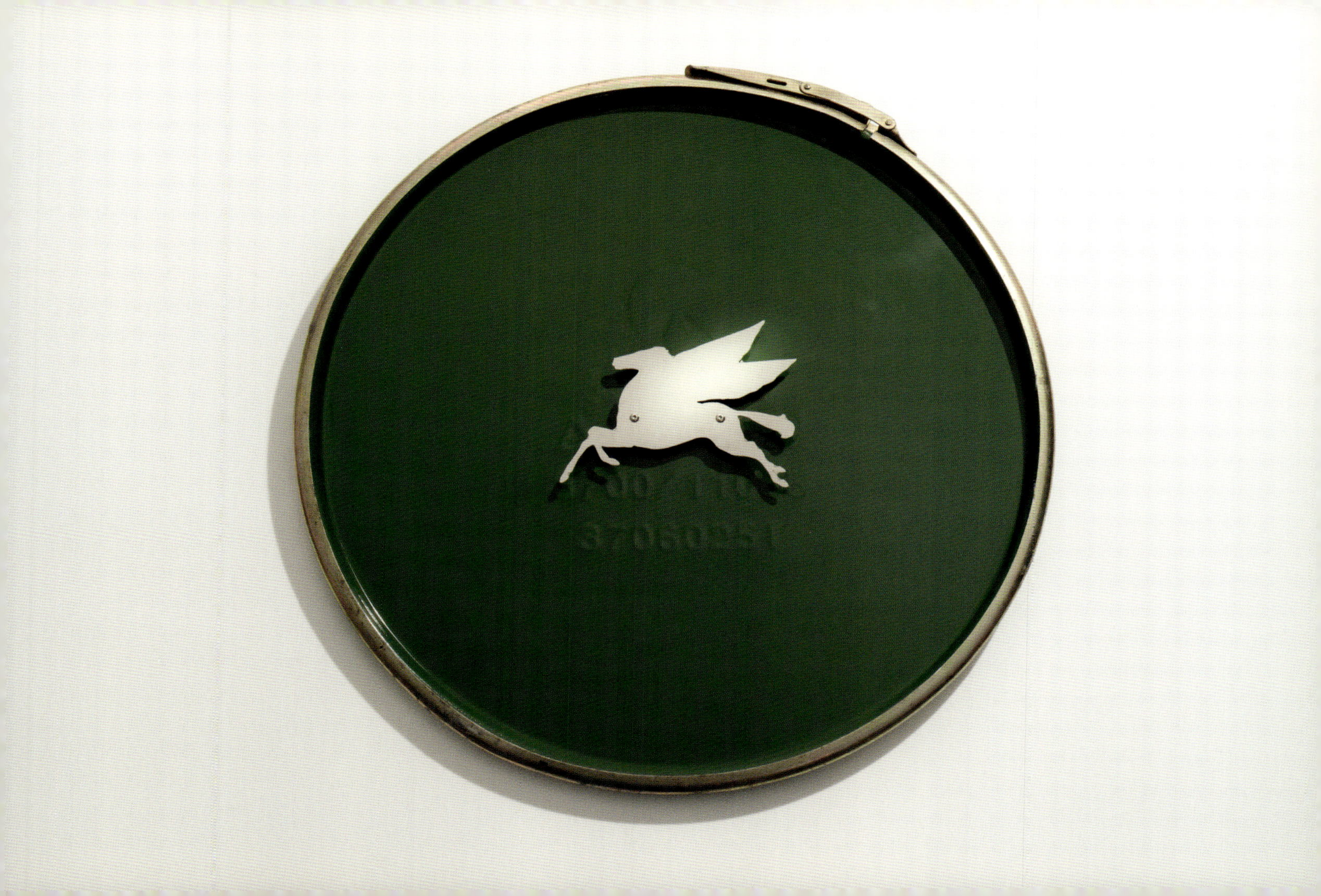

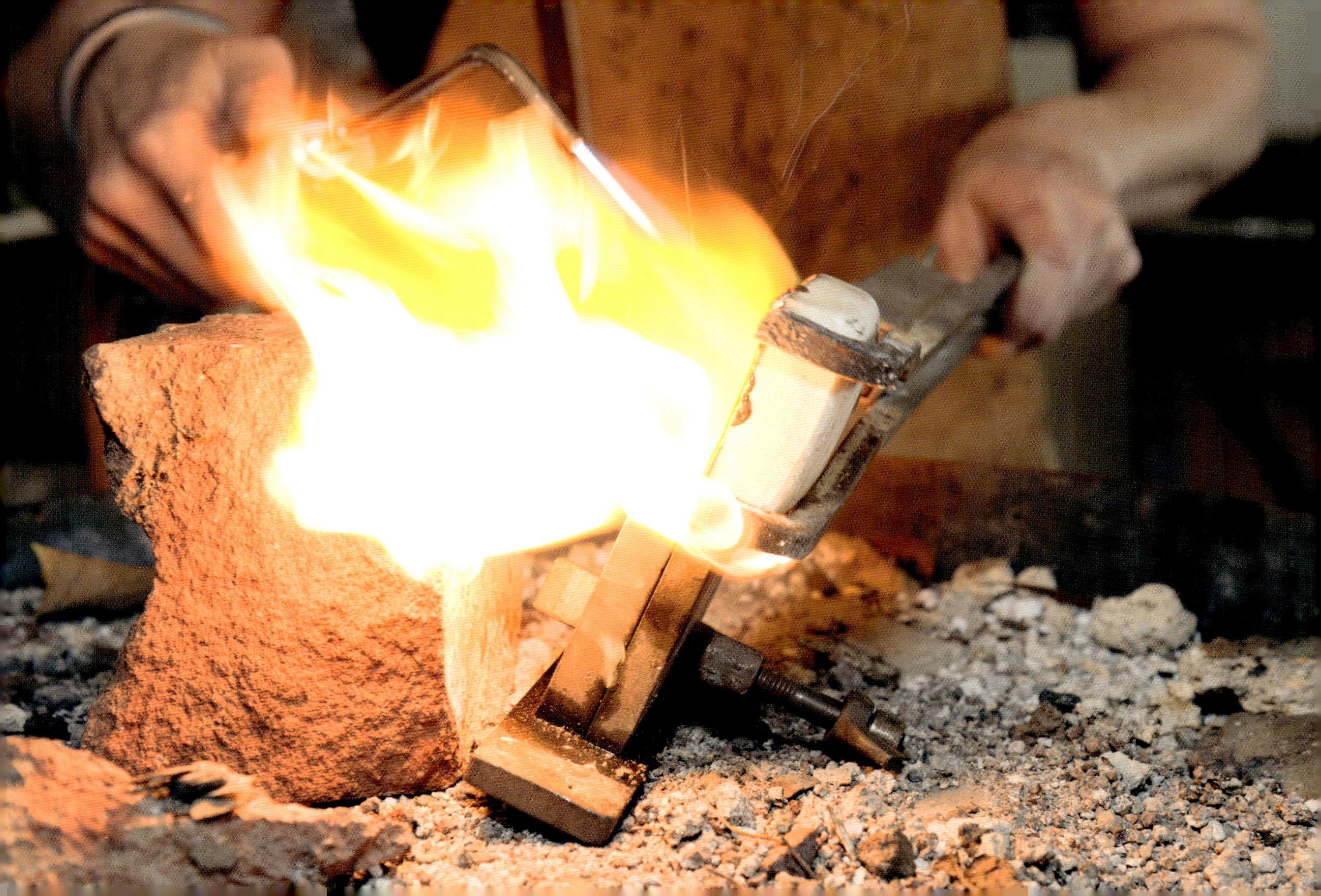

SABINE PAGAN

BORN 1972, NEUCHATEL, SWITZERLAND
LIVES QUEANBEYAN, NEW SOUTH WALES

STEEL IS EVERYWHERE. It supports soaring skyscrapers and enters the intimate spaces of our bodies as sophisticated medical instruments. Sabine Pagan works between these public and private spheres: she is alive to the ways our bodies inhabit the large shared built spaces of architecture, but also, with jewellery, embrace diminutive constructed objects that accompany us every day.

In each case it's the relationship between construction and flesh that matters: Pagan's jewellery demonstrates the productive tensions that exist between who we are and what we make, and even hint at ways each affect and inflect the other. As she noted about jewellery and architecture, 'Despite obvious differences in scale, purpose and function, these creative disciplines share a common aspiration for engaging us, as human beings, through our senses.'[1] The ring, *Site #2*, 2008 has become an iconic statement of this idea – the small pristine gold cube sits atop a sturdy shank made of surgical steel, its form perhaps suggesting a dwelling placed on a sloping hill, but its title equally valid for architecture or jewellery – the hand is a most personal 'site'.

More than simply borrowing architectural forms, Pagan considers how studying architecture can suggest new ways of thinking about wearing jewellery:

My interpretations of architectural qualities into jewellery is applied through subtle elements, prompting both the wearer and viewer to experience them over time and depending on the 'conditions' of the environment they find themselves in. Standing inside, outside, moving the hand, grasping things with the hand, shaking hands are all elements that will affect the conditions in which the embodied characteristics of the ring are lived and experienced.[2]

Pagan is unusually attentive then, to the physical and relational aspects of jewellery as part of lived experience, with all the baggage of memory this brings with it. As part of her research into the affect of jewellery, she asked participants to live with her jewellery over a period, both wearing it and observing it off the body, and recording their reactions to it. *Anew*, 2014, is a fine example of this practice, having altered over time through wear: it embodies the sensory life of its wearer.[3]

Given that built forms are such a crucial inspiration for Pagan, most recently in the work of the Swiss architect Peter Zumthor[4], it's nice that her key jewellery project at this time is the ring, amongst the smallest of jewellery items and the one that lives on the active making hand. As Pagan says, 'I am particularly drawn to the intimate scale of rings and their performative roles when both worn and detached from the body.'[5] With Pagan's rings, we have a window onto the world, in miniature.

Pagan's education as a jeweller and gemmologist has been long and unusually thorough. Originally undertaking an apprenticeship, then formal training in jewellery at the esteemed CIFOM, Ecole d'Art Appliques, at La Chaux-de-Fonds in her native Switzerland, she later emigrated to Australia, living in Sydney, Wagga Wagga and now Canberra. Over the last two decades Pagan has taught at various university art schools and has recently completed her PhD at the School of Art, Architecture and Design, University of South Australia.

PREVIOUS PAGE
Sabine Pagan pouring an ingot in her studio in Quenbeyan, Australia Capital Territory.
Photo: courtesy the artist

◥
Site #2, 2009
9k yellow gold, surgical steel, sterling silver, 350 x 36 x12
Photo: Emily Snadden

◢
Sabine working at her jewellers bench.
Photo: courtesy the artist

▸▸
In situ, 2015
18k yellow gold, fine silver, steel (old bell), 59 x 75 x 26
Photo: Grant Hancock

1 Pagan, S. 'Contemporary Jewellery: a phenomenological approach to making informed by Architecture', 2014, http://acuads.com.au/conference/article/contemporary-jewellery-a-phenomenological-approach-to-making-informed-by-architecture, accessed September 2016.

2 Pagan, S. 'Crafting new spatial and sensorial relationships in contemporary jewellery.' *Craft • Material • Memory, craft + design enquiry*. Issue 6, 2014.

3 Email from Sabine Pagan to the author, 4 September, 2016.

4 Pagan has made an extended study of work in Europe of the distinguished Swiss architect Peter Zumthor (b. 1943), winner of the 2009 Pritzker Prize and the 2013 RIBA Medal, especially his 1999 thermal baths at Vals, Switzerland, which used Vals stone extensively. See Pagan, S. *On Milieu*, (self-published) 2016, pp. 62-65.

5 See Pagan, S. *On Milieu*, (self-published), 2016, pp. 36.

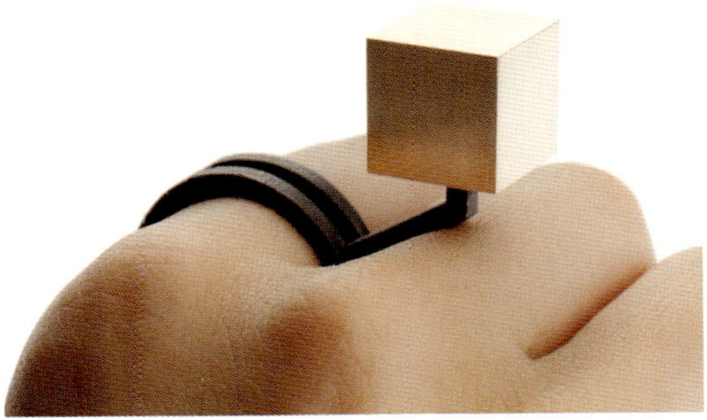

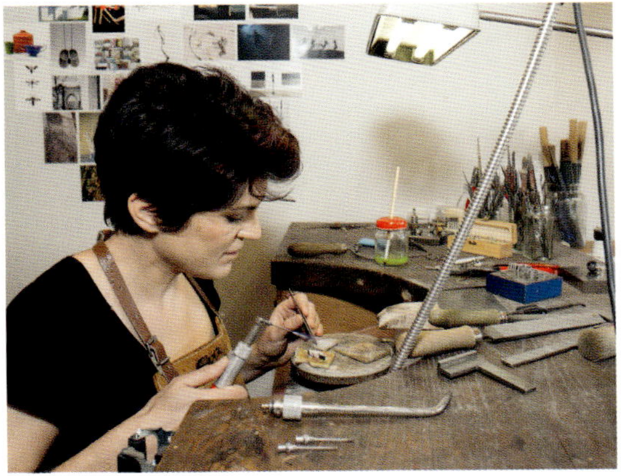

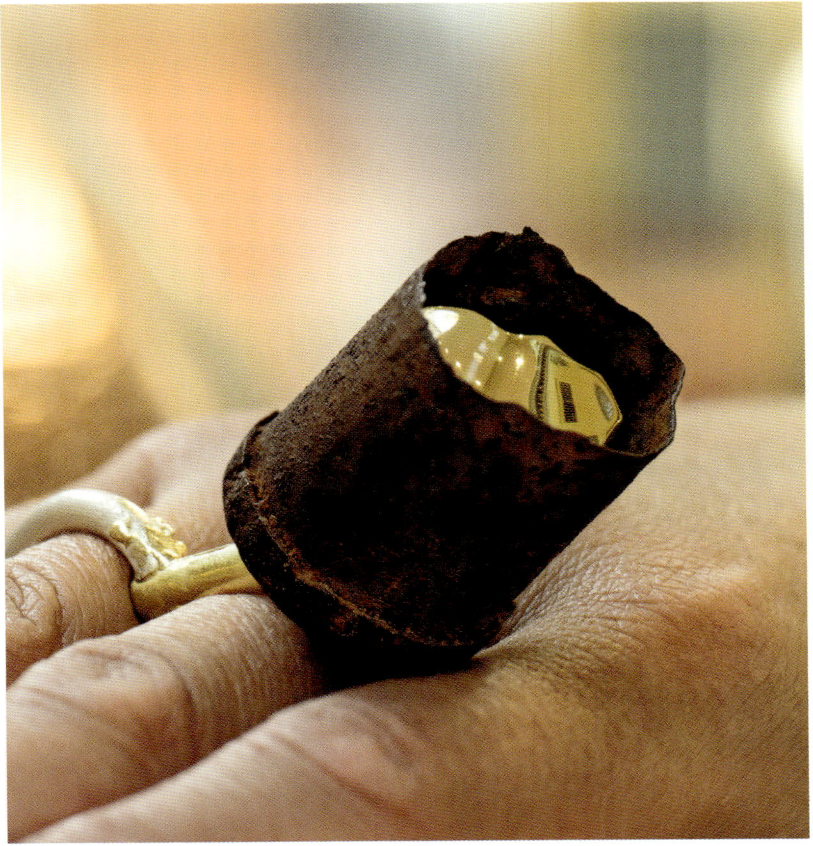

ANEW, UNDERPASS, UNTITLED, AND INSITU

Sabine Pagan considers with great thoughtfulness the structural relationships between each component of her pieces. This is evident in her rings, which encompass a great variety of materials and forms and, therefore, methods of construction. Employing materials such as surgical steel, sterling silver, gold, monel, corian and different stones, Pagan investigates the spaces and volumes of the rings with both panache and discretion, always setting these rigorously geometric forms, expressed in obdurate materials, against the soft mobile flesh of the supporting hand.

Many works take their inspiration from actual physical and historical sites: *Anew,* 2015, features the distinctive Vals rock, gneiss from Vals in Switzerland where she studied Peter Zumthor's architecture – its many minerals make Vals rock sparkle. The fine silver 'walls' of *Underpass*, 2016, have been imprinted with a piece of Vals rock, and is accompanied by the very piece of rock (*Untitled*, 2016) that served as the mould for the *Underpass* ring.

In Situ, 2015, incorporates a fragment of an old steel bell, responding to Pagan's 2012 visit to a collaborative work by Zumthor and the late Louise Bourgeois in Vardø, Norway, that commemorates victims of witchcraft trials that took place in the 17th century. Here culture is coupled with nature, as buildings are married to sites. And here, too, memory comes from the lived senses. ■

JULIE EWINGTON

OVERLEAF
Left:
Anew, 2015
surgical steel, monel, patinated copper, Vals rock (gneiss), stainless steel screws, 33 x 39 x 15
Photo: Grant Hancock

Right:
Underpass, 2016
fine silver, monel, mild steel, 40 x 40 x 14

Untitled (mould for *Underpass*), 2016
Vals rock (gneiss), 40 x 30.5 x 12
Photo: Grant Hancock

▸

Site specific, 2014
18k yellow gold, monel, patineted sterling silver
Photo: Grant Hancock

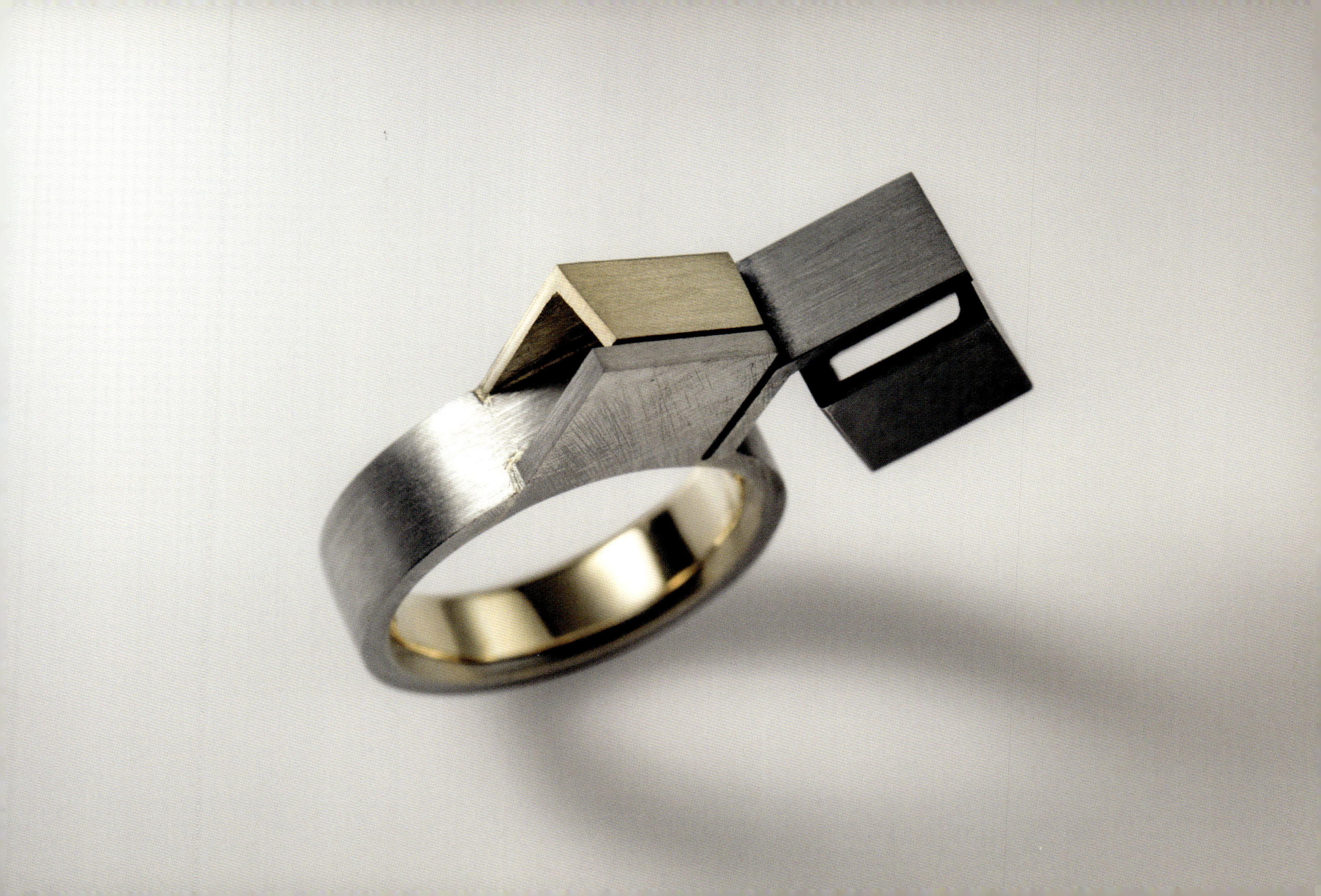

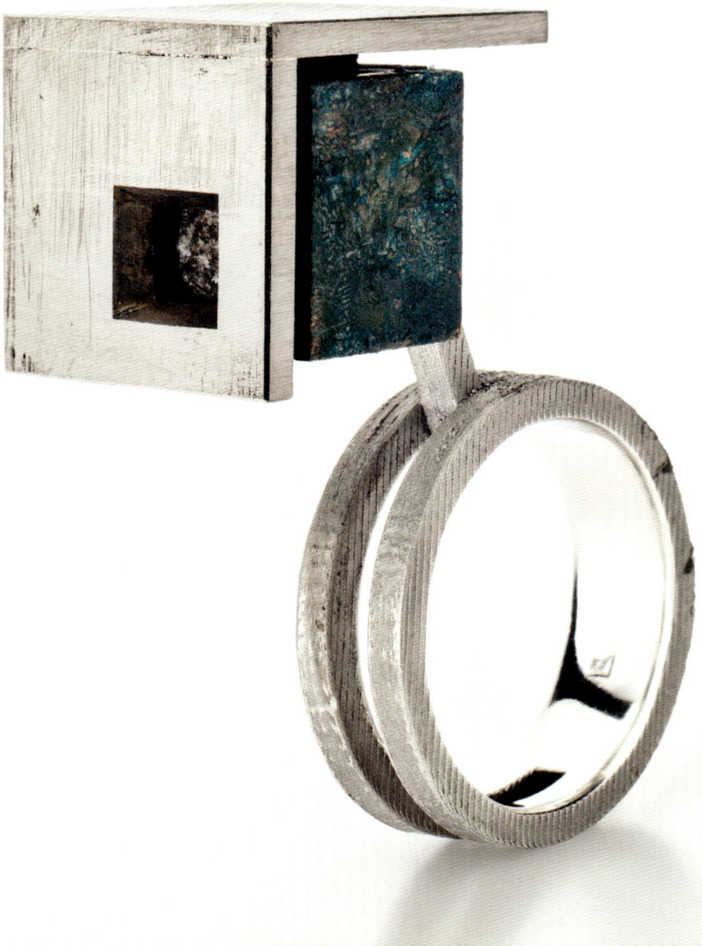

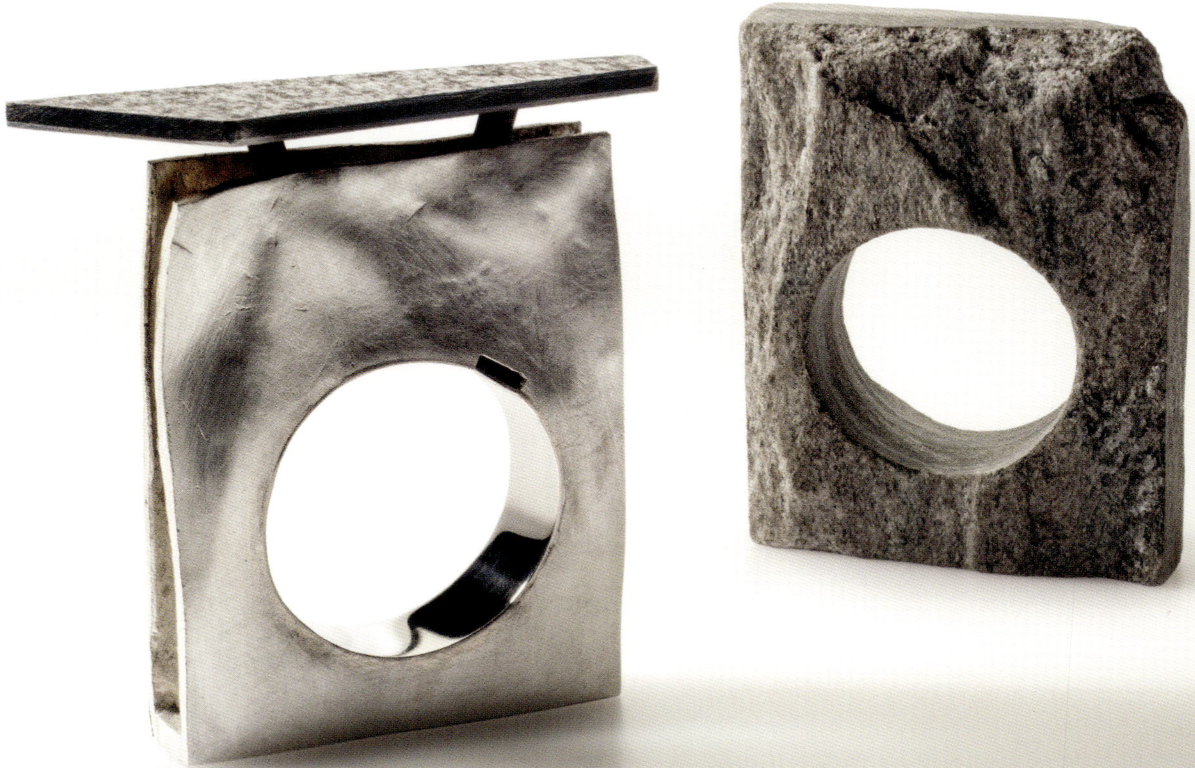

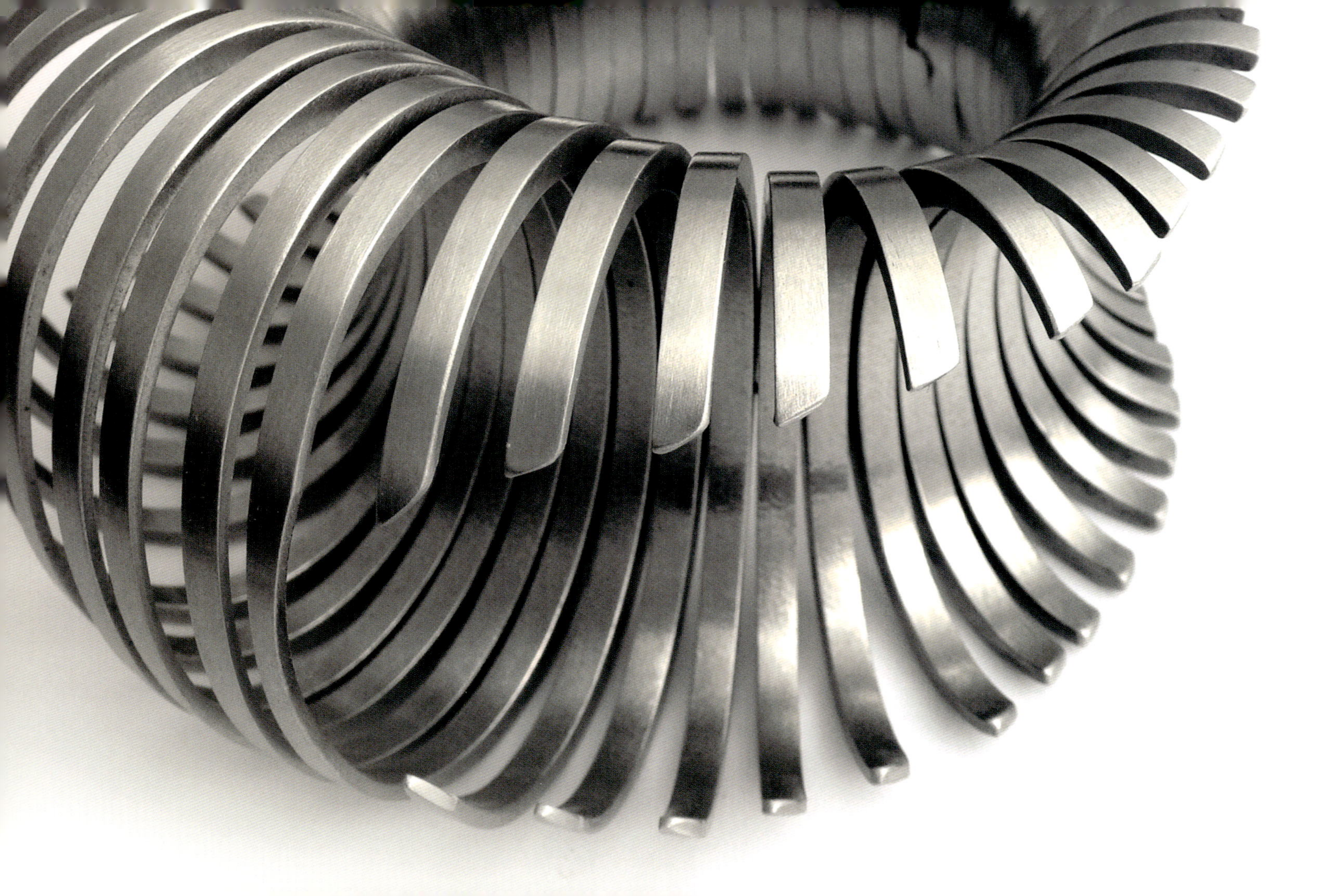

SEAN O'CONNELL

BORN 1972, SYDNEY, NEW SOUTH WALES
LIVES SYDNEY, NEW SOUTH WALES

ANY MISCONCEPTIONS of steel's static, fixed nature are exploded by the work of Sean O'Connell. He creates striking images and stunning examples of kinetic jewellery that express the possibilities of how steel can respond to the triggers created in his Bundeena studio, surrounded by the heathlands of the Royal National Park south of Sydney.

O'Connell studied Gold and Silversmithing at the School of Art, Australian National University and has recently completed his PhD at Sydney College of the Arts, University of Sydney. Noting inspirations as diverse as Andrei Tarkovsky, Amon Tobin and Dr Seuss, O'Connell says his work is an abstraction of the forces that are present in his life and self. His work employs stainless steel, tantalum, gold, bearing balls and engineering bits and pieces crafted by a metal lathe, a TIG welder, a 3-phase metal linisher and a hammer, resulting in elegantly simple renderings of form and movement.

O'Connell's kinetic jewellery pieces are small expressions of energy and possibility, graceful objects that suggest the range of interior motions aided by but not limited to the movement of the wearer.

The jewellery I make is turned on the lathe, manually, without CNC or digital readouts, and all under my own hand. Or I cut links of chains laboriously by hand, like some idiot machine, doing the same thing over and over (my hands hurt as I think about it...!) I make moving elements, usually with balls, sometimes with links, occasionally with springs and pivots, and the finished jewellery is playful and fiddly. Fun to wear.[1]

Alongside this range of works, O'Connell also creates explorations of the energetic potential of steel, through spark discharge images. Each material has a complex electrical character – it is not simply a matter of seeing what conducts best and makes the biggest spark, but rather to explore the individual energetic character of each material.

I take various steel samples and apply high voltage electricity to them while they are resting on a large format negative film in the dark, and develop the film normally to reveal the way the energetics of the electricity flows through the steel. There is no camera – the sparks dance across the actual film and that makes the image.

O'Connell works across a diverse range of processes and substances, and his practice involves a deep investigation into the structure of matter. His work with steel is a fine example of his scientific and creative process.

The pieces are designed and developed slowly and after many iterations new designs evolve naturally. Stainless steel is the ideal material to use as it is well behaved, very strong in small sections, does not corrode, is easy to wear, and can be welded, turned, filed, tapped, hammered or cut. While it is hard, it is very well behaved, except when heated, when it tends to warp and buckle.

Like many artists, O'Connell's work is the culmination of inquiry and process, resulting in expressions of possibility. His reasons for creating are simple.

I am compelled to make – it is a way of making sense of the world.

GLEN MARTIN

1 The quotes in this profile were recorded by the author in an interview with Sean O'Connell.

[redacted]

PREVIOUS PAGE
Profile bracelet, 2015
stainless steel, nitinol wire,
200 x 60 x 40
Photo: Sean O'Connell

[redacted]

left to right:
Stainless chain bracelet, 2015
hand cut and welded stainless steel links, 13 x 13 x 230
Photo: Sean O'Connell

Balltrack kinetic rings, 2015
stainless steel, 10 x 25 each
Photo: Sean O'Connell

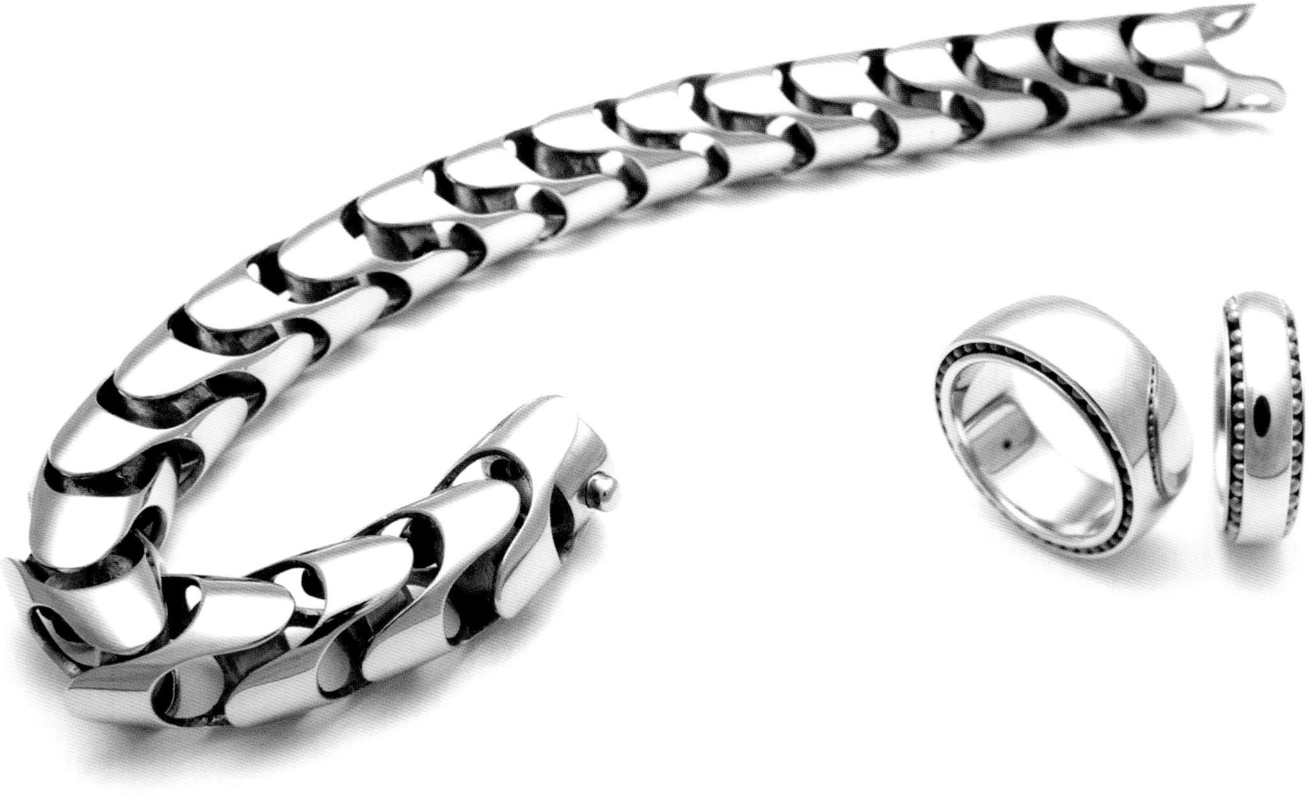

FORCES

'*Forces*, 2016, explores the energetic qualities of steel. Five different steel samples are imaged directly over negative film, saturated with high voltage electricity, tuned in frequency and intensity, to reveal their individual energetic signatures. The samples are mild steel, DF-2 tool steel, 316 stainless steel, layered nickel and carbon Damascus steel, and meteoric steel from Namibia.

Using high frequency electricity to create ionised spark trails directly onto photographic film, the resulting image creates a document of the energy moving through each sample. These images reveal the internal structures of steel in different forms – the soft even structure of everyday mild steel, the tightness of hardened high-carbon tool steel, the strong alloyed elements of stainless steel, the layered foldings of tough Damascus steel, and the distinctive crystalline structure of meteoric iron that cooled four billion years ago in the depths of deep space. The way the electricity moves through each sample and out across the photographic film, allows us to glimpse inside their internal structures, and track the movement of forces within their solid matter.' ■

SEAN O'CONNELL

OVERLEAF
Mild steel spark image, 2016
40,000V DC and AC over foma 100 emulsion, 200 x 250
Photo: Sean O'Connell

▶
Meteroic steel spark image, 2016
50,000V DC and AC over ilford ortho emulsion, 200 x 250

Mild steel spark image, 2016
20,000V DC over lithographic emulsion, 150 x 150

Mild steel spark image, 2016
40,000V DC, multiple strikes, over lithographic emulsion, 150 x 150

Tool steel spark image, 2016
35,000V DC over lithographic emulsion, 150 x 150
Photos: Sean O'Connell

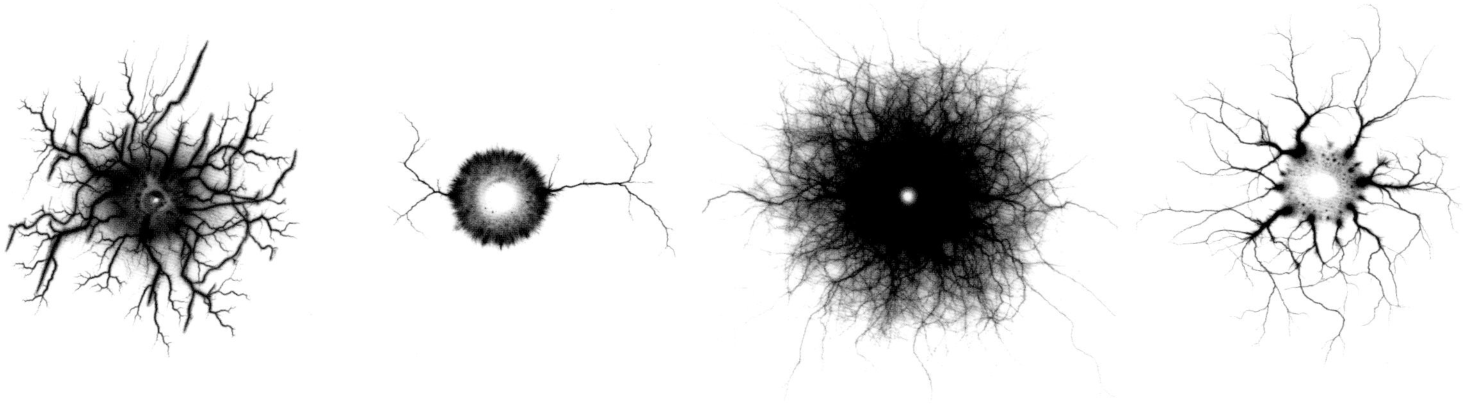

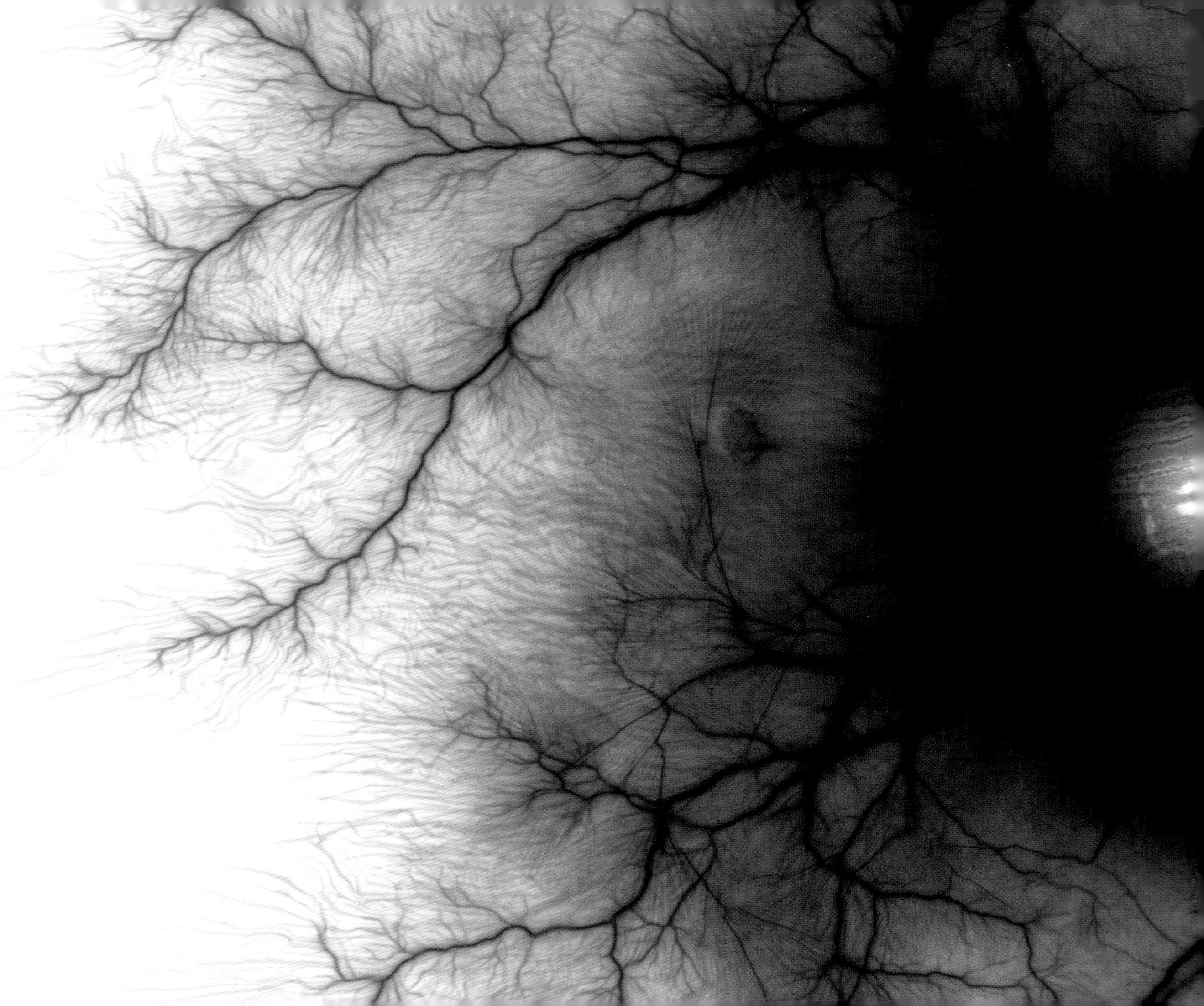

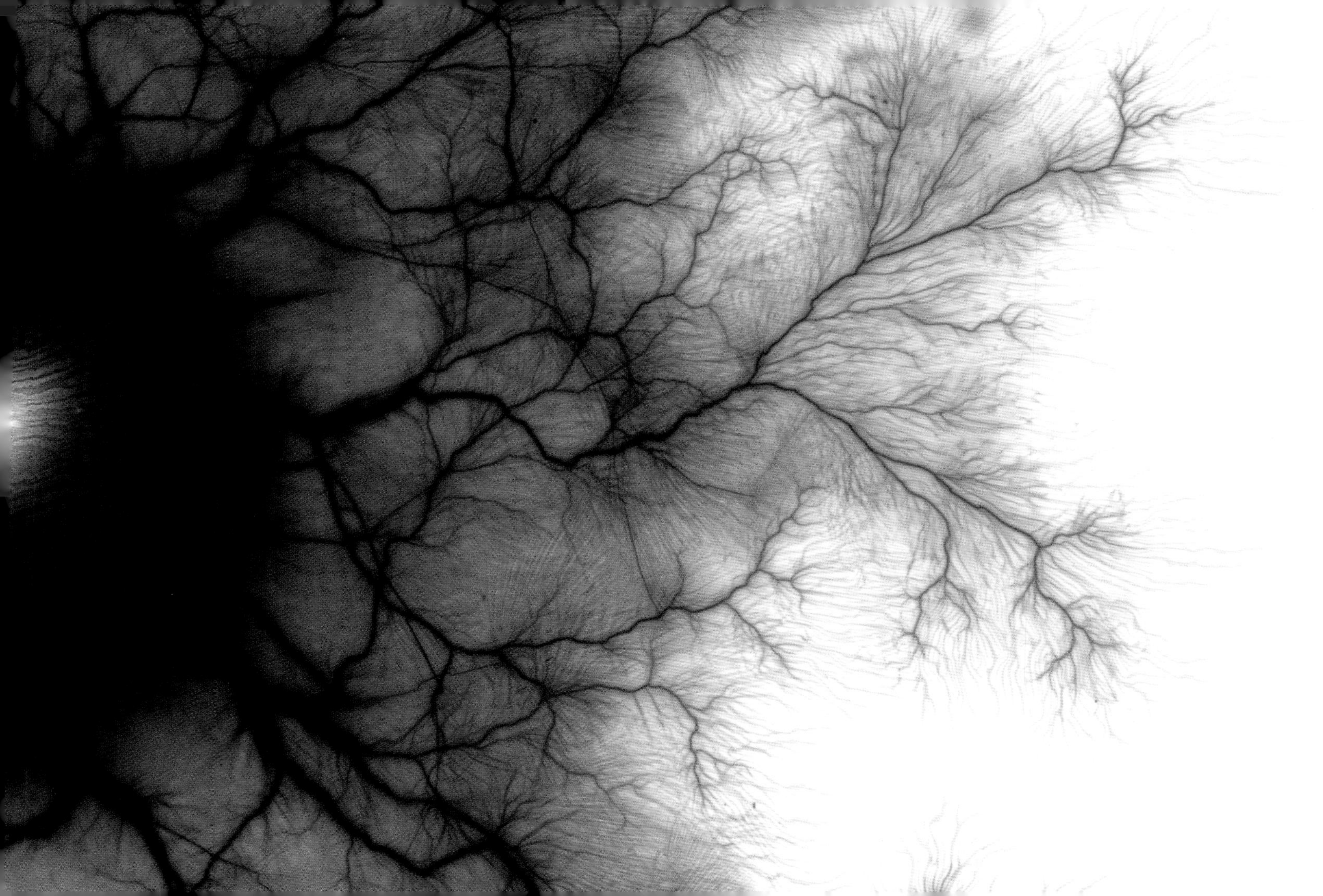

Sketches.
Paperclip DNA.

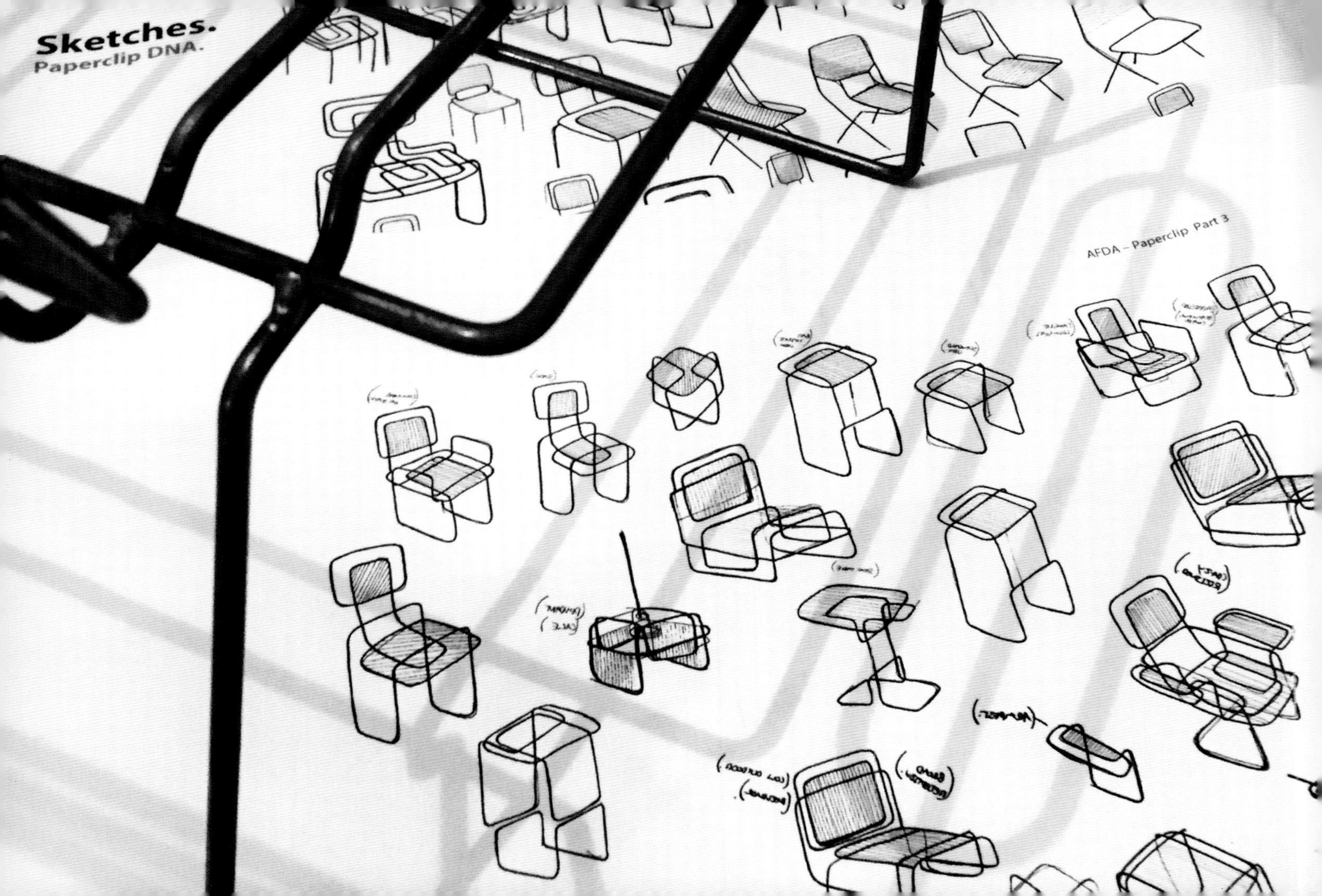

SEATON MCKEON

BORN 1988, SYDNEY, NEW SOUTH WALES
LIVES SYDNEY, NEW SOUTH WALES

SEATON MCKEON recently came to national attention after winning the inaugural Australian Furniture Design Award, 2015, presented by JamFactory and Stylecraft. The Sydney-based designer was one of six finalists shortlisted from 150 entrants in the prestigious new biennial prize, impressing the judges with his *The Sun The Moon and Me*, 2015. An innovative study in LED technology, this freestanding light and mirror typifies the designer's strong conceptual approach and intelligent design thinking. As part of his prize, McKeonundertook a residency at JamFactory's Furniture Studio and 2016 saw him develop a new design collection through to commercial production.

It's a rapid career trajectory for someone who only graduated with a Bachelor of Industrial Design (Honours) from the UNSW Australia the previous year. But Mckeon has been working as an industrial designer since 2011 and is currently in-house Industrial Designer at Blue Sky Design Group. Within the past few years he has featured in the *Workshopped* exhibition three times, was a finalist in *Launchpad 2013* and during that same year won the Northern Lights competition, presented by Great Dane and &tradition, with his *Press pendant*, 2013.

While this lighting design is iconic in its simple, bold form, Mckeon is most well known for his Alfred range produced in collaboration with DesignByThem (pg135). Comprising a magazine rack and umbrella stand, this powder coated aluminium collection is unapologetically utilitarian, making it one of the most popular items in the Sydney-based design brand's effortlessly modern portfolio.

As Mckeon explains it, his work falls into two stylistic groups that he continues to develop simultaneously. The first is a 'machine aesthetic' that is minimal and stripped of any unnecessary embellishment to make products appear clean and efficient.

The *Alfred* collection, his *Nexus*, 2013, coathanger and, to a lesser extent, *The Sun The Moon and Me* fall into this grouping and highlight Mckeon's strong graphic sensibilities. On the other hand, his 'organic' works are softer in appearance, with an emphasis on curved lines and round forms (instead of hard edges and sharp angles), as exemplified by his *Gravity*, 2016, dumbbells, *Rocket*, 2014, kitchenware and *Knot*, 2016, skipping rope.

The latter group reveals Mckeon's expert exploration of luxe materials and his firm understanding of their inherent textural qualities. Combining European beech and natural vegetable tanned leather in *Knot*, cleverly reinvents an otherwise everyday fitness item, while the gunmetal construction of *Gravity* elevates the product to high-end object. McKeon is currently extending both of these collections, but his practice isn't solely limited to industrial design, with a portfolio that also includes packaging design, technical illustration, wayfinding and image retouching.

This desire to not become pigeonholed by one particular product category or industry sector is influenced by Marc Newson – a designer Mckeon drew inspiration from early on in his career. For Mckeon, the 'design rock star' paved the way for the younger generation of Australian designers, encouraging them to believe they could not only make it locally, but also be successful on an international stage.

Mckeon enjoys working across multiple sectors and his achievements to date can also be attributed to this ability to reach a broad range of different people. As he continues to build a portfolio that resonates with intelligence and clear vision, his work becomes all the more appealing, not only for its formal attributes, but for its intuitive functionality as well.

PREVIOUS PAGE
Sketches and scale model of the *Paperclip*, 2015
Photo: Seaton McKeon

◥

Robotic welding arm.
Photo: Seaton McKeon

◢

CNC wire bending mandrel.
Photo: Seaton McKeon

▸▸

Adjusting the backrest of the lounger chair to make for greater comfort.
Photo: Seaton McKeon

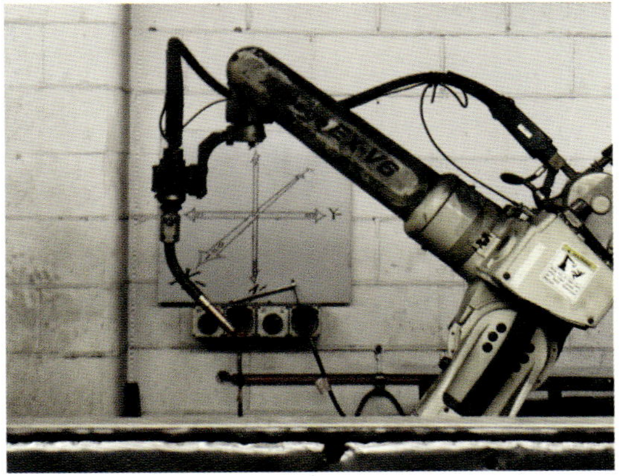

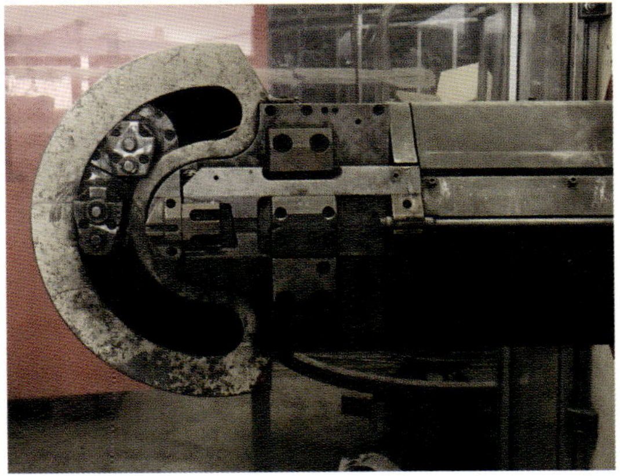

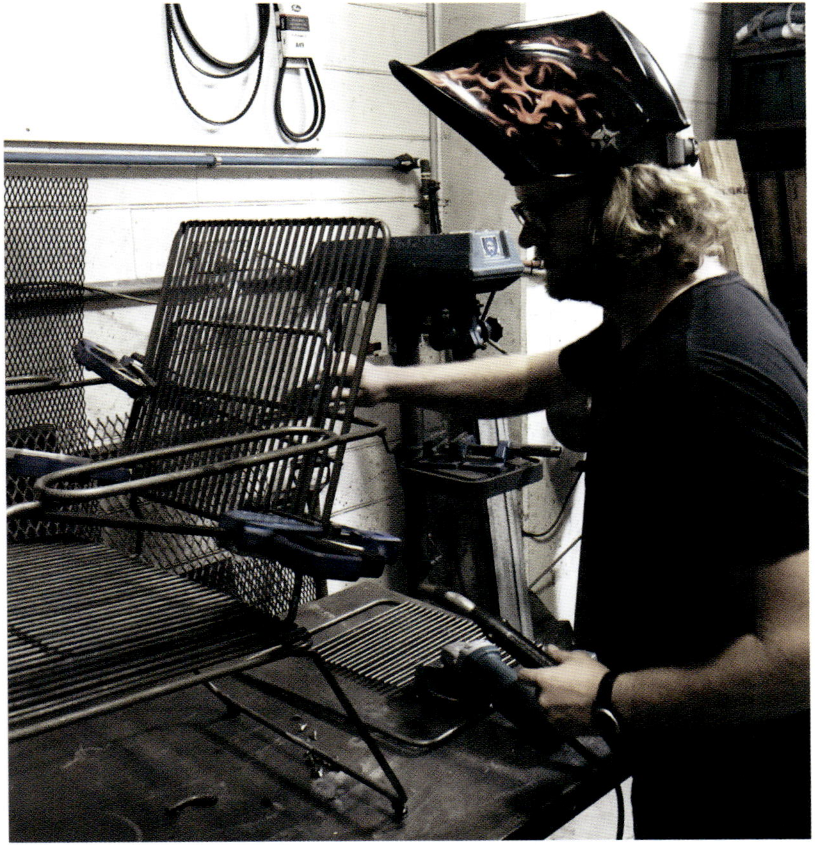

PAPERCLIP COLLECTION

As part of his Australian Furniture Design Award prize in 2015, Mckeon was given the opportunity to work with JamFactory's Furniture Studio and its Creative Director Jon Goulder to develop a new design through to commercial production. *Paperclip*, 2017, collection is the result of this residency – comprising six pieces of furniture, including three stools in different heights, the *School* chair, *Lounger* chair and a cafe table.

Mckeon's 'machine aesthetic' is at play within *Paperclip* collection as he reinterprets the classic school chair of the 1920s. The concept is nostalgic and evokes a sense of narrative, however the pieces' clean, minimal construction is what immediately appeals. Communicating the essence of making through pared back forms is what lends the collection its robustness, despite the lightness of the material palette. The use of steel is beneficial from a production perspective, but it's also advantageous when creating such lightweight frameworks.

While simple geometries inform the collection's appearance, it's softened by each piece's curved edges, which makes them as utilitarian as they are elegant. When Mckeon was brainstorming names for his 'wire-based design' he imagined bending a paperclip into the form of the *School* chair. Calling the collection *Paperclip* owes as much to this crude resemblance as it does to a warm nostalgia for bygone times.

The *Paperclip* collection is inherently versatile and would not look out of place in either a residential, hospitality or office environment. It will be available through Stylecraft showrooms in both Australia and Singapore. ■

LEANNE AMODEO

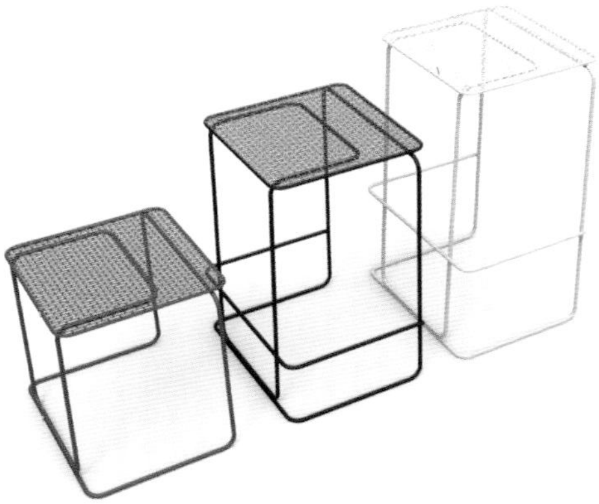

▶ ▶▶

Seaton McKeon's computer renders of the *Paper Clip* collection, 2017. The collection includes stacking outdoor tables, school chair and lounger.

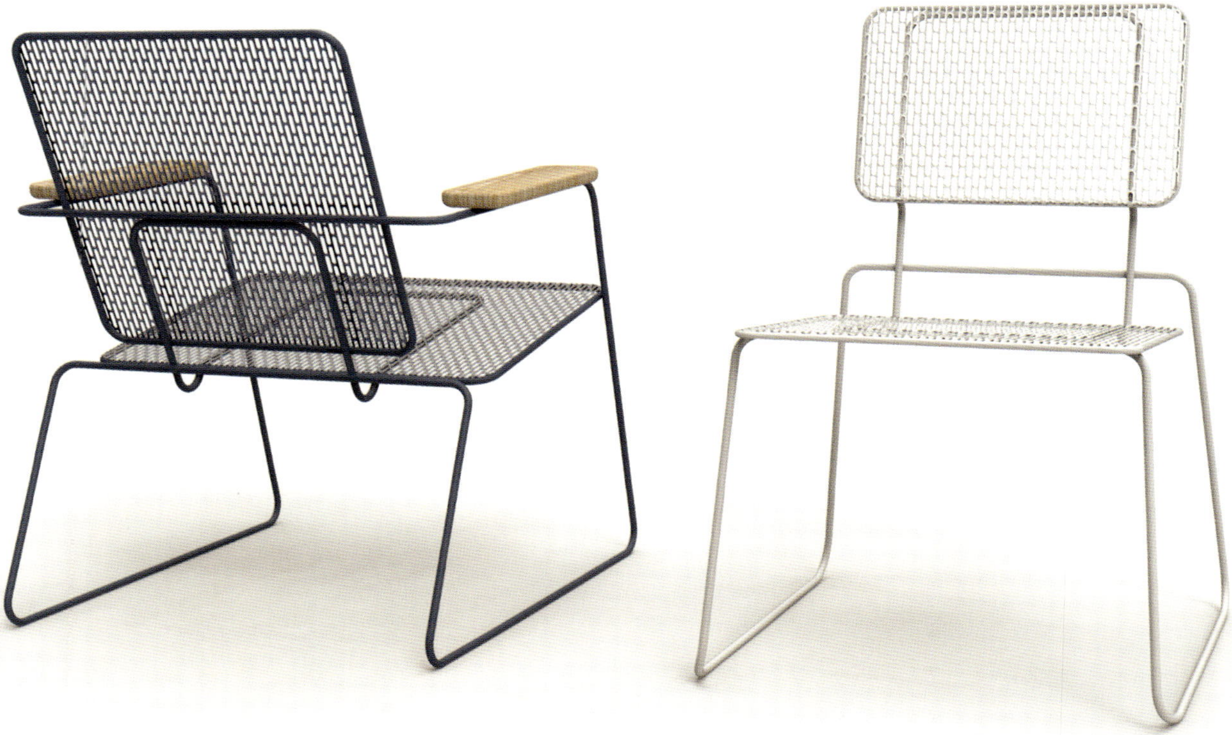

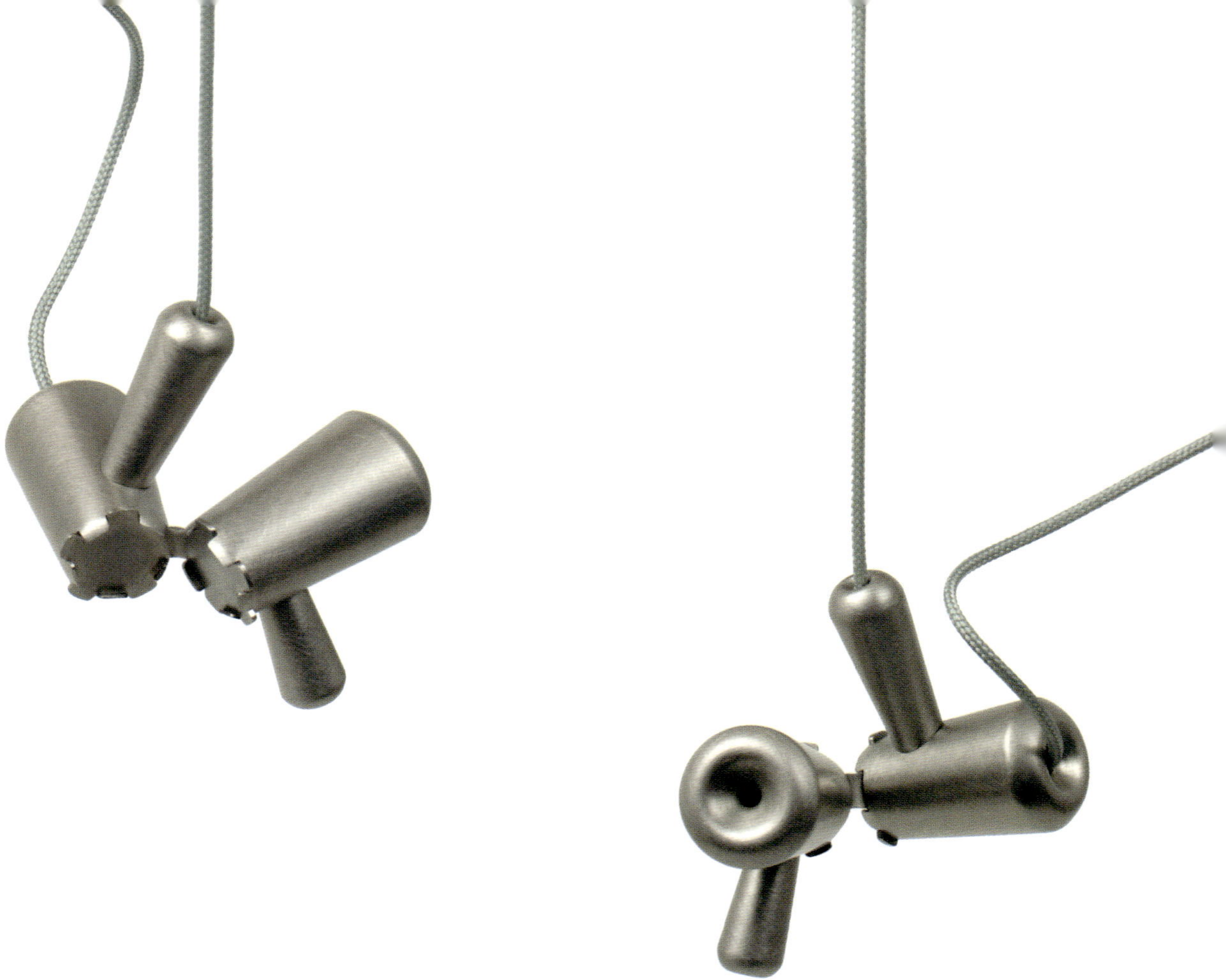

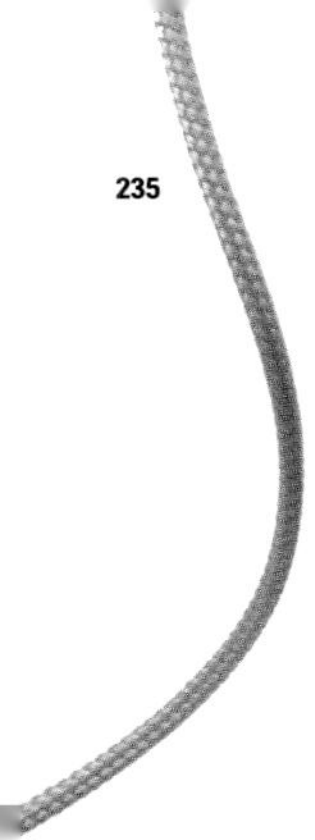

SIMON COTTRELL

BORN 1975, MELBOURNE, VICTORIA
LIVES CANBERRA, AUSTRALIAN CAPITAL TERRITORY

SIMON COTTRELL works almost exclusively in Monel 400, a nickel alloy beloved by jewellers and spectacle-makers for its strength and adaptability. Originally patented in the United States in 1906, Monel has been used in aircraft and rocket bodies, marine valves and pumps, and for chemical processing. Monel is also resistant to wear. As Cottrell says, 'It is more stainless than stainless steel,'[1] does not corrode and can be welded at low temperatures. Its stringent elegance speaks to the material's origins in advanced manufacturing technology and there is an echo of this functional history in Cottrell's tubular forms: many sit within the Modernist imagery of industrialization, some recalling the splendid solid mechanical bodies of the early-twentieth century French painter Fernand Léger. One of Cottrell's brooches was even included in a 2016 National Gallery of Australia display exploring the art of the 'machine age'.

Monel is also beautiful. It polishes up to exquisite soft greys, and its dense seductive surface quickly warms in the hand. It is perfect for Cottrell's interests, which persistently circle around ambiguity. In brooches and pendants he employs a repertoire of simple forms that nevertheless multiply and tumble, advancing and retreating from each other. Many works, such as the brooches *Doubled barrelled bud bud*, 2013, and *Doubled circles on circles, white*, 2013, comprise pairs of forms that play with each other, sometimes mirroring the other. To further complicate this, *Doubled circles on circles, white* is impeccably powder coated with the colour of the title, but as this paint is bio-phosphorescent, the brooch glows green in the dark.

This play with the conditions of visuality encapsulates Cottrell's fascination with the processes of perception and creation. He wrote: 'The more you look the more you see'[2], and subtle references in his works insist viewers come to their own readings.

The pendant *Paired uneven double*, 2015, for instance, might be fragments of a human or a machine, or both, as these abbreviated acrobats turn and hang upon their own truths. As Cottrell says, 'I always try to create pieces that feel somewhere between organic growths and built architectonics, among many other subtle contrasts in their physical qualities.'[3] Witty as well as wise, some recent works are deceptively simple: the pendant *Reflex Protrusion Bent*, 2016, might equally suggest a floral generative form, perhaps a pistil, or else a sort of switch, even a whistle, but in any case, the crucial point is that two finely made forms, which bear a general family resemblance but are precisely different, meet mid-way. At which point one might reasonably ask, what is the orientation of the piece? Moreover, from how many perspectives may one see it?

Cottrell studied Gold and Silversmithing at RMIT University, achieving his Masters in 2010, and has exhibited both in Australia and overseas since 1996. He has taught at both RMIT University and Monash University in Melbourne, and in Singapore, New Zealand and the United States. He currently lectures at the School of Art, Australian National University in Canberra. Cottrell's works are held in numerous private and public collections in Australia and internationally.

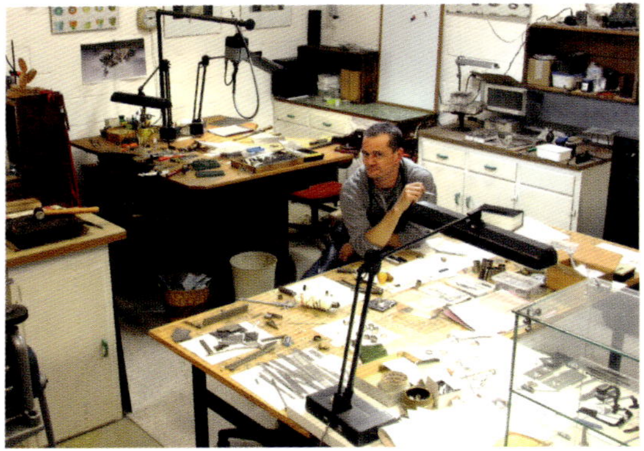

▲

Simon Cottrell in the studio at Australian National Capital Artists (ANCA) Canberra.
Photo: Simon Cottrell

PREVIOUS PAGE

Paired uneven double pendant, 2015
monel, stainless steel,
woven nylon chord, 45 x 40 x 35
Photo: Simon Cottrell

▶

Reflex Protrusion Bent pendant, 2015
monel, stainless steel,
woven nylon chord, 130 x 35 x 35
Photo: Simon Cottrell

▶▶

Doubled circles on circles, white brooch, 2013
monel, stainless steel,
powder coating, synthetic
bio-phosphorescence, 70 x 40 x 40
Photo: Simon Cottrell

1 Interview with Susan Cummins, 21 October 2013, in Art Jewelry Forum, https://artjewelryforum.org/artists/simon-cottrell-surface-depths, accessed August 2016.

2 'Statement', http://klimt02.net/jewellers/simon-cottrell, accessed August 2016 and also the fine exposition of Cottrell's interests in perception in Marjorie Simons, 'Intuitive Flow of Determinate Form: The Jewelry of Simon Cottrell', *Metalsmith*, Vol. 33, no 5, pp.40-7.

3 https://artjewelryforum.org/artists/simon-cottrell-surface-depths, accessed August 2016.

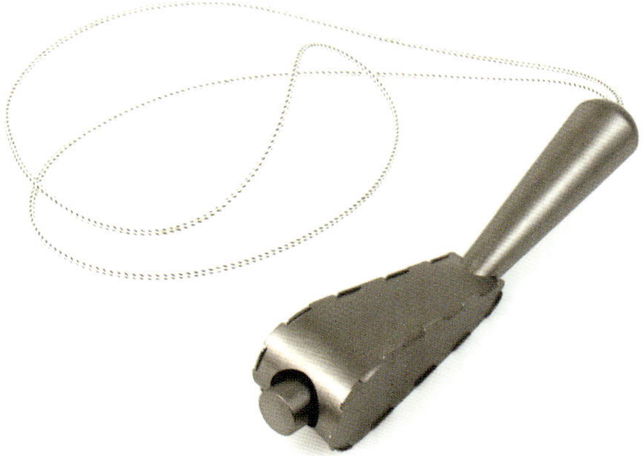

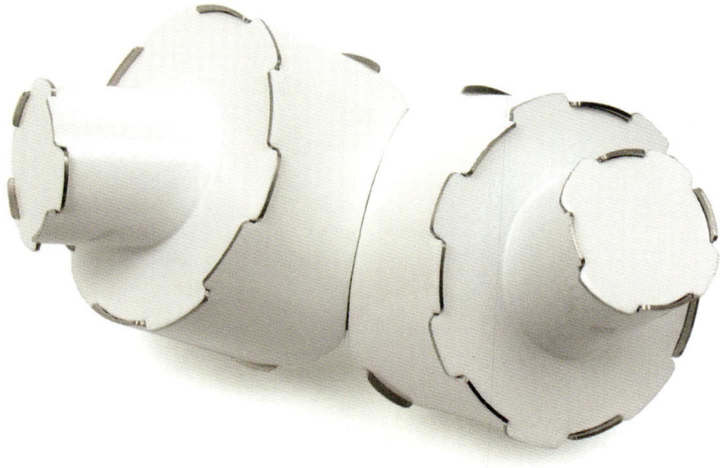

SIX LOOSE FORMS FOCUSSING AND FOUR FOCUSSED BARRELLED DROPS

Of all Simon Cottrell's works shown here, *Six loose forms focussing*, 2014, is perhaps the most elaborate. The title insists on complexity: six elements, all different in size, finished in one of two characteristic ways – welded and polished to form perfect integrated shapes, or flanged together, so that one must take notice of the way the metal sheets embrace each other. The six forms float down the supporting body, and on closer inspection one sees that, starting with one completely integrated form, it is the flanging that links them together. This minor magic reminds us that the human body, the support for Cottrell's jewellery, is (usually) composed of six connected parts – head, torso, four limbs – that cohere perfectly. It is 'focus', the other term in the title of the work, which provides the motivation for the body's ability to make its loose forms work together. The other complex work here is the hilarious *Four focussed barrelled drops*, 2011, where all the forms are smoothly welded, at the same time as they seem to cast about wildly, even sightlessly, for information. Neither work is anthropomorphic, exactly, but Cottrell's achievement is to slyly suggest we should be more attentive to how we see our own bodies, as well as those of others. ■

JULIE EWINGTON

▸

Four focussed barrelled drops brooch, 2011
monel, stainless steel, 85 x 60 x 40
Photo: Simon Cottrell

▸▸

Six loose forms focussing, 2014
monel, stainless steel, 95 x 65 x 40
Photo: Simon Cottrell

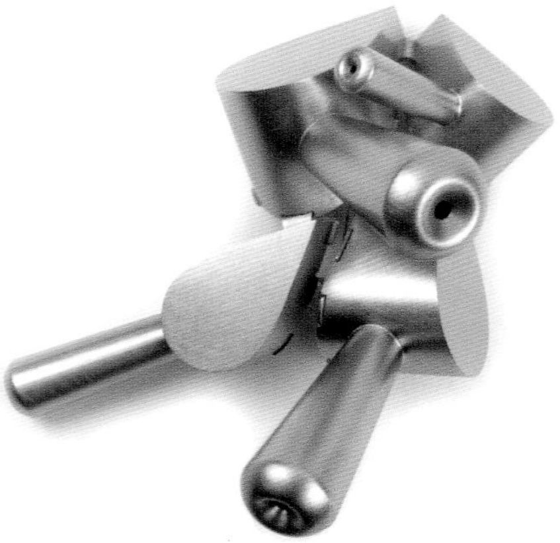

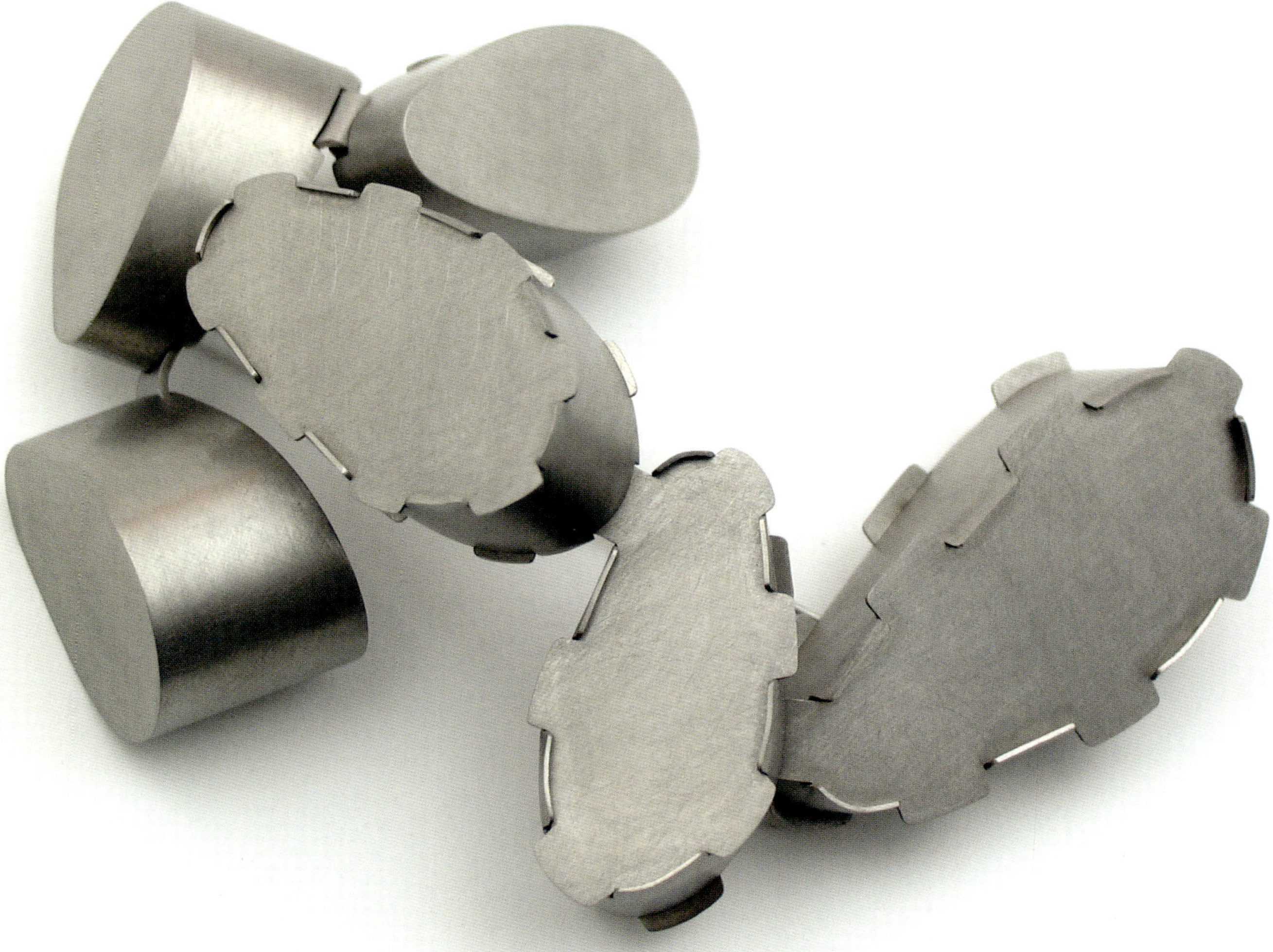

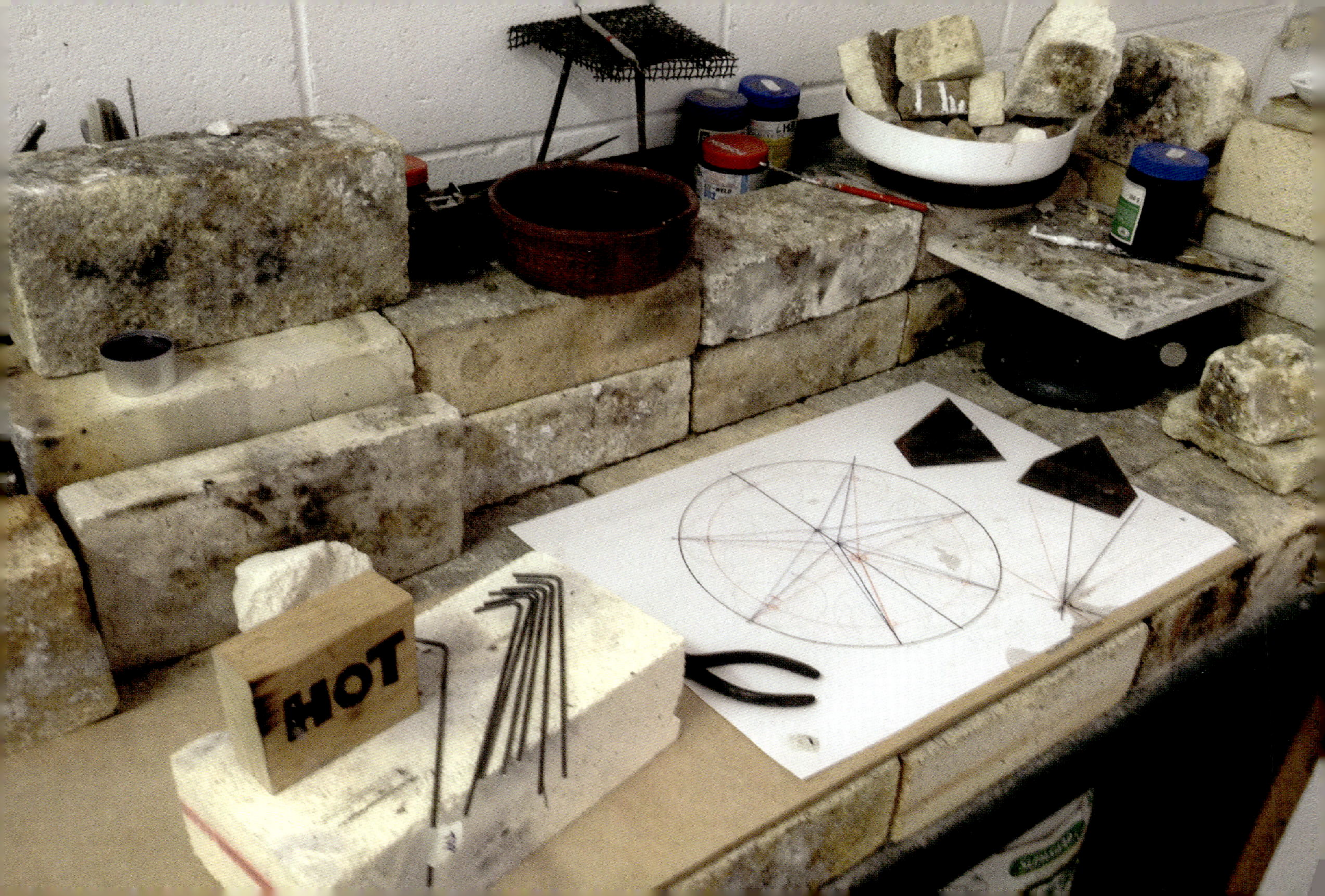
HOT

SUE LORRAINE

BORN 1955, MELBOURNE, VICTORIA
LIVES ADELAIDE, SOUTH AUSTRALIA

SUE LORRAINE has worked with steel for more than two decades. Abandoning precious metals to favour this common industrial material, she first used corten steel, but since her 1998 solo exhibition, *disembody*, she has settled into a long, fruitful investigation of mild steel. Lorraine says, 'I like the graphic quality of it once it's heat-coloured, I like the simplicity of sanding blasting and heating the metal to get this finish. It suits my minimal, graphic style and I have been able to find different ways to work with it over the years. Sometimes I use it for its weight, sometimes strength, sometimes colour...'[1] Precisely. Lorraine has made numerous jewellery series in mild steel – the sumptuous solid *Petal*, 2000 brooches, the delicate *Fly Strings,* 2008, the ravishing little *Black pearl rings*, 2012 – turning the malleability and even the resistant quality of steel to her interrogative wit.

From 2009, Lorraine has matched fine heat-treated steel rods with painted wood, the Cuisenaire rods usually found in the classroom where they are used for teaching maths to children. The *Stick insect* brooches of 2009, with their plump, coloured wooden bodies and springy spindly steel legs, were the first manifestation of her matchmaking with these materials, each an equally artificial component of the confected creature. In 2009 Lorraine wrote: 'My *Stick Insect* brooches were inspired by a collection of spectacular plasmids (stick insects) I saw at the National Museum of Natural Sciences in Taichung, Taiwan. These specimens captivated my imagination by their structural qualities, by their design adaptations for camouflage and by the permanent reminder they were of the fragility of nature.'[2] Lorraine has nailed it: there is something poignant about the splendid improbability of these highly-adapted creatures.

More recently, Lorraine has used Cuisenaire rods and steel in table-top sized sculptures that take leave from structures and forms embodied in nature: she's interested in growth

1 Email to the author, 21 August 2016.

2 Email to the author, 21 August 2016.

3 The Fibonacci number sequences, known in India for over 2,000 years, are named for their first publication in Europe in 1202 by the Italian Leonardo of Pisa, known as Fibonacci. Very simply, in this series a number is found by adding up the two numbers before it; starting with 0 and 1, the sequence goes 0, 1, 1, 2, 3, 5, 8, 13, 21, 34, and so on.

4 Email to the author, 21 August 2016. Lorraine noted, 'Cuisenaire rods are named after their inventor, Georges Cuisenaire a Belgian primary school teacher (1891-1976).' They are still used in Australia today.

[redacted]

PREVIOUS PAGE
Sue Lorraine's work bench at Gray Street Workshop, Adelaide, South Australia.

patterns, mathematical sequences including the Fibonacci sequence[3], anything that might elucidate the logic of natural structures. The *Cuisenaire trees* series from 2013 onwards make this enquiry, and the original use of the rods themselves, explicit. The colour of each rod corresponds to a certain length from 1-10cm, so children quickly learn size and scale by working with them, later absorbing more complex ideas about inter-relationships, proportions and structures. Lorraine remembers Cuisenaire rods from home and primary school as 'a nostalgic and memorable part of my childhood education.'[4]

As so often with Lorraine's work, this conjunction of wood and steel carries a double message: Cuisenaire rods and steel nicely conjoins wood, the most ancient material used for human-built structures, with the incomparable durability of Modernity's most important industrial product. So this is nature and culture, twice over: natural and manufactured materials, natural structures and human curiosity. Elegant.

Lorraine been a partner in Gray Street Workshop, Adelaide's enduring jewellery institution, since its foundation in 1985. Over more than three decades she has produced numerous bodies of works for solo and group exhibitions, and her works are held in major public collections nationally and internationally. From 1999-2008 Lorraine was also Creative Director of JamFactory's Metal Design Studio.

[redacted]

◥
Black pearl rings, 2012
heat coloured mild steel,
ball bearings, 10 x 20 x 20 each
Photo: Grant Hancock

◢
Dragon flies 2013
heat coloured mild steel,
Staedtler Mars Technico
clutch pencil, 150 x 130 x 10 each
Photo: Grant Hancock

[redacted]

◥◥
Rubber band brooches, 2006
heat coloured mild steel,
dimensions variable
Photo: Grant Hancock

◢◢
Petal brooches, 2000
heat coloured mild steel,
60 x 60 each
Photo: Grant Hancock

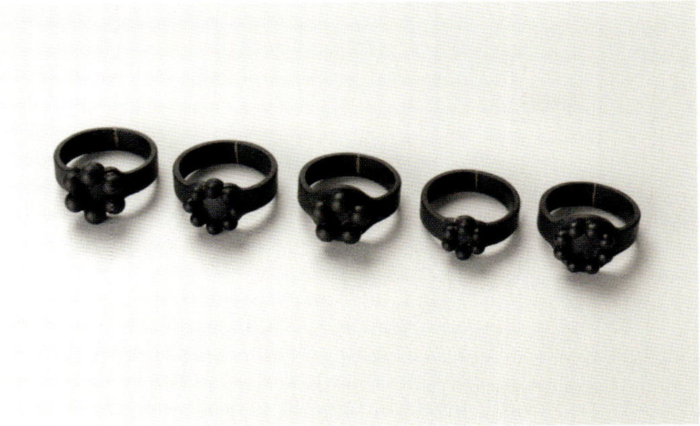

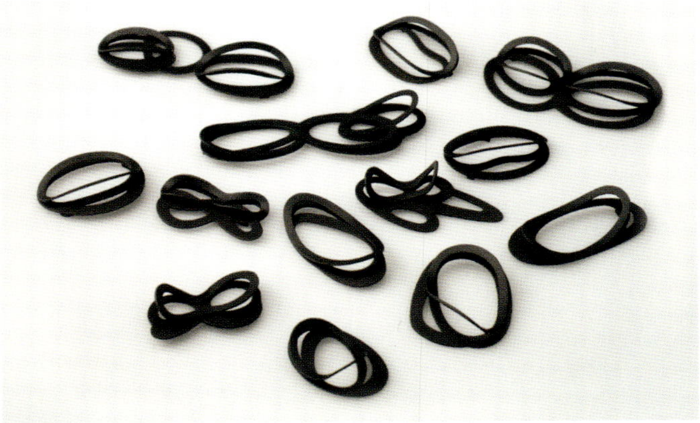

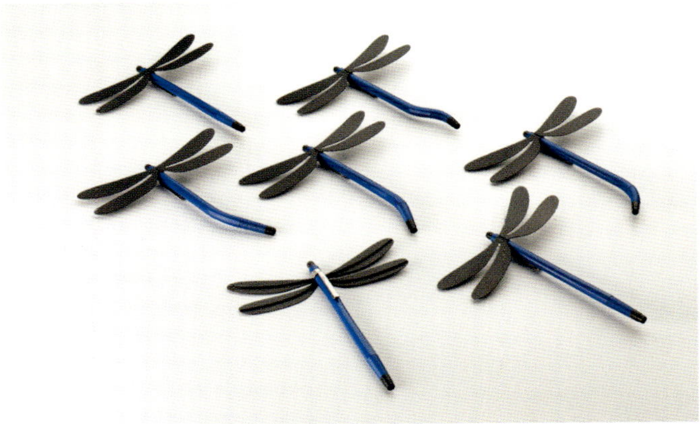

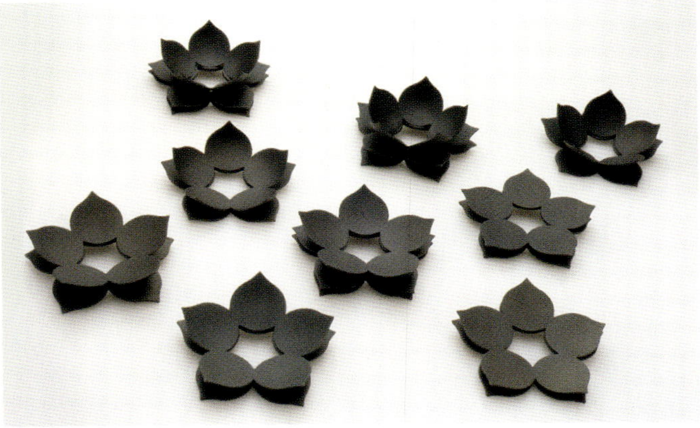

CUISENAIRE TREES

In her several series of *Cuisenaire trees*, Sue Lorraine registers the intelligent play that she remembers from her own education, then principally used in mathematics but also more recently in linguistics. Each little tree sports bright twiggy branches made from vintage wooden Cuisenaire rods, which are arranged according to particular structural principles. In the 2013 versions, the branches were applied to the steel trunks in odd, even, and Fibonacci number series configurations. *Cuisenaire trees*, 2016, continue to explore the various possible arrangements of the coloured rods: one tree references the Fibonacci spiral or snail shell spiral, another has two bases and trees joined together, hinting at human relationships, and a third has a simple skeletal structure, together with what the artist calls 'a chaotic arrangement' of Cuisenaire rods. About the latter, Lorraine writes '...in this case I think I'll use the magnetic properties of the steel to hold the rods which also means the elements can be rearranged in whatever way!' (Some modern plastic Cuisenaire rods are magnetised for classroom use on whiteboards).

Whatever the arrangements of the branches, Lorraine's *Cuisenaire trees* demonstrate the variety and adaptability of natural forms. But they also speak to the jeweller's ingenuity as she investigates the nature world we inhabit. ■

JULIE EWINGTON

[redacted]

▸

Tree model – odds, evens, Fibonacci, 2013
heat coloured mild steel,
Cuisenaire rods,
painted wooden base,
left: 350 x 150 x 140
centre: 380 x 200 x 85
right: 330 x 140 x 120
Photo: Grant Hancock

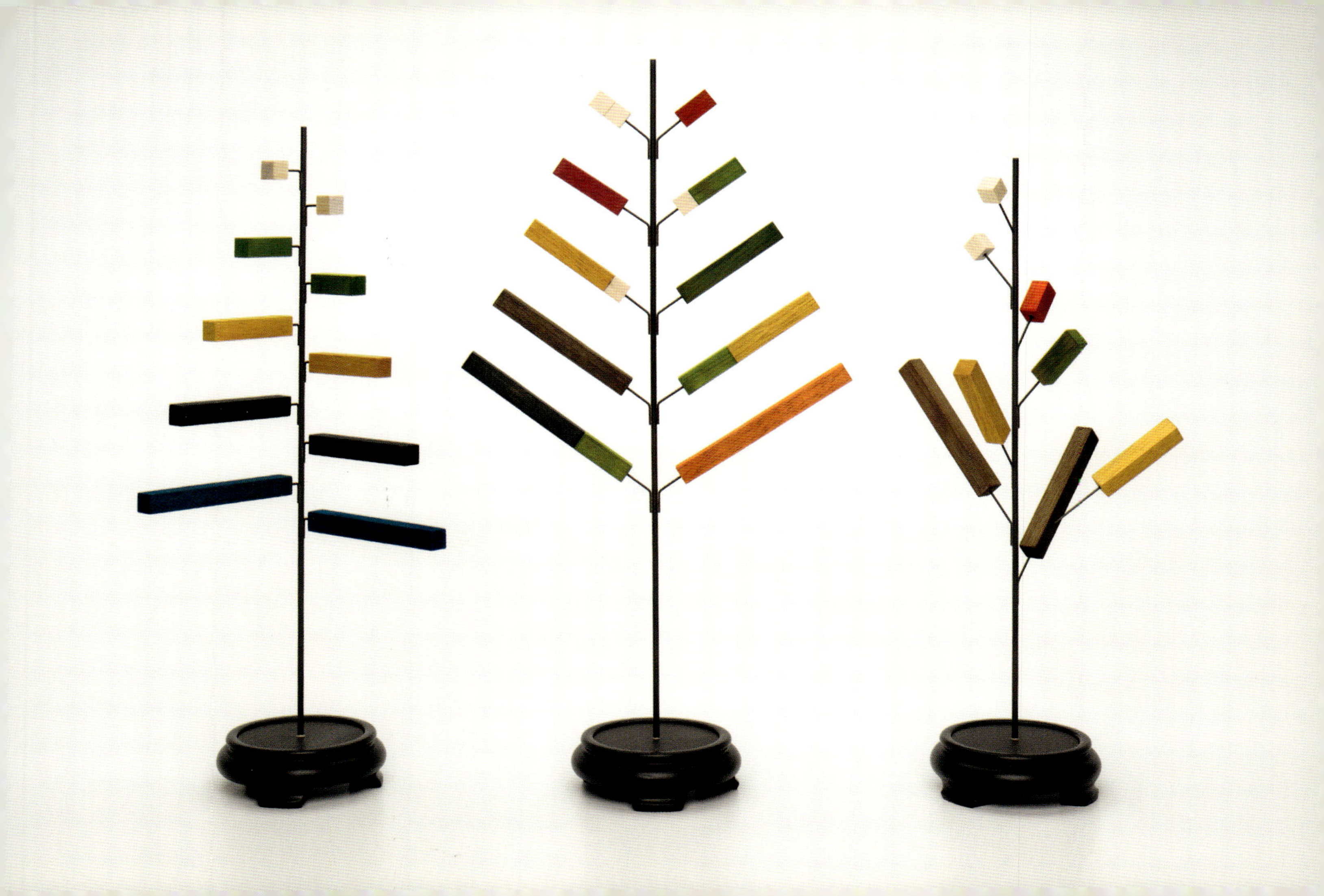

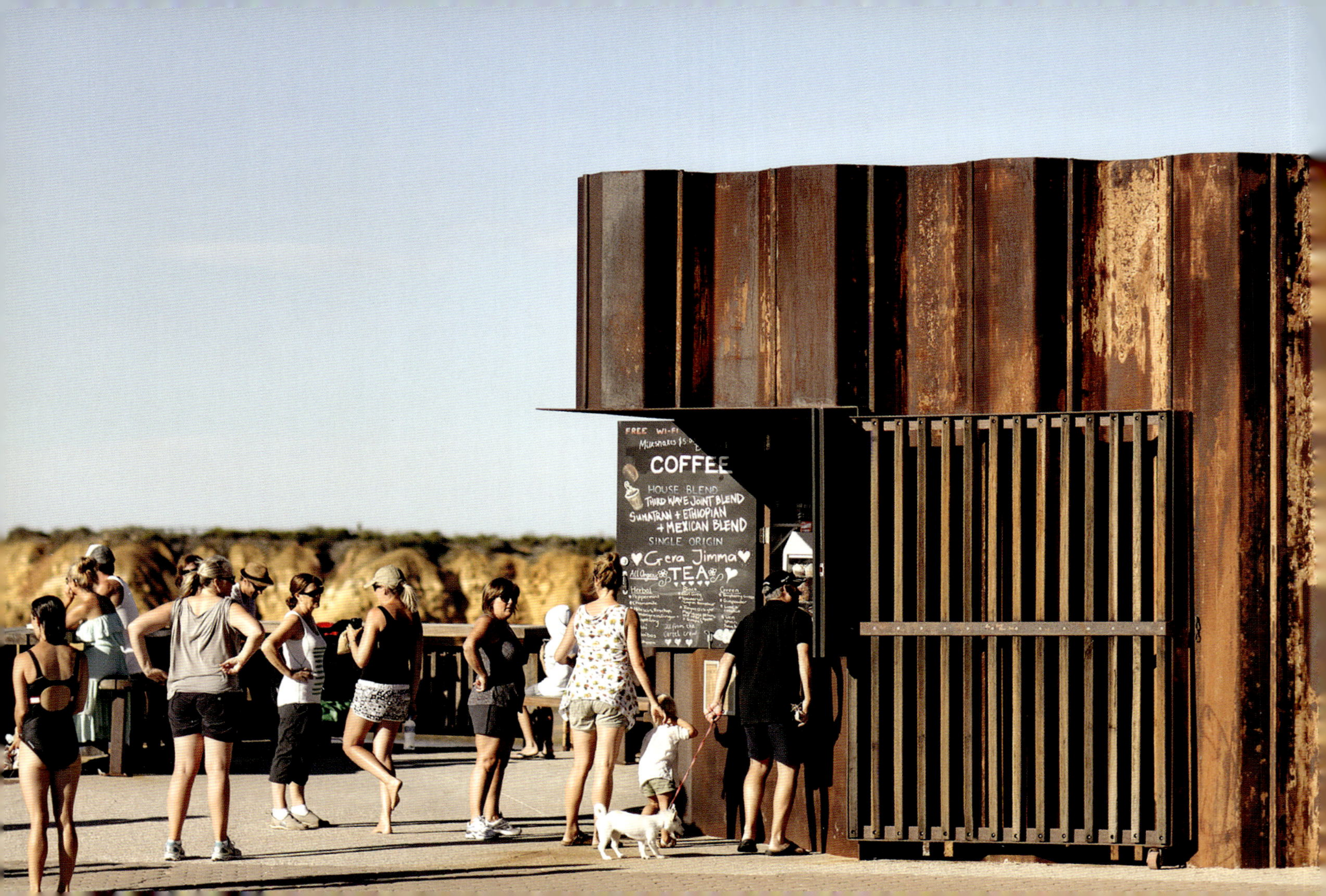
COFFEE
HOUSE BLEND
THIRD WAVE JOINT BLEND
SUMATRAN + ETHIOPIAN
+ MEXICAN BLEND
SINGLE ORIGIN
Gera Jimma
TEA

TONY HOBBA ARCHITECTS

ESTABLISHED 1993,
BELLS BEACH, VICTORIA

TONY HOBBA
BORN 1952, MOUNT GAMBIER,
SOUTH AUSTRALIA
LIVES BELLS BEACH, VICTORIA

ANY DISCUSSION on Tony Hobba Architects (THA) seems somewhat incomplete without mentioning the practice's most well known project, Third Wave Kiosk, 2012 The rusted steel-clad canteen in Torquay, Victoria, continues to capture people's imagination with its bold form and dynamic materiality, making it one of the most well-respected examples of coastal architecture in Australia. However, THA's portfolio isn't limited to small-scale amenities, with the four-strong team working across multiple sectors and also specialising in urban design and master planning.

Architect Tony Hobba founded the Bells Beach-based practice in 1993 and is proudly embedded in the very region (the iconic Surf Coast of Victoria, just off the Great Ocean Road) he committedly serves. Designing for Australia's unique coastal environment has allowed him to develop a particular architectural vernacular that is best expressed in projects such as Third Wave Kiosk. Sensitivity to place and an awareness of the site's specific conditions allow Hobba to create structures that promote passive design, are resilient and exhibit empathy for their surrounds.

He takes inspiration from the Great Otway National Park and local surf beaches, and because of the location of many THA projects, the view is central to the overall scheme. His residential projects, in particular, are configured to allow the best possible sightlines, which more often than not is an integral part of the client's brief.

Many of the practice's projects are the outcome of a master planning commission, such as the Anglesea Recreation Camp, 2007, allowing for an intuitive response underpinned by a holistic design approach. This project revealed what the practice can achieve on a modest budget and also reinforces its commitment to community. Hobba is actively involved in both local and State government planning bodies in order to champion better architecture for Victoria's coastal regions. He is also part of the Surf Coast Planning Committee, the author of the *Surf Coast Design Guide*, 2009[1], and regularly consults for the Surf Coast Shire on urban planning and design.

THA embraces a collaborative design approach and while Hobba places emphasis on building strong client-architect relationships, he equally values the partnerships formed with the wider Surf Coast community. A network of artists, environmentalists, contractors and regulatory authorities regularly contribute to the practice's projects, creating highly responsive outcomes. The Lighthouse, 2006, best exemplifies THA's collaborative spirit, with a number of stone, metal and glass artists engaged to refurbish the existing interior. Finishes reference the local beach while a high level of craftsmanship is expressed through the textural qualities of the natural material palette.

Hobba navigates potentially tricky terrain when dealing with the authoritative bodies required to approve his public coastal architecture. The regulations and restrictions make any one of these projects a potential minefield to develop. But it's testament to his reputation and attitude that challenges are kept to a minimum and structures are fully realised to great effect. It ensures a growing portfolio of strong environmentally responsive designs that are welcomed by locals and tourists alike.

1 The Surf Coast Shire engaged Hobba to produce this guide, the result of a 12-month research commission. In 2010, the project was reviewed and currently takes the form of the *Surf Coast Sustainable Design Book*.

[redacted]

PREVIOUS PAGE
Third Wave Kiosk,
Torquay, Victoria, 2012
Photo: Rory Gardiner

[redacted]

◥
Detail of the external interlocked recycled sheet piles typically used in seawalls.
Photo: Rory Gardiner

◢
The weathered steel palette of reds and ochres harmonise with the colours of the coastal dune.
Photo: Rory Gardiner

▸▸
The building nestled within its surroundings.
Photo: Rory Gardiner

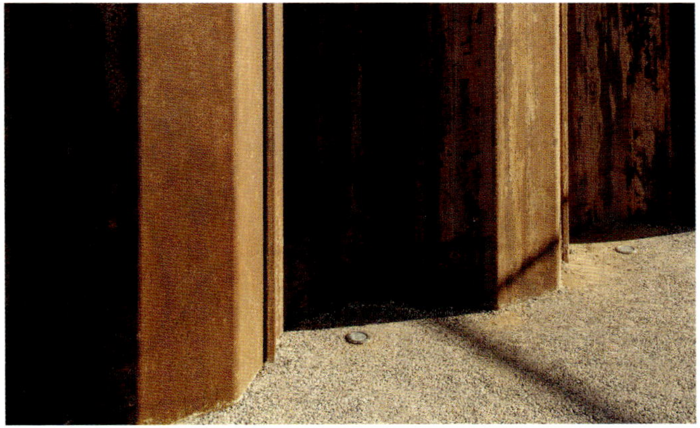

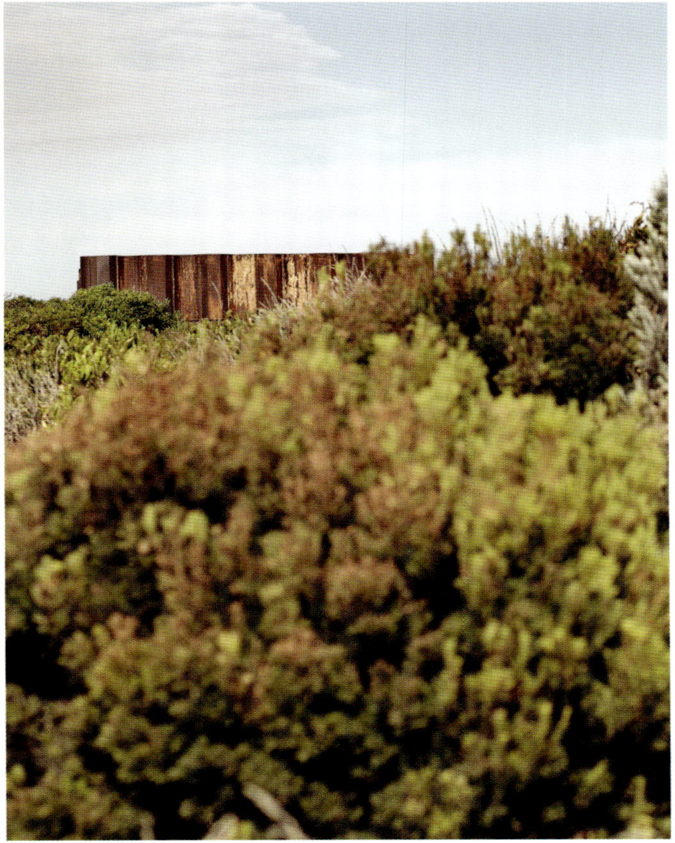

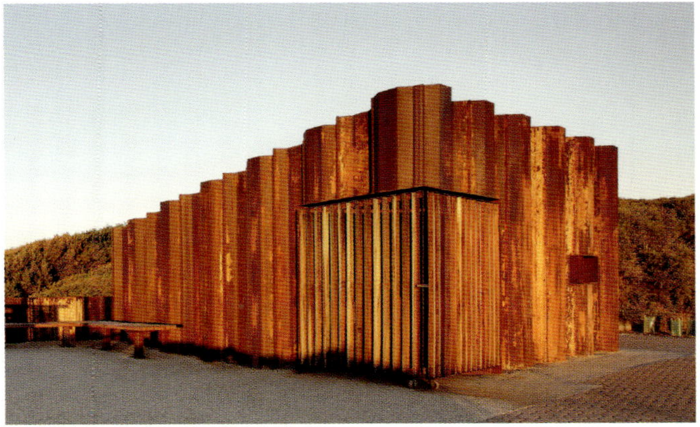

THIRD WAVE KIOSK

The Third Wave Kiosk, 2012, by Tony Hobba Architects serves as a much talked about public facility on The Esplanade at Torquay, Victoria. What could have been a nondescript modestly-sized block of toilets, change rooms and a canteen is elevated to landmark status via a strikingly sculptural envelope of recycled sheet piles. These sheets are typically used for seawalls and were procured from the Victorian floods of 2011, where they were installed for flood protection works along the Murray River.

In their current innovative application they function as retaining walls for Third Wave Kiosk's alfresco terrace and lookout, and provide permanent formwork for the building as well as function as the primary structure and facade. The system of construction was extremely efficient, cost-effective and ultimately respectful of the local coastal environment and the current Victorian Coastal Strategy. Hobba intentionally left the weathered steel in its original condition and the rusted finish complements the surrounding cliffs. There's nothing precious about this cladding and its robust materiality is designed to withstand the harshest weather conditions.

Third Wave Kiosk is visible from the beach and water's edge, although it doesn't impose itself upon the site. The structure's undulating profile references the ocean and rolling coastline, while its angled roof makes for a bold silhouette that echoes the form of the stairs leading down over the sand dune and to the beach. From certain viewpoints it looks like something that was washed up long ago, making its patina all the more interesting as an expression of the site's natural elements. ■

LEANNE AMODEO

[redacted]

▸ The shape of the building take cues from the tiered stairway leading to the beach.
Photo: Rory Gardiner

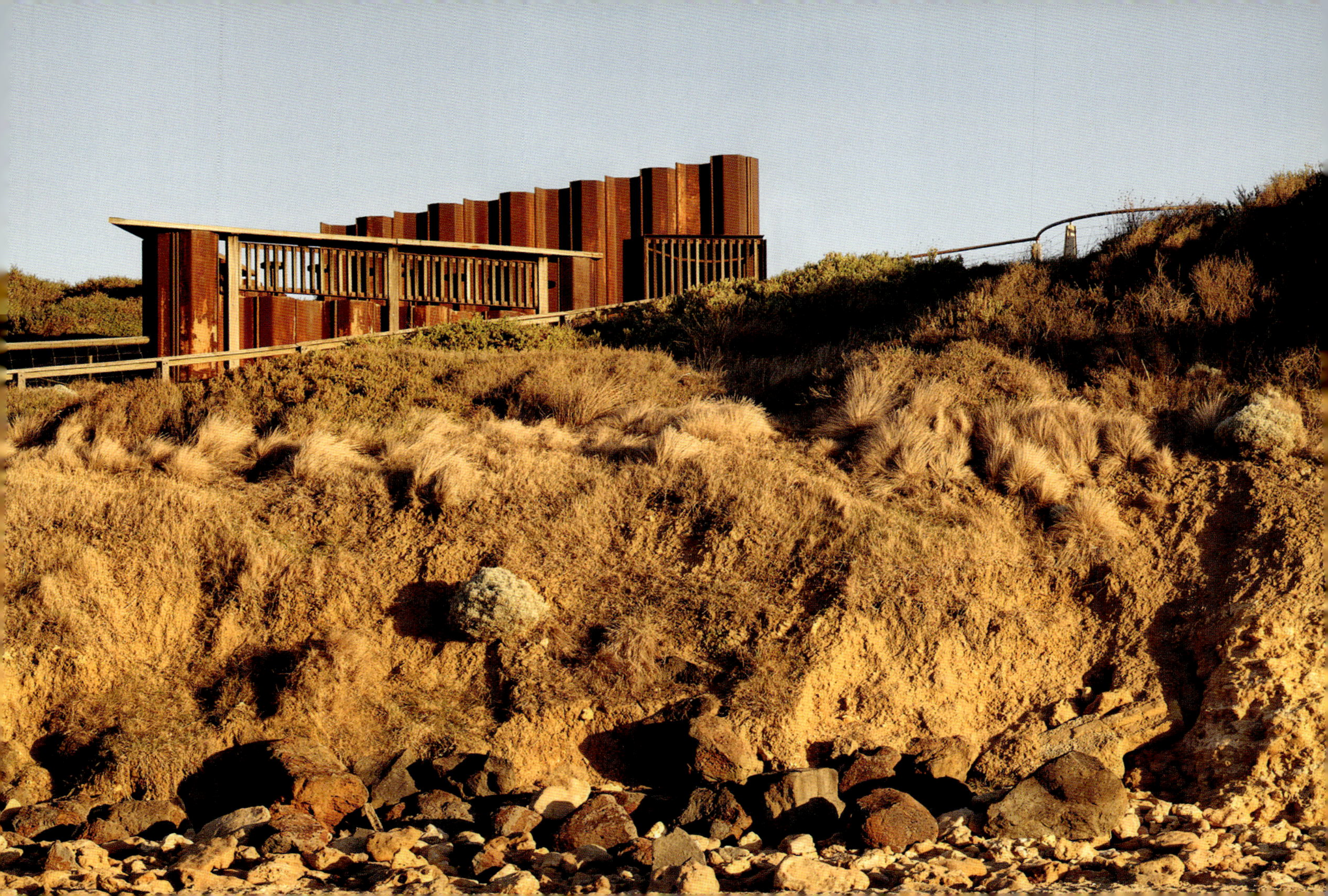

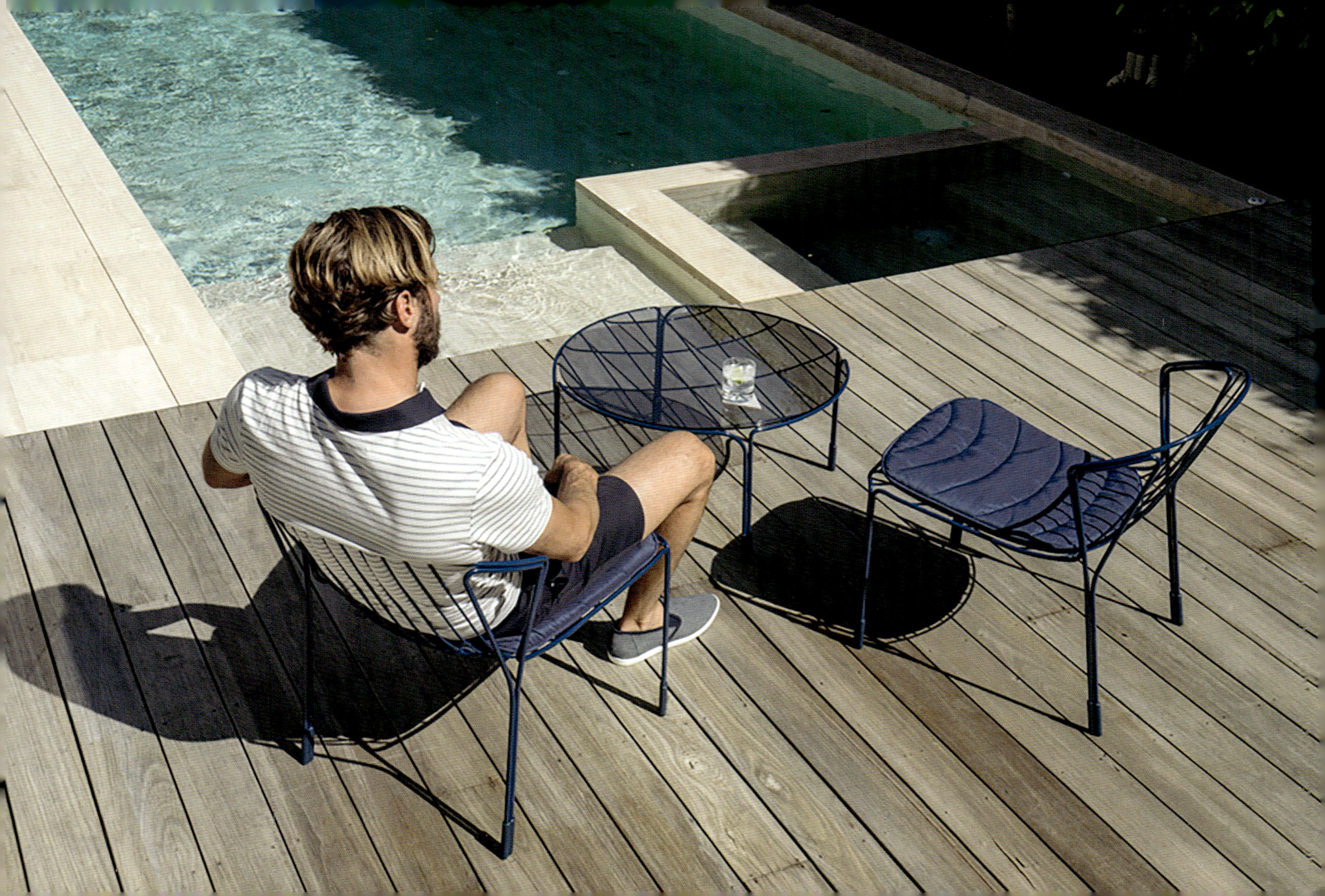

TRENT JANSEN

BORN 1981, WOLLONGONG, NEW SOUTH WALES
LIVES THIRROUL, NEW SOUTH WALES

SINCE GRADUATING IN 2004 with a Bachelor of Design from the College of Fine Arts, UNSW Australia, Trent Jansen has quickly become one of Australia's leading, thought provoking and passionate designers. With experience, opportunities, and accolades amassed throughout Australia, Japan and Europe Jansen's practice is focused on creating sustainable design through developing pieces that maintain a lasting relationship with their user.

To develop these relationships, he imbues his designs with references to some of the most powerful human relationships, such as the bond between mother and child (*Pregnant Chair*, 2008, produced by Moooi), lovers (*Kissing Pendants*, 2008) and partners (*Nuptial Pendants*, 2010) or with rich narrative content.

This narrative content has been of particular importance in recent works. In a process he describes as 'Design Anthropology,' Jansen mines the archives for primary and secondary sources to unveil unknown stories and interrogate Australian mythologies. He explains:

This method was devised to move design beyond the stark pragmatism of modernism and its incongruence with the beautiful imperfection of humanity. Design Anthropology focuses on these imperfections, studying the history and culture of human societies and taking design inspiration from the rich stories that punctuate human heritage. The ideas that result from this method are richly symbolic and tell innately human stories.[1]

Design Anthropology is most apparent in one of his most celebrated designs, the *Briggs Family Tea Service*, 2011, for Broached Commissions. Founded by creative director Lou Weis and Vincent Aiello Broached Commissions is an Australian design company that works closely with curators, writers and a select team of leading Australian designers, to create bespoke and limited edition design pieces. Using Australia's history and isolation

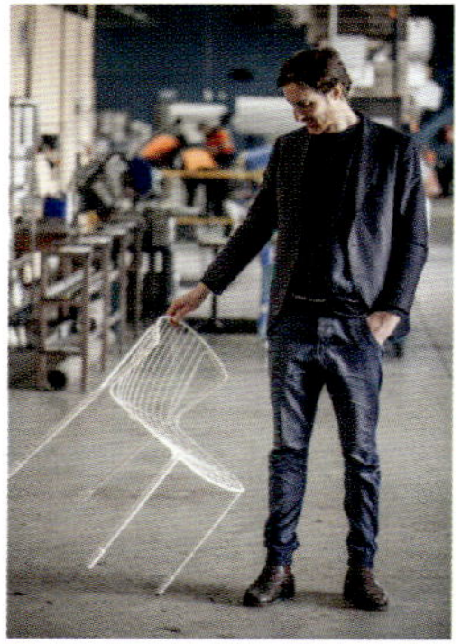

as an impetus for design, the *Briggs Family Tea Service* was part of the Broached Colonial collection.

Wishing to look at the multifaceted relationships that make a family unit and the impact of colonisation on Aboriginal people the tea service references the complex cross-cultural identity of a family living in Tasmania in early 19th Century. The union between Tasmanian sealer, George Briggs, and his wife Woretermoeteyenner of the Pairrebeenne people, was the first marriage between a free white settler and an Aboriginal woman. The burgeoning hybridised culture the union harbingered is explored in the work. Employing materials and archetypal design Jansen fuses the kalikina (bull kelp) rikawa (water carriers) of Tasmanian Aboriginal people with the porcelain tea services produced by British potteries.

Aligning himself with companies that have similar core values and design ethos is important to Jansen's practice. Recently he collaborated with Melbourne based company Tait. Founded in 1992 by Managing Director Gordon Tait and Creative Director Susie Tait, the company is committed to supporting local designers and manufacturers in the production of their range of residential and commercial outdoor furniture. Selected for an invitation-only design competition, Jansen was drawn to the challenge of designing a commercial range. Impressed with Gordon's skilled knowledge of metal, its uses and capabilities as well as his hands-on approach to the business, Jansen pitched the *Tidal collection*, 2015, a series of outdoor furniture that investigates the 60s and 70s surf culture of Australia: hot summers at the beach, long boards, Kombi vans, camping, sunburn and freedom.

Drawn nostalgically to their own childhood memories, Gordon and Susie were taken by Jansen submission, that he describes developed through a form of enquiry closer to fieldwork rather than any formal research. Having grown up in the beachside suburb of Kiama, Jansen unlike many of his friends and cousins, had an aversion to the water, therefore to create this range he spent time talking with surfers and mates, examining their unique jargon and specialised surf knowledge.

PREVIOUS PAGE
Tidal collection designed by Trent Jansen for Tait, 2015
powder coated stainless steel
Tidal Lounger: 560 x 710 x 710
Tidal Coffee Table: 350 x 730
Photo: Haydn Cattach, on location in Melbourne

Trent Jansen designer of the *Tidal collection* for Tait.
Photo: Mark Chew

Prepping parts for manufacture of the *Tidal collection* by clamping stainless steel together using modified vice grips in Tait's Thornbury factory, 2015.
Photo: Mark Chew

Welding stainless steel parts for manufacture of the *Tidal collection* in Tait's Thornbury factory, 2015.
Photo: Mark Chew

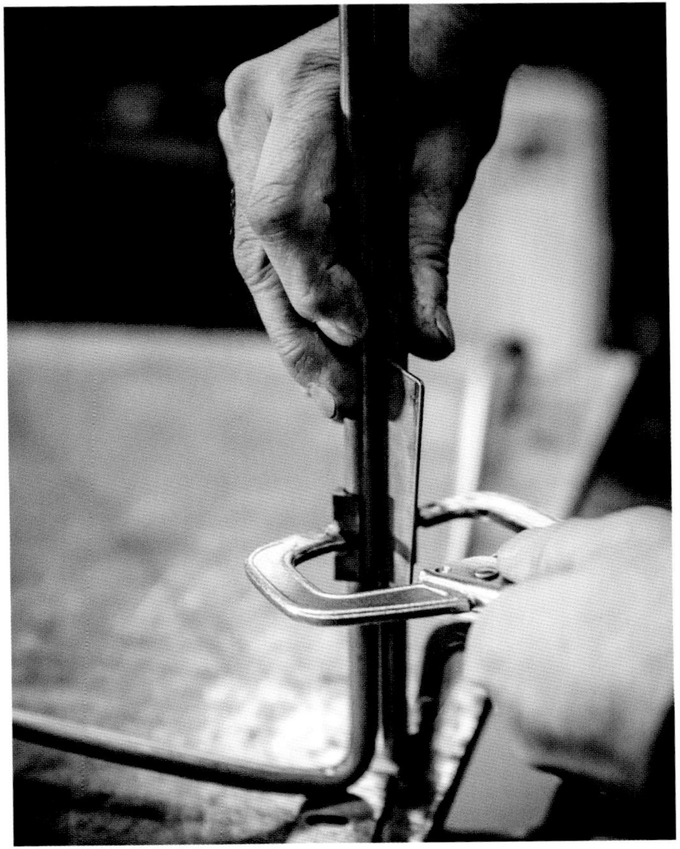

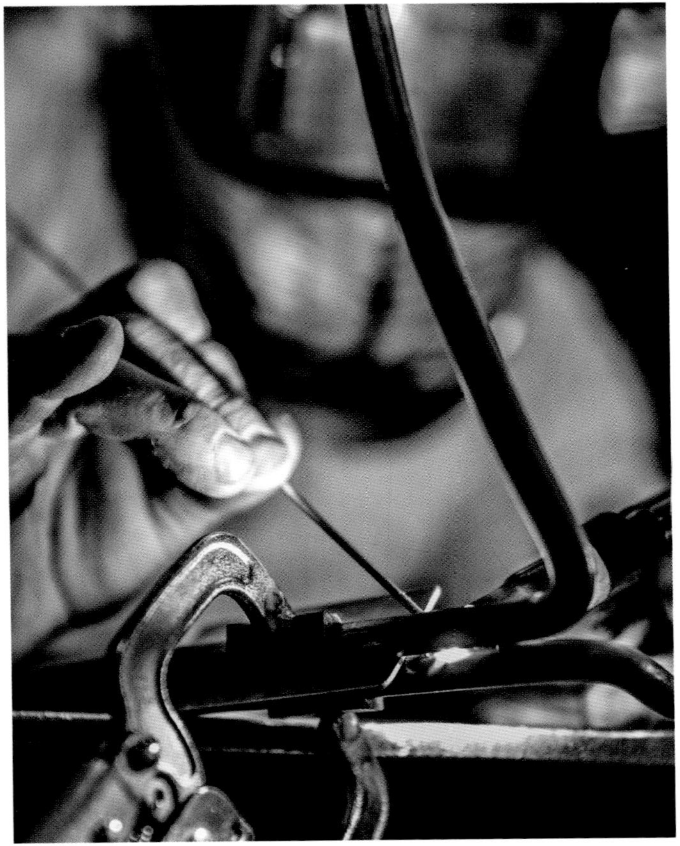

1 http://www.architectureanddesign.com.au/features/comment/in-profile-trent-jansen, accessed September 2016.

2 http://trentjansen.com/, accessed September 2016.

3 Ibid.

▸

The Tidal Coffee Table, 2015
powder coated stainless steel, glass, 350 x 730
Photo: Haydn Cattach

▸▸

The Tidal Lounger, 2015,
powder coated stainless steel,
560 X 710 X 710
Photo: Haydn Cattach

TIDAL COLLECTION

The Tidal collection, 2015, is the first range developed under Tait's new Research & Development Program that sees invited designers pitch concepts based on a formal brief developed in response to market demand. The 2015 brief identified the need for an Australian product collection for poolside and coastal environments.

The *Tidal collection* uses stainless steel wire and comes in a range powder coated finishes. Jansen chose the material for its strength, recyclability and durability in scenarios where it would be exposed to UV light, chlorine and salt water. The use of stainless steel wire is also a point of difference to other outdoor furniture ranges often made of aluminium, iron or wood.

The graphic qualities of the wire within the three chairs of the *Tidal* range take its cues from wave diagrams tracing the stages of wave formations as they form, crest and crash their way to the shore. As Jansen describes: '*Tidal Sun Lounge* is the thick, laid back wave at the back of the set; the *Tidal Lounger* is a curling wave at the place in the set where surfers usually lurk; and the *Tidal Chair* is the close-out that breaks on the sand.'[2]

In addition to the chairs Jansen has created four tables. Their design is based on 'the less common occurrence of waterspouts, which sometimes touch down on the ocean during a storm. Like a waterspout, these tables twist as they ascend, inspired by the spout's spiralling water.'[3] ■

MARGARET HANCOCK DAVIS

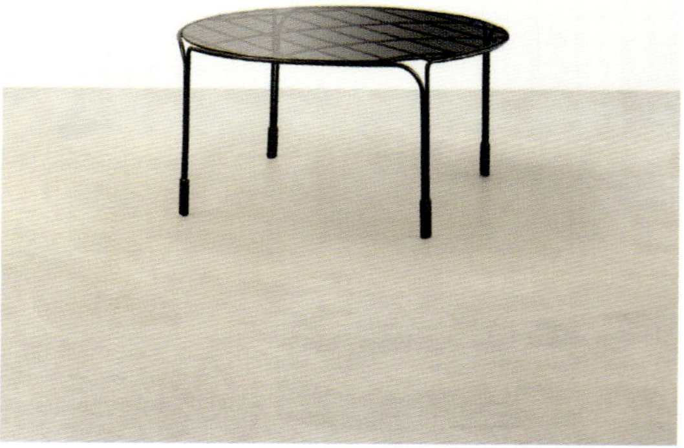

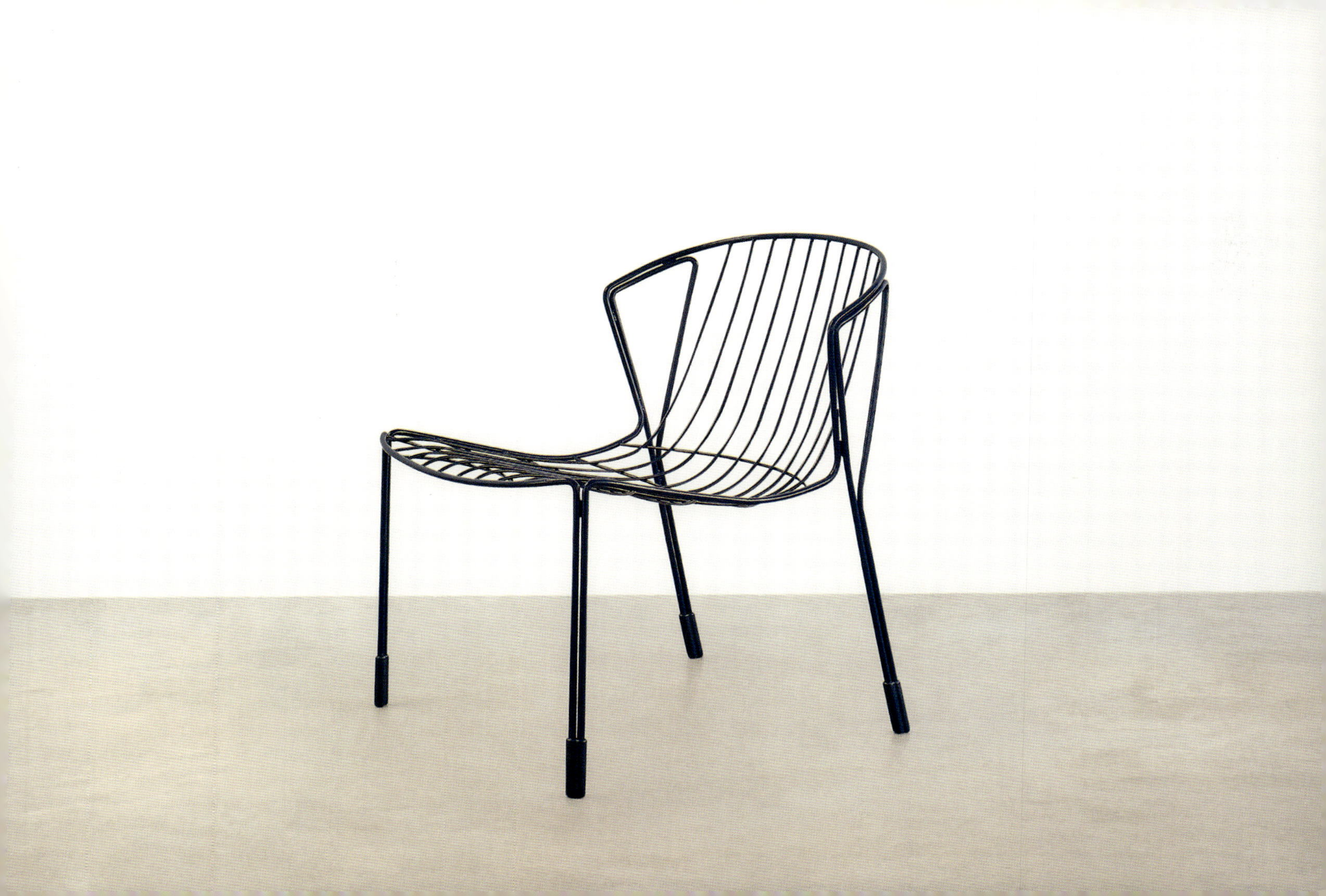

CONTRIBUTORS

Margaret Hancock Davis (curator, essay writer) is Senior Curator at JamFactory. Her curatorial projects include: *From the earth: Contemporary Indigenous ceramics* (2008), and *Prototyping: Making ideas* (2011), the international exhibition *Southern Stars: Northern Lights* (2009) for Blue Coat Liverpool, UK, as well as the touring exhibitions *Stephen Bowers: Beyond Bravura* (2013 -15), *Gerry Wedd : Kitschen Man* (2016 -19), and the Visions of Australia-funded exhibitions *Designing Craft/Crafting Design: 40 years of JamFactory* (2013 -16) and *GLASS: art design architecture* (2015-18). Prior to her role as Senior curator at JamFactory, she was Project Coordinator of the International Craft Initiative, which presented Australian craft and design at key international events including SOFA (Chicago), Collect (London) and Talente (Munich). In addition to her curatorial practice, Margaret has written texts for a number of exhibition catalogues and magazines. Her qualifications include a Graduate Diploma of Art History, Graduate Diploma of Art Administration and a Bachelor of Visual Arts and Applied Design.

Stephen Goddard (catalogue and exhibition designer, essay writer) is a multi-disciplinary designer, design lecturer, and Creative Director of Project Two. He has worked with many of Australia's largest cultural institutions and galleries on projects spanning publication, interpretation and exhibition design, for which he has won many awards. More recently Goddard has curated a number of exhibitions, including *I Spy* (2013) and *Happyness* (2016), both in collaboration with Meryl Ryan at Lake Macquarie City Art Gallery. Goddard teaches design at UNSW Australia Art & Design and Raffles Institute, and is currently undertaking a Master of Design (Research) at UNSW Australia. *STEEL: art design architecture* is the third in a series of exhibitions, all of which he designed for JamFactory.

Leanne Amodeo (profile writer) is a content director, media consultant and educator. A former editor of *Monument* and *(inside)* magazines, she has 20 years experience as a writer and editor on design, architecture and art. Leanne regularly contributes to national and international design publications, including *Indesign*, *Houses*, *ICON*, *Australian House & Garden*, *Habitusliving*, *Artichoke* and *Urbis*. She has lectured at University of South Australia, where she developed a number of research courses for the Bachelor of Interior Architecture program.

Penny Craswell (essay writer) is a writer and editor specialising in design and architecture, and a communications consultant working with a range of design studios, including Koichi Takada Architects, M Moser, Bijl Architecture and Frost Collective. A former editor of Artichoke magazine, she is Contributing Editor of *AR* and *Mezzanine* magazines, writes for *Frame*, *Mark* and *Azure* magazines internationally and is the founder of *The Design Writer* blog. She is currently working on a Master of Design (Research) at UNSW Australia.

Julie Ewington (profile writer) is a writer, curator and broadcaster working in Sydney. Between 1997-2014 she was lead curator in Australian Art at Queensland Art Gallery|Gallery of Modern Art, and between 1996-2012 contributed to the *Asia-Pacific Triennial of Contemporary Art*. Since 2014 Julie has written essays for catalogues and journals; reviewed exhibitions in Australia and internationally, including for *The Monthly and Artforum*; and is curating a survey exhibition for the late sculptor Bronwyn Oliver for TarraWarra Museum of Art.

Glen Martin (profile writer) is a Canberra based writer and marketer who has written on art, design, sports and popular culture for a number of titles including *Australian Art Monthly*, *Vive*, *Luxe*, *Australian Creative*, *Muse Art Monthly* and *The Roar*. He has curated and co-produced events including *Pecha Kucha* Canberra and music festivals such as *Electric Lake*, the *You Are Here Laneway* and *Gangbusters*. Glen is currently at work on a PhD through the Australian National University Centre for Art Theory and Art History.

Kimberley Moulton (profile writer) is a Yorta-Yorta woman and curator. She is Senior Curator of South Eastern Aboriginal Collections, Melbourne Museum and alumni of National Gallery of Australia Indigenous Arts Leadership Program. Kimberley is also an alumni of the British Council ACCELERATE program UK and 2015 National Gallery of Australia international fellow at the Kluge-Ruhe Aboriginal Collection USA. Kimberley was a judge for 2016 Telstra National Aboriginal and Torres Strait Islander Art Awards and participant of the 2016 Australia Council Indigenous Curators delegation USA.

Kate Rhodes (essay writer) is Curator at RMIT Design Hub. Kate has worked on art, craft and design exhibitions, workshops and creative activities both in Australia and internationally. Kate was Creative Director of the State of Design Festival and has held the position of Curator at Object: Australian Design Centre, Craft Victoria and the National Design Centre. She was Assistant Curator of Photography and Contemporary Art at the National Gallery of Victoria for five years and Editor of *Artichoke* magazine. Kate is a founding member of the Office for Good Design.

Danielle Robson (profile writer) is Director and Co-founder of ArtsPeople, a curatorial consultancy with offices in Sydney and Tokyo. Specialising in contemporary art and design, she was the Creative Programs Manager at Object: Australian Design Centre, where she curated major touring exhibitions *CUSP: Designing into the Next Decade* (2013-15) and *HYPERCLAY: Contemporary Ceramics* (2012-14). Danielle co-curated *SafARI* (2010, 2012) the 'unofficial' fringe festival to the Biennale of Sydney. Her qualifications include a Master of Art Administration and a Bachelor of Laws and Media.

Mark Thomson (essay writer) is a writer, designer and maker, working in the field of resourceful problem-solving cultures, championing the meaning and benefits that flow from those activities. He is the author of a number of books including *Blokes & Sheds*, *Makers, Breakers & Fixers*, *Rare Trades* and *The Lost Tools of Henry Hoke*. He is the founder and research director of the slightly prestigious Institute of Backyard Studies.

Serena Wong (profile writer) is an emerging freelance writer and curator. She is Co-Director at the Artist-Run-Initiative FELTspace where she runs the Writers Program and co-produced such projects as FELTpublic. She has written for a number of publications and curated independent projects including the four-part series *The Success of Failure* (2015), in AEAF 24:7 and *Transfiguring* (2015) at FELTspace. In 2013-14 she was the Assistant for the Adelaide Biennial of Australian Art.

ACKNOWLEDGEMENTS